Mareva Injunctions and
Anton Piller Relief   OLD EDITION

Mareva Injunctions and Anton Piller Relief

Second Edition   OLD EDITION

Steven Gee MA (Oxon)
Of the Middle Temple, Barrister
Sometime open scholar of Brasenose College, Oxford
Standing Junior Counsel to the Department of
Trade and Industry, Export Credits Guarantee
Department

Foreword to the 2nd Edition by
The Right Honourable Lord Justice Bingham

Foreword to the 1st Edition by
The Right Honourable Lord Denning

© Steven Gee 1990

Published by
Longman Law, Tax and Finance
Longman Group UK Ltd
21–27 Lamb's Conduit Street
London WC1N 3NJ

Associated offices
Australia, Hong Kong, Malaysia, Singapore, USA

ISBN 0 85121 514 9

O 171721

A CIP catalogue record for this book is available from the British Library.

Printed and bound in Great Britain

Contents OLD EDITION

Preface

Fifteen years or so ago no-one knew of Mareva injunctions or Anton Piller orders. Now they form part of the everyday tools of the trade for lawyers practising in different areas of the law and different courts of the land. There has been much development and refinement of the principles. Substantial changes and developments have taken place. The case law has grown and multiplied, and not all of it is from England. Part is to be found from other common law countries. In the development of the Mareva to apply to assets worldwide, the Australian courts have led the way.

I have been privileged to have a foreword written by Lord Justice Bingham. Also included is Lord Denning's original foreword to the first edition.

I am grateful for the unceasing enthusiasm and encouragement of my friend, Anthony Grabiner QC. His advice has been beyond price.

I must record a debt of gratitude to my parents, Dr Hilda Elman and Dr Sidney Gee, who have in their individual ways each made an invaluable contribution. To them, this book is dedicated.

The law is stated as at 1 January 1990.

Steven Gee
4 Essex Court
Temple
London EC4

Acknowledgements

I would like to acknowledge all the assistance and support which I have had in writing this book from others. Geraldine Andrews co-authored the first edition and has researched much of the unreported Court of Appeal case law. My pupil, Khamal Mukhi has been a faithful aide. Andrew Faiers and Susan Taylor of the Crown Prosecution Service helped me with Chapter 20. Much help has also been given to me by my clerk, David Grief, and his team and the staff at Longman.

Foreword to the Second Edition by The Right Honourable Lord Justice Bingham

Experience since the first Mareva injunctions and Anton Piller orders were granted in 1974 and 1975 has fully vindicated the boldness of counsel in seeking the orders and the percipience of the courts in making them. Properly used, the orders protect the rights of the plaintiff and so promote the interests of justice. But experience has also shown that these orders, powerful weapons in the arsenal of the plaintiff, can be oppressive and prejudicial to the defendant, whose privacy may be invaded and his business and family life blighted, all by orders made without notice to him. As the proliferating case law has defined how and when applications should be made, so it has plotted the potential pitfalls. Applicants who have lacked an existing cause of action, or failed to make full disclosure on their *ex parte* application, or mistaken the proper purpose of an order, or overlooked the legitimate interests of the third parties, or obtained relief excessive in its scope, or failed to pursue their actions after the grant of interlocutory relief have all in their different ways come to grief. It is a foolhardy practitioner who nowadays ventures into this field, save in the most straightforward case, without pausing (in the limited time often available) to make sure that his case is sound and his tackle in order.

To the prudent practitioner this book will be a godsend. It deploys in an accessible way the fruits of Steven Gee's exhaustive research and considerable practical experience. It discusses the impact of recent statutes such as the Civil Jurisdiction and Judgments Act 1982, the Financial Services Act 1986, the Insolvency Act 1986, the Drug Trafficking Offences Act 1986 and the Criminal Justice Act 1988. Above all, it states the underlying principles and illuminates the hazards. Steven Gee has made, in this substantially re-written book, an invaluable contribution to the literature on this still-developing topic.

London
November 1989

Foreword to the First Edition by The Right Honourable Lord Denning

Every legal practitioner knows that there is a great difference between Getting a Judgment against your Adversary: and Enforcing it against him. Often the practitioner has to advise his client that it is not worthwhile to sue the debtor; 'He's not worth powder and shot' or 'You cannot get blood out of a stone'.

But it is even worse when the creditor has got judgment against his adversary and then finds that meanwhile the debtor has got rid of all his assets or put his money into an overseas bank account where the creditor cannot get at it. The debtor has in the proceedings made all sorts of excuses for not paying. He has put in a dilatory plea so as to gain time for his evasive actions. And then, when the creditor gets judgment, all has gone.

Until recently the law of England gave no aid to the creditor. It gave all its aid to the defaulting debtor. A creditor could do nothing against a debtor until he got judgment against him and sought to enforce it: only to find that by that time the debtor had put all his assets out of reach.

In this respect the law of England lagged behind the laws of most other commercial countries. On the Continent they have a process called '*Saisie Conservatoire*' by which, at the very outset of proceedings, the assets of a debtor can be seized so as to preserve them for the creditor. Very often the debtor lodges security and gets the goods released. And the security is there to meet the judgment.

Now the law of England has been remedied so as to correspond closely to the European process. It has been done by means of an injunction called the Mareva Injunction. It freezes the assets of the debtor—especially his bank account—and stops him dealing with them. So that he can no longer spirit them away before judgment.

The remedy of a Mareva is so important, and its ramifications are so extensive, that it is essential for all practitioners to be familiar with it. So Steven Gee and Geraldine Andrews have written this book for the purpose. Steven Gee is well qualified to do it. He is a practising member of the Bar, doing commercial cases, and in daily touch with Marevas. And Geraldine Andrews is in the same chambers. Their writing, as you will see, is not in the solid style of the *White Book*. It is in the conversational style of a master instructing his pupils. It reminds me of the book on *Practice* written by the famous Special Pleader, William Tidd, 150 years ago. It was so celebrated that it finds a place in Dickens' *David Copperfield* (Chapter XVI).

The young David comes upon the lawyer's clerk, Uriah Heep. 'I found Uriah reading a great fat book, with such demonstrative attention, that his lank forefinger followed up every line as he read, and made clammy tracks along the page (or so I fully believed) like a snail. "I am improving my legal knowledge, Master Copperfield," said Uriah. "I am going through Tidd's Practice. Oh, what a writer Mr Tidd is, Master Copperfield!" '

That rapturous exclamation, as Dickens described it, can be said of this book by Steven Gee and Geraldine Andrews.

I feel an especial interest in the book because it was in my court in 1975 that the Mareva started on its way. The first case is reported as *Nippon Yusen Kaisha* v *Karageorgis* [1975] 2 Lloyd's Rep 137. I remember it well. It was on a Monday afternoon, 22 May 1975. I was sitting as Master of the Rolls with Lord Justice Browne and Lord Justice Geoffrey Lane (now Lord Chief Justice). As soon as we took our seats, counsel rose from the junior bar and told us that his clients, the Japanese shipowners NYK, were owed a large sum of money by Greek charterers for the hire of a ship. But their whereabouts were unknown. Their office in Piraeus was closed. Yet they had a large sum of money in a London bank. It was feared that they would withdraw the money before NYK could stop them. The judge below had refused to intervene. But we did so. We granted an injunction to stop the Greek charterers disposing of the money. We said our order was to be notified to the bank. The application only took a quarter of an hour. It was effective. The shipowners got their money.

The news flashed round the temple. Here indeed was a find of prodigious scope. The commercial bar seized upon it. Four weeks later, on 23 June 1975, a similar emergency arose with an Italian ship, the *Mareva*. This time before me, Lord Justice Roskill and Lord Justice Ormrod. The case is reported in [1975] 2 LLR 509. Again at 2 o'clock we heard an application for an injunction. The facts were similar. The shipowners were owed money for charter-hire. The charterers had not paid but had money in a London bank. Again we granted an injunction to stop it being disposed of. It took half an hour. Again it was effective.

That second case gave its name to the process. It was known as the Mareva Injunction. We had launched in the City of London a new legal process which was destined to take the legal fraternity by storm and to give the city merchants and traders a much-needed remedy against shifty customers and delaying or defaulting debtors.

In both those cases we heard one side only. The applications were *ex parte* by the shipowners. We did not hear both sides until March 1977. It was in *Rasu* v *Perusahann (The 'Pertamina')* [1978] 1 QB 644. We then examined the law and affirmed the decisions.

But in those cases the defendants were abroad and out of the jurisdiction. Only their money was here in the bank. The question arose: did the Mareva only extend to cases where the defendant was here and could be served here? Again we intervened. Again in an application at 2 o'clock. Again *ex parte*. A lady came from the Persian Gulf to England. She bought a large house in Hampshire and had £20,000 in a bank in England in her own name. There was a danger that the assets or money might disappear and be taken out of the reach of the creditors. Again we granted a Mareva. The case was not reported in the Law Reports but the shorthand writer took it down and it is in a transcript in the Bar Library. You will find it quoted in the *Third Chandris case* [1979] 1 QB at p 667.

Afterwards, to remove any doubts, Parliament endorsed the Mareva by s 37 of the Supreme Court Act 1981.

Alongside the Mareva, there was a parallel development on the Chancery side which Steven Gee and Geraldine Andrews describe well too. It is called the Anton Piller Order. It came before the Court of Appeal in 1975—the same year as the Mareva. It is reported in [1976] Ch 55. An English company got to know that their German competitors were infringing their copyright. If they issued a writ and served it on the defendants, they feared that the German competitors would destroy or dispose of the infringing material so as to defeat the ends of justice. So the plaintiffs applied *ex parte* for an order against the German competitors to enable their premises in England to be searched before the writ was served. We granted it.

So the Mareva takes its place as a leading case of the same order as *Ashby* v *White* (1703) 2 Lord Raymond 938. It illustrates the maxim, *ubi jus ibi remediam*. The words of Sir John Holt, the Chief Justice, are still applicable: 'If the plaintiff has a right, he must of necessity have a means to vindicate and maintain it, and a remedy if he is injured in the exercise or enjoyment of it: indeed it is a vain thing to imagine a right without a remedy: for want of right and want of remedy are reciprocal.'

If any of you are interested in legal history, the Mareva is as revolutionary an invention as the Action on the Case was long ago. It has been invented by the judges to give a remedy where there had been none before. So it is worthy of study: and this book by Steven Gee and Geraldine Andrews is the best book in which to study it.

January 1987

Table of Cases

Table of Statutes

Table of Statutory Instruments

Chapter 1

Evolution of the Mareva injunction and Anton Piller relief

(1) The Mareva jurisdiction

The Mareva injunction was regarded as a new concept when the modern jurisdiction emerged in 1975. However, an historical antecedent may be found in a process called 'foreign attachment' which was available as part of the custom of the City of London as far back as the late 15th century. If a citizen of London issued a plaint of debt against the defendant in the Court of the Mayor and Aldermen of London, and the latter was not to be found within the jurisdiction of the court, the plaintiff was able to make an application to attach any effects of the defendant, whether money or goods or debts in the hand of third parties, to be found within the jurisdiction of the court. If a certain procedure was followed, after the defendant had failed to appear, his goods were appraised and delivered to the plaintiff up to the value of the amount demanded. The plaintiff had to give security that he would make restitution if the defendant appeared before the court within a year and a day, and proved that he owed nothing to the plaintiff at the time when the plaint was made, or that he owed only part of the debt. The debt had to be owed in London, and the defendant had to be 'foreign' in the sense of being 'not civic', ie out of the jurisdiction of the London court. He need not have been abroad.[1]

By the middle of the 19th century, the process of foreign attachment was riddled with fictions (*Mayor, etc of London* v *London Joint Stock Bank*). The absence of notice to the defendant was contrary to modern notions of natural justice, and the procedure raised difficulties as to the jurisdiction of the London Court over defendants abroad. The procedure fell into disuse, although it thrived in the United States.[2] There the Supreme Court[3] has limited the use of the procedure for the purpose

---

1 For a detailed description of the process see Bohun, *Privilegia Londini* 3rd ed, 1723, pp 253–289; Pulling, *The Laws, Customs, Usages and Regulations of the City and Port of London*, 2nd ed, 1842, pp 187–192. See also *Mayor and Aldermen of the City of London* v *Cox* (1866) LR 2 HL 239; *Mayor, etc of London* v *London Joint Stock Bank* (1881) 6 App Cas 393 (HL); (1880) 5CPD 494(CA).

2 *Ownby* v *Morgan* 256 US 94 at p 104 (1921).

3 *Shaffer* v *Heitner* 433 US 186 (1977); *Rush* v *Sarchuk* 444 US 320 (1980).

of founding jurisdiction for the court to determine the merits of the case.

Apart from the special customary procedure of foreign attachment, which was mirrored in many European countries, it appeared for many years that there was no procedure available to a plaintiff suing in England whereby he could seize the money or other assets of a defendant before obtaining judgment against him so as to prevent him from dissipating them (see eg, *Mills* v *Northern Railway of Buenos Aires Co* (1870) LR 5 Ch App 621, per Lord Hatherley LC at pp 627–628). The courts were also not prepared to grant an injunction to restrain the defendant from parting with his property (see *Mills* v *Northern Railway of Buenos Aires Co* (above); *Robinson* v *Pickering* (1881) 16 Ch D 660; *Lister & Co* v *Stubbs* (1890) 45 Ch D 1 and a number of other cases cited in argument on behalf of the defendant in *Rasu Maritima SA* v *Perusahaan Pertambangan* [1978] QB 644 at p 650). However, none of the cases appeared to consider the position where a foreign defendant was abroad and has assets within the jurisdiction which he was likely to remove at short notice (see *Rasu Maritima*, above at p 659).

(2) The Anton Piller jurisdiction

The granting of Anton Piller orders dates from 1974, the first reported case in which one was granted being *EMI Ltd* v *Pandit* [1975] 1 WLR 302 and the jurisdiction to grant the relief was first upheld by the Court of Appeal in *Anton Piller KG* v *Manufacturing Process* [1976] Ch 55, in which the procedure was distinguished from that of granting search warrants. The order itself gives no authority to the plaintiff or his solicitor to enter premises. The plaintiff must obtain the defendant's permission to enter and search for documents or other evidence. The defendant is made subject to a mandatory order of the court requiring him to give permission to a limited number of persons including the plaintiff's solicitors to enter the relevant premises within certain hours to search for evidence, property or other material falling within the ambit of the categories defined in the order and to remove the material found there so that it can be safeguarded. It is of the essence of the procedure that the application is made *ex parte*, and the hearing is conducted in chambers in the Queen's Bench Division, or in camera in the Chancery Division. In the Court of Appeal, an application will usually be heard in camera, but may occasionally be made in open court if the identity of the respondents to the application can be satisfactorily concealed from the public.

Often application is made so as to safeguard vital evidence which is needed to prove the plaintiff's claim but the procedure can be invoked so as to obtain necessary information required to safeguard the plaintiff's rights, or to locate assets upon which a judgment might be enforced, or to preserve property which otherwise might be dissipated or destroyed.

Because the application for the relief is made *ex parte*, the emergence of the jurisdiction has focused special attention on the content of the duty of the applicant to make full disclosure to the court, and the practice and procedure to be followed on an application to discharge the order. When the defendant is served with an Anton Piller order, after a short period allowed to him for the purpose of taking legal advice, he becomes under an immediate obligation to comply with the order, otherwise he will be in contempt of court, and be liable to be penalised even if subsequently he succeeds in having the order set aside.[4]

The plaintiff is required to give undertakings to the court as to how the order is to be executed, and breach of these undertakings constitutes a contempt of court. The plaintiff's solicitors have an onerous personal responsibility when they take on the conduct of an application for Anton Piller relief and execution of the order. Failure to adhere to the requisite professional standards is liable to result in criticism from the court, penal orders in relation to costs and possibly the making of a disciplinary complaint either to the court or under the Solicitors Act 1974.

The jurisdiction has also given rise to consideration by the courts of the ambit of the privilege at common law and under s 14 of the Civil Evidence Act 1968 against self-incrimination, in particular in and following the decision of the House of Lords in *Rank Film Distributors Ltd* v *Video Information Centre* [1982] AC 380. There has also been intervention by statute in the form of s 72 of the Supreme Court Act 1981.

As with the power of the courts to grant Mareva relief, the jurisdiction to grant Anton Piller relief is widely recognised in common law jurisdictions throughout the world, including Australia, New Zealand, Hong Kong, Singapore and Canada.

(3) Emergence of the Mareva jurisdiction

Even prior to 1975, the apparent absence of an available remedy to prevent foreign defendants from removing their assets from the jurisdiction so as to render useless any judgment which the plaintiff might obtain, was beginning to come to the attention of the courts.

The final report of the Committee on the Supreme Court Practice and Procedure (1953: Cmnd 8878) proposed that the writ of *ne exeat regno* (under which a defendant is arrested in order to prevent him leaving the jurisdiction) should become available post-judgment in order to prevent a judgment debtor from leaving the jurisdiction so as to evade his judgment creditor. This proposal was not acted upon. In *Felton* v *Callis* [1969] 1 QB 200, Megarry J held that the writ was not available for the purpose of preserving assets within the jurisdiction, but indicated that it would be appropriate for consideration to be given to a change to the law in this

---

4 *Wardle Fabrics Ltd* v *G Myristis Ltd* [1984] FSR 263; *Columbia Pictures Inc* v *Robinson* [1987] Ch 38 at pp 71–72.

area. Subsequently, the Committee on the Enforcement of Judgment Debts (1969: Cmmd 3909) recommended reform of the law.

The breakthrough came in 1975 when in two cases the Court of Appeal granted injunctions prohibiting the defendants from disposing of money by removing it from the jurisdiction. Those cases were *Nippon Yusen Kaisha v Karageorgis* [1975] 1 WLR 1093, and *Mareva Compania Naviera SA v International Bulkcarriers SA* [1975] 2 Lloyd's Rep 509, the case from which the Mareva injunction derives its name. In both cases the 'assets' which were made the subject of the injunction were bank accounts; the defendants were resident out of the jurisdiction and the applications were made and granted *ex parte*. The Court of Appeal derived jurisdiction to grant the relief sought from s 45 of the Supreme Court of Judicature (Consolidation) Act 1925, which provided as follows: 'A *mandamus* or an injunction may be granted or a receiver appointed by an interlocutory order of the court in all cases in which it shall appear to the court to be just or convenient.' The jurisdiction to grant such relief was affirmed by the Court of Appeal in the case of *MBPXL Corporation v International Banking Corporation Ltd* (unreported) Court of Appeal (Civil Division) Transcript No 411 of 1975 (28 August 1975), although it was described as 'exceptional'. Subsequently, the existence of the jurisdiction was challenged on an *inter partes* basis in *Rasu Maritima SA v Perusahaan Pertambangan* [1978] QB 644. The Court of Appeal held that the order could be granted in principle, and that in order to obtain such relief, the plaintiff need not show that he could obtain summary judgment, but merely that he had a 'good arguable case'.

In the course of his judgment Lord Denning MR reviewed the history of pre-trial attachment and the cases decided before the emergence of the Mareva jurisdiction (pp 657–661). The *Lister v Stubbs* line of authority was distinguished on the basis that it did not apply to foreign defendants who were abroad but who had assets within the jurisdiction which were liable to be removed at short notice.

(4) Gradual extension of the principle to English defendants

For some time there was considerable doubt whether Mareva relief could be obtained against English defendants resident within the jurisdiction. In *Van Weelde v Homeric Marine Services* [1979] 2 Lloyd's Rep 117, Lloyd J held that there was a settled practice against the granting of a Mareva injunction against a defendant resident within the jurisdiction, referring to an earlier case of *Adler Cosmetica v Minnahurst Ltd* (unreported) in which he had refused such relief, and the Court of Appeal had upheld his judgment (*inter alia*) on that point.

In *Chartered Bank v Daklouche* [1980] 1 WLR 107, the Court of Appeal held that the temporary presence of a defendant within the jurisdiction would not prevent the court from granting Mareva relief, and this was approved in dicta in *Third Chandris Shipping Corporation v Unimarine SA*

[1979] QB 645. Yet in *Bank Leumi (UK) Limited* v *Ricky George Sportain (UK) Limited,* Court of Appeal (Civil Division) Transcript No 753 of 1979 (1 November 1979) Ormrod LJ, with whom Brandon LJ agreed, stated that a Mareva injunction could not be obtained against a defendant within the jurisdiction.

In *Siskina* v *Distos SA* [1979] AC 210, the Mareva jurisdiction was considered for the first time by the House of Lords. Lord Hailsham pointed out the unjustifiable distinction between English and foreign-based defendants and observed that either the position of a plaintiff making a claim against an English-based defendant would have to be altered, or the principle of the Mareva cases would have to be modified. However, the House of Lords did not decide whether or not there was jurisdiction to grant Mareva injunctions, which at that time had been based by the courts on s 45 of the Supreme Court of Judicature (Consolidation) Act 1925. The decision of the House of Lords was that the plaintiffs in that case could not bring their claim within the former RSC Order 11, r 1(1)(i) then in force and that consequently there was no jurisdiction to entertain the claim on the merits or to maintain an interlocutory injunction in relation to that claim. Subsequently, in *Barclay-Johnson* v *Yuill* [1980] 1 WLR 1259, Sir Robert Megarry VC granted a Mareva injunction in respect of the assets of an English defendant temporarily absent abroad, but ordinarily resident within the jurisdiction.

The Mareva jurisdiction was further extended by the Court of Appeal in *Rahman (Prince Abdul) bin Turki al Sudairy* v *Abu-Taha* [1980] 1 WLR 1268. In that case, the Court of Appeal granted a Mareva injunction in terms which prohibited the dissipation of the defendant's assets within the jurisdiction, as well as their removal from the jurisdiction.

The jurisdiction of the courts to grant Mareva injunctions was put beyond doubt by s 37(3) of the Supreme Court Act 1981, which provides as follows:

The power of the High Court under subs(1) to grant an interlocutory injunction restraining a party to any proceedings from removing from the jurisdiction of the High Court, or otherwise dealing with, assets located within that jurisdiction shall be exercisable in cases where that party is, as well as in cases where he is not, domiciled, resident or present within that jurisdiction.

Section 37(1) of the Supreme Court Act 1981 replaced s 45 of the Supreme Court of Judicature (Consolidation) Act 1925 as the statutory source of the power to grant Mareva relief. It provides as follows: 'The High Court may by order (whether interlocutory or final) grant an injunction or appoint a receiver in all cases in which it appears to the court to be just and convenient to do so.'

Similar powers are conferred on the county court in cases falling within its jurisdiction by virtue of s 38 of the County Courts Act 1984. In addition, Mareva relief may be obtained in aid of arbitration proceedings in England (s 12(6)(*h*) of the Arbitration Act 1950) and under s 25 of the

Civil Jurisdiction and Judgments Act 1982, the High Court is empowered to grant Mareva injunctions in aid of proceedings before the courts of other contracting states to the European Judgments Convention.

The Mareva injunction is now one of the most commonly sought forms of interlocutory relief. Its efficacy in appropriate cases is undoubted. However, the frequency with which Mareva injunctions are now being sought and granted has led to tighter practical controls being imposed by the courts, in order to prevent abuse of the procedure. The plaintiff's duty to make full and frank disclosure of all material facts has been of particular concern. Since the consequences of a Mareva injunction can be very serious for the defendant, applications for Mareva relief require considerable forethought and careful preparation, despite the constraints of time which are often faced.

(5) The appointment of receivers

In *Hart* v *Emelkirk* [1983] 1 WLR 1289, Goulding J made an order appointing a receiver in a pre-judgment case in respect of assets in which the plaintiff claimed no proprietary interest and in respect of which the plaintiff had no entitlement to have them used in any particular way. The appointment was made simply on the basis that it was 'just and convenient' to do so, and that s 37(1) of the Supreme Court Act 1981 conferred jurisdiction to enable the appointment to be made. It is now clearly established (pp 139–141, below) that a receiver may be appointed irrespective of the nature of the plaintiff's claim in the action and whether before or after judgment. The emergence of the Mareva jurisdiction is also likely to lead to the law becoming more flexible in relation to the appointment of receivers by way of equitable execution (pp 142–143, below).

(6) Ancillary orders

The courts have also used s 37 of the Supreme Court Act 1981 as the statutory basis for the jurisdiction to make a wide variety of different types of order in aid of Mareva relief (p 12, below). A defendant may be required to give information to the plaintiff about his assets falling within the scope of the Mareva injunction for the purpose of assisting the plaintiff in ensuring that the Mareva relief can be made effective in safeguarding the relevant assets. That information may have to be provided on affidavit or by discovery of documents, and the defendant may be ordered to attend the court for cross-examination concerning the information provided. The defendant may be ordered to provide the plaintiff with authority to ask banks about assets, and he may in an extreme case be ordered to surrender his passport so that he cannot leave the country.

(7) Mareva relief granted worldwide

The courts have now departed from the original rule[5] that Mareva relief would only be granted in respect of assets situated within the jurisdiction. In this they[6] have followed the initiative taken in certain Australian courts[7] and taken into account the provisions for international reciprocity in granting interim relief in aid of substantive proceedings abroad and in recognising orders made by way of interim relief by foreign courts. This change in practice has given rise to the need to consider the extent (if at all) to which third parties are bound to respect a Mareva order in so far as it applies to assets abroad. This was the first done by the Court of Appeal in *Babanaft Co SA v Bassatne*.

(8) The carrying on of business and making payments out of assets subject to Mareva relief

As a consequence of the emergence of the Mareva jurisdiction the courts have laid down the principles which are to be applied in deciding whether or not assets are to be released from a Mareva injunction to be used for a particular purpose.[8]

(9) Effects on third parties

The granting of Mareva relief is liable to have an impact on third parties who deal with the relevant defendant or are involved in dealing with assets falling within the scope of the order. The courts have evolved rules of practice concerning undertakings to be provided by the plaintiff in favour of third parties and the drafting of the terms of the order, and have laid down principles as to the effect of Mareva relief on third parties and the extent to which their interests are to be taken into account when a court decides whether to grant or continue Mareva relief.

(10) Criminal law

The Mareva jurisdiction has provided the context for evolution of rules concerning the freezing of alleged proceeds of crime at common law. Statutory provisions are also in force providing for the making of restraint orders in connection with the prosecution of drug offences and other crimes.

---

5 Set out in *Ashtiani* v *Kashi* [1987] QB 888.
6 *Babanaft Co SA* v *Bassatne* [1989] 2 WLR 232; *Republic of Haiti* v *Duvalier* [1989] 2 WLR 261; *Derby & Co Ltd* v *Weldon (No 1)* [1989] 2 WLR 276; *Derby & Co Ltd* v *Weldon (Nos 3 and 4)* [1989] 2 WLR 412.
7 *Ballabil Holdings Pty Ltd* v *Hospital Products Ltd* (1985) 1 NSWLR 155; *Coombs and Barei Construction Pty Ltd* v *Dynasty Pty Ltd* (1986) 42 SASR 413; *Re Clunies-Ross, ex parte Totterdell* (1987) 72 ALR 241.
8 *Iraqi Ministry of Defence* v *Arcepey Shipping Co SA (The 'Angel Bell')* [1981] QB 65.

(11) The Civil Jurisdiction and Judgments Act 1982

Under Art 24 of the European Judgments Convention it is recognised that the courts of a contracting state may grant interim relief in respect of claims made before the courts of another state, and under s 25 of the Civil Jurisdiction and Judgments Act 1982, statutory jurisdiction now exists in cases falling within the section for the courts to grant interim relief, including Mareva injunctions and Anton Piller relief, in respect of proceedings on the merits which have been commenced or are to be commenced abroad. This has made a substantial inroad into the rule of practice laid down in *Siskina* v *Distos SA* whereby Mareva relief could only be granted in respect of a claim which was entertained on its merits by a tribunal or court within the jurisdiction.

Chapter 2

Nature of Mareva relief

(1) General principles

A Mareva injunction is an interlocutory order[1] of the court granted either before judgment, or in aid of execution of a judgment, which restrains the party enjoined from disposing of or dealing with his own assets. The assets covered by the order may be specified, but more usually are assets falling within one or more categories of asset set out in the order, and may be assets wherever situated (pp 122–124, below), even if they are outside the jurisdiction of the court.

The injunction does not confer on the plaintiff a pre-trial attachment or any form of security,[2] nor is the jurisdiction to be used for the purpose of putting pressure on the defendant to secure the claim.[3] The purpose of the exercise of the jurisdiction includes preventing a defendant from taking action 'designed to ensure'[4] that either a subsequent judgment or order of the court or an existing judgment or order is rendered less effective than would otherwise be the case. The circumstances in which Mareva relief may be appropriate include those where there is reason to believe that the defendant intends to cheat[5] the plaintiff of the fruits of a judgment, but are not so confined. There is no necessity to prove 'nefarious intent' on the part of the defendant (pp 117–121, below).

Mareva relief is relief *in personam* in the sense that it is directed to the defendant personally and does not confer upon the plaintiff any proprietary rights over or in assets which fall within its ambit. In the case of an injunction in the usual form, which is expressed not to apply to the assets in question in so far as their value exceeds a stipulated sum, then in the event of the value exceeding the stipulated sum, the injunction

---

1 'Interlocutory' includes the period after final judgment, see *Smith* v *Cowell* (1880) 6 QBD 75 and *Orwell Steel* v *Asphalt Ltd* [1984] 1 WLR 1097.
2 *Cretanor Maritime Co Ltd* v *Irish Marine Ltd* [1978] 1 WLR 966; *Bank Mellat* v *Kazmi* [1989] QB 541.
3 *Derby & Co Ltd* v *Weldon* (Nos 3 and 4) [1989] 2 WLR 412 at p 419; *K/S A/S Admiral Shipping* v *Portlink Ferries* [1984] 2 Lloyd's Rep 166.
4 *Derby & Co Ltd & Weldon* (Nos 3 and 4) above at p 422, per Lord Donaldson MR.
5 *PCW (Underwriting Agencies)* v *Dixon* [1983] 2 Lloyd's Rep 197 at pp 201–202, per Lloyd J.

allows the enjoined party to deal with the assets in relation to the excess value.

In *Cretanor Maritime Co Ltd* v *Irish Marine Ltd* [1978] 1 WLR 966, Buckley LJ said that in relation to a body of unspecified assets the injunction 'must be capable of having an ambulatory effect' so as to apply to assets from time to time coming within its ambit. Buckley LJ distinguished Mareva relief from an attachment ([1978] 1 WLR 966 at p 974):

. . . [I]t is, I think, manifest that a *Mareva* injunction cannot operate as an attachment. 'Attachment' must, I apprehend mean a seizure of assets under some writ or like command or order of a competent authority, normally with a view to their being either realised to meet an established claim or held as a pledge or security for the discharge of some claim either already established or yet to be established. An attachment must fasten on particular assets . . .

A Mareva injunction, however, even if it relates only to a particularised asset . . . is relief *in personam* . . . . All that the injunction achieves is in truth to prohibit the owner from doing certain things in relation to the asset. It is consequently, in my judgment, not strictly accurate to refer to a Mareva injunction as a pre-trial attachment.

However, a third party with knowledge of the injunction must not deliberately aid and abet a breach of its terms. The third party is not himself enjoined by the injunction, but the court will not 'allow its process to be set at naught and treated with contempt'.[6] Thus, for example, a bank with knowledge of a Mareva injunction must not honour cheques drawn on an account covered by the order.[7] To that extent the injunction can be said to operate as if it had an effect on an asset *in rem*, namely that the defendant is precluded from dealing with the assets, and third parties with knowledge of the order must not aid and abet a breach. Furthermore, it would appear that a third party is at risk of being held in contempt for participating in acts which are contrary to the terms of the order, even when the party enjoined does not yet know of the granting of the injunction.[8] This is on the ground that the court order takes effect as soon as it is pronounced, and even though the defendant would not be in contempt of court if he acted inconsistently with the terms of the injunction without knowledge that it had been made, nevertheless the third party would be guilty of conduct which deliberately caused the court order 'to be set at naught'.

The number of applications for Mareva injunctions has steadily increased since the emergence of the jurisdiction in 1975 and they are now commonplace. However, the relief is not to be granted except in circumstances when the court is satisfied that:

---

6 *Seaward* v *Paterson* [1897] 1 Ch 545 at p 555, per Lindley LJ. See also *Lord Wellesley* v *Earl of Mornington* (1848) 11 Beav 180; *Acrow (Automation) Ltd* v *Rex Chainbelt Inc* [1971] 1 WLR 1676; and *Z Ltd* v *A-Z and AA-LL* [1982] QB 558.

7 *Z Ltd* v *A-Z and AA-LL* (above).

8 Eg, a bank with knowledge of the order paying a cheque drawn by the defendant before the injunction was made: see *Z Ltd* v *A-Z and AA- LL* (above).

(1) the plaintiff has a good arguable case against the defendant;

(2) there is a real risk that judgment will go unsatisfied by reason of the disposal by the defendant of his assets, unless he is restrained by court order from disposing of them; and

(3) it would be just and convenient in all the circumstances of the case to grant the relief sought.

The drastic nature of Mareva relief has led to it being described somewhat graphically as 'one of the law's two "nuclear" weapons', the other being the Anton Piller order, per Donaldson LJ in *Bank Mellat* v *Nikpour* [1985] FSR 87 at p 92.

Since the Mareva injunction gives the plaintiff no proprietary rights over the defendant's assets, a bona fide purchaser (or assignee for value) or chargee of the assets without notice of the injunction will obtain good title or good security. Similarly, anyone with an existing charge over the assets is entitled to enforce it, although he will probably need the sanction of the court to do so. The same applies to bona fide judgment creditors of the defendant: in principle they can execute their judgment against any of his assets. In practice, if they have notice of the injunction they may need to obtain a specific variation to enable them to do so. For example, if a judgment creditor wishes to garnishee a bank account which is subject to a Mareva injunction then, unless the injunction is varied, the garnishee may object to making payment to the judgment creditor. However, strictly speaking, execution under a court order would not amount to a breach of the injunction. This is because the dealing with the assets is by order of the court and not by an act of the defendant. See further the dicta of Robert Goff J in *Iraqi Ministry of Defence* v *Arcepey Shipping (The 'Angel Bell')* [1981] QB 65 at p 72, and of Parker J in *A* v *B (X intervening)* [1983] 2 Lloyd's Rep 532 at p 534, which appear to suggest that a judgment creditor does not need to seek a variation of the Mareva injunction before executing the judgment on the assets. On the defendant's insolvency the plaintiff will rank *pari passu* with other unsecured creditors.

(2) 'Disposing of or dealing with' assets

A Mareva injunction is ordinarily expressed in terms which enjoin the defendant from 'disposing of' or 'dealing with' assets falling within the ambit of the order except in certain defined circumstances, eg payment of living expenses. In *Z Ltd* v *A-Z and AA-LL* Lord Denning MR said ([1982] QB 558 at p 574) that if an asset is covered by the terms of a Mareva injunction a third party who holds the asset and knows of the injunction must 'do what he reasonably can to preserve the asset. He must not assist in any way in the disposal of it. He must hold it pending further order . . .'

It might have been the case that the courts gave the terms of a Mareva injunction which precluded 'disposing of' or 'dealing with' assets abroad meaning so as, for example, to preclude the defendant from causing chattels to be removed by him from a bailee, or allowing a debt which was due to be paid to him. For debts, this appears to have been what was envisaged by Lord Denning MR in *Z Ltd* v *A-Z and AA-LL* when he referred to a bank 'freezing' a bank account. Such an approach would have the merit of making the position clear to third parties as to where they stood as a result of the injunction, and would tend to promote efficacy of the injunction because third party debtors or bailees would retain the relevant asset in the same form, pending further order of the court.

However, in *The Law Society* v *Shanks* [1988] 1 FLR 504, the defendant was an individual who was subject to a Mareva injunction which restrained him 'by himself, his servants, or agents or otherwise . . . from disposing pledging or transferring or dealing with any assets' of his within the jurisdiction including any gratuity to be received from the Ministry of Defence, which had been the employer of the defendant. The Ministry did not pay the defendant either the gratuity or his pension. Sir John Donaldson MR, with whom the other members of the court agreed, refused to follow the observations of Lord Denning MR in two passages ([1982] QB 558 at pp 572 and 574E) of his judgment in *Z Ltd* v *A-Z and AA-LL* saying that:

. . . I know of no authority other than this particular passage [ie the passage at p 574E] for the proposition that [the injunction] prevents anybody handing the asset over to the owner of the asset, in this case the defendant. That does not amount to a dissipation or a disposal of any kind whatsoever. In special circumstances, where it is known that the sole purpose of requiring the asset to be handed over to the defendant is to facilitate a dissipation of that asset, different considerations may arise . . . . That would be a very peculiar case indeed.

. . . [W]hilst [the two passages] are entitled to the greatest possible respect as coming from Lord Denning, they do not in my judgment represent a general statement of the law which is applicable in any ordinary case.

The court was clearly concerned in that case with the fact that the injunction contained no provision for payment by the defendant of his living expenses, and that even had provision been made, the injunction as interpreted by the Ministry in reliance on the observations of Lord Denning MR was taken as preventing payment to the defendant within the jurisdiction of money due to him.

In *Bank Mellat* v *Kazmi* [1989] QB 541, the defendant had been convicted of defrauding the plaintiffs who had obtained judgment against him. A question arose as to the effect of a Mareva injunction which restrained the defendant from 'disposing [of], pledging, transferring or otherwise dealing with any assets he may have within the jurisdiction of this court', and whether that injunction ought to be varied. The defendant had made a claim for supplementary benefit and an adjudication officer had determined that he was entitled to receive a substantial sum from the Secretary of State for Social Services who had thereby become a debtor of the defendant. The plaintiff judgment creditors wanted the money to be paid to one of the defendant's bank accounts, but the defendant wanted the money to be paid to him directly. The Secretary of State sought to intervene in the proceedings and asked for directions as to what he should do. Nourse LJ, with whom the other members of the court agreed, after citing from the judgment of Sir John Donaldson MR in *Law Society* v *Shanks* said (at p 547) that:

... Mere notice of the existence of a Mareva injunction cannot render it a contempt of court for a third party to make over an asset direct. Otherwise it might be impossible, for example, for a debtor with notice to pay over to the defendant even the most trivial sum without seeking the directions of the court. A distinction must be drawn between notice of the injunction on the one hand and notice of a probability that the asset will be disposed of or dealt with in breach of the order on the other. It is only in the latter case that the third party can be in contempt of court. No general test can be propounded for the latter class of case, although the facts here suggest that it may not be quite as peculiar as Sir John Donaldson MR thought.

Accordingly, it appears that although a Mareva injunction is expressed as restraining any 'dealing with' an asset, the court will interpret this as not preventing any conduct of the defendant which merely results in the same asset, or in the case of a debt the financial proceeds of the debt, being held by the defendant himself. However, the injunction will restrain the defendant from disposing of the asset when held by him or the financial proceeds of the debt. Consequently, if a plaintiff wishes to prevent the defendant from receiving payment of a debt due or accruing due to him from a third party, it is necessary to make an application for special wording to be inserted in the injunction expressly prohibiting the defendant from giving directions for, accepting or receiving payment of the relevant debt due or to become due from the third party.[9] On the basis of the approach adopted by the Court of Appeal in these two cases it would appear that the effect of a Mareva injunction in standard form is simply to prevent dissipation or disposals of assets.[10]

The position which has been reached is not entirely satisfactory. A defendant in respect of whom it has been thought appropriate to grant Mareva relief should not be accorded the right to require substantial sums in cash to be paid to him by his debtors. A third party should not be placed in the position where there is not a clearly correct course, and he has to seek to judge whether or not a payment can be made to the defendant. The question also arises as to whether a defendant who was subject to Mareva relief confined to his assets within the jurisdiction could require a bank or other third party consistently with Mareva relief granted in the

---

9 This was done by the plaintiffs in *Deutsche Schachtbau-und Tiefbohrgesellschaft GmbH* v *Ras Al Khaimah National Oil Co (No 1)* [1987] 3 WLR 1023 (CA); [1988] 3 WLR 230 (HL) in a separate application to Bingham J on 24 July 1986, and in consequence the wording of the injunction was varied.

10 An analogy can be drawn with the ambit of s 127 of the Insolvency Act 1986 which contains a provision formerly contained in s 227 of the Companies Act 1948 and s 522 of the Companies Act 1985. See in particular *Re Gray's Inn Construction* [1980] 1 WLR 711 at pp 715–716, and *Re Leslie Engineers Co Ltd* [1976] 1 WLR 292. Contrast the effect of a criminal restraint order; see p 254 below.

usual form to pay money to him from an account within the jurisdiction to an account (or in cash) outside the jurisdiction. It might be said that the payment would not itself constitute a 'disposal of' or 'dealing with' the asset, and that once the proceeds of the debt were outside the jurisdiction, they would not constitute an asset falling within the ambit of the injunction.

(3) When the defendant has a claim against a third party

A plaintiff who has obtained Mareva relief against a defendant who also happens to be a party to some other proceedings before the court is not regarded as having sufficient direct interest in the other proceedings to entitle him to intervene in those proceedings under RSC Order 15, r 6(2): see *Woodstock Shipping Co* v *Kyma Compania Naviera SA (The 'Wave')* [1981] 1 Lloyd's Rep 521. The plaintiff may be liable to be affected financially by the result of the other proceedings. Thus, for example, the other proceedings may involve a chose in action which represents all or a substantial part of the assets of the defendant. However, it would be impracticable to allow a plaintiff, who merely asserts a claim, to intervene in proceedings when he has no direct interest in the subject matter as such, but only a commercial interest in the outcome of the litigation. The fact that a Mareva injunction is obtained which applies to the chose in action which is the subject of the other proceedings, does not confer on the plaintiff a direct interest in the subject matter of those proceedings: see *Sanders Lead Inc* v *Entores Ltd* [1984] 1 WLR 452 (CA). This is the case even though an adverse result in the other proceedings is liable to leave the Mareva injunction without subject matter—the chose in action having been nullified by an adverse judgment.

The position is different once the plaintiff becomes a judgment creditor. He may then be able to obtain a garnishee order *nisi* if the subject of the other proceedings is an alleged debt: see *Sanders Lead Inc* v *Entores Ltd* above, per Kerr LJ at p 461. Alternatively, he may apply to the court to appoint a receiver by way of equitable execution to pursue the other proceedings in the name of the judgment debtor. As a further option, it may be possible for the plaintiff to commence winding-up proceedings or bankruptcy proceedings against the defendant. A liquidator or trustee in bankruptcy would then have the opportunity of taking over the conduct of the other proceedings.

A Mareva injunction in standard form would appear to preclude a defendant from settling other proceedings in which he is a claimant if the chose in action is an asset falling within the ambit of the injunction. This is because the chose in action is liable to be destroyed or altered by the settlement. In such circumstances the defendant should seek a variation of the Mareva injunction under the principles established in *Iraqi Ministry of Defence* v *Arcepey Shipping Ltd (The 'Angel Bell')* [1981] QB 65, before concluding the settlement.

In *Normid Housing Association Ltd* v *Ralphs and Mansell* [1989] 2 Lloyd's Rep 265, the plaintiffs had a substantial claim against the defendant architects for negligence and breach of contract in the design of certain works. The defendants had professional indemnity cover, and the insurers had made a comparatively small offer to settle the claims against them by the defendant architects. The plaintiffs desired to prevent the defendants from compromising the claim with the insurers, and obtained an injunction restraining them from doing so. The plaintiffs originally sought to uphold the injunction on the basis that they had a legal or equitable interest in the insurance claim by reason of the Third Parties (Rights Against Insurers) Act 1930. However, this Act only has the effect of transferring an insurance claim to a third party in the events[11] set out in s 1 of the Act—for example, in the event of an individual assured becoming bankrupt or making a composition or arrangement with his creditors or in the event of a winding-up order being made in respect of a company. None of those events had occurred. Section 3 of the Act afforded protection to third parties against settlements made after the commencement of bankruptcy or winding up, but not against settlements concluded beforehand. Accordingly, the Court of Appeal declined to uphold the injunction by reference to the Act (at pp 267–274). The plaintiffs then sought to uphold the injunction by reference to Mareva principles, arguing that the claim of the architects against the insurers was an asset and that the defendants should be precluded from dealing with that asset. The insurers and the architects submitted that the pending claim of the defendants against the insurers was not an asset for Mareva purposes. The Court of Appeal found it unnecessary to deal with this submission,[12] however it is considered to be misconceived. Mareva injunctions are commonly granted in respect of choses in action as such,[13] and in the context of the appointment of receivers, it is well established that a receiver may be appointed over a claim or potential claim against a third party.[14] However, the court did decide that the compromise of the claim by the architects would be a transaction entered into 'in the ordinary course of business' in the sense that it was not suggested that the proposed settlement was in any way collusive, nor was it a case in which the defendants were 'putting their assets or seeking to put their assets beyond the plaintiffs' reach' (at p 276, per Lloyd LJ). Accordingly, no Mareva injunction should be granted to prevent the compromise.

It was also sought to be suggested by the insurers that there should not be an injunction because if a settlement was entered into by the architects for the purpose of prejudicing the interests of the plaintiffs, it could

---

11 See generally *Firma C-Trade SA* v *Newcastle Protection and Indemnity Association* [1989] 1 Lloyd's Rep 139 at pp 250, 258 and 263.

12 *Normid Housing Association Ltd* v *Ralphs and Mansell (No 2)* [1989] 2 Lloyd's Rep 274 at p 275.

13 An obvious example is a bank account.

14 *Bourne* v *Colodense* [1985] ICR 291; *Maclaine Watson & Co* v *International Tin Council* [1988] Ch 1 at p 21; and see also [1989] Ch 253 at p 271.

subsequently be impugned under s 423 of the Insolvency Act 1986. The Court of Appeal did not deal with this argument, which goes to the manner in which the discretion was to be exercised. However, the consideration that if a settlement were to proceed the plaintiff may be able subsequently to have it set aside under s 423 cannot in itself preclude the granting of Mareva relief. If there are substantial grounds for believing that the intended settlement is not bona fide, then it is likely to be appropriate to prevent it being concluded. Prevention may well be better than a possible future cure.

Accordingly, as a general rule, Mareva relief granted to a plaintiff who is not a judgment creditor, will be varied so as to leave the defendant free to deal with claims against third parties including the prosecution of litigation and the negotiation and conclusion of any settlement. Exceptionally, relief may be available pre-judgment if the circumstances indicate that, for example, the defendant is seeking to rush through a disadvantageous settlement in the hope of spiriting away the proceeds. The fact that relief may be available under ss 423 to 425 of the Insolvency Act 1986 is no more than a factor which may fall to be taken into account in the exercise of the discretion of the court. Indeed, if the relevant third party is outside of the jurisdiction, any subsequent claim under those sections to impeach a settlement may be one which it would be difficult to prosecute or enforce.[15] The same is in principle applicable to an application by a plaintiff before judgment to have a receiver appointed over the claim, with authority to negotiate a settlement, prosecute litigation and collect any proceeds. The appointment of a receiver would only be appropriate in circumstances which justified the granting of relief by way of Mareva injunction, and as a matter of discretion should not be granted in circumstances where the granting of an injunction would itself not be just and convenient. However, if the plaintiff is a judgment creditor then he will be entitled to look to the claim for the purpose of satisfying the judgment.

(4) Courts in which Mareva injunctions can be obtained

Mareva injunctions can be obtained in any of the three Divisions of the High Court, although in view of the special statutory powers to grant relief in certain matrimonial actions derived from s 37 of the Matrimonial Causes Act 1973, they are less frequently sought in the Family Division than in the Queen's Bench or Chancery Divisions.

A Mareva injunction in aid of arbitration proceedings must usually be sought from a judge of the Commercial Court. The application must be made to a judge: a master or registrar does not have jurisdiction to grant a Mareva injunction within RSC Order 32, r 11(1)(*d*). Nevertheless, RSC

---

15 In *Normid Housing Association Ltd* v *Ralphs and Mansell* (above) it would appear that, although the insurers were foreign, there was no reason to suppose that there would be any special difficulties in making a claim under s 423.

Order 73, r 6(1) does not make it obligatory to apply under s 12(6) of the Arbitration Act 1950 to a commercial judge—this is because the requirement of making the application to a judge is not imposed by RSC Order 73, rr 2 or 3. In borderline commercial actions (ie those which fall within the definition of a 'commercial action' as set out in RSC Order 72, r 1, but which could equally well be dealt with in the ordinary Queen's Bench list) the plaintiff may prefer to start the proceedings in the Commercial Court and risk later transfer, for purely practical reasons. It usually takes less time to obtain a Mareva injunction in the Commercial Court than it does elsewhere, and the judges of the Commercial Court have considerable experience of such applications.

It is possible to obtain Mareva relief in the county court if the plaintiff's claim falls within the county court limits.[16] The source of the jurisdiction is s 38 of the County Courts Act 1984. In *Sions* v *Ruscoe-Price* (Court of Appeal (Civil Division) Transcript No 1027 (30 November 1988)), the Court of Appeal was concerned with a case in which the judge had refused Mareva relief on the ground (among others) that the sum involved was only £2,000. The court upheld the decision of the judge, Woolf LJ observing that in general it was inappropriate for Mareva relief to be granted in respect of a relatively small sum, particularly in view of the costs which might be involved and Staughton LJ emphasising that Mareva relief should not be granted as a matter of routine in every case of an unpaid debt, the risk of removal or dissipation of assets must be viewed in the context of the importance of the case and the sum involved. Accordingly, Mareva relief should not be granted in relation to a relatively small claim unless the court is satisfied that in all the circumstances of the case the possible adverse consequences of the relief sought are in proportion to the objective sought to be achieved.

(5) Mareva injunctions are available before and after judgment

The nature of Mareva relief is such that the majority of applications are made at a very early stage, usually before the writ has been issued. However, if it emerges during the course of a case that the defendant may be about to remove his English assets from the jurisdiction, there is no reason in principle, why the plaintiff should not make an application for Mareva relief at that time. Furthermore, the court has jurisdiction to extend a Mareva injunction which has been granted initially 'to judgment or further order', to cover the period between judgment and satisfaction of the judgment. A Mareva injunction may be granted to a judgment creditor in aid of execution of his judgment even if he did not apply for or obtain a Mareva injunction originally.[17] The injunction is granted in the

---

16 For examples see *Naz* v *Kaleem* [1980] CLY 409 and *Vanse* v *Bray* [1987] CLY 2997.
17 *Stewart Chartering* v *C&O Managements SA (The 'Venus Destiny')* [1980] 1 WLR 460; *Hill Samuel & Co Ltd* v *Littaur* (1985) 135 NLJ 57; *Orwell Steel (Erection and Fabrication) Ltd* v *Asphalt and Tarmac (UK) Ltd* [1984] 1 WLR 1097.

action in which the plaintiff has obtained judgment. Assets acquired by the defendant after judgment and prior to satisfaction will fall within the scope of any Mareva injunction extended or granted in aid of execution: see *TDK Tape Distributor (UK) Ltd* v *Videochoice Ltd and others* [1986] 1 WLR 141. This is because in the case of a Mareva injunction which refers to unspecified assets it has 'an ambulatory effect so as to apply to all assets of the defendant which at any time while the injunction remains on foot may be within the ambit of the assets covered by the injunction' per Buckley LJ in *Cretanor Maritime* v *Irish Marine Management Ltd* [1978] 1 WLR 966 at p 973.

If a plaintiff has become a judgment creditor this is liable to have an important effect on the exercise of discretion by the court on an application by the defendant to have the injunction varied to enable assets to be dealt with or disposed of for a particular purpose. Thus, before judgment a plaintiff who appears to have a clear right to be paid by the defendant still cannot insist on his claim being paid or secured either in priority to or *pro rata* with payment of other claims made against the defendant. In *K/S A/S Admiral Shipping* v *Portlink Ferris Ltd* [1984] 2 Lloyd's Rep 166, the plaintiffs had a good arguable claim against the defendants, and it appeared that the business of the defendants had been sold to a third party and that the assets of the defendants would probably only suffice to pay ordinary trade creditors, leaving the plaintiffs if and when they established their claim with nothing. The plaintiffs could not apply to wind up the defendants because the claim was a disputed one for unliquidated damages, and the statutory provisions in relation to setting aside preferences were unlikely to be applicable in due course, in particular because of the statutory time limit of six months.[18] The plaintiffs sought an order which, whilst the defendants would be permitted to pay their trade creditors, would be subject to sums being set aside which would be available to be paid towards discharging the plaintiff's claim if and when this was established. The Court of Appeal held that the injunction should be varied to enable trade creditors to be paid without there being any provision being made for a fund to be established to meet the plaintiffs' claim. It would be inappropriate for the Mareva jurisdiction to be used to produce a 'quasi-winding up' of the defendants in advance of judgment being obtained.[19]

However, once the plaintiff has obtained judgment the position is different. He may then be in a position to make an individual defendant bankrupt or have a corporate defendant wound up. Furthermore, he will be in a position to enforce the judgment by executing it on assets of the defendant. In these circumstances the injunction is granted or continued in aid of execution or, as may be the case, bankruptcy or winding-up proceedings. It will not be a good answer to execution for a defendant to say that he

---

18 The provisions now applicable are to be found in ss 239, 240 and 241 of the Insolvency Act 1986.
19 Applying *Iraqi Ministry of Defence* v *Arcepey Shipping (The 'Angel Bell')* [1981] QB 65. See also *Investors and Pensions Advisory Service Ltd* v *Gray* (1989) 139 NLJ 1415 at pp 1415–1416.

wishes to use the asset in question to pay another creditor. Nor in principle should it be a good reason for a judgment debtor to seek a variation to a Mareva injunction which has been granted in aid of execution. Thus, in *Deutsche Schachtbau-und Tiefbohrgesellschaft GmbH* v *Ras Al Khaimah National Oil Company (No 1)* [1987] 3 WLR 1023 (CA); [1988] 3 WLR 230 (HL), the Court of Appeal upheld Mareva relief granted in aid of enforcement of an arbitration award against a foreign company. Judgment had been obtained but was not yet enforceable under the rules of court, and it was contemplated that garnishee proceedings would be taken in relation to the relevant asset which was a debt due or accruing due from a third party. In these circumstances Sir John Donaldson MR, with whom the other members of the court agreed, observed that the injunction was not strictly speaking an injunction which fell into the Mareva category, but was an injunction granted as protection for a judgment creditor, under a jurisdiction recognised[20] before the emergence of the Mareva jurisdiction. 'The purpose of the injunction was . . . to maintain the status quo during the period covered by the stay of execution and not to preserve assets against the probability that DST might at some later date be able to establish its claim—the ordinary Mareva situation.' In the House of Lords the appeal against the injunction was dealt with at the same time as the appeal against the garnishee order, which was set aside on the grounds that if upheld it would place the garnishee at the risk of having to pay the same debt twice, and thus would be inequitable. In those circumstances the injunction could not be justified on precisely the same ground, namely that it would be inequitable to the third party debtor.

It is thought that the purpose for which the injunction has been granted, or for which the injunction is being maintained, may be an important consideration in the exercise of any discretion as to whether that injunction should be varied or discharged so as to release assets to be dealt with by the enjoined party. This is in line with the observations of the Master of the Rolls in the Court of Appeal, and is unaffected by the decision of the House of Lords. Thus, for example, if an injunction is granted in contemplation of the presentation of a winding-up petition then it may well be appropriate only to permit dispositions of the assets of the company which are validated by the court under s 127 of the Insolvency Act 1986.[21] Similarly, if an injunction is being maintained in aid of execution, the purpose of the injunction is likely to be of substantial, if not determinative, importance on any application by the judgment debtor to pay trade creditors. If, however, the judgment creditor has deliberately refrained from petitioning for the winding up of a company which is

---

20 Eg in *Bullus* v *Bullus* (1910) 102 LT 399.
21 This course was adopted by the Court of Appeal in *United Bank Ltd* v *Claybridge SA* (1980) 14 LMLN (15 May 1980); 16 LMLN (12 June 1980); unreported (9 March 1981) Court of Appeal (Civil Division) Transcript No 143 of 1987, the relevant statutory provision being then s 227 of the Companies Act 1948.

continuing to trade, then it may be inequitable for the court not to permit the judgment debtor to continue its business and pay its trade creditors notwithstanding the existence of the judgment.

(6) Mareva injunction in respect of land

If Mareva relief has been granted in an action pre-judgment the order is not one made 'for the purpose of enforcing a judgment' within the meaning of s 6(1) of the Land Charges Act 1972. The plaintiff may not obtain a final judgment to enforce.[22] Accordingly, the plaintiff is not entitled to register a land charge, or, in the case of registered land, a caution. Once the plaintiff obtains and seeks to enforce a judgment the position is different.[23]

The position in relation to Mareva relief is to be contrasted with the position when a receiver is appointed over land. In those circumstances a land charge or a caution may be registered (see p 147, below).

(7) Types of claim for which Mareva relief is available

A Mareva injunction is designed to protect the plaintiff against the dissipation of assets against which he might otherwise execute judgment whether immediately or in the future. It follows that Mareva relief is only suitable when the plaintiff's claim is one which would result in his being able to enforce judgment against the defendant's assets. If there is a claim to the assets themselves, the jurisdiction is not strictly 'Mareva' jurisdiction but an analogous jurisdiction under which the court is more ready to make orders requiring the defendant to state where the assets are located and preserving those assets.[24] A plaintiff who seeks purely declaratory relief will be unable to invoke the court's jurisdiction to grant him Mareva relief. See, for example *The Steamship Mutual Underwriting Association (Bermuda) Ltd* v *Thakur Shipping Co Ltd* [1986] 2 Lloyd's Rep 439.

However, there are no constraints on the nature of the plaintiff's cause of action or on the types of monetary relief which he may seek: his claim may be for payment of a debt, or damages, or an account, or even for statutory compensation. Mareva injunctions have been granted in actions for damages for nuisance, actions brought by husbands or wives for maintenance, and even in actions for damages for personal injuries: *Allen* v *Jambo Holdings* [1980] 1 WLR 1252. A Mareva injunction has been granted in an action by a former employee for damages for wrongful dismissal: see *Quinn* v *Marsta Cession Services Ltd* (1981) 133 DLR (3d) 109 (High Court of Ontario).

---

22 *Stockler* v *Fourways Estates Ltd* [1984] 1 WLR 25.
23 *Re Overseas Aviation Engineering GB Limited* [1963] Ch 24.
24 *Bankers Trust Co* v *Shapira* [1980] 1 WLR 1274; *A* v *C (No 1)* [1981] QB 956; *Mediterranea Raffineria Siciliana Petroli SpA* v *Mabanaft GmbH* Court of Appeal (Civil Division) Transcript No 816 of 1978 (1 December 1978); and *London and County Securities Ltd* v *Caplan* (unreported) Templeman J (26 May 1978), referred to in *Bankers Trust Co* v *Shapira* (above) and *A* v *C (No 1)* (above). See also p 65, below.

Under the Financial Services Act 1986 provision is made for the bringing of proceedings for the benefit of persons who have suffered loss as a
result of infringements of the requirements of the Act. In proceedings
brought by the Securities and Investment Board acting in pursuance of
powers delegated to it by the Secretary of State for the benefit of such persons, Mareva relief has been granted to the Board in respect of the total
losses suffered by those affected.[25] Thus, in principle, Mareva relief can be
obtained in respect of a statutory cause of action put forward by the plaintiff for the benefit of others, and the injunction will be granted by reference
to final relief which the plaintiff claims in the action. It is therefore open to
a plaintiff who puts forward a claim based on ss 423, 424 and 425 of the
Insolvency Act 1986 for the benefit[26] of the 'victims' of a transaction
defrauding creditors to obtain Mareva relief which is not confined to such
losses that he personally may have suffered by reason of the transaction
sought to be impugned. The Mareva relief to be granted will be related to
the nature of the final relief likely to be obtained by way of an order made
under s 423 of the Act.

Mareva relief is also available in respect of an order for costs to be taxed
even though the costs have not yet been taxed,[27] and in respect of damages
or other sums which are liable to be the subject matter of an order to pay
based on an undertaking which has been given to the court.[28]

(8) Claims against the crown

In proceedings against the crown, the court cannot issue an injunction of
any description by reason of the Crown Proceedings Act 1947, s 21(1),
proviso (a). The court cannot grant an injunction against an officer of the
crown if the effect would be to give relief against the crown which could
not have been obtained against the crown directly.

If a defendant subject to Mareva relief is entitled to receive money from
the crown, then in principle the crown could intervene in the proceedings
in appropriate circumstances to seek directions, and the court would have
jurisdiction to give directions concerning payment of the money by the
crown.[29] An order made in such circumstances directing the crown to pay

---

25 *Re DPR Futures Ltd* [1989] 1 WLR 778 at p 782; *Securities and Investment Board* v *Pantell SA*
[1989] 3 WLR 698.
26 Every application made for an order under s 423 is required by s 424(2) to be treated as
made 'on behalf of every victim of the transaction'. Accordingly, the order to be made
under s 423 will take into account the interests of all the 'victims' and not merely the
limited personal interest of an applicant who is a 'victim'.
27 *Faith Panton Property Plan Ltd* v *Hodgetts* [1981] 1 WLR 927.
28 *Commodity Ocean Transport Corpn* v *Basford Unicorn* [1987] 2 Lloyd's Rep 197 at p 200. (See
also *Yandil Holdings Pty Ltd* v *Insurance Company of North America* (1986) 7 NSWLR 571
(Supreme Court of New South Wales) in relation to a personal undertaking given by an
individual in respect of costs which had resulted in an order for costs being made against
the individual.)
29 *Bank Mellat* v *Kazmi* [1989] QB 541.

the money into a designated bank account or into court is not 'execution or attachment or process in the nature thereof . . . for enforcing payment by the crown of . . . money'[30] because the crown is ready, willing and able to pay the money, and is simply seeking a direction as to how the money is to be paid.[31] Accordingly, such a direction is not precluded by s 25(4) of the Crown Proceedings Act 1947.

(9) Claims against foreign states: State Immunity Act 1978

Section 13(2) of the State Immunity Act 1978 provides as follows:

Subject to subsections (3) and (4) below:
  (a) relief shall not be given against a state by way of injunction or order for specific performance for the recovery of land or other property; and
  (b) the property of a state shall not be subject to any process for the enforcement of a judgment or arbitration award or, as an action *in rem* for its arrest, detention or sale.

Under the State Immunity Act 1978 there are a number of different types of proceedings in which states are not immune from suit. This is because states only enjoy restrictive immunity. Nevertheless, s 13(2)(*a*) contains an absolute bar against the granting of an injunction against a state. Under s 14(1) and (4) of the Act a state includes the sovereign or other head of state in his or her public capacity, the government of the state, any department of the government, and the state's central bank, (reversing the effect of the decisions in *Trendtex* v *Central Bank of Nigeria* [1977] QB 529 and *Hispano Americana Mercantile SA* v *Central Bank of Nigeria* [1979] 2 Lloyd's Rep 277) or monetary authority. However, other state-owned or controlled entities are not immune from the granting of Mareva relief and whether an injunction is to be granted is a matter of discretion: see *Et Esefka International* v *Central Bank of Nigeria* [1979] 1 Lloyd's Rep 445; the 1978 Act did not apply in this case and the court refused to grant an injunction as a matter of discretion. Such entities may have immunity from suit in relation to proceedings relating to acts done by the entity 'in the exercise of sovereign authority': s 14(2). In view of the wording of s 13(2)(*a*) the courts may not grant a Mareva injunction even against assets of a state which are in use or intended for use for 'commercial purposes' and even after a judgment has been given against the state.

If a state intervenes in an action to seek a variation of a Mareva injunction so as to take outside its ambit any property which is asserted to belong to the state, then the mandatory terms of s 13(2)(*a*) make it inappropriate for the court to postpone determination of any issue as to whether the assets are the property of the state. Such a delay might otherwise have been appropriate: *SCF Finance* v *Masri* [1985] 1 WLR 876. In view of the terms of the section the court should not be willing to risk

---

30 Section 25(4) of the Crown Proceedings Act 1947.
31 *Bank Mellat* v *Kazmi* (above).

interfering with the state's enjoyment of its property simply by continuing an injunction granted against a third party.

(10) Types of asset which can be subject to a Mareva injunction

It appears clear that Mareva injunctions are available to prevent the disposal or removal from the jurisdiction of almost any type of asset, ranging from cash, goods, ships and aircraft to industrial machinery: *Rasu Maritima* v *Perusahaan Pertambangan* [1978] QB 644 (CA), the goodwill of a company: *Darashah* v *UFAC (UK) Ltd* (1982) *The Times*, 30 March, (CA), choses in action such as insurance policies: *TDK Tape Distributor (UK) Ltd* v *Videochoice Ltd and others* [1986] 1 WLR 141, and the proceeds of sale of a flat: *Barclay-Johnson* v *Yuill* [1980] 1 WLR 1259, or other interests and estates in land.

(a) Mareva injunctions over ships and aircraft

A plaintiff may obtain a Mareva injunction in respect of a ship even in circumstances in which he could not arrest it, and there is nothing as a matter of policy, or in the International Convention for the Arrest of Seagoing Ships 1952, or the statutes which have given effect to it, which prevents him from so doing: *The 'Rena K'* [1979] 1 QB 377, especially at p 409. The circumstances in which an action *in rem* can be brought against an aircraft are narrowly circumscribed: ss 20(2) and 21 of the Supreme Court Act 1981. It is possible that these will be widened if and when the United Kingdom ratifies the Convention on the International Recognition of Rights in Aircraft (which was signed at Geneva on behalf of the United Kingdom on 19 June 1948: see generally ss 90 and 91 of the Civil Aviation Act 1982), or the Rome Convention for the Unification of certain Rules relating to the Precautionary Arrest of Aircraft, 1933. It is doubtful whether the extension of the jurisdiction to arrest aircraft would have any effect upon the plaintiff's right to seek Mareva relief—certainly the courts have been willing to grant such relief in respect of aircraft in the past: see eg *Allen* v *Jambo Holdings* [1980] 1 WLR 1252. However, s 89 of the Civil Aviation Act 1982 excludes the availability of Mareva relief (or any relief involving seizure) in connection with certain patent claims in respect of aircraft and spare parts. This gives effect to Art 27 of the Chicago Convention 1944.

(b) Bills of exchange

A bill of exchange can be made the subject of a Mareva injunction restraining a party from dealing with the bill. The court will usually grant a plaintiff summary judgment on a bill of exchange. Furthermore, the court will refuse a counterclaiming defendant a stay of execution, save in exceptional circumstances: *Nova (Jersey) Knit Ltd* v *Kammgarn Spinnerei GmbH* [1977] 1 WLR 713. Nevertheless, the court may grant an injunction restraining dealings with the proceeds of a bill of exchange or a judgment founded on a bill of exchange even at the suit of the party liable on the bill: *Montecchi* v *Shimco (UK) Ltd* [1979] 1 WLR 1180. If an action is brought in England on the bill of exchange then the defendant can compel the plaintiff to produce the original bill of exchange within the jurisdiction under RSC Order 24, r 10(1).

(c) Judgment debts

A Mareva injunction is capable of applying to a judgment debt owed by a third party to the defendant. However, if the injunction is to be limited to assets within the jurisdiction, it is undesirable that the wording of the order should leave it to the defendant to decide for himself whether the relevant judgment debt is properly to be regarded, for the purposes of the injunction, as located within the jurisdiction. The defendant should know precisely what he is prohibited from doing from the face of the order (see p 178, below). It is considered that an English judgment debt is to be regarded as located within the jurisdiction for the purposes of a Mareva injunction (see: *A-G* v *Bouwens* (1838) 4 M&W 171 at p 191), and that an injunction limited to assets within the jurisdiction should be formulated so as to expressly include any relevant English judgment debt within its ambit. If a judgment debt is made subject to Mareva relief, the better view is that it does not preclude enforcement of the judgment, provided that the result of enforcement will be simply to provide proceeds which are also subject to the injunction. Although the effect of successful enforcement would be to discharge the judgment debt, overall the value of the defendant's assets held subject to the injunction is unaffected (see also pp 11–14, above).

(d) Claims under letters of credit, performance bonds and bank guarantees payable on demand

The circumstances in which a bank can be enjoined from making payment under a performance bond, letter of credit or bank guarantee payable on demand are very circumscribed. The general principle is that the court will not grant an injunction restraining payment under such a commercial instrument unless there is a strong *prima facie* case of fraud or the validity of the instrument itself is the subject of a substantial challenge.[32] A plaintiff who was concerned directly or indirectly in the provision of the relevant commercial instrument cannot use the Mareva procedure to

---

32 See generally: *Hamzeh Malas* v *British Imex Industries Ltd* [1958] 2 QB 127; *Discount Records* v *Barclays Bank* [1975] 1 WLR 315; *Howe Richardson Scale Co Ltd* v *Polimex-Cekop* [1978] 1 Lloyd's Rep 161; *Harbottle* v *National Westminster Bank* [1978] QB 146; *Edward Owen* v *Barclays Bank* [1978] QB 159; *Intraco* v *Notis Shipping* [1981] 2 Lloyd's Rep 256; *UCM* v *Royal Bank of Canada* [1983] 1 AC 168 at pp 182–188; *Bolivinter Oils* v *Chase Manhattan Bank* [1984] 1 WLR 392; *United Trading* v *Allied Arab Bank* [1985] 2 Lloyd's Rep 554; and *Siporex* v *Banque Indosuez* [1986] 2 Lloyd's Rep 146; see also *Elian* v *Matsas* [1966] 2 Lloyd's Rep 495, in which the Court of Appeal granted an injunction in the absence of an allegation of fraud. However, the decision can be regarded as one in which there was a dispute as to the continuing validity of the bank guarantee given the subsequent conduct of the beneficiary.

prevent payment under that instrument if he would not be entitled to an injunction against the bank. The courts have yet to consider whether a party seeking Mareva relief who has no connection with the letter of credit transaction, is in any different position. *Prima facie* payment under the instrument would not amount to the type of dissipation of assets or removal of assets from the jurisdiction which such relief is designed to prevent, and the court would refuse to interfere with a genuine business transaction.

Whether the general principle applies depends upon the construction of the commercial instrument and whether in substance it amounts to an independent undertaking by the bank to pay the beneficiary which is not conditional or dependent upon the actual performance of the underlying transaction. For cases involving such a question of construction see *Esal (Commodities) Ltd* v *Oriental Credit* [1985] 2 Lloyd's Rep 546; *Siporex* v *Banque Indosuez*, above, at pp 157–158; and *Hortico (Australia)* v *Energy Equipment Co (Aus)* (1985) 1 NSWLR 545. Such undertakings are almost invariably payable on demand or against presentation of certain documents. The precise form of a demand required to operate an undertaking is also a question of construction (*IE Contractors Ltd* v *Lloyds Bank plc* [1989] 2 Lloyd's Rep 205). Thus, for example, it may be necessary for the demand to contain a statement that there has been a breach of the underlying transaction (*Esal Commodities Ltd* v *Oriental Credit* [1985] 2 Lloyd's Rep 546 at p 550 (per Ackner LJ)). In transactions involving the provision of a bank's unconditional undertaking the only implied term is that the beneficiary will not seek to enforce the undertaking unless he has an honest belief that he is entitled to do so.[33] For the fraud exception to apply the plaintiff must show clear evidence of fraud by the beneficiary and that the bank has knowledge of that fraud (*Bolivinter Oil* v *Chase Manhattan Bank* [1984] 1 WLR 392). The uncorroborated evidence of the plaintiff will not be sufficient. The test appears to be whether the plaintiff has established (with the assistance of strong corroborative evidence) that the only realistic inference on the evidence presently available appears to be that there is fraud by the beneficiary. This does not require the plaintiff to show that there is no possibility whatsoever of the beneficiary having acted honestly: *United Trading* v *Allied Arab Bank* [1985] 2 Lloyd's Rep 554 at p 561. The plaintiff may be able to obtain an injunction even though not in direct contractual relations with the bank concerned, on the grounds of a threatened breach of a duty of care owed in tort.

A question which has been raised is whether the court is limited in considering the extent of the knowledge of the bank at the date of the issue of the writ. In principle it is desirable that the court should take into account all of the evidence available regardless of when that evidence came into

---

33 *United Trading* v *Allied Arab Bank* [1985] 2 Lloyd's Rep 554 following *State Trading Corporation of India* v *ED & F Man (Sugar)* [1981] Com L Rep 235, see also *Dodsal PVT Ltd* v *Kingpull Ltd* Court of Appeal (Civil Division) Transcript No 345 of 1985 (1 July 1985).

existence. On the other hand, the plaintiff must have a cause of action against the bank at the date of the issue of the writ. The difficulty can be surmounted by the plaintiff issuing a new writ on conclusion of the *inter partes* hearing before the court, by which time the bank will have notice of all the evidence before the court. The relevant questions will then be:

(1) whether the plaintiff has produced sufficient evidence to establish a clear *prima facie* case of fraud on the part of the beneficiary (albeit not excluding altogether the possibility of an innocent explanation); and

(2) whether on a balance of convenience it is appropriate to grant an injunction against the bank.

A Mareva injunction may be granted to restrain the defendant from assigning his right to receive the proceeds of the letter of credit, performance bond, or bank guarantee, or to restrain dealings with the proceeds after payment has been made. See *Intraco Ltd* v *Notis Shipping Corporation (The 'Bhoja Trader')* [1981] 2 Lloyd's Rep 256; *Power Curber International Ltd* v *National Bank of Kuwait SAK* [1981] 1 WLR 1233 at pp 1241–1242; and *Hortico (Australia)* v *Energy Equipment Co* (1985) 1 NSWLR 545 in which such an injunction was refused on the grounds that on the facts there was no more than 'the usual likelihood of a defendant who is being sued so organising his assets that any judgment . . . [would] be frustrated'. For a similar case see *Dodsal PVT Ltd* v *Kingpull Ltd* Court of Appeal (Civil Division) Transcript No 345 of 1985 (1 July 1985).

Even if a Mareva injunction is granted, there is a strong probability that it is unlikely to be of much assistance to the plaintiff. It is common practice for a trading organisation to raise finance by assigning its right to receive payment under a letter of credit or bank guarantee to a bank, in return for a loan; such transactions usually take place a long time before the plaintiff is in a position to challenge the validity of the documents tendered for payment under the letter of credit, or before the plaintiff discovers that the goods are not what he contracted to buy. Naturally, the bona fide assignee will have a better right to the assets than the defendant, and he can usually obtain the discharge of the Mareva injunction by producing evidence of the assignment: *Pharaoh's Plywood Co Ltd* v *Allied Wood Products*, Court of Appeal Transcript (Civil Division) No 217 of 1980 (18 January 1980). This is so whether or not notice of the assignment has been given to the bank liable on the letter of credit, performance bond or guarantee.

Therefore, there are many commercial transactions in which Mareva or other injunctive relief is either unobtainable or ineffective.

(11) Effect of statutes which preclude any assignment or charge on certain assets

There are statutory provisions which prevent certain assets being assigned or being made the subject of a charge. Mareva relief does not as such effect an assignment of or a charge on an asset covered by the scope of the injunction (see pp 9–10, above). However, such statutory provisions can be relevant to whether Mareva relief is to be granted because it must be considered for what *purpose* Mareva relief is sought. If the position is that the plaintiff will not be able to obtain execution on the relevant asset even if he obtains a judgment then it would be wrong in principle to grant Mareva relief pre-judgment or post-judgment in relation to that asset for the purpose of safeguarding the asset in anticipation of possible execution proceedings.[34] Furthermore, even if it may eventually be possible to reach an asset by execution, or through bankruptcy or winding-up proceedings[35] there will still be the question whether it is just and equitable that the asset should be the subject of a restraint in the meantime.

(12) Joint ownership of assets

In *Z Ltd* v *A-Z and AA-LL* ([1982] 1 QB 558 at p 591, Kerr LJ said that in cases in which a Mareva injunction is granted over a joint bank account, the order should include a specific reference to the account. The practice has grown up of drafting Mareva injunctions in wide terms so as to cover 'moneys held to the account of the defendant whether in his own name or jointly with some other party' and injunctions are commonly granted in this or in a similar form. It is well established that a judgment creditor cannot obtain a garnishee order over a joint bank account.[36] However, each joint account holder has a right of property in the chose in action represented by the account: *Welch* v *Bank of England* [1955] Ch 508 at p 532; *Baker* v *Barclays Bank* [1955] 1 WLR 822 at pp 830–831. This right of property is an asset which in principle can be the subject of a Mareva injunction. However, the plaintiff should be prepared to demonstrate to the court that the asset may be available for execution of a judgment or that the asset may be available for distribution through bankruptcy or winding-up proceedings. Thus, for example, if the defendant is solely beneficially interested in a joint bank account (the other joint account holder being merely a nominee) then the plaintiff may eventually be able to have a receiver appointed by way of equitable execution over the account. The usual position on a joint account is that each account holder is entitled independently to draw on the account. In such circumstances a plaintiff who has a cause of action against only one of the joint account holders should not normally be allowed to prevent the other account holder from drawing on the account. For this reason it will only be in comparatively rare circumstances that it will be justifiable to grant a Mareva injunction against a joint bank account: *Z Ltd* v *A-Z Ltd* [1982] QB 558 at p 591, per Kerr LJ.

---

34 Eg see the position under s 203 of the Army Act 1955, and the decisions in *Walker* v *Walker* [1983] Fam 68 and *Bank Mellat* v *Kazmi* (above).

35 *DST* v *Ras Al Khaimah* [1988] 3 WLR 230 at 262G.

36 See eg *Hirschorn* v *Evans* [1938] 2 KB 801; *Macdonald* v *Tacquah Gold Mines Co* (1884) 13 QBD 535; *Catlin* v *Cyprus Finance Corporation* [1983] QB at p 769.

In the case of joint interests in land, there is a trust for sale with each party having an interest in the proceeds of sale. Such an interest may be the subject of a Mareva injunction and, after judgment, be the subject matter of a charging order: *Harman* v *Glencross* [1986] Fam 81. Joint ownership of an asset is to be distinguished from the position where an asset is in joint names, but there is good reason for supposing that the asset in fact is owned beneficially by the defendant to the substantive claim. In these circumstances the court may grant Mareva relief against both parties in whose names the asset is held.[37] If the position is that the plaintiff is entitled to seek to set aside a transaction under which a third party acquired a joint interest in an asset together with the defendant (eg an interest acquired by a spouse), then again in principle the court may grant Mareva relief against both the defendant and the third party (see pp 132–134, below).

---

37 *SCF* v *Masri* [1985] 1 WLR 876 and see pp 126–127, below.

Chapter 3

Forms of the Mareva injunction

(1) Introduction

When the Mareva jurisdiction was beginning to develop, the form of injunction adopted usually had no financial limitation. In addition, some of the early injunctions merely prohibited the defendant from removing his assets from the jurisdiction, thus leaving it open for him to contend that he was not precluded from paying off debts within the jurisdiction, or otherwise dealing with his assets in a manner designed to ensure that there were none left when the plaintiff obtained judgment.

(2) Prohibition on dealings with assets

The usual form of order which is granted prohibits the defendant and his servants or agents from 'removing from the jurisdiction, disposing of, charging, encumbering, or otherwise dealing with howsoever' any of his assets within the jurisdiction and then goes on to specify particular assets which are included. In appropriate cases, a particular form of 'dealing' may be expressly prohibited, eg if one of the assets is real property or a vessel, a specific prohibition on mortgaging assets may be included. A specific prohibition on the assignment of assets is usually unnecessary because 'disposing' includes sale or assignment, but it may be preferable to spell this out in cases involving debts or other choses in action. If the plaintiff is aware of the existence of specific assets (such as bank accounts) they should be referred to with as much particularity as is possible, so as to enable third parties on whom notice of the injunction is served to identify them and comply with the terms of the order. If a joint account is to be included, the order must say so (see generally the guidelines laid down by Kerr LJ in *Z Ltd v A-Z and AA-LL* [1982] 1 QB 558 at pp 587–592).

It was also said by Kerr LJ in *Z Ltd v A-Z and AA-LL*, that a Mareva injunction should not apply to shares or title deeds which a bank may hold as security or articles in a safe deposit which a bank may hold in the name of a defendant. The justification for the view is that it would place too great a burden on banks for them to be placed in the position of assessing the value of unspecified assets with reference to the maximum sum specified in the injunction. The current practice is not to exclude such assets from the terms of the *ex parte* order. If a bank considers itself to be placed in an embarrassing position then it may apply to the court for specific directions to be given concerning such types of asset. On such an application the court could decide to exclude such types of asset from the ambit of the injunction or, preferably, could grant an injunction confined to the particular assets held by the bank which is not limited to a maximum sum. If the court adopted the latter course then:

(1) it would be open to the defendant to place evidence of value before the court with a view to having certain items excluded by reference to the maximum amount of the plaintiff's claim; and

(2) the court could grant an ancillary order (for discovery of documents or information, concerning the value to be provided by the defendant). The court could then reconsider the scope of the Mareva injunction in the light of the information obtained under the ancillary order.

If the bank does not wish to place before the court information as to what assets it holds, it may make the application by calling attention to the omission of words in the Mareva order specifically referring to the types of asset referred to by Kerr LJ. Such an application could not be regarded as a breach of the duty of confidentiality owed by the bank to its customer.

It appears that a Mareva injunction in the standard form is interpreted by the court as only prohibiting *disposal* of chattels, and therefore it would seem that a bank may be bound to release to its customer share certificates, title deeds or articles in a safe deposit, unless the bank knows that this is a step taken as a preliminary to a disposal (see pp 11–14, above).

(3) 'Maximum sum' orders

It is now rare for a Mareva injunction to be granted without a financial limitation (see *Z Ltd* v *A-Z and AA-LL*, above). The rationale behind this is that the plaintiff's claim is only for a limited amount, and there is no justification for freezing assets which are in excess of that limit if the purpose behind the order is simply to preserve sufficient assets to satisfy the judgment. In determining the limit to be placed on the injunction, the court will usually adopt the quantum of the plaintiff's claim (or such of it as is likely to succeed), or, if appropriate, the total of all cumulative claims, together with an estimate of the interest likely to accrue on that sum until judgment. If the plaintiff has alternative claims, the court will assess the maximum sum by reference to the highest claim in amount in respect of which the plaintiff has a good arguable case. By way of analogy, see the practice of assessing the amount of security in an Admiralty action *in rem* in *The 'Moschanthy'* [1971] 1 Lloyd's Rep 37. At one time doubts were expressed as to whether it would be appropriate to include an element for the plaintiff's costs (on the grounds that this would be tantamount to ordering a defendant to put up security for costs), but in practice nowadays an element for recoverable costs is usually included. The way in which a 'maximum sum' order is expressed may vary and there are two main versions. The first restrains dealings with assets up to the value of the financial limit; the second restrains dealings with assets save in so far as they exceed in value the financial limit.

(4) Unlimited orders

Unlimited orders are rarely justifiable in ordinary Mareva cases. However, in tracing cases, for example where the plaintiff is seeking to trace into the defendants' bank accounts the proceeds of an alleged fraud, it may be appropriate for the court to place no financial limitation on the injunction, either because the full quantum of the plaintiff's claim is unascertainable, or because it is just and equitable that all assets should be preserved until investigations have been carried out with a view to ascertaining which are arguably subject to a trust and which are not. Similar considerations may apply in cases where the plaintiff is claiming for the breach of intellectual property rights (eg breach of copyright, infringement of trade marks or patents), where the extent of the plaintiff's claim may be impossible to predict and the number of infringing copies in circulation is unknown.

(5) Orders limited to specific assets

It is possible to obtain orders which do not relate to the defendant's assets generally, but which are limited to specific assets. These are particularly appropriate where the plaintiff knows that the defendant has one asset, eg a diamond necklace, which is worth as much as, or more than, the plaintiff's claim. If the injunction can be confined to a particular asset, this may have the advantage of limiting the exposure of the plaintiff to claims under his cross-undertaking in damages. It is possible for the court to confine the scope of a Mareva injunction to specific assets after it has been granted in wider terms, if sufficient information about the defendant's assets has been revealed pursuant to an order for discovery, or voluntarily.

(6) Ancillary orders

The Mareva injunction may be granted in an order which includes ancillary orders to assist the efficacy of the injunction, eg orders for the disclosure of assets, Anton Piller orders relating to documents or articles which require preservation, orders under the Bankers Books (Evidence) Act 1879, or even orders restraining the defendant personally from leaving the jurisdiction (see generally: Chapter 17).

Chapter 4

Comparison of Mareva relief with other forms of order preserving assets

(1) Admiralty rights *in rem*

The right to proceed against a vessel or aircraft *in rem* is governed by ss 20–24 of the Supreme Court Act 1981, which provide an exclusive statutory code. Certain of the claims which can be enforced by action *in rem* give rise to a maritime lien (eg salvage and collision claims). A maritime lien is available against the vessel even though ownership of the vessel has been subsequently transferred to a bona fide purchaser for value (*The 'Ripon City'* [1897] p 226 at p 241) and even though this has occurred prior to the commencement of the action. Under English law the right to a maritime lien is a matter of procedure and is to be determined according to the *lex fori*: *Bankers Trust Ltd* v *Todd Shipyards* [1981] AC 221. In the case of other rights to proceed *in rem* against a vessel, the Admiralty jurisdiction is invoked when the writ is issued (*Re Aro Co* [1980] Ch 196) and the right to arrest the vessel continues notwithstanding a change in ownership of the *res* after the issue of the writ: *The 'Monica S'* [1986] P 741. The right to arrest is available before or after judgment and the warrant of arrest is granted upon an *ex parte* application supported by affidavit when the *res* is within the jurisdiction. The measure of priority afforded by the right *in rem* depends upon the nature of the cause of action. Thus, for example, a claim in respect of salvage takes priority over a mortgage. For a list of priorities see McGuffie, *Admiralty Practice*, British Shipping Laws, 1, 1964 ed chapter 39.

The practice of the Admiralty Court is not to determine priorities until after the vessel has been sold. If bail is not provided, the court will usually order a sale *pendente lite*. See generally on this *The 'Myrto'* [1977] 2 Lloyd's Rep 243; however, such a sale may not be ordered if the plaintiffs do not stand to obtain some financial benefit in terms of security for their claim: *The 'Marco Reefer'*, 50 Lloyd's Maritime Law Newsletter (19 August 1981). In the event of the defendant wishing to secure the release of the vessel from arrest he may provide bail by RSC Order 75, r 16, which is assessed upon the basis of the plaintiffs' claim, interest and costs: *The 'Moschanthy'* [1971] 1 Lloyd's Rep 37 at pp 46–47. More usually, a vessel is released from arrest by agreement of the parties upon provision of a letter of guarantee acceptable to the plaintiffs. Interference with a vessel under arrest is a contempt of court: *The 'Jarvis Brake'* [1976] 2 Lloyd's Rep 320.

(2) Garnishee procedure

This is a procedure available under RSC Order 49, r 1 and the Supreme Court Act 1981, ss 40 and 139, for execution of a judgment for a liquidated sum, upon debts due or accruing due, National Savings, deposit and withdrawable share accounts by including assets expressed in foreign currency: *Choice Investments Ltd* v *Jeromnimon* [1981] QB 149. The procedure is only available after judgment (even an order for costs to be taxed will not suffice) and is by way of order *nisi* granted *ex parte* on affidavit evidence, subsequently converted into an order absolute. It has been said that it is only possible to garnishee debts which are recoverable and therefore situated within the jurisdiction: *Richardson* v *Richardson* [1927] P 228 and *Brooks Associates Inc* v *Basu* [1983] QB 220 at pp 222–223. However, this view has been doubted in *SCF* v *Masri (No 2)* [1987] QB 1002, in which the matter has been said to be a question of discretion (eg the order will not be made if the garnishee would be at risk of having to pay twice: *Martin* v *Nadel* [1906] 2 KB 26).

The order *nisi*, takes effect when it is served upon the garnishee. In the event of the order being made absolute, the garnishee is bound to pay the debt or hold the asset for the judgment creditor. Meanwhile, once served with an order *nisi*, the garnishee cannot pay the debt or transfer the asset without incurring the risk of having to pay twice.

The making of a garnishee order is a matter of discretion exercised upon the same principles as those which apply to charging orders. Thus, the order will be made unless there are special factors making it inequitable to grant it: *Roberts Petroleum Ltd* v *Bernard Kenney Ltd* [1983] 1 AC 192. The mere fact that a judgment debtor wishes to use the asset to satisfy other debts is insufficient; but, if the judgment debtor is bankrupt or insolvent, the asset will be released for distribution *pro rata* among the creditors. In order to found jurisdiction to make a garnishee order, it is sufficient if the garnishee has agreed to submit to the jurisdiction or is within the jursidiction when the application is made for an order *nisi*: *SCF* v *Masri (No 2)*, above.

If the intended garnishee would in fact be subjected to a substantial practical risk of having to pay twice, which cannot be protected against, then this will be liable to constitute good grounds for not making the order. Thus, in *Deutsche Schachtbau-und Tiefbohrgesellschaft GmbH* v *Shell International* [1988] 3 WLR 230, the plaintiff judgment creditors were refused a garnishee order when the intended garnishees had been successfully sued by the judgment debtors for the debt in foreign court proceedings. Although the relevant foreign court had no jurisdiction over the matter under English rules of conflicts of law, nevertheless there was a serious risk of the foreign judgment being successfully enforced against the intended garnishees, and therefore it would be inequitable to the intended garnishees to grant a garnishee order.

(3) Charging orders

The grant of a charging order by the court provides a means by which judgment for a liquidated sum may be executed upon an interest in land, funds in court, or shares. The procedure, which is very similar to that for garnishee orders, has been considerably extended by the Charging Orders Act 1979. A charging order is only available after judgment.

In the event of the order being made absolute the plaintiff acquires a judicial charge over the asset as from the date of the order *nisi*. The charge is realised by fresh proceedings for the sale of the asset and distribution of the proceeds.

(4) Appointment of a receiver

The court has power to appoint a receiver over any type of asset (including, for example, a claim for unliquidated damages) and even over assets situated outside the jurisdiction. The court may appoint a receiver over an asset at any stage of proceedings; the statutory power to appoint a receiver by interlocutory order whenever it is just and convenient to do so, is contained in the same section as that conferring jurisdiction to grant Mareva injunctions: s 37 of the Supreme Court Act 1981, preserving the jurisdiction previously exercised under s 45 of the Supreme Court of Judicature (Consolidation) Act 1925.

The order does not confer upon the plaintiff any priority not enjoyed previously. However, the appointment of the receiver is usually made for the purpose of protecting some interest or rights of the plaintiff in or concerning the underlying assets. The development of the Mareva jurisdiction from s 45 of the Supreme Court of Judicature (Consolidation) Act 1925 opened the way for the courts to appoint a receiver in the absence of the plaintiffs asserting rights relating to the underlying assets. Since the Supreme Court Act 1981, the courts have appointed receivers on an interlocutory basis even though the plaintiff does not claim any right to the underlying assets.

(5) Summary of comparison

(1) A Mareva injunction can be obtained both before and after judgment in the action. When it is obtained after judgment it is granted as an aid to execution. A warrant of arrest *in rem* and an order appointing a receiver are likewise obtainable before or after judgment. Charging orders and garnishee orders, however, can only be obtained after judgment.

(2) There are no restrictive rules relating to the nature of the cause of action in respect of which Mareva relief can be granted, although the plaintiff will not be entitled to Mareva relief if he cannot demonstrate that he will be entitled to enforce any judgment he may obtain against the defendant's assets. A warrant of arrest *in rem* can only be obtained in the circumstances covered by ss 20–24 of the Supreme Court Act 1981.

(3) A Mareva injunction may be granted and a receiver may be appointed in relation to assets of the defendant, wherever situated. A warrant of arrest is limited to an asset within the jurisdiction. A garnishee order may only be made over a garnishee who has been served with a garnishee order *nisi* within the jurisdiction or who has voluntarily submitted to the jurisdiction. It is not limited to debts which can be said to be located within the jurisdiction, but it is a mode of execution in respect of which there has to be a connection between the intended garnishee and the jurisdiction. Charging orders are not limited to assets which can be described as located within the jurisdiction, although the categories of asset on which a charging order can be sought are limited by statute and rules of court.

(4) By way of contrast to other forms of order preserving assets, a Mareva injunction does not affect the defendant's proprietary interest in his assets. The plaintiff gains no priority over any other creditor of the defendant and no proprietary interest in or charge over the assets which are subject to the injunction. He will only obtain security if the defendant puts up security in order to achieve the release of the injunction. On the other hand, the issue of a writ *in rem* may lead in due course to the plaintiff obtaining security, eg by the arrest of the vessel followed by provision of bail, a bank guarantee, or some other suitable form of security for the release of the vessel, or by the sale of the vessel *pendente lite*. Charging orders when made absolute also give the plaintiff security. A garnishee order absolute entitles the garnishee to enforce and receive payment of the garnished debt. But it does not transfer or assign the attached debt to the garnishor.[1]

(5) The court may decide to vary or discharge a Mareva injunction for reasons of commercial convenience, or to enable the defendant to pay debts or even to meet moral obligations. See generally, *Iraqi Ministry of Defence* v *Arcepey Shipping (The 'Angel Bell')* [1981] QB 65. The court is most careful to ensure that third parties are not unduly burdened by the granting of Mareva relief. See, eg *Galaxia Maritime SA* v *Mineralimport/export* [1982] 1 WLR 539.

---

1 *Re Combined Weighing and Advertising Machine Company* (1890) 43 ChD 99.

This is not the position with a warrant of arrest. Indeed, as previously noted, the arrest will be maintained notwithstanding the fact that the vessel was sold to a bona fide purchaser after the writ was issued but before it was served: *The 'Andria' (now renamed The 'Vasso')* [1984] QB 477; *The 'Monica S'* above. Accordingly, a third party with no knowledge of the dispute in relation to which the vessel was arrested may find himself in the unfortunate position of having to provide security to obtain the release of his ship. The risk of arrest, however, has been treated by the courts as one of the normal incidents of the ownership of vessels, and the purchaser of a vessel should be prepared to face such an event if the arrest causes him substantial financial or commercial hardship. See *The 'Helene Roth'* [1980] QB 273.

In the event of the plaintiff seeking the appointment of a receiver as a means of facilitating the operation of a Mareva injunction, in circumstances where the plaintiff claims no proprietary interest in the assets, it is likely that third party rights would be taken into consideration by the court in accordance with the normal principles affecting the grant of Mareva relief.

(6) Third parties with notice of the Mareva injunction may not aid or assist the defendant to break the order. The same principle applies to an order appointing a receiver and a warrant of arrest. Garnishee orders and charging orders operate *in rem* upon the relevant asset.

(7) A Mareva injunction does not produce the effect that an asset is attached or seized by an officer of the court. The defendant remains in possession or with a legal right of control, albeit that he is restrained from actually exercising his rights to deal with the asset unless the court permits him to do so.

(8) A Mareva injunction or an order appointing a receiver can be made over almost any type of asset. Warrants of arrest, charging orders and garnishee orders only apply to special types of asset.

(9) A Mareva injunction does not result in possession of an asset being transferred. If this is to be achieved it must be done under an ancillary order. An order appointing a receiver ordinarily has the objective of putting the receiver into possession of the asset and may give him powers of management. A garnishee order attaches the relevant debt and entitles the garnishor to receive payment of the debt. A charging order does not alter the right to possession of the asset but may result in a judicial sale.

Chapter 5

The jurisdiction to grant Mareva and Anton Piller relief

In *Siskina* v *Distos SA* [1979] AC 210, the House of Lords construed the former RSC Order 11, r 1(1)(*i*) then in force as not providing justification for service out of the jurisdiction of proceedings making a claim in respect of which Mareva relief was sought covering assets within the jurisdiction. The leave to serve the writ out of the jurisdiction was set aside, as was the Mareva relief which could only have existed in that case by way of an interlocutory injunction granted in an action on the merits of the substantive claim of the plaintiff. The position has been substantially changed as a result of the enactment of s 25 of the Civil Jurisdiction and Judgments Act 1982 and in summary is as follows.

(1) Section 37(1) of the Supreme Court Act 1981 enables interlocutory relief to be granted, including Mareva or Anton Piller relief, whenever an action on the merits is proceeding before the English court.

(2) Even if an action on the merits has been stayed, the court is not bound to discharge or set aside interlocutory relief which has been granted.

(3) Mareva or Anton Piller relief may be granted under s 12(6) of the Arbitration Act 1950 in respect of English Arbitration Proceedings.

(4) Mareva or Anton Piller relief may be granted under s 25(1) of the Civil Jurisdiction and Judgments Act 1982 in relation to proceedings on the merits which have been or are to be commenced in another contracting state to the European Judgments Convention.

(5) Such relief may also be granted under s 25(1) in respect of proceedings on the merits which have been or are to be commenced in any other part of the United Kingdom (eg Scotland).

(6) There is statutory provision which has not yet been utilised by Order in Council, for conferring jurisdiction on the court to grant interim relief, including Mareva and Anton Piller relief, in relation to proceedings on the merits commenced or to be commenced in other foreign courts or before a foreign arbitration tribunal.

(7) Relief may be granted in contemplation or in aid of the commencement of English winding-up or bankruptcy proceedings.

(8) If the plaintiff has obtained a foreign judgment or arbitration award which is to be enforced by an English court, Mareva or

Anton Piller relief may be granted in contemplation of, or in aid of, such enforcement.

(9) If the intended application falls in none of the above categories or only within category (6) above, then no Mareva or Anton Piller relief can be granted.

(1) Action on the merits before the English court

Mareva and Anton Piller relief can be granted before and after judgment. In a case in which leave is required to serve the substantive proceedings out of the jurisdiction, s 24(1)(a) of the Civil Jurisdiction and Judgments Act 1982 expressly confers jurisdiction on the court to grant interim relief when the question of jurisdiction on the merits is in issue in the proceedings. Thus, Mareva relief is commonly granted *ex parte* in an action against a defendant who is to be served out of the jurisdiction under the provisions of RSC Order 11, r 1(1), and it is equally clear that the court has jurisdiction to grant Anton Piller relief against such a defendant, and that such relief may be granted in respect of premises abroad.[1] However, as a matter of discretion, the court may decide to suspend the operation of the Anton Piller order so as to give the foreign defendant the opportunity to challenge the jurisdiction of the court to entertain the proceedings on the merits.[2]

In exercising the discretion whether or not to make an immediately effective Anton Piller order against a foreigner who is to be served under the provisions of RSC Order 11, r 1 the factors to be taken into account include the following.

(1) 'The moment a person is properly served under . . . [Order 11] that person, so far as the jurisdiction is concerned, is precisely in the same position as a person in this country'.[3] This principle has been regarded as applying at a time when the relevant person has not yet been served but leave to serve him has been granted.[4] The fact that the relevant person may apply to the court to set aside the leave does not impeach the jurisdiction of the court in the interim.[5] However, if there are substantial doubts as to the granting of leave under RSC Order 11, this is plainly a factor to be taken into account in relation to whether or not Anton Piller relief should be granted.

---

1 *Cook Industries* v *Galliher* [1979] Ch 439.
2 *Alertext Inc* v *Advanced Data Communications Limited* [1985] 1 WLR 547 at p 463, in which the decision of Goulding J in *Protector Alarms Ltd* v *Maxim Alarms Ltd* [1978] FSR 442 was considered.
3 *Re Liddell's Settlement Trusts* [1936] Ch 365 at p 374 per Romer LJ.
4 *Republic of Haiti* v *Duvalier* [1989] 2 WLR 261 at p 273, a case in which the *ex parte* relief granted against the defendants included mandatory disclosure orders (see para (4) of the order made by Knox J on 3 June 1988).
5 Section 24 of the Civil Jurisdiction and Judgments Act 1982.

(2) If the premises in question are situated in England then *prima facie* the English court should deal with the application on its merits.

(3) If the premises in question are situated abroad (as was the case in *Alertext Inc* v *Advanced Data Communications Ltd*) then the court exercising jurisdiction at that location is likely to be the appropriate court to which an application should be made. In *Denilauler* v *Snc Couchet Frères* [1980] ECR 1553, the European Court of Justice said (at p 1570):

> The courts of the place or, in any event, of the contracting state, where the assets subject to the measures sought are located, are those best able to assess the circumstances which may lead to the grant or refusal of the measures sought or to the laying down of procedures and conditions which the plaintiff must observe in order to guarantee the provisional and protective character of the measures ordered. The Convention has taken account of these requirements by providing in Article 24 that application may be made to the courts of a contracting state for such provisional, including protective, measures as may be available under the law of that state, even if, under the Convention, the courts of another contracting state have jurisdiction as to the substance of the matter.

> This is particularly true of complex relief such as Anton Piller relief which is liable to give rise to local difficulties including questions of local custom and practice, as well as those of language.

(4) Since an Anton Piller order is granted *ex parte* it will not be capable of recognition and enforcement by the courts of another contracting state to the European Judgments Convention, even if made in proceedings falling within Art I of the Convention ie proceedings in civil and commercial matters.[6] This is because it is only after the defendant has had an opportunity to resist an order that it is capable of qualifying for enforcement and recognition. In the context of premises situated in contracting states to the European Judgments Convention it is to be expected that an application for *ex parte* Anton Piller relief would ordinarily have to be made to the courts of that state pursuant to Art 24 of the Convention. For premises situated in a non-contracting state, in principle it is similarly to be expected that the application will ordinarily be made to the courts of that state.

(5) If the premises in question are abroad, the circumstances of the case may nevertheless make it desirable for the English court to deal with the application for relief. In the analogous context of Mareva relief, the English courts may, in the exercise of their discretion, grant a Mareva injunction over assets abroad even though the courts having jurisdiction at the place where the assets are located might themselves have dealt with the application. Thus in *Republic of Haiti* v *Duvalier* [1989] 2 WLR 261 at pp 272–273, the

---

6 *Denilauler* v *Snc Couchet Frères* [1980] ECR 1553; *Babanaft Co SA* v *Bassatne* [1989] 2 WLR 232 at pp 245–246 per Kerr LJ.

Court of Appeal upheld Mareva relief which had been granted over assets abroad despite the principle that, in general, the courts having jurisdiction at the location of the assets are those 'best able to assess the circumstances', because in that case it was not known at the time of the *ex parte* application in what jurisdiction or jurisdictions the assets might be found. It is thought that in certain circumstances it may be appropriate for the English court to grant *ex parte* Anton Piller relief in respect of premises abroad. In order to justify the granting of such relief the English court ought to satisfy itself that in the circumstances it is the appropriate tribunal to deal with the application notwithstanding the considerations set out in (3) above, which have particular force in the context of the granting of mandatory relief which has as its objective the obtaining of entry to premises for purposes of searching them. If relief is granted then it should be directed solely to the defendant and expressed not to have an effect on third parties. This is because the English court's sole justification for granting such relief is that it has jurisdiction over the defendant in respect of the claim on the merits. In addition, plainly the English Court should neither authorise nor require to be carried out acts which may be illegal at the location in question.[7] It is thought that any Anton Piller relief granted should contain a specific provision to this effect, and should only be granted on the plaintiff's undertaking to comply with the law in force at the relevant location.

(2) If an action is to be stayed or has been stayed

A distinction can be drawn between actions which are subject to a mandatory stay by virtue of statute (eg under s 1 of the Arbitration Act 1975) and those in which a stay is to be granted on discretionary grounds. A distinction can also be drawn between on the one hand attaching conditions to the granting of a stay (eg a condition that an undertaking is given to the court in the terms of the Mareva relief or an undertaking that a guarantee or other security is provided), and on the other hand maintaining Mareva relief in the action itself notwithstanding the existence of a stay.

If a stay is to be granted on discretionary grounds (eg because of the existence of a foreign jurisdiction clause or on the grounds of '*forum non conveniens*') then the stay may be granted subject to conditions and it will ordinarily be the case that the court would only grant the stay if it is satisfied that the plaintiff's position in relation to the Mareva relief will be adequately protected. In the context of granting a stay on the grounds of *forum non conveniens*, in *Spiliada Maritime Corporation* v *Cansulex* [1987] AC 460 at

---

7 See RSC Order 11, r 5(2) in relation to service of a writ abroad, and RSC Order 11, r 9(7) which makes that provision applicable to service of other documents including court orders.

p 483, Lord Goff referred to the analogous situation in which security had been obtained for the plaintiff through the commencement of proceedings on the merits in England, eg by means of threatening or effecting the arrest of a vessel in admiralty proceedings *in rem*,[8] and said that:

It would not, I think, normally be wrong to allow a plaintiff to keep the benefit of security obtained by commencing proceedings, while at the same time granting a stay of proceedings in this country to enable the action to proceed in the appropriate forum. Such a conclusion is, I understand, consistent with the manner in which the process of *saisie conservatoire* is applied in civil law countries; and cf s 26 of the Civil Jurisdiction and Judgments Act 1982, now happily in force

The reference to s 26 of the Civil Jurisdiction and Judgments Act 1982 is to an express statutory provision[9] which enables the court notwithstanding that an action is stayed or dismissed so that the claim can be adjudicated upon either in arbitration or by a court outside England and Wales, to retain the *res* as security or to order that the stay or dismissal (as the case might be) is conditional upon the provision of security. Even prior to s 26 coming into force in cases where a stay was being granted as a matter of *discretion* (eg because of the existence of a foreign jurisdiction clause) the court could and usually did make the granting of the stay in an admiralty action *in rem* conditional upon the provision of alternative security.[10]

Although the granting of Mareva relief does not involve conferring security on the plaintiff for his claim, the relief does have as its purpose giving the plaintiff a measure of protection against being left with an unsatisfied judgment. To this extent a direct parallel is to be drawn with security obtained in an admiralty action *in rem*, and in principle the same approach on the exercise of discretion is to be applied, namely that in general the plaintiff is not to be prejudiced in relation to the Mareva relief by virtue of the court deciding, in the exercise of its discretion, that the claim on the merits ought to be determined elsewhere.

In the case of a mandatory stay directed by statute the court will not be entitled to attach conditions to the stay in the absence of statutory provisions enabling it to do so.[11] If the stay is to enable the claim to be

---

8 Usually this will result in the provision of a guarantee either to forestall such an arrest as to procure release of the vessel. If security is not provided by way of a guarantee, nevertheless by invoking the admiralty jurisdiction of the court by commencing an action *in rem*, the plaintiff does obtain the status of secured creditor, at least for certain purposes: *Re Aro Co Ltd* [1980] Ch 196 at p 209, in which leave was granted to the plaintiff to continue with admiralty proceedings *in rem* against a ship and *in personam* against the owner of the ship, which was a company under compulsory liquidation, under the statutory provision now contained in s 130(2) of the Insolvency Act 1986.

9 For the difficulties under the law as it stood in relation to retaining security in an action *in rem* which was subject to a mandatory stay under s 1 of the Arbitration Act 1975, prior to s 26 coming into force see *The 'Rena K'* [1979] QB 377 at pp 396–401.

10 *The 'Rena K'* [1979] QB 377 at p 398; and *The 'El Amria'* [1981] 2 Lloyd's Rep 119 at pp 123–124 and 128.

11 *The 'Rena K'* [1979] QB 377 at p 400.

brought in English arbitration proceedings then there is jurisdiction to grant or continue the Mareva relief under s 12(6) of the Arbitration Act 1950.[12] This is the case regardless of whether the stay is being granted as a mandatory stay required by s 1 of the Arbitration Act 1975 or is being granted as a matter of discretion.

If, however, a stay is granted in relation to a foreign arbitration clause then the court will not have jurisdiction to grant or continue the Mareva injunction under s 12(6) of the Arbitration Act 1950. Nevertheless, it seems to be the case that the court would still have power to maintain the Mareva injunction (in the action which has been stayed) for the purpose of preventing the defendant from dissipating assets before the plaintiff eventually obtains judgment in the English action. This may occur following removal of the stay after completion of the foreign arbitration. This view is supported by the reasoning of Brandon J in *The 'Rena K'* which was to the effect that a vessel could be retained under arrest in an Admiralty action *in rem* notwithstanding that the action had been stayed pending arbitration. There is no power to arrest a vessel as security for an arbitration claim. However, the judge maintained the arrest on the ground that there was a distinction to be drawn between the choice of forum on the one hand and the right to security on the other. See also *Law* v *Garrett* (1878) 8 ChD 26 at p 38 and *Marazura Navegacion SA* v *Oceanus Mutual* [1977] 1 Lloyd's Rep 283. In due course there might be a judgment in an Admiralty action after the stay was removed following arbitration. The Supreme Court of Western Australia has allowed this procedure to be used in connection with a claim which was the subject of arbitration proceedings in England brought by the plaintiff against an Australian company. The defendant unsuccessfully sought to have the injunction discharged on the grounds that a stay of the proceedings would be granted: *Sanko Steamship* v *DC Commodities* [1980] WAR 51.

Similarly, a court would have power to grant or continue a Mareva injunction even though the English proceedings are stayed or left in abeyance pending the outcome of foreign court proceedings. Under s 34 of the Civil Jurisdiction and Judgments Act 1982, a judgment in the foreign court precludes the plaintiff from suing on the underlying cause of action in England provided that the foreign judgment is enforceable and entitled to recognition in England. The fact that a foreign judgment would result in the English proceedings becoming moribund does not preclude the court from either granting or continuing Mareva relief in the interim.[12A]

Accordingly, it appears that regardless of whether a stay is made under the mandatory provisions of a statute or is granted as a matter of discretion, there is still jurisdiction to continue or grant Mareva relief or indeed other interlocutory relief, such as the appointment of a receiver.[13]

---

12 *The 'Rena K'* [1979] QB 377; *Third Chandris* v *Unimarine SA* [1979] QB 645 at p 663.
12A *House of Spring Garden* v *Waite* [1984] FSR 277.
13 *Law* v *Garrett* (1878) 8 Ch D 26 at p 38.

Whether or not the relief is to be maintained is a matter of discretion for the court. In principle this discretion ought to be exercised in accordance with the same approach as that applicable to the attaching of conditions when a stay is to be granted on discretionary grounds. In effect, the maintaining of Mareva relief in the action or imposing conditions on the granting of a stay (where this is possible) are simply different procedures open to the court for achieving the same overall objective.

If an action has already been stayed and a plaintiff wishes to obtain Mareva relief for the first time in connection with the claim which is the subject of the proceedings, then the court has jurisdiction to entertain the application, and whether it is to be granted will depend upon the circumstances of the case. Attempts have been made to seek Mareva relief in an action in England newly brought on the merits for the purpose of seeking the relief when the court has jurisdiction to entertain the claim on the merits, but is not the appropriate court to do so. These are in cases falling within the scope of RSC Order 11, r 1, and not covered by s 25 of the Civil Jurisdiction and Judgments Act 1982. In *Baidini* v *Baidini* [1987] FLR 463, there were matrimonial proceedings on the merits in Michigan in which an interlocutory order had been made against a husband in respect of his assets. The wife sought to commence proceedings in England on the merits. Even though the proceedings fell within RSC Order 11, r 1, the Court of Appeal held that there should not be service out of the jurisdiction purely to enable Mareva relief to be granted by the English court. Similarly, in *A/A D/S Svendborg* v *Maxim Brand* Court of Appeal (Civil Division) Transcript No 39 (23 January 1989), the Court of Appeal held that no leave should be granted under RSC Order 11, r 1 and discharged Mareva relief which had been granted, Kerr LJ saying that it had been faintly argued that an action could be brought in England and stayed, leaving the Mareva relief in place. 'However I cannot see the slightest ground for acceding to such an extraordinary application.'[14]

(3) Section 12(6) of the Arbitration Act 1950

A Mareva injunction may be granted by the High Court upon the application of a party to an arbitration which is taking place or which is due to take place within the jurisdiction. The power is derived from a combination of s 37(3) of the Supreme Court Act 1981 and s 12(6) of the Arbitration Act 1950, which provides as follows:

s 12(6) The High Court shall have, for the purpose of and in relation to a reference, the same power of making orders in respect of:
   (*e*) the preservation, interim custody or sale of any goods which are the subject matter of the reference;
   (*f*) securing the amount in dispute in the reference;
   (*h*) interim injunctions or the appointment of a receiver;

---

14 See pp 50–51 in relation to s 25(3) of the Civil Jurisdiction and Judgments Act 1982.

as it has for the purpose of and in relation to an action or matter in the High Court.

A Mareva injunction obtained in aid of arbitration proceedings is usually granted until a specified period after the final award is made. The successful claimant can then make an application for an extension of the injunction. The court may grant a Mareva injunction in aid of the enforcement and subsequent execution of an English arbitration award in exactly the same way as for a judgment; the only difference is that an English arbitration award must be converted into a judgment before it can be executed, and it may take longer to enforce an arbitration award than a judgment in an action for this reason. The successful party has two options; he can bring an action in the High Court founded on the award (which proceeds in the normal way), or he can apply to the court for an order for summary relief under s 26 of the Arbitration Act 1950. The latter course is speedy and cost-effective, but is unsuitable for cases in which there are proceedings pending to set aside the award, or where the respondent is seeking to object to the validity of the award.[15]

Where the claimant has been unsuccessful in the arbitration but still wishes to appeal to the High Court, it is thought that the court would still have jurisdiction to continue relief under s 12(6) of the Arbitration Act 1950 pending the outcome of the appeal. Thus, in the High Court there is jurisdiction to grant or continue a Mareva injunction pending the outcome of an appeal to the Court of Appeal.[16] A Mareva injunction is an 'interim injunction',[17] and it is considered that the granting of the relief is made 'in relation to a reference', namely the reference in which the arbitration award has been made, which is subject to challenge on appeal and may be varied or set aside.

If the respondent to an arbitration has unsuccessfully defended the arbitration then Mareva relief can be granted or continued by the court in aid of proceedings to enforce the award. If the unsuccessful respondent seeks leave to appeal, the court has the power to impose conditions upon the granting of leave to appeal, and in suitable cases leave can be granted on terms that the amount in dispute is paid into court. That is more satisfactory than a Mareva injunction, in that the amount paid in will be security for the respondent's claim: *WA Sherratt* v *John Bromley (Church Stretton) Ltd* [1985] QB 1038.

Similarly, if the unsuccessful party to an award seeks to have it set aside for misconduct, the court is empowered under s 23(3) of the Arbitration

---

15 *Middlemiss & Gould* v *Hartlepool Corporation* [1972] 1 WLR 1643.
16 *Erinford Properties Ltd* v *Cheshire County Council* [1974] Ch 261 at pp 262–267; *Orion Property Trust Ltd* v *Du Cane Court Ltd* [1962] 1 WLR 1085. There is also jurisdiction in the court of first instance to grant a stay pending appeal of an injunction granted as final relief: *E I Du Pont de Nemours & Co* v *Enka BV* [1988] RPC 497, which is similar in that the court is granting interim relief after trial to preserve the position pending appeal.
17 *Orwell Steel (Erection and Fabrication)* v *Asphalt and Tarmac (UK)* [1984] 1 WLR 1097; *Siskina* v *Distos SA* [1979] AC 210.

Act 1950 to order that the amount of the award be paid into court or otherwise secured pending the determination of the application. This is a most useful provision, although it apparently only applies where the challenger wishes to have the award set aside, and not where he merely seeks to have it remitted.

Scott v *Avery* arbitration clauses are commonly found in certain standard form contracts. There are two distinct types, namely:

(1) a clause including a provision that no action shall be brought until an arbitration has been conducted and an award made; and

(2) a clause including a provision that the only obligation of the defendant shall be to pay such sum as the arbitrator shall award.

Scott v *Avery* clauses have long been accepted as valid and effective. A *Scott* v *Avery* clause postpones accrual to the plaintiff of a cause of action which can be successfully pursued in court proceedings. If a plaintiff brings court proceedings by writ before obtaining an arbitration award then he has no cause of action.

In Australia it had been decided by the Supreme Court of New South Wales[18] that Mareva relief could be granted, notwithstanding that the plaintiff had no existing cause of action because of the clause. In England fortunately (see p 43), under s 12(6) of the Arbitration Act 1950, the court has power to grant Mareva injunctions in relation to a claim advanced in arbitration under a *Scott* v *Avery* clause. Depending upon its precise wording, the clause may also have the effect of precluding either party from bringing any legal proceedings at all in relation to the claim pending the making of the award as in *Mantovani* v *Carapelli* [1980] 1 Lloyd's Rep 375, distinguishing *Marazura Navegacion SA* v *Oceanus Mutual* [1977] 1 Lloyd's Rep 283.

In such a case as *Mantovani* v *Carapelli*, substantial damages have been awarded against a claimant who, in breach of the clause, sought security for the claim. Would such a clause prevent the court from granting a Mareva injunction under s 12(6) of the Arbitration Act 1950? The opening words of s 12(6) state: 'The High Court shall have, for the purpose of and in relation to a reference, the . . . power . . .'. These words make it clear that the power of the court is to make orders ancillary to the conduct of the reference, and accordingly the better view would appear to be that even though the claimant has to launch separate proceedings by originating summons to obtain an injunction, nevertheless those proceedings are in substance only ancillary to the reference and therefore do not give rise to a breach of the clause. However, even if a clause did seek to preclude the bringing of proceedings for a Mareva injunction, the court would still have jurisdiction to grant an injunction, albeit that the existence of the clause would be a factor to take into account on discretion.

Anton Piller relief is also capable of coming within s 12(6) of the

18 *Construction Engineering (Australia) Pty Ltd* v *Tamber* [1984] 1 NSWLR 274.

Arbitration Act 1950. Which paragraph of s 12(6) is applicable will depend upon the purpose for which the order is sought. Thus, for example, if the applicant wishes to search for documents which would assist in proving his claim in the reference then this would fall within s 12(6)(b) of the Act and if the applicant wishes to preserve a valuable object which he is claiming in the reference then this would fall within s 12(6)(g) of the Act. It is also the case that relief can be granted by virtue of s 12(6)(h) on the grounds that the order is an interim injunction[19] which in High Court proceedings is justified by s 37 of the Supreme Court Act 1981.

(4) Section 25(1) of the Civil Jurisdiction and Judgments Act 1982

This section has the practical effect of taking cases falling within its ambit outside the scope of the decision of the House of Lords in *Siskina* v *Distos SA* [1979] AC 210. It confers jurisdiction on the court to grant 'interim relief', which is defined in s 25(7), when the court is not seized with jurisdiction on the substance of the matter, provided such proceedings 'have been or are to be commenced in a contracting state other than the United Kingdom or in a part of the United Kingdom' outside England and Wales.

The definition of 'interim relief' in s 25(7) provides that the term:

means interim relief of any kind which [the High Court] has power to grant in proceedings relating to matters within its jurisdiction, other than:
> (a) a warrant for the arrest of property; or
> (b) provision for obtaining evidence.

Section 25(7)(a) excludes arresting a ship in an Admiralty action *in rem* from the jurisdiction conferred on the court by s 25(1). Admiralty arrests are the subject matter of s 26 of the Act (see p 41, above). Section 25(7)(b) excludes measures directed to 'obtaining evidence' for the substantive hearing of the case. Thus in *Republic of Haiti* v *Duvalier: re an application by Mr Turner and Mr Matlin* Court of Appeal (Civil Division) Transcript No 490 (7 June 1988),[20] a mandatory order was upheld by the Court of Appeal requiring the defendants 'acting by Messrs Turner and Matlin, to disclose' certain information to the plaintiffs' solicitors relating to assets held by the defendants, so that orders could be obtained freezing those assets. The objection was raised that the information required was 'evidence' falling within s 25(7)(b) of the Act. But this was rejected because the information was required for the purpose of seeking to freeze dealings with assets, and not as evidence to be used for the purpose of the

---

19 *Distributori Automatici* v *Holford Trading Co* [1985] 1 WLR 1066 at p 1073; *Rank Film Ltd* v *Video Information Centre* [1982] AC 380 at p 417, per Templeman LJ; *Third Chandris* v *Unimarine SA* [1979] QB 645 at p 669, per Lord Denning MR.

20 The hearing was held in camera on 7 June 1988 before Lord Donaldson MR, Woolf LJ and Sir John Megaw, and the judgment was subsequently released. It is referred to by Staughton LJ in the subsequent appeal in the case by Jean-Claude Duvalier, his wife and his mother: [1989] 2 WLR 261 at pp 265–266.

substantive hearing. If the information obtained did reveal large, unexplained cash balances or other valuable assets it seems likely that this would have been relevant to the prosecution of the case on the merits, which had been commenced before the Tribunal de Grande Instance at Grasse.[21] However, while s 25(7)(*b*) precludes an application made under s 25(1) for the purpose of obtaining evidence for the prosecution of the claim on the merits, it does not preclude the making of an order for the purpose of preserving assets, even if a consequence of compliance with the order may be to provide the applicant with information and material which would be of assistance to him in the prosecution of the substantive claim.

As a result of s 25(7)(*b*) of the Act, the scope for the granting of Anton Piller relief under s 25(1) does not include applications made for the purpose of 'obtaining evidence'. However, an application made, for example, for the purpose of preserving assets which are in jeopardy, would fall within s 25(1).

It was also sought to be argued by Messrs Turner and Matlin that s 25(7) only included within 'interim relief', orders which related to assets, or other subject matter within the territorial jurisdiction of the court. In relation to this submission, Lord Donaldson MR, with whom the other members of the Court of Appeal agreed, said:

What [s 25(7)] is saying is not that the court can make no orders relating to the subject matter outside the geographical limits of this country, but that it cannot make orders which it could not make in support of proceedings properly begun in the English courts.

If there were some unusual form of ancillary relief available in the French courts, as indeed there is of course in the United States courts in the form of pre-trial examination of witnesses, the English courts, in accordance with subsection (7), have no power to grant that relief. They can only do in support of foreign proceedings what they can do in support of their own proceedings.

Section 25(1) of the Civil Jurisdiction and Judgments Act 1982 confers on the High Court a jurisdiction permitted[22] by Art 24 of the European Judgments Convention. This provides that:

Application may be made to the courts of a contracting state, for such provisional, including protective, measures as may be available under the law of that state, even if, under this Convention, the courts of another contracting state have jurisdiction as to the substance.

Section 25(1) also extends to certain cases falling outside the scope of the European Judgments Convention, provided that the subject matter of the proceedings on the merits are within the scope of Art I of the Convention. Thus, for example, if proceedings are intended to be commenced in the courts of another contracting state against an intended defendant who

---

21 The defendants disputed the jurisdiction of the French court to entertain the claim on the
   · merits and at the time of the English proceedings that dispute had not been resolved.
22 *Siskina* v *Distos SA* [1979] AC 210 at pp 259–260.

is not domiciled in a contracting state, and those proceedings are not within Art 16 of the Convention, s 25(1) enables the High Court to grant 'interim relief', provided that the intended substantive proceedings come within Art I of the Convention. Thus, the jurisdiction conferred by s 25(1) is in fact wider than that envisaged by Art 24 of the Convention. In *CHW v GJH* [1982] ECR 1189 the European Court of Justice held that Art 24 did not apply to provisional measures applied for in relation to substantive proceedings on the merits which fell outside the provisions of the Convention concerning jurisdiction (in that case the substantive proceedings were brought by a wife against her husband in respect of his management of her property and fell outside Art I). However, s 25(1) applies provided that the substantive proceedings concern subject matters within the scope of Art I, even though the Convention itself does not have 'effect in relation to the proceedings' (s 25(1)(*b*) of the Act). Any extension of the application of s 25(1) by means of an Order in Council made pursuant to s 25(3) will still be limited by the requirement that the subject matter of the relevant substantive proceedings must come within the scope of Art I of the Convention.

Under s 25(1) 'interim relief' can be granted in respect of assets outside of the jurisdiction,[23] and the relief can be granted against parties whether or not they are domiciled in England and Wales. In the case of a defendant who is domiciled in any part of the United Kingdom or any other 'Convention territory' as defined in RSC Order 11, r 1(4), proceedings can be served out of the jurisdiction on that defendant without leave pursuant to RSC Order 11, r 1(2).[24] In the case of a defendant who falls outside of RSC Order 11, r 1(2)(ii), then if service of the proceedings is to be effected out of the jurisdiction, leave will have to be obtained to do this under the provisions of RSC Order 11, r 1(1). If Mareva relief is to be sought restraining the intended defendant from doing certain acts within the jurisdiction, then notwithstanding that the injunction is necessarily an interlocutory one,[25] it has been held[26] that leave can be granted under RSC Order 11, r 1(1)(*b*) notwithstanding that the wording of that provision is identical to the former RSC Order 11, r 1(1)(*i*) (see also pp 134–138, below). If Anton Piller relief is to be sought in relation to premises in England in circumstances falling within s 25(1), then in principle such an order would contain an 'injunction' within the meaning of RSC Order 11, r 1(1)(*b*). Thus, this sub-paragraph in the context of Mareva relief has been construed as including an interlocutory injunction, and

---

23 *Republic of Haiti* v *Duvalier* [1989] 2 WLR 261.
24 *Republic of Haiti* v *Duvalier* (above) at pp 267–269.
25 *Siskina* v *Distos SA* [1979] AC 210; *Orwell Steel (Erection and Fabrication)* v *Asphalt and Tarmac UK* [1984] 1 WLR 1097.
26 *X* v *Y* [1989] 3 WLR 910 (Mr Anthony Diamond QC sitting as a Deputy High Court Judge).

it is considered that an Anton Piller order is properly to be regarded as a form of interlocutory injunction,[27] for the purposes of this provision.

Whether or not, and if so in what terms an order is to be granted, is a matter of discretion for the court. Section 25(2) expressly provides that the court may refuse to grant the relief if the court is of the opinion that the fact that the court has no jurisdiction on the substantive claim 'makes it inexpedient for the court to grant it'.

Section 25(1) of the Act is not directed to a situation in which the English court is being asked to enforce an order for protective measures made by the court having jurisdiction over the claim on the merits. The decisions of the European Court of Justice in *de Caval* v *de Caval (No 1)* [1979] ECR 1055 and *Denilauler* v *Snc Couchet Frères* [1980] ECR 1553, are consistent with and support the proposition[28] that the court having jurisdiction on the merits of the substantive claim has jurisdiction to make an order for provisional measures in relation to assets located in another contracting state. Such an order, even though only interlocutory, is to be enforced by the courts of other contracting states under the European Judgments Convention.[29] Furthermore, an order made for provisional measures by a court without jurisdiction over the substantive claim on the merits, is itself an order which, provided that it has been made in accordance with the applicable provisions of the Convention,[30] will itself be entitled to recognition and enforcement by the courts of other contracting states.[31] Accordingly, in exercising its discretion under s 25(1), the High Court is entitled to proceed upon the basis that relief granted or continued, otherwise than *ex parte*, will be recognised and enforced by the courts of other contracting states.[32] This is a factor to be taken into account in relation to the exercise of the discretion under s 25(1) and whether it would be 'inexpedient' within s 25(2) to grant relief in the circumstances of the particular case in question.

The jurisdiction under s 25(1) can be exercised post-judgment. Thus, in the context of Mareva relief in relation to proceedings in England it is established that there is jurisdiction to grant or continue the relief after judgment (see p 17), and s 25(7) imports the equivalent jurisdiction where the substantive proceedings have been commenced which come within s 25(1). Furthermore, the fact that the judgment is to be enforced

---

27 *Distributori Automatici* v *Holford Trading Co* [1985] 1 WLR 1066 at p 1073; *Rank Film Ltd* v *Video Information Centre* [1982] AC 380 at p 417, per Templeman LJ; *Third Chandris* v *Unimarine SA* [1979] QB 645 at p 669, per Lord Denning MR.

28 *The Territorial Reach of Mareva Injunctions* by Lawrence Collins (1989) 105 LQR 262 at pp 290–292.

29 Articles 1, 25, 26 to 28 and 31 of the Convention, and the comments of Professor Jenard on Title III of the Convention in the Official Journal, 1979, No C59 at p 42 and following. *Babanaft Co SA* v *Bassatne* [1989] 2 WLR 232 at p 244.

30 The order must have been made *inter partes* or at least after the defendant has been given notice of the application: *Denilauler* v *Snc Couchet Frères* [1980] ECR 1553.

31 *Babanaft Co SA* v *Bassatne* (above) at p 249, per Kerr LJ.

32 See generally *The Territorial Reach of Mareva Injunctions* by Lawrence Collins (above).

by the courts of another contracting state does not preclude the granting of Mareva or Anton Piller relief designed to assist in the enforcement process. Article 24 justifies the High Court in exercising the jurisdiction conferred upon it by s 25(1), and Art 16(5) of the Convention is not directed to precluding the granting of such relief.[33]

In *Republic of Haiti* v *Duvalier*, the proceedings seeking relief under s 25(1) were commenced by writ. However, it is considered that by virtue of RSC Order 5, r 3, proceedings seeking relief under the section must be commenced by originating summons. It would be appropriate to refer to s 25(1) in the title to the proceedings, however, there is no necessity to do so, at least in proceedings to be commenced in the Chancery Division.[34]

(5) Section 25(1) and proceedings on the merits which have been or are to be commenced in any other part of the United Kingdom (eg Scotland)

Section 25(1) enables the High Court to grant 'interim relief' when proceedings on the merits have been or are to be commenced in any other part of the United Kingdom, for example in Scotland. Mareva injunctions and Anton Piller orders are 'provisional measures' within s 18(5)(*d*) of the Civil Jurisdiction and Judgments Act 1982 and accordingly do not qualify for enforcement by other courts in the United Kingdom under s 18 of the Act.

However, s 25 applies to the High Court in Northern Ireland, and a similar jurisdiction has been conferred on the Court of Session in Scotland under s 27 of the Act. Accordingly, if for example the High Court in England granted Mareva relief in relation to assets located in Scotland or Northern Ireland, in proceedings on the merits commenced or to be commenced in England, the Court of Session or the High Court in Northern Ireland (as the case might be) could itself entertain an application for and grant relief following within s 27(1) or s 25(1) of the Act respectively. The granting of Mareva relief in England would not be a pre-condition to the exercise of the jurisdiction. Similarly, the granting of provisional measures by the Court of Session or the High Court in Northern Ireland is not a pre-condition to the exercise of jurisdiction by the High Court in England under s 25(1).

(6) Section 25(3) of the Civil Jurisdiction and Judgments Act 1982

Section 25(3) enables the power of the High Court to grant interim relief to be extended by Order in Council so as to make it exercisable in relation to proceedings commenced or to be commenced otherwise than in a contracting state (which is defined in s 1(3) of the Act), proceedings whose

---

33 *Babanaft Co SA* v *Bassatne* (above).
34 *Practice Direction (Chancery: Procedure)* [1983] 1 WLR 4 (at paragraph 2), preserved at [1987] 1 WLR 93, at p 100.

subject matter is not within Art I of the Convention and arbitration proceedings. No Order in Council has yet been made in pursuance of s 25(3). Attempts have been made in cases falling within RSC Order 11, r 1(1) to seek to persuade the court to grant leave to serve proceedings out of the jurisdiction for the purpose of enabling the court to grant Mareva relief, even though it is intended that the substantive claim on the merits will be determined elsewhere. However, the Court of Appeal has rejected those attempts (see p 43, above). The position now is that Parliament, by means of ss 12(6) of Arbitration Act 1950 and 25(1) of the Civil Jurisdiction and Judgments Act 1982, has made provision in specific categories of case for the court to grant interlocutory injunctions and other relief in relation to cases in which the substantive claim is not to be adjudicated upon by the High Court. Furthermore, in s 25(3), Parliament has created the statutory machinery to enable the power conferred by s 25(1) to be extended to the categories of case at present excluded from its scope. In these circumstances it is considered that it would be wrong in principle for the courts to 'indulge in parallel creativity'[35] by allowing Mareva or Anton Piller relief to be granted in cases falling within RSC Order 11, r 1(1) when the substantive claim on the merits is to not be determined in England. Thus, the fact that the plaintiff wishes to obtain Mareva or Anton Piller relief does not qualify the substantive claim on the merits as a proper case for service out of the jurisdiction under RSC Order 11, r 4(2).

(7) Winding-up or bankruptcy proceedings

In *United Bank* v *Claybridge SA*,[36] Robert Goff J had granted a Mareva injunction against a Panamanian company which was chartering in vessels and sub-chartering them. In the Commercial Court the injunction was qualified so as to enable the defendant company to pay trading debts and expenses.[37] However, the plaintiffs appealed to the Court of Appeal against an order enabling the defendant to pay out certain moneys, and in the course of the appeal, Templeman LJ suggested that the plaintiffs should petition for the winding up of the company. In contemplation of the commencement of winding-up proceedings, the injunction was modified so as to restrain the defendant from making any payment except

---

35 This phrase was used by Hoffmann J in *Chief Constable of Leicestershire* v *M* [1989] 1 WLR 20 at p 23, when he declined to extend the principles established in relation to the common rights of constables to detain the proceeds of crime on the ground (among others) that the matter was already the subject of statutory intervention in the form of the Drug Trafficking Offences Act 1986, and the Criminal Justice Act 1988 (which at that time was not yet in force but which has subsequently come into force).

36 (1980) 14 LMLN (15 May 1980); 16 LMLN (12 June 1980); and (1981) *The Times*, 13 March, also in Court of Appeal (Civil Division) Transcript No 143 of 1981 (9 March 1981).

37 Applying *Iraqi Ministry of Defence* v *Arcepey Shipping Co SA* (*The 'Angel Bell'*) [1981] QB 65.

payments validated by the Companies Court under s 227 of the Companies Act 1948, which is now s 127 of the Insolvency Act 1986.

In the *United Bank* case there were substantive proceedings on the merits of the plaintiffs' claims pending before the Commercial Court. However, the existence of such substantive proceedings is not a precondition for the exercise of the jurisdiction. Section 37(1) of the Supreme Court Act confers a jurisdiction on the High Court which can be exercised in the context of winding-up proceedings. Thus, in *Re Oriental Credit Ltd* [1988] Ch 204, an order was made under s 561 of the Companies Act 1985[38] for the attendance at a private examination of a director and shareholder in a company which was in creditors' voluntary liquidation. The director had left the jurisdiction prior to the commencement of the liquidation. An injunction was granted by Harman J restraining the director from leaving the jurisdiction until after the completion of the private examination, pursuant to the order made for attendance under s 561. This injunction was granted under s 37(1) of the Supreme Court Act 1981 as being in aid of and ancillary to the order which had been made by the court for the attendance of the director. Accordingly, s 37(1) of the Supreme Court Act 1981 is applicable to the winding-up jurisdiction of the court, and in principle Mareva or Anton Piller relief can be granted in aid of or ancillary to the exercise of that jurisdiction by the court.[39] If assets of the company are in jeopardy then the court may appoint[40] a provisional liquidator under s 135 of the Insolvency Act 1986 and this may be done *ex parte* on sufficient cause being shown. Ordinarily in such a case the applicant will be required to give an undertaking in damages, although this requirement was dispensed with by Sir Robert Megarry VC in *Re Highfield Commodities*, where the application was made by the Secretary for Trade and and Industry for the purpose of enforcing the law and in pursuance of his public duty.[41]

Winding-up proceedings may be successfully brought in England against a foreign company under Part V of the Insolvency Act 1986.[42] This is so even when such a company does not have assets within the jurisdiction, provided that[43] there is sufficient connection with England of the affairs of the company in question, and there is a reasonable possibility of

---

38 Subsequently repealed, and now replaced by s 236 of the Insolvency Act 1986.

39 See also *Deutsche Schachtbau-und Tiefbohrgesellschaft GmbH* v *Shell International* [1988] 3 WLR 230 at p 262 per Lord Goff where the possibility was addressed of granting an injunction in aid of winding-up proceedings but the injunction was refused on discretionary grounds.

40 *Re Highfield Commodities Ltd* [1985] 1 WLR 149 at pp 158–159; *Re Union Accident Insurance Co Ltd* [1972] 1 All ER 1105.

41 By analogy to the principle applicable to interlocutory injunctions discussed in *F Hoffman–La Roche & Co AG* v *Secretary of State* [1975] AC 295.

42 *Re Compania Merabello San Nicholas SA* [1973] Ch 75 *Re Allobrogia Steamship Corporation* [1979] 1 Lloyd's Rep 190; *Re Eloc Electro-Optiek and Communicate BV* [1982] Ch 43; *Re A Company (No 00359 of 1987)* [1988] Ch 210.

43 *Re A Company (No 00359 of 1987)* [1988] Ch 210 at pp 225–226.

benefit for the creditors from the winding up. The petition may be presented and proceeded with, regardless of whether the claim on which the petition is based could have been made the subject of a substantive action on the merits for which leave to serve proceedings out of the jurisdiction could have been obtained.

A Mareva injunction will not improve the plaintiff's position as regards other creditors in a liquidation and those with prior claims are entitled to a variation of the injunction which will enable the liquidator to satisfy their claims eg, *Cretanor Maritime Co Ltd* v *Irish Marine Management Ltd* (*The 'Cretan Harmony'*) [1978] 1 WLR 966. However, if the defendant has put up security (eg a bank guarantee) in return for the release of the Mareva injunction, the plaintiff is in an improved position on the defendant's insolvency eg, the comments of Donaldson LJ in *Hitachi Shipbuilding & Engineering Co Ltd* v *Viafiel Compania Naviera SA* [1981] 2 Lloyd's Rep 499 at p 509.

The circumstances in which a bankruptcy petition may be presented against a debtor are set out in s 265 of the Insolvency Act 1986. A petition may be presented in respect of an individual even though he is neither domiciled in England and Wales, nor personally present within England and Wales on the day of presentation of the petition, if in the period of three years ending with the day on which the petition is presented, he was ordinarily resident or has had a place of residence in England and Wales, or he has carried on business in England and Wales. The debtor may have carried on business himself, or by a firm or partnership of which he is or was a member, or by an agent or manager acting for himself, or for the firm or partnership. Again there is no requirement that in relation to the debt on which the petition is founded, this could have been made the subject of substantive proceedings for which leave to serve out of the jurisdiction could have been obtained. Under s 286 of the Insolvency Act 1986, the court has jurisdiction to appoint an interim receiver 'if it is shown to be necessary for the protection of the debtor's property' and such an appointment may be made at any time after presentation of the petition. Section 37(1) of the Supreme Court Act 1981 is applicable to the jurisdiction of the court in bankruptcy and it is considered that Mareva and Anton Piller relief may be granted in aid of or ancillary to the exercise of that jurisdiction by the court. If Mareva relief were to be granted in relation to bankruptcy proceedings then it would not be appropriate for the injunction to have an unqualified exception to allow the payment of debts of the debtor, but would ordinarily allow payments sanctioned by the court under s 284(1) of the Insolvency Act 1986.

(8) Mareva or Anton Piller relief in contemplation of, or in aid of, enforcement of a foreign judgment or arbitration award

In the case of a plaintiff who had obtained a foreign judgment which he wishes to register in England, the procedure is set out in RSC Order 71.

Such a plaintiff is not entitled to seek to execute the foreign judgment for a period of time after registration (RSC Order 71, r 10). Once the plaintiff has obtained a foreign judgment, he is entitled to commence substantive proceedings in England for the registration of that judgment, and upon completion of those proceedings he will have a final judgment which can be executed in England. In principle therefore, the plaintiff is entitled to apply for Mareva relief in connection with those substantive proceedings immediately prior to or upon commencement of those proceedings. Thus, Mareva relief is available in cases in which the foreign judgment is to be enforced within the jurisdiction by registration. In New Zealand this has been decided to be the case in relation to provisions corresponding to the Foreign Judgments (Reciprocal Enforcement) Act 1933: *Hunt* v *BP Exploration Company (Libya) Ltd* [1980] 1 NZLR 104. In that case the original *ex parte* injunction (granted on *ex parte* registration of the judgment) was maintained even though the overseas judgment was subject to an appeal, and an application to set aside the registration of the judgment had been adjourned pending the outcome of the appeal (pursuant to the provision corresponding to s 5(1) of the Foreign Judgments (Reciprocal Enforcement) Act 1933). In *Deutsche Schachtbau-und Tiefbohrgesellschaft GmbH* v *Ras Al Khaimah National Oil Company* (No 1) [1987] 3 WLR 1023, the Court of Appeal upheld an injunction granted by Bingham J in proceedings to enforce a foreign arbitration award by registration. In that case Bingham J had made an order *ex parte* pursuant to RSC Order 73, r 10 and s 3(1)(*a*) of the Arbitration Act 1975 granting leave to the plaintiffs to enforce the arbitration award as a judgment. Under RSC Order 73, r 10(6), the award is not immediately enforceable in the same manner as a judgment or order, but the injunction was granted for the purpose of preserving assets pending the award becoming enforceable and execution being sought. In the interim period, it was regarded by Sir John Donaldson MR (with whom the other members of the court agreed) as 'at least doubtful' whether the injunction was to be regarded as a Mareva injunction or an injunction granted to a judgment creditor in aid of execution, albeit that by reason of RSC Order 73, r 10(6) the right to levy execution was 'subject to a suspension', and that the order made *ex parte*, granting leave to enforce, might subsequently be set aside.

Under RSC Order 11, r (1)(*m*) there is jurisdiction in the court to grant leave to serve out of the jurisdiction proceedings in which the claim is brought to enforce any judgment or arbitral award, and RSC Order 11, r 1(2) enables service out of the jurisdiction to be effected without leave on a defendant domiciled in any part of the United Kingdom or any other Convention territory (as defined in RSC Order 11, r 1(4)) of proceedings to enforce a judgment under Art 31 of the Convention or a judgment under s 18 of the Civil Jurisdiction and Judgments Act 1982 (judgments and arbitration awards from another part of the United Kingdom).

If a judgment or award cannot be enforced by registration, it may still be open to the party seeking to enforce, to bring an action at common law on the judgment or the award, and Mareva and Anton Piller relief may be granted in those proceedings.[44]

The fact that proceedings to enforce the relevant judgment against the assets in question have been commenced or are to be commenced before the courts of another contracting state to the European Judgments Convention does not preclude the High Court from granting Mareva or Anton Piller relief in aid of the enforcement proceedings: in particular Art 16(5) of the Convention does not prevent the High Court from granting such provisional measures.[45]

(9) An intended application which falls only within a category of case for which provision has not been made by Order in Council under s 25(3) of the Civil Jurisdiction and Judgments Act 1982, or otherwise

Mareva and Anton Piller relief is not available in these circumstances, which remain governed by the decision of the House of Lords in *Siskina* v *Distos SA* [1979] AC 210.

---

44 *NEC Corporation* v *Steintoon* (1986) 52 OR 201, also reported at 5 CPC (2nd) 187 (Ontario).
45 *Babanaft Co SA* v *Bassatne* [1989] 2 WLR 232.

Chapter 6

Preservation of assets: other types of relief

The use of the Mareva injunction has become so widespread that it is now regarded as probably the foremost type of interlocutory relief for the preservation of assets. However, the courts do have other procedures available, and the power to grant other forms of interlocutory relief in circumstances in which Mareva relief is inappropriate, or liable to be ineffective.

(1) Buyers' claims on contracts for the sale of a ship

A recurring problem in practice has been that of purchasers who believe that a vessel which is about to be delivered under a concluded sale agreement (usually on the Norwegian Sale Form) suffers from defects. If the vessel is delivered in this condition, the buyer may have a claim for damages under the sale agreement. This, of course, depends upon the terms of the agreement; although the terms as to the fitness for purpose and merchantable quality implied by ss 13 and 14 of the Sale of Goods Act 1979 are capable of being implied in a ship sale contract, such sales are nowadays more often concluded on an 'as is' basis. Accordingly, if the buyer has a claim at all, it is more likely that it would arise in respect of a breach of an express term of the sale agreement. For example, in *Ninemia Maritime Corporation* v *Trave Schiffahrtsgesellschaft GmbH (The 'Niedersachsen')* [1983] 1 WLR 1412, the claim was in respect of, *inter alia*, the alleged breach of the term providing for the vessel to be delivered 'free of average damage affecting class'.

A buyer, who has reason to believe that he would have a good claim for damages if he took delivery of the vessel, will often have in mind the following considerations.

(1) The buyer, for commercial reasons, wishes to take delivery of the vessel.

(2) The buyer does not wish to be left with an unsecured claim for damages against the seller. The seller is often a company which is selling its only known asset.

(3) The proceeds of the sale may be payable to a bank which holds a mortgage over the vessel, and has first claim over the sale proceeds.

(4) The provisions of sale agreement usually entitle the seller (a) to serve a notice making time of delivery of the essence, and (b) to forfeit the buyer's deposit and cancel the contract in the event of the buyer failing to comply with such a notice.

(5) The buyer may not be entitled to reject the vessel, even if he wished to do so.

(6) The buyer may not even have reliable detailed information about the suspected defects, upon which to consider the position and decide what prospects he has of legitimately rejecting the vessel, or to assess the quantum of his prospective liability in damages if he makes the wrong decision.

Attempts have been made by buyers to deal with these considerations by proceeding to take delivery of the vessel and applying for a Mareva injunction over the sale proceeds within the jurisdiction either before or after delivery. The courts have shown a marked reluctance to assist buyers with Mareva relief before delivery.

In relation to an application before delivery of the vessel is accepted by the buyer, two major objections have arisen. First, it is often the case that the buyer will not acquire a right of action in damages until he has accepted delivery. Secondly, it is said that the buyer should now be allowed to use the Mareva injunction procedure to set a 'trap' for the unwary seller, who gives the vessel up, only to find the sale proceeds immediately frozen in his hands.[1]

The first objection is based upon the principle that Mareva relief is not available unless and until the plaintiff has an accrued cause of action. The courts have consistently refused to grant Mareva injunctions to assist a plaintiff who has strong grounds for believing that the potential defendant will break his contract with the plaintiff or commit a tort against him. In *Siporex Trade SA* v *Comdel Commodities Ltd* [1986] 2 Lloyd's Rep 428, Bingham J refused to grant a Mareva injunction to a plaintiff who had not yet acquired a cause of action. However, upon the plaintiff acquiring a cause of action (by making a payment to the defendant) Bingham J subsequently granted, *ex parte*, an injunction restraining the defendant from dealing with (*inter alia*) the fund resulting from the payment. Modern telecommunications resulted in the fund being successfully preserved within the jurisdiction before the defendant was able to remove it from the jurisdiction, and the injunction was maintained by Bingham J *inter partes*. A Mareva injunction can only be granted as interlocutory (and thus merely ancillary) relief in an action claiming final, substantive relief: *Siskina* v *Distos SA* [1979] AC 210 at p 254 per Lord Diplock. If the plaintiff has not issued his originating process at the time of the application, he is required

---

1 *Z Ltd* v *A-Z and AA-LL* [1982] QB 558 per Kerr LJ at p 585; *Ninemia Maritime Corporation* v *Trave Schiffahrtsgesellschaft GmbH (The 'Niedersachsen')* [1983] 1 WLR 1412 at p 1419 per Kerr LJ citing with approval a passage from Mustill J whose judgment is reported at [1983] 2 Lloyd's Rep 600.

to give an undertaking to the court that he will do so. If the plaintiff does not yet have a cause of action then there is no final relief properly being claimed to which the Mareva injunction is simply ancillary. In *Steamship Mutual Underwriting Assn (Bermuda)* v *Thakur Shipping*[2] Sir John Donaldson MR said:

What [the plaintiff] really wants is security for a future cause of action . . . a cause of action which will give rise to entitlement to monetary relief. I think that that would be contrary to a long line of authority which says that s 37 is to be used in support of an existing legal or equitable right . . . if we extended it to this case, even assuming we have jurisdiction to do so, it would be difficult to see what possible limits there could be to be Mareva jurisdiction.

In that case the Court of Appeal refused to grant an *ex parte* injunction sought by a P and I Club who believed that one of their members would fail to honour obligations owed to a third party leaving the Club liable under a guarantee to the third party. The Club had a right of indemnity against the member which had not yet become exercisable, and feared that the member would renege on the indemnity.

The refusal to grant Mareva relief in respect of a cause of action which a plaintiff expects to acquire in the near future is inconvenient. It is liable to involve the plaintiff making an immediate, urgent application to the judge upon acquiring the cause of action. However, in the meantime, the intended defendant may remove assets from the jurisdiction or deal with those assets. If the assets have yet to be acquired by the intended defendant, he may nevertheless enter into a valid equitable assignment, which will bind the assets when they are acquired and defeat the Mareva when it is eventually granted: *Pharaoh's Plywood Co Ltd* v *Allied Wood Products* Court of Appeal (Civil Division) Transcript, No 217 of 1980 (18 January).

In Australia the courts have declined to impose a rigid requirement that the plaintiff has to have an existing maintainable cause of action (see pp 110–112, below). Furthermore, such a requirement is in contrast to the result sought to be achieved by the court on the exercise of the *quia timet* jurisdiction, where injunctive relief is granted to prevent the commission of future wrongs. That jurisdiction enables the court to grant final relief in the form of a negative or a mandatory injunction,[3] and s 37 of the Supreme Court Act 1981 gives jurisdiction to the court to grant (*inter alia*) an interlocutory injunction *quia timet*. Mareva relief is necessarily only by way of interlocutory injunction whether granted before or after judgment and so is to be distinguished from the *quia timet* jurisdiction. In addition, under the *quia timet* jurisdiction it can justifiably be said that the plantiff has an *existing right* to be protected against future wrongs which it is feared

---

2 [1986] 2 Lloyd's Rep 439 at p 440. A similar statement was made by Mustill J in *Ninemia Maritime Corporation* v *Trave Schiffahrtsgesellschaft GmbH (The 'Niedersachsen')* [1983] 2 Lloyd's Rep 600 at p 602.

3 *Hooper* v *Rogers* [1975] Ch 43; *Morris* v *Redland Bricks* [1970] AC 652.

will be committed. Despite the distinctions to be drawn between the granting of relief *quia timet* and an application for Mareva relief in anticipation of acquiring an existing cause of action, there is a similarity. In each case the objective of the plaintiff is to prevent or forestall injustice being done to him by the defendant in the future.

In *A* v *B* [1989] 2 Lloyd's Rep 423, the plaintiffs sought an injunction to freeze sums in a joint account prior to taking delivery of a vessel and were granted an injunction to take effect if and when delivery of the vessel took place, this injunction to be served on the defendants before delivery of the vessel. In granting this order Saville J followed the established rule,[4] but avoided the inconvenience involved in the plaintiff only being allowed to make the application *ex parte* to the judge after delivery had been made. The application to Saville J was made after prior notice had been given to the shipowners and the mortgagees.

The second objection raises the question whether the court should be willing to grant a Mareva injunction unless the buyer is prepared to disclose the existence of the injunction to the seller before delivery of the vessel. If the court insists upon such a disclosure being made, the buyer will run the risk that the seller may refuse to complete the transaction unless the injunction is discharged. However, if the buyer waits until after taking delivery of the vessel before seeking Mareva relief, the sale proceeds may be paid away before the injunction can be made effective. Furthermore, there is the consideration that it would not in principle be proper for the injunction to be kept secret in circumstances where the buyer is encouraging the seller to complete, in the expectation that he will obtain free use of the purchase money. In effect the buyer in such a case would himself not be acting entirely consistently with good faith in his dealings with the seller, and might also himself be acting in breach of contract (dependent on its terms) by not giving the seller free use of the funds. In *Negocios Del Mar SA* v *Doric Shipping SA* [1979] 1 Lloyd's Rep 331, the buyers obtained a Mareva injunction *ex parte* from Mocatta J without disclosing their plan to keep the injunction secret pending completion. The injunction was discharged by the judge *inter partes* in view of the non-disclosure, and because he felt that the buyers had acted unfairly to the sellers in not disclosing the existence of the injunction to them before completion. Mocatta J refused to give 'the blessing of this court to what happened at the Eastcheap Branch of Lloyds Bank whilst a copy of [the] order was being . . . shown to the National Bank of Greece at Bevis Marks'. The Court of Appeal upheld the judge's discretion on the same grounds, Shaw LJ observing that:

. . . discretionary relief which is designed to prevent injustice is not to be sought by

---

4 The plaintiffs accepted that the rule applied.

or accorded to a party whose conduct appears to have been governed by the principle of catch as catch can.

In *Z Ltd* v *A-Z and AA-LL* Kerr LJ [1982] QB 552 at p 585,[5] observed that even disclosure of the intention to use the injunction 'as a means of setting a trap for the payee' should not suffice to justify the grant of the injunction in such cases. If the payer, 'appreciating the implications', is willing to make the payment then 'the courts should not assist him to safeguard the payment in advance by means of a Mareva injunction. However, this is a special type of situation, and, like all others in this field, [is] ultimately a matter for the discretion of the judge'. Nevertheless, the court may still grant Mareva relief *ex parte* on the basis that it will only be disclosed to the seller after delivery of the vessel. Thus, in *Ateni Maritime Corporation* v *Great Marine Ltd* (unreported (25 May 1989)), Phillips J in chambers made an order *ex parte* which contained an undertaking by the plaintiffs to give notice of the order 'immediately after (but not before) the completion of the Ship Sale Agreement and delivery of the vessel'.

Even leaving aside these difficulties there are further considerations which may render Mareva relief unsatisfactory to the buyer:

(1) If the vessel is mortgaged (and most trading vessels are) the mortgagees would be entitled to receive the sale proceeds towards discharge of their mortgage. The mortgagees would have a prior claim over the sale proceeds which cannot be defeated by a Mareva injunction.

(2) Even if the vessel is not mortgaged, the proceeds of the sale may be whittled away by Angel Bell orders enabling the seller to meet legal fees or other debts and expenses.

(3) The seller may assign his right to receive the sale proceeds to a third party before the Mareva injunction is granted. A bona fide assignee would be entitled to have the injunction discharged.

(4) Depending upon the terms of the contract of sale the sellers may say that there has not been payment of the price in compliance with the contractual requirements (eg if there is a requirement that the plaintiff is to have free use of the purchase money). If justified, this could involve as a consequence the sellers having the right of cancelling the contract, forfeiting the deposit and claiming damages.

The court has jurisdiction to grant an injunction *quia timet* to restrain the seller from rendering delivery of a defective vessel until the defects

---

5 See also the observations of Mustill J in *Ninemia Corporation* v *Trave Schiffahrtsgesellschaft GmbH (The 'Niedersachsen')* [1983] 2 Lloyd's Rep 600 at p 612, cited with approval by the Court of Appeal, reported in [1983] 1 WLR 1412 at p 1419 (where it was said 'there is something unattractive about the idea' of the buyer ostensibly paying the full price to obtain the vessel while 'preparing . . . behind the seller's back to deprive him of part of the price').

have been remedied, but in practice such jurisdiction would rarely, if ever, be exercised, because damages would usually be considered an adequate remedy. Furthermore, the application would necessarily be interlocutory; the court would not be in a position to make findings of fact in relation to the state of the vessel, and the granting of *quia timet* relief would effectively suspend delivery of the vessel pending resolution of the dispute. This could put serious and unjustifiable financial pressure on the seller.

(2) Possible alternative remedies available to buyers

If the vessel does suffer from defects upon delivery in breach of the sale agreement, then at common law the buyer has a right to abate the price payable for the vessel under the principles established by *Mondel* v *Steel* (1841) 8 M&W 858 (see further, *Modern Engineering* v *Gilbert-Ash* [1974] AC 689). If the buyer tenders what he considers to be an appropriately abated price, first the seller is unlikely to give delivery of the vessel, and secondly the buyer may not have sufficient details of the defects to enable an accurate assessment to be made of the quantum of the abatement. Accordingly, the buyer runs the risk of the seller cancelling the agreement and forfeiting the deposit. However, if the buyer could have proceedings heard and determined prior to delivery of the vessel, it would be possible to obtain an appropriate declaration as to the extent of the abatement which could legitimately be made. Has the court jurisdiction to preserve the position by interim order pending resolution of the claim to abatement of the price?

This is a different approach from that which the buyers have adopted in the Mareva cases. Thus, instead of seeking to freeze the seller's assets in respect of a claim for damages, the buyer is seeking to claim that the seller only has the legal right to be paid an amount lower than the price set out in the sale agreement. The buyer is therefore seeking an order preserving the position pending the quantification of the seller's claim for the price, that quantum being a matter of dispute.

The ship sale agreements which come before the courts almost invariably contain a London arbitration clause and are therefore usually expressly or impliedly governed by English law. Section 12(6) of the Arbitration Act 1950 expressly confers upon the court the power to make orders for the preservation of 'any property which is the subject of the reference' (s 12(6)(g)) or 'securing the amount in dispute in the reference' (s 12(6)(f)) as well as the power to grant interim injunctions. These powers are equivalent to (and may overlap with) the powers of the court conferred by s 37 of the Supreme Court Act 1981 and under RSC Order 29.

The court could make an order freezing an amount equivalent to the part of the purchase price in dispute pending resolution of the abatement issue. Thus it can be said that such an order 'secures the amount in dispute in the reference'—the 'amount in dispute' being the disputed amount of the price. It is envisaged that such an order would require payment of the amount in dispute into a joint bank account or into court. The buyer, by complying with the order and tendering the balance of the price to the seller, would then place the seller under a contractual duty to give delivery of the vessel. If the seller refused to give delivery, this would constitute a breach of contract on his part. Consequently he would not be entitled to forfeit the deposit, and would be at risk that the buyer might accept his conduct as a repudiation of the contract.

That s 12(6)(*f*) is in principle applicable to the case is supported by dicta of Brandon J in *The 'Rena K'* [1979] QB 377 at p 408. Even if s 12(6)(*f*) is to be limited in scope to securing a specific fund in which the applicant claims an interest,[6] the position is that the buyer is saying that he is entitled to retain that part of the purchase price which is equivalent in amount to his claim.

Alternatively, the order could be upheld by reference to s 12(6)(*h*) of the Arbitration Act 1950. This section justifies the granting of Mareva relief in relation to arbitration proceedings which have been or are to be commenced.[7] In *Seven Seas Properties Ltd* v *Al-Essa* [1989] 1 WLR 1272, the plaintiffs obtained an order against the defendant for specific performance of a contract of sale in respect of leasehold property. That order contained a provision for retention by the sellers of a substantial sum out of the purchase money payable under the contract. This part of the order was upheld by Hoffmann J on the grounds that it could be justified by reference to the Mareva jurisdiction of the court, and it would be 'excessively formalistic' to require two separate orders, one being for specific performance and the other being by way of a Mareva injunction. Such an injunction could have ordered the defendants to permit the plaintiffs to retain a certain amount of the purchase money pending further order of the court, and could have restrained the defendants from receiving that sum from the plaintiffs.

If, notwithstanding the order of the court concerning retention of part of the purchase money, the sellers declined to give delivery of the vessel, it is thought that in an appropriate case the buyer could seek specific performance of the contract from the arbitrators and it would be open to him to seek an order by way of interim specific performance[8] from the court under s 12(6)(*h*) of the Arbitration Act 1950.

A preservation order of the kind described above may also be of assistance to buyers of other types of goods where the terms of sale produce

---

6 As was the position in *Richco International* v *International Industrial* [1989] 2 Lloyd's Rep 106 at p 109, that case falling within RSC Order 29, r 2(3).

7 *The 'Rena K'* [1979] QB 377 at p 408; *Third Chandris* v *Unimarine SA* [1979] QB 645 at p 663.

8 *Astro Exito Navegacion SA* v *Southland Enterprise Co Ltd (The 'Messiniaki Tolmi') (No 2)* [1982] QB 1248 (CA) affirmed at [1983] 2 AC 787 (HL).

similar considerations. However, where payment is to be made by means of a letter of credit, or where there is a bank guarantee or performance bond, the matter is unlikely to be straightforward. As a general rule the court will refuse to intervene and prevent payment under a letter of credit, bank guarantee or performance bond, unless the person seeking such an order can produce very exceptional reasons justifying this course of action. Generally, only a strong *prima facie* case of fraud will suffice.

(3) Disappearing assets

A Mareva injunction will be of no value to the plaintiff if it is in respect of an asset of the defendant which is liable to perish or disappear before judgment can be obtained (eg a chose in action liable to become time-barred). The statutory source of the Mareva jurisdiction provides that the court has power to appoint receivers by interlocutory or final order 'in all cases in which it appears to the court to be just and convenient to do so'. Prior to the emergence of the Mareva jurisdiction, unless the plaintiff asserted a right in the underlying assets, courts would not appoint a receiver over assets of the defendant unless the plaintiff had already obtained judgment, or at the very least an untaxed order for costs, eg *Cummins* v *Perkins* [1899] 1 Ch 16.

However, this approach was based upon the reasoning which apparently precluded the granting of Mareva injunctions (see Kerr on *Injunctions*, 6th ed, at pp 613–4). It is now clear from the decision of the Court of Appeal in *Derby & Co Ltd* v *Weldon (Nos 3 and 4)* [1989] 2 WLR 412 (also see pp 139–141, below) that s 37(1) of the Supreme Court Act 1981 enables the court to appoint a receiver before judgment when it is just and right to do so. The remedy of appointment of a receiver is likely to be particularly appropriate when the asset in question needs to be managed, preserved or exploited. For example, if the asset consists of the controlling shareholding in a company which in turn holds assets, then a Mareva injunction granted in respect of the shares will not be effective in itself to prevent the defendant from dissipating the assets of the company. One approach to this problem is for the court to grant Mareva relief directly against the company under the principles discussed in Chapter 11. That approach would not in itself enable the company's assets to be managed.

Another approach would be for the court to appoint a receiver by way of interlocutory relief over the shares.[9] This approach would also be appropriate when the relevant asset consists of a claim against a third party, and active steps need to be taken to preserve the claim and in due course obtain proceeds. For example a receiver could be appointed so as

---

9 This was done in Hong Kong in *Asean Resources Ltd* v *Ka Wah International Merchant Finance Ltd* (1987) 8 IPR 241.

to take steps to protect the claim against the expiry of applicable time limits.[10]

(4) Interim specific performance and mandatory injunctions

The court has wide powers to make interim orders to preserve the position as between parties, so that in due course, if appropriate, an effective order for specific performance of a contract can be granted. The form of these orders is by no means limited to negative injunctions. It may be necessary to grant mandatory relief, simply to enable a plaintiff to obtain or preserve the possibility of specific performance.

A recent example of a situation justifying such an order is to be found in the case of *Astro Exito Navegacion SA* v *Chase Manhattan Bank (The 'Messiniaki Tolmi')* [1983] 2 AC 787 (HL). In that case the plaintiffs had agreed to sell a vessel to the defendants and deliver her at Kaohsiung Harbour, Taiwan. Payment was to be made under a letter of credit. The defendants made a late amendment to the letter of credit (accepted under protest by the plaintiffs), requiring the notice of readiness (which was one of the documents to be tendered under the letter of credit) to be signed and accepted by the buyers' agents. The defendants refused to accept the notice of readiness and the plaintiffs brought proceedings for specific performance which were then stayed, pending arbitration, on the defendants' application. However, Parker J ordered the defendants to sign the notice of readiness before the letter of credit expired, so that the money payable under the letter of credit could be released into a joint account until further order. The court also made provision in the order for a Master of the Supreme Court to sign the notice of readiness if the buyer's agents did not. This in fact happened. The bank refused to pay under the letter of credit. The House of Lords held that the judge had jurisdiction to make the interlocutory order, which he did under ss 45 and 47 of the Supreme Court of Judicature (Consolidation) Act 1925, the predecessor of the 1981 Act, and that, in view of the fact that he thought, rightly, that it was a strong case for ordering specific performance in favour of the sellers, he was entitled in his discretion to make an order in those terms. In principle, the court would also be able to appoint a receiver in pursuance of bringing about the position whereby a final decree of specific performance could in due course be granted at trial.

It will be seen, therefore, that the jurisdiction of the court to grant immediate specific performance by interlocutory order, subject to suitable undertakings should it subsequently appear that the order was unjustified, is particularly useful where the plaintiff is caught in time difficulties, for example if a letter of credit is about to expire. Although it might be a strong step to exercise this jurisdiction, a refusal to entertain such

---

10 For example giving timeous notice to an insurer so that the claim is not barred under the terms of the insurance policy—see the facts in *The Vainqueur Jose* [1979] 1 Lloyd's Rep 557.

applications could have the effect of causing serious injustice. Another example of a case where mandatory interlocutory relief was granted is *Continental Grain Company* v *Islamic Republic of Iran* [1983] 2 Lloyd's Rep 620, in which a mandatory interlocutory injunction was granted directing the second defendants, who were in control of a vessel carrying the plaintiff's goods, to discharge the goods at the nearest safe port, in order to give effect to the plaintiff's rights of stoppage *in transitu* and preserve the property pending the outcome of a dispute with the first defendants, who had agreed to buy them. However, a mandatory injunction will only be granted in a clear case when the court feels a high degree of assurance that at the trial, it will appear that the injunction was rightly granted.

It has also been said that the court will be required to be satisfied that if a mandatory injunction is granted it will be susceptible of enforcement.[11] However, the apprehension that a defendant will not or may not obey an injunction is not a good justification for refusing to grant it simply on the ground that its grant would be a mere *brutem fulmen*.[12]

Accordingly, there are circumstances in which merely negative relief by way of a Mareva injunction will be inappropriate because it is insufficient for the plaintiff's purposes, and where consideration will need to be given to seeking relief which requires active steps to be taken by the defendant in respect of the assets in question so as to preserve or maintain them in tact pending trial.

(5) Assets subject to a trust

A court has never hesitated to use the strongest powers to protect and preserve a trust fund in interlocutory proceedings.

There are many reported cases in which relief broadly similar to Mareva relief has been granted by the courts, where the plaintiff is claiming a proprietary interest in the assets which he seeks to preserve. Such cases range from the more straightforward trading cases (eg where the plaintiff has sold goods to the defendant, subject to a retention of title clause, and the defendant fails to pay him) to cases involving allegations of fraud. The court has a broad equitable jurisdiction to preserve trust assets, regardless of whether or not those assets are situated within the jurisdiction, and regardless of whether the trust arises from an express declaration or from operation of law by way of constructive trust (as in cases of fraud).[13] A parallel jurisdiction exists in such cases under RSC Order 29, r 3. It is

---

11 *Locabail International Finance* v *Agroexport (The 'Sea Hawk')* [1986] 1 WLR 657.
12 *Castanho* v *Brown & Root (UK) Ltd* [1981] AC 557 at p 574.
13 See eg *London and Counties Securities* v *Caplan* (unreported) 26 May 1978, referred to at [1981] QB 958; *Mediterrania Raffineria Sicilana Petroli SpA* v *Mabanaft GmbH* Court of Appeal (Civil Division) Transcript No 816 of 1978 (1 December 1978); *Bankers Trust* v *Shapira* [1980] 1 WRL: 1274; *A* v *C* (No 1) [1981] QB 956; *Bekhor* v *Bilton* [1981] QB 293 (especially at pp 937–939); and *PCW (Underwriting Agencies) Ltd* v *Dixon and another* [1983] 2 Lloyd's Rep 197, and p 20 above.

also well established that in such cases the court may grant an interlocutory order appointing a receiver over foreign assets: *Re Maudslay Sons and Field* [1900] 1 Ch 602; *Duder* v *Amsterdamsch Trustees* [1902] 2 Ch 132. As with Mareva relief, an injunction will not be made if its effect would be unduly oppressive, and it is subject to modification in the discretion of the court to allow the defendant to draw on frozen moneys to pay his ordinary living expenses or other debts: *PCW (Underwriting Agencies) Ltd* v *Dixon (PS)* [1983] 2 All ER 158, at p 697.

In a trust case, therefore, it is possible to obtain orders preserving assets situated abroad and ancillary orders for discovery of their whereabouts (see eg *Cook Industries* v *Galliher* [1979] Ch 439) inspection of the contents of an apartment in Paris; furthermore, third parties (eg banks) may be required to provide information concerning the whereabouts of such assets and their proceeds (see *Bankers Trust* v *Shapira* (above); and *A* v *C (No 1)*).

(6) Family law relief

In the Family Division of the High Court, special jurisdiction is available to the courts in relation to certain cases involving family law under s 37(2) of the Matrimonial Causes Act 1973. This provides as follows:

s 37(2)   Where proceedings for financial relief are brought by one person against another, the court may, on the application of the first-mentioned person:
  (*a*) if it is satisfied that the other party to the proceedings is, with the intention of defeating the claim for financial relief, about to make any disposition or to transfer out of the jurisdiction or otherwise deal with any property, make such order as it thinks fit for restraining the other party from so doing or otherwise for protecting the claim;
  (*b*) if it is satisfied that the other party has, with that intention, made a reviewable disposition and that if the disposition were set aside financial relief or different financial relief would be granted to the applicant, make an order setting aside the disposition;
  (*c*) if it is satisfied in a case where an order has been obtained under any of the provisions mentioned in subs (1) above by the applicant against the other party, that the other party has, with that intention, made a reviewable disposition, make an order setting aside the disposition;
and an application for the purpose of para (*b*) above shall be made in the proceedings for the financial relief in question.

'Financial relief' is defined in s 37(1) and means an order for maintenance of or for the provision of money for the benefit of children, under ss 22, 23, 24, 27, 31 or 35 of the Act.

The application must be made by the spouse or ex-spouse in question in proceedings for financial relief as defined by s 37(1).

It will be noted that the jurisdiction is wider than the jurisdiction to grant Mareva relief, in that the court has actually been empowered to undo transactions after they have been completed. However, the rights of a bona fide purchaser for value without notice remain unaltered (s 37(4)), so that an order will not be made by the court if it would affect the equitable rights of a mortgagee who is a purchaser for value without notice.

The statutory jurisdiction under s 37(2) and its predecessors, s 32(1) of the Matrimonial Causes Act 1965, and s 16(1) of the Matrimonial Proceedings and Property Act 1970 rendered obsolete a number of decisions to the effect that an injunction would not be granted to restrain the disposal of property by a spouse against whom no maintenance order had yet been made, or whose payments under such an order had not fallen into arrears: *Burmester* v *Burmester* [1913] P 76; *Fanshawe* v *Fanshawe* [1927] P 238; and *Scott* v *Scott* [1951] P 193. This line of authorities is likewise no obstacle to ordinary Mareva relief in a family law case.

Section 37(2)(*a*) of the Act confers an express jurisdiction on the court to restrain a party from making a disposition or transfer if the court is satisfied that such disposition or transfer would be made with 'the intention of defeating the claim for financial relief'. This requirement of intent is not a pre-condition for the granting of Mareva relief.

Section 37(2) is capable of applying to property wherever situated,[14] as is now the case in relation to the granting of Mareva relief.[15]

(7) Section 423 of the Insolvency Act 1986

Unlike s 37(2) of the Matrimonial Causes Act 1973 there is no statutory provision in s 423 of the Insolvency Act 1986 for restraining a transaction before it has been entered into by the parties. The statute itself only applies once a transaction has been entered into for one of the purposes set out in s 423(3), namely putting assets beyond the reach of a person who is making or may at some time make a claim, or of otherwise prejudicing the interests of such a person. It appears that s 423 is capable of applying to assets or property wherever situated. Thus, s 436 of the Act defines 'property' to include 'money, goods, things in action, land and every description of property where situated' and s 425 of the Act must be read with this definition of property incorporated into it.[16] Furthermore, the jurisdiction of the courts under s 423 is to be exercised *in personam* against those who entered into the impugned transaction, and any relevant third parties, and in principle it is to be expected that a jurisdiction which is *in personam* will not be restricted, in the absence of express provision to the

---

14 *Hamlin* v *Hamlin* [1986] Fam 11.

15 *Babanaft International Co SA* v *Bassatne* [1989] 2 WLR 232; *Derby & Co Ltd* v *Weldon* [1989] 2 WLR 276; *Republic of Haiti* v *Duvalier* [1989] 2 WLR 261; *Derby & Co Ltd* v *Weldon* (Nos 3 and 4) [1989] 2 WLR 412.

16 *Attorney-General* v *Corporation of Worcester* (1846) 15 LJ Ch 398 at p 399, per Lord Cottenham LC; *Phoenix General Insurance Co of Greece* v *Administratia Asigurarilor de Stat* [1986] 2 Lloyd's Rep 552 at pp 556–557.

contrary, to property or other assets located within the territorial jurisdiction of the court.[17]

A cause of action vests under s 423 in a 'victim' immediately upon a 'transaction' being entered into, and 'transaction' is defined in s 436 as including an 'agreement or arrangement'. 'Accordingly, it appears to be the case that as soon as even an informal 'arrangement' is made, although it is not legally binding, the court would have jurisdiction under s 423(2) of the Act to make such order as it thought fit for protecting the interests of persons "who are victims". Section 423(5) defines "a victim" in terms which include a person who is capable of being prejudiced' by the arrangement. Thus, it appears to be the case that although s 423 does not have an express provision for restraining dispositions or transfers before they occur, nevertheless it is sufficiently wide to catch an intended disposition or transfer as soon as an arrangement is made for it to occur.

It may also be the case that the court also has jurisdiction *quia timet* to restrain a disposition or transfer before it is carried out. Thus, it is clear that under the section the court would have power to undo a transaction the moment it was carried out, and in principle it cannot be correct[18] that the court must wait until the damage is done before it can act so as to undo that damage pursuant to the statute.

The jurisdiction under s 423 only applies in respect of transactions entered into for a purpose specified in s 423(3) and thus, in this respect, it is narrower than the Mareva jurisdiction. However, it is likely to be of particular relevance when the plaintiff wishes to seek to restrain dealings with assets held in the name of third parties or claimed by third parties who are closely connected with the defendant, and who have apparently received the assets from the defendant in circumstances giving rise to a strong inference that the assets were transferred to the third party for the purpose of prejudicing creditors (see pp 132–134, below).

(8) Stay of execution under RSC Order 47, r 1(1)(a)

It may be that a plaintiff company has a claim against a defendant who in turn has a claim against a third party company, which is in the same group of companies as the plaintiff company. In such circumstances, the plaintiff company might be entitled to seek a Mareva injunction over (*inter alia*) the chose in action against the third party. However, the courts have recognised that in such a situation it may be appropriate to allow the third party company a stay of execution on a judgment obtained by the defendant against the third party, pending the outcome of the plaintiff's claim.[19] A stay of execution has the advantage that the plaintiff's group of

---

17 Compare the analogous position under s 37 of the Matrimonial Causes Act 1973: *Hamlin v Hamlin* [1986] Fam 11 at pp 18 and 22–23.
18 *Re Oriental Credit Ltd* [1988] Ch 204.
19 *Burnett v Francis Industries plc* [1987] 1 WLR 802; *Canada Enterprises v McNab Distilleries Ltd* [1987] 1 WLR 813; *Orri v Moundreas* [1981] Com L Rep 168.

companies does not have to pay over to the defendant money in satisfaction of the stayed judgment. Even if the money has to be paid into court as the price of a stay the plaintiff has greater control over the future disposal of the fund than would be the case with a Mareva injunction (which is liable to be discharged or varied under the *'Angel Bell'* principle). Thus the stay of execution granted to the third party enables the third party, acting in the interests of the plaintiff, to prevent the defendant from executing the judgment, obtaining thereby, and thereafter dissipating, the fruits of that judgment.

The discretion will only be exercised when the court is satisfied that there are 'special circumstances' which render it 'inexpedient' to enforce the judgment. These circumstances may be found to exist if there is a risk that unless the stay is granted the defendent may obtain the fruits of the judgment and dispose of them with the result that in due course the plaintiff may obtain and be left with an unsatisfied judgment against the defendant. In exercising the discretion in such circumstances, the factors to be taken into account include the following:[20]

(1) Ordinarily the third party judgment debtor will be required as a term of any stay to pay money into court[21] or otherwise to give security for the judgment debt. Unless this is done a stay of execution may result in the defendent being deprived in due course of the fruits of the judgment. If there is any substantial risk of this occurring it would be a powerful (if not conclusive) factor against the jurisdiction being exercised ([1987] 1 WLR at p 811 (see the seventh matter listed by Bingham LJ)).

(2) The jurisdiction is an exceptional one and it is not sufficient for the third party judgment creditor to identify the claim by the plaintiff against the defendant, and to offer to give security for the judgment ([1987] 1 WLR at p 809).

(3) The onus of satisfying the court that the jurisdiction should be exercised in any particular case lies on the applicant third party, who accordingly has the burden of proving the facts on the basis of which the jurisdiction is to be exercised.[22]

(4) The claim by the plaintiff must be one of substance on the merits. The stronger the claim the greater is the risk of prejudice if a stay is not granted ([1987] 1 WLR at p 811).

(5) The court is entitled to have regard to whether there are co-defendants to the claim. In considering the relevance of there being co-defendants, the court should take into account whether the plaintiff's claim could fail against them and yet succeed against the

---

20 In *Burnett* v *Francis Industries plc* [1987] 1 WLR 802 at p 811, Bingham LJ lists a number of matters which will call for consideration by the judge. The factors listed here include those matters.

21 There was an offer to pay money into court in *Burnett* v *Francis Industries plc* [1987] 1 WLR 802 at p 810 and in *Canada Enterprises* v *Mc Nab Distilleries Ltd* [1987] 1 WLR 813 at p 814.

22 This follows from the wording of RSC Order 47, r 1(1)(a).

relevant defendant, and the financial standing of the co-defendants ([1987] 1 WLR at p 810).

(6) The extent of any stay which may be ordered must be limited by the quantum of the plaintiff's claim against the defendant. The size of the claim is, in any event, relevant ([1987] 1 WLR at p 811).

(7) The discretion is to be exercised taking into account the closeness of the connection between the plaintiff and the third party, notwithstanding that this connection lies behind the corporate veil of the third party ([1987] 1 WLR at p 811). The relevant question is whether in the circumstances of the case, including that connection and its extent, justice demands that the stay be imposed.

(8) It is not necessary to show a connection between the transaction or circumstances giving rise to the plaintiff's claim against the defendant and the transaction or circumstances which gave rise to the judgment.[23] However, if there is a connection then the nature of that connection is likely to be a material consideration in deciding what the justice of the case demands ([1987] 1 WLR at p 811).

(9) The nature of the claim which gave rise to the judgment debt may be relevant. Eg if it is a claim on a bill of exchange or for freight, in which case it would follow that the application for a stay would rarely, if ever, succeed.

(10) The court should take into account the likely delay before the plaintiff's claim will be adjudicated upon and determined.

(11) The court should take into account the extent of any prejudice which may be suffered by the defendant as a result of stay of execution being granted.

(12) The court should take into account the extent of any prejudice which may be suffered by the plaintiff unless a stay is granted.

---

23 See the citation from the judgment of Mustill J in *Orri* v *Moundreas* set out in [1987] 1 WLR at pp 808–809.

Chapter 7

The *ex parte* application

(1) The application

The initial application for a Mareva injunction is almost invariably made *ex parte* without notice to the defendant, as knowledge by the defendant that such an application is pending may well defeat the very object which the plaintiff is trying to achieve. An application for Anton Piller relief is invariably made *ex parte*. The application for Anton Piller or Mareva relief must be made to a judge. In the Queen's Bench Division of the High Court (including the Commercial Court) the application is made to a judge in chambers; in the Chancery Division it is made on motion to the judge in open court, although the court will usually sit in camera, in particular for Anton Piller applications: *Colombia Picture Industries and others* v *Robinson and others* [1987] Ch 38 at p 71.

Save in the most urgent cases, the affidavit in support of the application and a draft minute of the order sought should be lodged with the court by a specified time in advance of the hearing. In the Queen's Bench Division they should be lodged by 3pm on the day before (or on the Friday before if the hearing is to be on a Monday) (see *Practice Direction* (*Judge in Chambers: Procedure*) 30 March 1983, [1983] 1 WLR 433 and Appendix 2). This rule is strictly enforced, and unless the plaintiff's counsel is prepared to certify that the matter is so urgent that it must be heard on the same day, notwithstanding that the papers were not lodged on time, the application will not be heard. In cases where the papers have not been lodged, the plaintiff's counsel is required to sign a form to indicate that in his or her opinion the matter is sufficiently urgent to warrant a hearing that day. However, if (as is frequently the case) there is difficulty about lodging a sworn affidavit in time, the court will accept a draft affidavit. This can then be sworn later in the afternoon or, if it proves to be impossible to swear it before the hearing, there must be an undertaking that it will be sworn forthwith after the hearing in the terms of the draft. It is also permissible, in practice, to hand in a draft of the order sought on the morning of the hearing, provided that the affidavit was duly lodged on the day before.

In the Chancery Division, the notice of motion, affidavit and draft

71

minute of order should be lodged by 12 midday with the clerk of the lists, Room 163, Chancery Chambers, on the day before the hearing.[1]

The practice in the Queen's Bench Division of using only one or perhaps two judges to hear urgent applications often means a delay (sometimes lengthy) in obtaining the injunction which, in certain Mareva cases, could result in injustice to the plaintiff. Sometimes, when the queue is especially long, and the problem is explained, another judge may be found, but such instances depend upon the state of the lists. In the Commercial Court, however, it is usually much easier to find a judge who is available to hear an urgent *ex parte* application at short notice. If counsel is involved, an appointment is fixed through counsel's clerk, who will liaise with the Commercial Court Office. Applications are generally heard in the judge's private room, although occasionally they may be heard in the court where the judge happens to be sitting at the time. Since any of the judges sitting in the Commercial Court at a given time may be available, there is usually no problem with delay. The success and greater flexibility of the system adopted in the Commercial Court is heavily dependent upon the Commercial Court Office, and, of course, upon counsel and solicitors ensuring that they are kept well informed about the timing of a likely application. It should be noted that in the Commercial Court, as in the Queen's Bench Division generally, the Practice Direction should be adhered to whenever possible, and the papers should be lodged with the court in advance, save in truly urgent cases. It is beneficial if the judge can be provided with at least the draft affidavit and exhibits to look at overnight, because this saves a considerable amount of time when the application is made the next morning. It assists the court if counsel's clerk can give an indication, at the earliest possible opportunity, of when counsel wishes to make the application. Consequently, it is sensible for counsel to make an assessment, as soon as possible after receipt of the relevant instructions and papers, of how long it will take to prepare for the application (including the settling of any affidavit, if so instructed) and to estimate how long the application will take and to take steps to ensure that the Commercial Court Office is then informed of the intended timing of the application and of its estimated duration. Any changes in those estimates should also be notified as soon as possible.

In family proceedings which are transferable between the High Court and the county courts under ss 38 and 39 of the Matrimonial and Family Proceedings Act 1984, interlocutory applications involving Anton Piller or Mareva relief are ordinarily to be made in the Family Division of the High Court 'unless the nature of the issues of fact or law raised in the case makes them more suitable for trial in a county court than in the High

---

1 Practice Direction Ch D: *Motions Procedure (No 2)*, 18 January 1985, [1985] 1 WLR 244: see Appendix 2.

Court.'[2] This would appear also in principle to apply to family proceedings which involve an application for an injunction under s 37(2)(a) of the Matrimonial Causes Act 1973 which provides a procedure analogous[3] to that of the Mareva jurisdiction. In family proceedings the ordinary rule is that no undertaking as to damages will be required.[4] Although Anton Piller relief may be granted in matrimonial proceedings,[5] it is seldom appropriate, and it will only be granted on strong evidence.[6]

(2) Applications during vacation

The procedure for applications made during vacation is similar to that for applications made in the Queen's Bench Division during term-time, save that counsel must certify that the matter is sufficiently urgent to be classed as vacation business, and the papers are not necessarily lodged in advance. See generally RSC Order 64, rr 3 and 4 and *Practice Direction and Long Vacation Business* [1983] 1 WLR 432.

(3) Urgent applications

In practice, the orderly procedure envisaged in the various practice directions is rarely followed, particularly in the case of Mareva injunctions, which, by their very nature, tend to arise as a matter of urgency. It is not unusual for the affidavit to be placed before the judge in draft form, with an undertaking to swear it forthwith being given in the court and embodied in the order. In cases of extreme urgency, where there is no time even to draft the affidavit, the grounds on which Mareva relief is sought may be explained orally by the plaintiff's counsel, but this procedure should only be adopted if there is no realistic alternative (and, if it is, a very careful note should be kept of what was said to the judge, so that the affidavit which is compiled and sworn after the hearing is accurate). The decision whether to make an application on the basis of a draft affidavit or on limited information, or to wait until a more orderly procedure can be adopted or more information obtained, is often a difficult one for the plaintiff's legal advisers to take. Obviously, the longer they wait before making the application, the greater the risk that the defendant will remove the assets. On the other hand, a badly prepared or over-hasty application can have serious consequences for the plaintiff; the injunction may be refused, or the application may be adjourned for additional information to be gathered and placed before the court, or the application may be granted and the injunction subsequently discharged because the duty of

---

2 *Practice Direction (Family Division: Business Distribution)* [1988] 1 WLR 588 at p 559, para 2(2)(k).
3 *Derby & Co Ltd* v *Weldon (Nos 3 and 4)* [1989] 2 WLR 412 at 438, per Butler-Sloss LJ.
4 *Practice Direction (Injunction: Undertaking as to Damages)* [1974] 1 WLR 576.
5 *Emanuel* v *Emanuel* [1982] 1 WLR 669.
6 *Francis* v *Francis* Court of Appeal (Civil Division) Transcript No 197 of 1986.

full disclosure has not been complied with. It is usually preferable to be cautious than to be underprepared. Even a plaintiff who successfully obtains a Mareva injunction or Anton Piller relief may have his costs of doing so disallowed if the court takes the view that he made insufficient inquiries before embarking on the application.[7]

Mareva relief can be granted at any stage of the proceedings, including the stage at which the plaintiff wishes to execute judgment. However, especially in the situation where proceedings have already been issued, care must be taken to apply for Mareva relief with reasonable promptness, once all the facts and matters on which the application is founded are known to the plaintiff. Mareva injunctions, like any other form of inter-locutory relief, should be sought with reasonable swiftness: the failure of a plaintiff to make the application until several weeks after he could have done so may suggest to the court that his motive in seeking the relief is not to protect his position, but instead to put pressure on the defendant, and may lead to a refusal to grant the injunction. This should not be the case, however, if the delay arose from the plaintiff investigating matters relevant to the application, with a view to ensuring that he had sufficient information to support his case and that he had complied with his duty to make full disclosure of all relevant facts and matters. The latter point is of particular relevance in cases in which the plaintiff is a large organisation and several people are involved as sources of information.

(4) Documentation

It is of the utmost importance that as far as is possible the documents should be in good order for the judge. The affidavit and exhibits should be in a form complying with the Lord Chief Justice's Practice Direction.[8] This Practice Direction applies to all divisions of the High Court and to the Court of Appeal, and gives detailed directions as to the preparation of affidavits, exhibits and bundles of documents. In the event of the application being made by counsel he or she should be satisfied that the draft order is an appropriate one to place before the court: *Z Ltd* v *A-Z and AA-LL* [1982] QB 558 at p 578. It will often be helpful for the judge to be given a written outline chronology (in the form of a table of events) and a *dramatis personae*.

The Guide to Commercial Court Practice, in Section IV (see Appendix 2), states that paragraph 3 of the *Practice Direction* [1983] 1 WLR 433 (see Appendix 2) issued by the Lord Chief Justice concerning *ex parte* applications to the judge in chambers in the Queen's Bench Division is equally appropriate to the Commercial Court. Annexed to Section IV, in Annexe A of the Guide, is a standard draft order which may be suitable as

---

7 *Systematica Ltd* v *London Computer Centre Ltd* [1983] FSR 313 in which Whitford J so held in relation to an *Anton Piller* order. The reasoning appears equally apposite to Mareva cases.
8 *Practice Direction* [1983] 1 WLR 922: see Appendix 2.

an initial working draft to be used for the preparation of a draft order to be used on an *ex parte* application for Mareva relief.

In the Chancery Division draft minutes of order for Mareva and Anton Piller (see Appendix 2) relief have been made available by the court, and serve the same function.

(5) Sources of information and belief

Under RSC Order 41, r 5(2), an affidavit sworn for the purpose of being used in interlocutory proceedings[9] may contain 'statements of information or belief with the sources and grounds thereof.' Although in practice affidavits are often used which are defective in this respect, it is of particular importance that the requirements of RSC Order 41, r 5 are complied with on applications for Mareva or Anton Piller relief. On an *ex parte* application the plaintiff has a duty of full disclosure and this extends to all matters which the court would wish to take into account in the weighing operation which the court has to make in deciding whether or not to grant the order. To what extent a deponent knows matters of his own knowledge may be material. So in relation to matters outside his own knowledge, the relevant source of information or ground for his belief could be material. In the absence of a source or ground for belief being identified then, subject to contrary indication appearing from the evidence, the court may well proceed upon the basis that the matters deposed to are within the personal knowledge of the deponent.

Independent of the question as to whether there has been full disclosure by the applicant, is the question whether or not the court will act on material contained in an affidavit which is not within the personal knowledge of the deponent. RSC Order 41, r 5(2) is permissive in enabling statements of information and belief to be made with their sources and grounds respectively set out in the affidavit. The purpose of the rule is to enable a deponent to place before the court in interlocutory proceedings, frequently in circumstances of urgency, facts which he cannot personally prove, but which could in theory be proved by an appropriate means at a trial—for example by calling a witness or by proving matters under the Civil Evidence Act 1968. Affidavits ought not to contain material which is inadmissible—eg because it is mere opinion or relates to irrelevant matters.[10]

On the assumption that the material sought to be adduced in evidence by means of the affidavit is in principle admissible, then the sources and grounds of the statements of information and belief must be sufficient to enable the court to evaluate the material and form a judgment as to its

---

9 In the context of the rule, interlocutory proceedings in general include proceedings other than the trial of the action or final determination of the proceedings in the case of an originating summons or other originating process: *Savings Bank* v *Gasco BV (No 2)* [1988] Ch 422.

10 *Savings Bank* v *Gasco BV* [1984] 1 WLR 271.

weight. A broad general reference to 'documents in my possession' or 'inquiries I have made' is not sufficient for this purpose, and does not bring hearsay material within the scope of the rule. Thus in *Deputy Commission of Taxation* v *Ahern*[11] a Mareva injunction had been granted to the Deputy Commissioner of Taxation on the basis of evidence which included an affidavit by an employee of the Commissioner which set out the ambit of inquiries made by him and his conclusions. The deponent did not exhibit the documents seen by him nor did he list them, nor did he state what their contents were, nor did he seek to relate his conclusions to specific documents which he had seen or particular information which he had received. In these circumstances on appeal, the injunction was set aside, the court observing that to uphold the injunction would be 'to sanction trial by the averment of officials' and that:

In circumstances of great urgency a court may accept a general statement of sources as sufficient compliance with the rule, although this will more readily happen in the case of an interim rather than an interlocutory injunction. The question as to what is a sufficient disclosure of sources must be decided according to the exigencies of each particular case, and the court's discretion is not to be fettered. In the present case there were no apparent circumstances of urgency justifying the absence of disclosure of sources, and the bulk of the material may fairly be described as oppressive and embarrassing.

RSC Order 41, r 5(2) is in terms permissive in allowing hearsay evidence to be incorporated and it might be suggested that if material was placed before the court which did not sufficiently identify the sources of information and grounds of belief then this material would not fall within the scope of RSC Order 41, r 5, and that therefore it would be wholly inadmissible,[12] with the consequence that any order founded upon it should be set aside. However, in view of RSC Order 2, r 1, it is considered that the correct analysis is that hearsay material is in principle admissible in an affidavit, but the failure to indicate the sources of information and grounds of belief is a 'failure to comply with the requirements of these rules . . . in respect of . . . content or in any other respect' within RSC Order 2, r 1(1), so that it constitutes 'an irregularity' and does not 'nullify any order'. The court may make such order as it thinks fit for dealing with the position under RSC Order 2, r 1(2). If on an an *ex parte* application there is a failure to make adequate disclosure of sources of information or grounds of belief, then it is considered that the court has power to act on the defective material, and if it chooses to do so ordinarily the plaintiff should be required to rectify the position by incorporating the missing information in a further affidavit to be prepared as soon as possible. This approach is in line with the intended objective of the passage cited above

---

11 [1988] 2 Qd R 158 (Queeensland, Australia). In that case the Queensland Rules of Court contained in Order 41, r 3 are similar provisions to those to be found in RSC Order 41, r 5.
12 *Re JL Young Manufacturing Co Ltd* [1900] 2 Ch 753 at pp 754 and 755.

from *Deputy Commissioner of Taxation* v *Ahern (No 2)*, but does not involve the court in applying different standards in relation to what constitutes compliance with the requirements of RSC Order 41, r 5(2) according to the degree of urgency of the *ex parte* application.

(6) The Court of Appeal

If an *ex parte* application for Mareva relief or Anton Piller relief is refused in whole or in part then the applicant can renew the application *ex parte* to the Court of Appeal. The renewed application must be made within seven days of the refusal under RSC Order 59, r 14(3). It is treated as made when the applicant has lodged with the Civil Appeals Office a notice of *ex parte* application. By virtue of RSC Order 3, r 2(4) the period of seven days does not include weekends. Although the application is by way of an interlocutory appeal, under s 18(1)(*h*)(iii) of the Supreme Court Act 1981, leave to appeal is not required in cases 'where an injunction or the appointment of a receiver is granted or refused.' The granting of Anton Piller relief has been justified by reference to RSC Order 29, r 2.[13] However, it is considered that an order requiring the defendant to permit the plaintiff's representatives to have access to premises for certain defined purposes, is an interlocutory mandatory injunction,[14] and as such leave to appeal is not required.

In relation to an application for Anton Piller relief, the Court of Appeal have issued a *Practice Note* [1982] 1 WLR 1420 (see Appendix 2) as to the procedure to be followed if the applicant desires to make the application to the Court of Appeal in camera. The court also hears other applications in camera if it is necessary to do so,[15] including *ex parte* applications for Mareva relief. Even if an order is granted *ex parte* by the Court of Appeal, any application to discharge the order will be made to the court of first instance.

In an urgent case, the High Court can take the course of refusing an application for Mareva relief, but nevertheless granting an injunction pending appeal,[16] so as to preserve the position pending the hearing of the appeal. The Court of Appeal also has the same concurrent jurisdiction, which is 'incidental' to the appeal and therefore can be dealt with by a single judge of the Court of Appeal under s 58 of the Supreme Court Act 1981 and RSC Order 59, r 10(9). Ordinarily an application for the granting of relief pending appeal must be made in the first instance to the High

---

13 *EMI* v *Pandit* [1975] 1 WLR 302 at p 305, per Templeman LJ.
14 *Distributori Automatici Italia SpA* v *Holford General Trading Co* [1985] 1 WLR 1066; *Rank Film Ltd* v *Video Information Centre* [1982] AC at pp 417–418, per Templeman LJ; *Bayer* v *Winter* [1986] 1 WLR 497 at p 502, per Fox LJ.
15 This was done for example in *Republic of Haiti* v *Duvalier: Re an application by Mr Turner and Mr Martin* Court of Appeal (Civil Division) Transcript No 490 of 1988 (7 June 1988); see p 46, above.
16 *Erinford Properties Ltd* v *Cheshire County Council* [1974] Ch 261.

Court (or county court) judge who refused the relief, although another judge of the court of first instance does in fact have jurisdiction to deal with the application.[17] The application should not be made in the first instance to the single judge of the Court of Appeal, or the Court of Appeal, 'except where there are special circumstances which make it impossible or impracticable to apply to the court below (RSC Order 59, r 14(4)).'

---

17 This is the ordinary principle: *Warren* v *T Kilroe & Sons* [1988] 1 WLR 516 (a case on s 18(1)(*h*) of the Supreme Court Act 1981 and RSC Order 59, r 14(4)).

Chapter 8

The duty to make full and frank disclosure

(1) General principles

Any applicant to the court for relief to be granted *ex parte* must show the utmost good faith and disclose[1] to the court all matters which are material to be taken into account by the court in deciding whether or not to grant relief *ex parte*, and if so on what terms.[2] This is a general principle which applies to all applications for *ex parte* relief.[3] However, it applies with special force[4] to applications for Mareva or Anton Piller relief, which by their nature are particularly liable to cause substantial prejudice to a defendant or other parties. Thus Donaldson LJ in *Bank Mellat* v *Nikpour* [1985] FSR 87 at p 92 said:

The rule requiring full disclosure seems to me to be one of the most fundamental importance, particularly in the context of the Draconian remedy of the Mareva Injunction. It is in effect, together with the Anton Piller order, one of the law's two 'nuclear' weapons. If access to such a weapon is obtained without the fullest and frankest disclosure, I have no doubt at all that it should be revoked.

Therefore, the applicant is only permitted to apply *ex parte* provided that there is compliance with this duty, which has been described as being governed by the same principles which require an applicant for insurance

---

1 The applicant must also refrain from making misrepresentations. The same principles apply to material misrepresentation as apply to material non-disclosure. Both involve misleading the court in a material respect.

2 *R* v *Kensington Income Tax Commissioners, ex parte Princess Edmond de Polignac* [1917] 1 KB 486 at pp 504–506, 509, and 514–515; *Dormeuil Frères SA* v *Nicolian Ltd* [1988] 1 WLR 1362 at p 1368.

3 *Dalglish* v *Jarvie* (1850) [2 Mac & G 231], and see generally Kerr on *Injunctions* (6th edition) at pp 323, 637 and 661 and *Seton's Judgments and Orders* (7th edition) at pp 516–517 and the cases there cited.

4 In *A/A D/S Svendborg* v *Maxim Brand* Court of Appeal (Civil Division) Transcript No 39 of 1989 (23 January 1989), Kerr LJ said in relation to a case concerning an application to discharge leave to serve out of the jurisdiction granted under RSC Order 11 as well as Mareva relief that 'in principle the same duty of disclosure arises in relation to Order 11. But in practice such oversights are more likely to be penalised only in the form of costs, since it would not be right to drive the plaintiffs to an inappropriate jurisdiction or to bar a bona fide claim from a proper one. To that extent the practice may be different in relation to Order 11 from cases involving injunctions'.

to act in the utmost degree of good faith.[5] The duty extends to placing
before the court all matters which are relevant to the court's assessment of
the application,[6] and it is no answer to a complaint of non-disclosure that
if the relevant matters had been placed before the court, in fact the
decision would have been the same.[7] The test as to materiality is an objective one, and it is not for the applicant or his advisers to decide the question[7A]; hence it is no excuse for the applicant subsequently to say that he
was genuinely unaware, or did not believe, that the facts were relevant or
important.[8] All matters which are relevant to the 'weighing operation'
that the court has to make in deciding whether or not to grant the order
must be disclosed.[9]

   The duty to disclose is a strict duty and applies to matters known to the
plaintiff or his agents, or matters which ought to have been known, had all
inquiries been made which should reasonably have been made prior to the
application.[10] It has been held that even if the plaintiff has forgotten the
matters in question, nevertheless this does not justify the failure to disclose

---

5 *Dalglish* v *Jarvie* (1850) 2 Mac & G 231 at 243 per Rolfe B.
6 *R* v *Kensington Income Tax Commissioners ex parte Princess Edmond de Polignac* [1917] 1 KB 486
   at p 505 per Lord Cozens-Hardy MR citing the judgment of Rolfe B in *Dalglish* v *Jarvie*
   (above). *Brink's Mat Ltd* v *Elcombe* [1988] 1 WLR 1350 at p 1356 per Ralph Gibson LJ
   'The material facts are those which it is material for the judge to know in dealing with the
   application as made'. In *Siporex Trade SA* v *Comdel Commodities Ltd* [1986] 2 Lloyd's Rep
   428 at 437, Bingham J said that the applicant 'must disclose all facts which reasonably
   could or would be taken into account by the Judge in deciding whether to grant the application'. See also *Boyce* v *Gill* (1891) 64 LT 824, at p 825 'the court should be in a position
   to weigh all matters which might influence it so as to decide whether . . . an injunction
   should be granted'. For the equivalent test in relation to contracts of insurance, see *Container Transport International Inc* v *Oceanus Mutual* [1984] 1 Lloyd's Rep 476.
7 *Behbehani* v *Salem* [1989] 2 WLR 723 at p 729 per Woolf LJ; *Eastglen International Corpn* v
   Monpare SA (1987) 137 NLJ 56.
7A *Brink's Mat Ltd* v *Elcombe* [1988] 1 WLR 1350 at 1356 per Ralph Gibson LJ, citing *R* v
   Kensington Income Tax Commissioners ex parte Princess Edmond de Polignac [1917] 1 KB 486 at
   p 504; *Dalglish* v *Jarvie* 2 Mac & G 231 at p 238 and *Thermax Ltd* v *Schott Industrial Glass
   Ltd* [1981] FSR 289 at p 295.
8 *Brink's Mat Ltd* v *Elcombe* [1988] 1 WLR 1350 was a case in which the non-disclosure was
   'innocent in the sense that the plaintiffs did not intentionally omit information which they
   thought to be material' (see the passage in the judgment of Ralph Gibson LJ which is not
   in the report but which is cited by Woolf LJ in *Behbehani* v *Salem* [1989] 1 WLR 723 at
   p 728). Also see *Martigny Investments SA* v *Elmbranch* Court of Appeal (Civil Division)
   Transcript No 276 of 1985 (12 June 1985); *Siporex Trade SA* v *Comdel Commodities Ltd*
   [1986] 2 Lloyd's Rep 428 at p 437; *Thomas A Edison Ltd* v *Bullock* (1912) 15 CLR 679 at
   pp 681–682.
9 *Thermax Ltd* v *Schott Industrial Glass Ltd* [1981] FSR 289 at p 298, per Browne-Wilkinson J.
10 *Brink's Mat Ltd* v *Elcombe* [1988] 1 WLR 1350 at pp 1356–1357. The extent of the necessary inquiries depends on all the circumstances of the case including the nature of the case
   raised by the applicant, the order sought and its likely effects on the defendant and the
   degree of legitimate urgency, and the time available for the making of inquiries. See also
   Bank Mellat v *Nikpour* [1985] FSR 87. For an *ex parte* injunction case in which urgency justified not waiting for the outcome of an indirect approach which had been made to a
   defendant, see *Semple* v *The London and Birmingham Railway Co* (1838) 1 Ra Ca 480 (Lord
   Cottenham LC).

them.[11] However, this would be a relevant factor to be taken into account by the court in deciding what should be the consequences of the non-disclosure.[12]

It may not be a sufficient answer to an allegation of non-disclosure for a plaintiff to say that the relevant information giving rise to the defence was contained in an exhibit, though not referred to in the body of the plaintiff's affidavit in the context of a possible defence. Exhibits to such affidavits are often voluminous, and since *ex parte* applications for Mareva or Anton Piller relief are often dealt with comparatively shortly and the judge may not have had the opportunity of considering the papers in detail before the hearing, the applicant has the responsibility of ensuring that all relevant points are presented clearly and distinctly.[13] Thus in *Siporex Trade SA* v *Comdel Commodities Ltd* [1986] 2 Lloyd's Rep 428 at p 437, Bingham J said that the applicant must 'identify the crucial points for and against the application, and not rely on the mere exhibiting of numerous documents'. Any contractual provision (eg an exclusion clause) which is relevant to the court's consideration of the application should be referred to and preferably set out in the body of the affidavit.[14] It will not usually be sufficient simply to exhibit the entire contract.

Accordingly, it is of the utmost importance that the plaintiff carefully considers the nature of the cause of action and the facts on which it is based before formulating the application. A thorough check should be made to ensure that all defences actually raised by the defendant are identified and fairly summarised in the affidavit.[15]

The plaintiff must also identify any defences, which, although not yet taken, would have been available to be taken by the defendant had he been present at the application,[16] provided that:

---

11 *Clifton* v *Robinson* (1853) 15 Beav 355. This is regarded as an 'unnecessarily harsh view' in Spry on *Equitable Remedies* (3rd ed) at p 477. However, it is in line with the requirement that the applicant make all proper inquiries that the standard of the applicant's duty is one of due care. Furthermore, if the court considers that the applicant has not been guilty of culpable conduct this can be adequately dealt with in the context of what consequences should flow from the non-disclosure in question.

12 *Brink's Mat Ltd* v *Elcombe* [1987] 1 WLR 1350 at 1357, principle (6) stated by Ralph Gibson LJ, see p 89, below.

13 *O'Regan* v *Iambic Productions* (1989) 139 NLJ 1378, Sir Peter Pain said 'It is clearly the duty of Counsel and of the solicitor to point out to the Judge any points which are to their client's disadvantage, which the Judge should take into account in considering whether or not to grant the injunction. It is difficult for a Judge upon an *ex parte* application at short notice to grasp all the relevant points'. Sir Peter Pain went on to say that the Judge's attention should have been drawn to particular matters there in question.

14 *Bakarim* v *Victoria P Shipping* [1980] 2 Lloyd's Rep 193 at p 199.

15 *Third Chandris Corp* v *Unimarine SA* [1979] QB 645 at p 668; *Bank Mellat* v *Nikpour* [1985] FSR 87 at p 89; *Harbottle* v *Pooley* [1869] 30 LT 436; *Escott* v *Thomas* [1934] NZLR s 175.

16 *Lloyd's Bowmaker Ltd* v *Brittania Arrow* [1988] 1 WLR 1337 at pp 1341 and 1343, where Glidewell LJ says that the authorities cited support the proposition that the applicant 'must disclose any defence he has reason to anticipate may be advanced'. In advance of commencement of legal proceedings a defendant may not be in a position, or have yet

(1) the defence is one which can reasonably be expected to be raised in due course by the defendant;[17]

(2) the defence is not one which can be dismissed as without substance or importance[18] (eg an argument based on a misconceived interpretation of a statutory provision).

This is simply an aspect of the applicant's duty to give a fair account for the case for and against the defendant, identifying the crucial points for and against the granting of the application. Thus, if there is an obvious answer to the claim, such as a limitation point, the plaintiff should refer to it even if the defendant has not explicitly raised it.

It is often a difficult exercise to settle a suitable affidavit which achieves the right balance between full and fair disclosure and an overlong and far too detailed description of the facts, with perhaps too much generosity towards the defendant. The duty of disclosure does not require the plantiff to describe his case or the factual background in minute detail, nor does it require him to search for possible but unlikely defences.

One of the matters which should be carefully considered is whether the applicant is likely to be good for any damages which he may be required to pay on the cross-undertaking as to damages.[19] This is almost invariably required to be given on an application for Mareva or Anton Piller relief, and will only be dispensed with in exceptional circumstances (eg a claim by the Crown to enforce the law). In general it is strongly advisable for this matter to be expressly dealt with on the application with particulars given as to the applicant's solvency and worth. If nothing is said and an order is made, then the court will be proceeding upon the basis that there is no reason to doubt that the person giving the cross-undertaking will be good for the damages. If disclosure is made of facts which raise doubts and as to the likely worth of the cross-undertaking, should it be called upon, the court may nevertheless in the exercise of its discretion decide to grant the application if there are special circumstances which make it just to do so.[20] However, it is for the court to consider the matter, and decide questions of materiality, not the applicant or his legal advisers.

Thus in *Block* v *Nicholson* Court of Appeal (Civil Division) Transcript

---

sought, to set out all the defences which may arise. The ambit of the duty of disclosure is not limited to the defences (if any) which may have been indicated by the defendant up to the time of the *ex parte* application. In *Town & Country Sport Resorts* v *Partnership Pacific Limited* (1988) ATPR 49, 783 at 786, the full court of the Federal Court of Australia expressly referred to the duty of the applicant 'to place before the court all relevant matters including such matters which would have been raised by the [defendant] in his defence if he had been present'.

17 *The Electric Furnace Co* v *Selas Corporation of America* [1987] RPC 23; *Practice Direction* [1983] 1 WLR 433, at paragraph 3(2)(*d*).

18 *Weston* v *Arnold* (1873) LR 8 Ch App 1084 at 1090 per Sir WM James LJ; *The Electric Furnace Co* v *Selas Corporation of America* (above) at p 29, per Slade LJ citing with approval *BP Exploration Co (Libya) Ltd* v *Hunt* [1976] 3 All ER 879 at p 893, per Kerr J.

19 *Swedac Ltd* v *Magnet & Southerns plc* [1989] FSR 243 at p 251. *Manor Electronics Ltd* v *Dickson* [1988] RPC 618.

20 *Allen* v *Jambo Holdings* [1980] 1 WLR 1252, *Szentessy* v *Woo Ran* (1985) 64 ACTR 98 (Supreme Court of the Australian Capital Territory).

No 409 (17 April 1986), the plaintiff failed to disclose to the court on an *ex parte* application for Mareva relief that he had been arrested and charged with fraud prior to the application. This was a matter which was plainly relevant to whether the court on the *ex parte* application could safely accept the plaintiff's undertaking in damages and accordingly the judge discharged the relief granted on the grounds of non-disclosure, and his decision was upheld by the Court of Appeal. Similarly, in *Manor Electronics v Dickson* [1988] RPC 618, Scott J set aside an Anton Piller order which had been obtained without disclosure being made of facts concerning the plaintiff's financial status, saying (at p 623) that if no reference is made on the *ex parte* application to the plaintiff's worth then the assumption is made by the court that the plaintiff's financial status is 'adequate for the purpose of the cross-undertaking'.

In formulating an application it is appropriate to include all matters which could reasonably be regarded as capable of being relevant to the assessment of the application including what undertakings should be sought from the applicant and the precise terms of any order which might be made. Consideration should be given as to whether third parties are liable to be affected by the order sought and all relevant information should be given to the court for the purpose of enabling the court to assess what undertakings should be sought from the applicant at the *ex parte* stage. This has a particular importance when it is borne in mind that the court has no power to order a party to give an undertaking, or to modify the wording of an undertaking which has been given without the consent of the party who gave the relevant undertaking.[21] Accordingly, if a third party appears before the court subsequently, complaining that inadequate protection is given to him by the *ex parte* order, the court may find that meanwhile the *ex parte* relief is no longer required (eg the Anton Piller order has been executed, or the Mareva relief has been discharged). In such circumstances the court will not be in a position to extract a suitable undertaking as the price for continuance of the relief which was granted.[22]

Accordingly, it is right and proper that the court on the *ex parte* application should insist on full disclosure as to the position in relation to third parties so that adequate undertakings can be required to protect the position of third parties as the price of relief at the *ex parte* stage.[23]

If the plaintiff is engaged in open negotiations with the defendant this

---

21 *Commodity Ocean Transport Corpn v Basford Unicorn* [1987] 2 Lloyd's Rep 197 at p 200.
22 *Commodity Ocean Transport Corpn v Basford Unicorn* (above).
23 In relation to undertakings which have been thought appropriate to protect the position of third parties, see generally *Z Ltd v A-Z* [1982] QB 558; *Clipper Maritime v Mineral import/export* [1981] 1 WLR 1262 and *Searose v Seatrain UK Ltd* [1981] 1 WLR 894. Consideration should also be given as to whether proper disclosure is being made to enable the court to deal with whether the circumstances are such that it would be unjust to grant an injunction at all because of the likely prejudice to third parties—eg as in *Galaxia Maritime SA v Mineralimport/export* [1982] 1 WLR 539.

is a matter which is capable of being relevant to the exercise of the court's discretion as going to the question whether the plaintiff needs urgent *ex parte* relief. Thus, if the defendant is willing to attend an open meeting to discuss the claim, this may indicate a measure of responsibilty in relation to his legal obligations which would shed doubt on whether the case was suitable for Mareva relief. Accordingly, in considering what matters should be disclosed to the court, it is necessary that the applicant should include any facts which are relevant to the exercise of the discretion, regardless of whether they would also be relevant to the merits of the claim.

In the context of compliance with orders for discovery, a solicitor has a personal responsibility to ensure that the party for whom he is acting makes proper discovery of documents pursuant to the order,[24] and similarly it is thought that in principle a solicitor has a personal responsibility to take all proper steps to ensure that there is full and frank disclosure to the court on the application.[25] Thus, if the applicant's solicitor causes the application to proceed when he knows such matters are not being disclosed, he may well render himself liable to compensate the defendant in respect of loss which would be covered by the cross-undertaking.[26] This may be dealt with by the court under its inherent jurisdiction to order solicitors to pay compensation to the other party on the grounds of serious neglect or dereliction of duty on an application made against the solicitor personally.[27] The solicitor will not be made liable personally under the inherent jurisdiction of the court, if there has been a mere slip or accidental oversight, albeit that he has been at fault. But that jurisdiction is liable

---

24 *Myers* v *Elman* [1940] AC 282; *Rockwell Machine Tool Co Ltd* v *EP Barrus (Concessionaires) Limited* [1968] 2 All ER 98; *Woods* v *Martins Bank Ltd* [1959] 1 QB 55 at p 60; *EI Du Pont de Nemours & Co* v *Commissioner of Patents* (1987) 83 ALR 499 (Federal Court of Australia: General Division).

25 In *O'Regan* v *Iambic Productions* (1989) 139 NLJ 1378 at p 1379, Sir Peter Pain said 'I find [the solicitor's] attitude very disappointing coming from a solicitor. I could understand a litigant in person not familiar with the procedure adopting [that attitude] . . . but [the person in question] is a solicitor and an officer of the court. If the Anton Piller jurisdiction is to work at all, the court must rely on its officers to be very careful and lean over backwards to make sure there is full disclosure, especially if it is to the client's disadvantage . . . The point is that it is the duty of the solicitor to apprise the court of the facts so that the court can make up its own mind'. See also p 155, below.

26 In *Schmitten* v *Faulks* [1893] WN 64, a solicitor had not disclosed to the court on the *ex parte* application that he himself had commenced bankruptcy proceedings against his client. Although the non-disclosure was not committed in bad faith in the sense that the solicitor erroneously believed that the matter did not have to be disclosed because the solicitor had control over the bankruptcy proceedings, nevertheless on an application brought by the defendant against the solicitor, Chitty J ordered that the solicitor should pay the loss caused by the *ex parte* injunction, the cross-undertaking of the plaintiff being of no value.

27 *Udall* v *Capri Lighting Ltd* [1988] QB 907; *R & T Thew Ltd* v *Reeves (No 2)* [1982] QB 1283; *Myers* v *Elman* [1940] AC 282. *Re The Crown Court holden at Lewes* (1989) *The Times*, 15 November.

to be exercised when the conduct of the solicitor is 'inexcusable and such as to merit reproof'.[28]

Under RSC Order 62, r 11, the court has jurisdiction to impose responsibility for costs on a solicitor where 'costs are incurred improperly or without reasonable cause or are wasted by undue delay or by any other misconduct or default' and the solicitor is responsible for what has occurred either 'personally or through a servant or agent'. This jurisdiction only applies to costs but in *Sinclair-Jones* v *Kay* [1989] 1 WLR 114, the Court of Appeal has decided that the jurisdiction is not subject to a limitation that it is only exercisable in cases of gross misconduct. Accordingly, if the solicitor or his servant or agent has failed to act with reasonable competence and care, and this has resulted in an *ex parte* application being made in which there has been material non-disclosure, then the solicitor may be made personally responsible for the costs wasted or thrown away.

The duty to make full disclosure of material facts does not prevent the plaintiff from making adverse or unfavourable comment about the nature of the defendant's defences, provided that he does not mislead the court: indeed if he can show that the defences are spurious, this may assist him. However, when settling the affidavit, care must be taken not to seek to draw too strong an adverse inference from the fact that thin defences have been raised; it is one thing to say that the plaintiff believes that he has more than a good arguable case because the defences raised are thin, and that summary judgment may be given, but it is quite another to suggest that the defendant has not raised them bona fide and that they have been raised at the last minute as a means of putting off the day of payment. Allegations of the latter kind should only be made if there is sufficient evidence (eg the terms of communications between the parties) which would properly justify an interference of *mala fides* on the part of the defendant. If an applicant wishes to include in the application matters of prejudice against the defendant, he must take care to ensure that they are presented as fully as is necessary to be fair: the applicant cannot seek to 'pile on the prejudice' but only tell 'half of the story'.[29]

A question may arise as to the extent to which it is the applicant's responsibility on an *ex parte* application to direct the court's attention to legal source material which could have a bearing on the relevant legal arguments (eg provisions of an Act of Parliament or case law). If there is a provision in an Act of Parliament or a binding authority which is clearly determinative of the application then plainly the court's attention should be drawn to it.[30] However, in general the duty of disclosure is confined to material facts, and the court does not require disclosure of legal source

---

28 *Udall* v *Capri Lighting Ltd* [1988] QB 907 at p 917. Reliance upon advice from counsel does not necessarily exonerate the solicitor. Although it will be a factor to be taken into account, the solicitor may still be ordered to pay compensation where that advice was obviously wrong: *Davy-Chiesman* v *Davy-Chiesman* [1984] Fam 48.

29 *Lloyd's Bowmaker* v *Brittania Arrow* [1988] 1 WLR 1337 at p 1348 per Dillon LJ.

30 *Code of Conduct for the Bar of England and Wales* (4th edition) paragraph 22.5.

material which is only relevant to submissions as to the legal consequences flowing from the facts placed before the court.[31] Thus, it has been
held by the Court of Appeal that incorrect legal submissions, or what may
eventually prove to have been erroneous legal conclusions based on the
facts, or erroneous legal assumptions made without proper consideration
will not amount to non-disclosure or material misrepresentation provided
that such errors do not deprive the court of knowledge of any material
fact: *Hispanica de Petroleos* v *Vencedora Oceanica Navigacion ('Kapetan Markos')*
[1986] 1 Lloyd's Rep 211.

If an application is made *inter partes* then it is considered that the applicant for relief does not have a duty to make full disclosure of material
facts, but is under an obligation not knowingly to mislead the court. The
reason for the existence of the duty to make full disclosure on an *ex parte*
application is because the applicant is himself asking the court to undertake the hazardous course of granting relief against a party in his absence
and without the opportunity of presenting his case. This consideration
does not apply on an *inter partes* application namely on an application
made after adequate prior notice has been given to the defendant in
accordance with the Rules of Court by due service on him of a summons
or notice of motion, but the defendant has chosen not to appear.[32] If an
application is made *ex parte* on notice to the defendant, then if the defendant does not appear, the rule requiring full disclosure applies. Even if the
defendant is represented, this is liable not to be equivalent to the standard
of representation which would be achieved after there had been a full and
proper opportunity to prepare for the application, and it is considered that
unless the plaintiff expressly seeks and obtains dispensation from the court
from the need to comply with the duty, the requirement for compliance
still remains in place. If there is 'innocent' non-disclosure on such an
application which could and ought to have been corrected by the defendant or his representatives, this is liable to be a material factor for the court
in considering what should be the consequences of the non-disclosure.

(2) Disclosure of confidential information

The court can only act on information which can be revealed to the
defendant, albeit at a later stage, so that the defendant can have an opportunity of applying to discharge the relief granted *ex parte*.[33] One of the
matters which is clearly capable of being material on an application for
Mareva or Anton Piller relief is whether the plaintiff intends to commence
or has commenced proceedings abroad connected with his claim,

---

31 *Attorney-General* v *The Mayor of Liverpool* (1835) 1 My & C 171 at p 211 per Sir Charles
   Pepys MR (subsequently Lord Cottenham LC). Contrast the view stated in Spry on
   Equitable Remedies (3rd ed) at p 477.
32 *Maclaren* v *Stainton* (1852) 15 Beav 279 at p 290.
33 *WEA Records* v *Visions Channel 4 Ltd* [1983] 1 WLR 721 at p 724.

particularly proceedings in which relief may be sought or has been sought, to assist in the prosecution or enforcement of the plaintiff's claim.[34] If proceedings are intended to be launched abroad, it is often the case that the applicant will seek to have the proceedings commenced at the same time as the English proceedings, and there will be no difficulty in referring to the intended foreign application in the affidavit made in support of the application, or recording the information relied upon in the application.[35] However, it may be that intended foreign proceedings cannot be commenced immediately and that the applicant has good grounds for wishing his intentions not to be revealed immediately to the defendant. In these circumstances the applicant cannot justify failure to disclose his intentions to the court on the grounds that the defendant might, on obtaining this information, take steps designed to frustrate an order made by the foreign court.[36] The appropriate procedure is to inform the court on the *ex parte* application of the plaintiff's intentions. This could be done orally, with the information being set out in a separate document prepared by the applicant, which is intended to be served on the defendant following commencement of the foreign proceedings in question. This procedure results in full disclosure being made to the court on the *ex parte* application and does not involve the information being disclosed prematurely to the defendant.[37] On the other hand it will not involve infringement of the principle that the defendant is entitled, albeit at a later stage, to full information about what has occurred before the court on the *ex parte* application. However, once the defendant applies to have the order set aside, he must be told of all that took place on the *ex parte* application.

(3) Effects of non-disclosure or material misrepresentation

On *ex parte* applications not involving Mareva or Anton Piller relief, where there has been non-disclosure, courts have simply set aside the *ex parte* relief, leaving the applicant to make a fresh application.[38] In those

---

34 Eg *Behbehani* v *Salem* [1989] 1 WLR 723 at pp 730–734, 736–737.

35 The applicant 'must, for the protection and information of the defendant, summarise his case and the evidence in support of it by an affidavit or affidavits sworn before or immediately after the application': *Siporex Trade SA* v *Comdel Commodities Ltd* [1986] 2 Lloyd's Rep 428 at p 437. Thus, if further information is placed before the court beyond what is contained in the affidavit placed before the court on the *ex parte* application, this should be recorded in a further affidavit to be made following the application, and an undertaking should be proffered to the court that this will be done.

36 *Behbehani* v *Salem* [1989] 1 WLR 723 esp at pp 732 and 737.

37 Orders are frequently made under which the court requires the existence of the proceedings not to be revealed to the defendant for a relatively short period whilst the plaintiff takes steps to execute the *ex parte* relief which has been granted, eg *Republic of Haiti* v *Duvalier* [1989] 2 WLR 261 at p 265.

38 *R* v *Kensington Income Tax Commissioners ex parte Princess Edward de Polignac* [1917] 1 KB 486 at p 506, per Lord Cozens-Hardy MR; *Fitch* v *Rochfort* (1849) 18 LJ Ch 458 at p 460 (per Lord Cottenham LC, during argument).

circumstances the court has considered that the applicant has been deprived of any advantage obtained by the granting of the *ex parte* relief. However, the position is different in relation to Mareva and Anton Piller cases, because the applicant has in effect struck prematurely and the defendant's position might have been affected by the granting of *ex parte* relief in the interim. Thus, for example, in relation to Mareva relief the defendant might have disposed of assets but for the granting of the relief.[39] Furthermore, the position is not as simple as in cases where the consequences of setting aside *ex parte* relief and leaving the applicant free to renew his application merely results in delay for the applicant and consequences in costs. Thus, in the context of Mareva relief the question would arise as to whether the applicant could make an immediate application for relief in the same terms. If he could the consequences in costs would not be likely to be very severe[40] and he would in effect have had the benefit of a continuous period from the time of the original *ex parte* application when an appropriate injunction was in place. On the other hand if he was precluded from making an immediate application, the result could be very severe. The defendant would have a period during which he would be free to deal with and dispose of his assets. In relation to Anton Piller relief, damages on the cross-undertaking could be substantial if the order is set aside.[41]

In practice the courts have adopted an approach which enables all relevant factors to be taken into account whilst maintaining, as a matter of policy, a sufficiently penal approach[42] that would-be applicants for *ex parte* relief are deterred from not making full and frank disclosure to the court of all relevant matters.[43]

The applicable principles have been stated in the context of Mareva relief by Ralph Gibson LJ in *Brink's Mat Ltd v Elcombe* at p 1356:

(1) The duty of the applicant is to make 'a full and fair disclosure of all the material facts': see *Rex v Kensington Income Tax Commissioners,* 'Ex parte Princess Edmond de Polignac* [1917] 1 KB 486, 514, per Scrutton LJ.

(2) The material facts are those which it is material for the judge to know in dealing with the application as made: materiality is to be decided by the court and not by the assessment of the applicant or his legal advisers: see *Rex v Kensington Income Tax Commissioners, per* Lord Cozens-Hardy MR, at p 504, citing *Dalglish v Jarvie* (1850) 2 Mac & G 231, 238, and Browne-Wilkinson J in *Thermax Ltd v Schott Industrial Glass Ltd* [1981] FSR 289, 295.

(3) The applicant must make proper inquiries before making the application: see *Bank Mellat v Nikpour* [1985] FSR 87. The duty of disclosure therefore applies

---

39 *Bank Mellat* v *Nikpour* [1985] FSR 87 at p 91.
40 The defendant would be entitled to damages on the cross-undertaking for any loss suffered in the interim, but this might well not be substantial.
41 A common effect of an Anton Piller order is to close down or seriously damage the defendant's business: *Columbia Pictures Inc* v *Robinson* [1987] Ch 37 at p 73.
42 *Brink's Mat Ltd* v *Elcombe* [1988] 1 WLR 1350 at p 1359, per Slade LJ.
43 *Brink's Mat Ltd* v *Elcombe* [1988] 1 WLR 1350 at p 1358, per Balcombe LJ and p 1359, per Slade LJ; *Behbehani* v *Salem* [1989] 1 WLR 723 at pp 726–729, per Woolf LJ.

not only to material facts known to the applicant but also to any additional facts which he would have known if he had made such inquiries.

(4) The extent of the inquiries which will be held to be proper, and therefore necessary, must depend on all the circumstances of the case including (a) the nature of the case which the applicant is making when he makes the application; and (b) the order for which application is made and the probable effect of the order on the defendant: see for example, the examination by Scott J of the possible effect of an *Anton Piller* order in *Columbia Picture Industries Inc* v *Robinson* [1987] Ch 38; and (c) the degree of legitimate urgency and the time available for the making of inquiries: see per Slade LJ in *Bank Mellat* v *Nikpour* [1985] FSR 87, 92-93.

(5) If material non-disclosure is established the court will be 'astute to ensure that a plaintiff who obtains [an *ex parte* injunction] without full disclosure . . . is deprived of any advantage he may have derived by that breach of duty': see *per* Donaldson LJ in *Bank Mellat* v *Nikpour*, at p 91, citing Warrington LJ in the *Kensington Income Tax Commissioners'* case [1917] 1 KB 486, 509.

(6) Whether the fact not disclosed is of sufficient materiality to justify or require immediate discharge of the order without examination of the merits depends on the importance of the fact to the issues which were to be decided by the judge on the application. The answer to the question whether the non-disclosure was innocent, in the sense that the fact was not known to the applicant or that its relevance was not perceived, is an important consideration but not decisive by reason of the duty on the applicant to make all proper inquiries and to give careful consideration to the case being presented.

(7) Finally, it 'is not for every omission that the injunction will be automatically discharged. A *locus penitentiae* may sometimes be afforded': *per* Lord Denning MR in *Bank Mellat* v *Nikpour* [1985] FSR 87, 90. The court has a discretion, notwithstanding proof of material non-disclosure which justifies or requires the immediate discharge of the *ex parte* order, nevertheless to continue the order, or to make a new order on terms.

'when the whole of the facts, including that of the original non-disclosure, are before [the court, it] may well grant . . . a second injunction if the original non-disclosure was innocent and if an injunction could properly be granted even had the facts been disclosed': *per* Glidewell LJ in *Lloyd's Bowmaker Ltd* v *Britannia Arrow Holdings Plc* [1988] 1 WLR 1337 at pp 1343H–1344A.

The same principles apply in relation to Anton Piller relief. Often an application to discharge the order for non-disclosure will not be made until after the order has been fully executed, in which case it may be that it is appropriate for the application not to be dealt with until the trial. In such circumstances the court is not confronted with the same problem as arises when the question is whether Mareva relief should be set aside with the consequence that an otherwise meritorious plaintiff may not be able to enforce his claim. The consequences of setting aside the Anton Piller relief will be reflected in terms of costs and damages on the cross-undertaking. Whilst these could be a substantial burden for the plaintiff they may be less severe than in a Mareva case. It is thought that the likely severity of the consequences to a plaintiff of setting aside an order for non-disclosure is a factor which the court can properly have regard to in deciding whether in any particular case the order should be set aside.

If the relevant non-disclosure is such that the court on reviewing the matter *inter partes* is of the opinion that the *ex parte* relief was inappropriate and should not have been granted then plainly the court will discharge the order.[44] However, the 'acid test' as to whether or not the order will be discharged is not whether or not the original judge who granted the order *ex parte* would have been likely to have arrived at a different decision if the material matters had been before him.[45] It has been said that in considering whether to discharge for non-disclosure the answer to the question is not 'a matter of great significance unless the facts which were not disclosed would have resulted in a refusal of the order'.[46]

Whether or not the relevant non-disclosure was 'innocent' in the sense that there was no intention to omit or withhold information which was thought to be material is an important factor to be taken into account by the court.[47] If there has been non-disclosure which was otherwise than innocent in this sense then it would only be in the most exceptional circumstances that the court would decline to discharge the order. Thus in *Eastglen International Corporation* v *Monpare* (1987) 137 NLJ 56,[48] the original solicitor who had acted for the plaintiff, who was a non-resident foreigner, had sworn an affidavit which clearly omitted a most material fact. When the defendant applied to discharge the injunction, the plaintiffs changed solicitors, who discontinued the first action and started a fresh application in new proceedings for Mareva relief supported by an affidavit which made clear the failure to disclose in the original action. Gatehouse J discharged the order for non-disclosure, but his decision was reversed by the Court of Appeal on the grounds that the fault was wholly that of the first solicitor, and not that of the client.

Where the non-disclosure was 'innocent' in the sense used above, the court will take into account the degree of culpability of the applicant and his advisers in relation to the non-disclosure in question.[49] Hence it is considered that if the court concludes on the evidence that the applicant had genuinely forgotten the relevant information, this would be an important factor[50] in favour of not setting aside the order.

---

44 *Ali and Fahd Shobokshi Group* v *Moneim* [1989] 1 WLR 710.
45 *Behbehani* v *Salem* [1989] 1 WLR 723 at p 729, per Woolf LJ. See also *Boyce* v *Gill* (1891) 64 LT 824 at p 825 'what the court would have done if all the facts had been known, I cannot say'.
46 *Behbehani* v *Salem* (above) at p 729.
47 *Ali and Fahd Shobokshi* v *Moneim* [1989] 1 WLR 710 at pp 719–720; *Brink's Mat Ltd* v *Elcombe* [1989] 1 WLR 1350, at pp 1358 and 1360; *Behbehani* v *Salem* [1989] 1 WLR 723 at 728.
48 This case is highly exceptional, see *Lloyd's Bowmaker Ltd* v *Britannia Arrow* [1988 1 WLR 1337 at p 1347; *Behbehani* v *Salem* [1989] 1 WLR 723 at p 729.
49 *Behbehani* v *Salem* [1989] 1 WLR 723 at p 729.
50 See the facts in *Clifton* v *Robinson* (1853) 16 Beav 355, where Sir John Romilly MR declined as a matter of policy to give effect to this excuse, saying that otherwise it would be relied upon 'in every instance'. The court would be astute to ensure that if the excuse was put forward, all relevant particulars were made out, and if necessary the court could order cross-examination of the deponent to the relevant affidavit which set out the excuse. See also Spry on *Equitable Remedies* (3rd ed) at p 477.

The discretion either to maintain the order or to allow a new application for relief in the same terms as the original order, is one to be exercised 'sparingly'.[51] In *Yardley* v *Higson* [1984] FSR 304[52] an *ex parte* injunction had been granted in a passing off action for a period of three weeks. At the end of this period the plaintiffs applied to renew their injunction and brought to the attention of the court that there had been non-disclosure of material matters at the *ex parte* application. The judge granted a modified injunction on the *inter partes* application and his decision was upheld by the Court of Appeal. This case and the subsequent decision of the Court of Appeal in *Eastglen International Corporation* v *Monpare SA* (1987) 137 NLJ 56, in which an application for an injunction was also granted notwithstanding earlier non-disclosure, show how important it may be, on an application to grant a renewed injunction, that a plaintiff, who has been guilty of non-disclosure at the *ex parte* stage, puts matters fully and frankly to the court at the *inter partes* application concerning the earlier non-disclosure. In both of these cases the plaintiff adopted this course.

The principle should not be carried to extreme lengths, and it is important that the court should have in consideration the practical realities of the case, and not allow the principle to be used as a refuge of last resort[53] for litigants when the substantial merits of the case and the balance of convenience strongly favour maintaining the relief which has been granted, and when the likely consequences of setting aside the order could be very severe for the plaintiff. Such litigants should not be encouraged 'to search ingeniously for facts' which might be viewed as relevant, in order to mount an application to discharge the order for non-disclosure.[54]

In the case of Anton Piller relief which has been set aside on an interlocutory application the question may arise as to whether, nevertheless, the plaintiff should be able to use the material obtained, for example in order to make an application for an interlocutory injunction. In general a consequence of an Anton Piller order being set aside will be that the plaintiff will be obliged to return all the documents, items and other material obtained under the order, to the defendant, and the plaintiff will be precluded from utilising any information acquired under and by virtue of the Anton Piller order. However, the court retains a discretion to allow the material or part of it to be used, albeit that this discretion is not to be exercised save for good reason, particularly if the relevant non-disclosure was serious and substantial.[55]

---

51 *Brink's Mat Ltd* v *Elcombe* [1988] 1 WLR 1350 at p 1358 per Balcombe LJ.

52 This was heard after *Bank Mellat* v *Nikpour* [1985] FSR 87 had been decided.

53 *Brink's Mat Ltd* v *Elcombe* (above) at p 1359 per Slade LJ; *Dormeuil Frères SA* v *Nicolian Ltd* [1988] 1 WLR 1362 at p 1369; *Swedac Ltd* v *Magnet & Southerns plc* [1989] FSR 243 at p 250.

54 *Citibank NA* v *Express Ship Management Services Ltd* [1987] HKLR 1184 (Court of Appeal of Hong Kong).

55 *Guess? Inc* v *Lee* [1987] FSR 125 at p 132.

(4) Effect of new developments after the *ex parte* application, including fresh information

The duty of the applicant for *ex parte* relief to act with the utmost good faith towards the court does not cease with the granting of the *ex parte* application. The court is exercising a jurisdiction which is obviously a very hazardous one and which is liable to cause serious prejudice to the defendant or third parties.[56] The granting of *ex parte* relief is an exception to the general rule that no order is to be made to the prejudice of a party unless he has had the opportunity of being heard in his defence. Furthermore, with Anton Piller orders, there will be almost invariably a period between the granting of the order and when the plaintiff is ready to execute it at the premises concerned. With Mareva relief there may similarly be a not insubstantial period between the making of the order and when the defendant is notified of it, whilst the plaintiff is giving notice of it to banks and other third parties and possibly also obtaining information from third parties under the order in respect of the defendant's assets.[57]

These considerations show that when the court grants *ex parte* relief of this nature, it is in effect entrusting the applicant with its order, at least for the period immediately following the application, upon the basis that the applicant will be using the order to forward the interests of justice. It is not for the applicant to act as a judge in his own cause and decide what effect, if any, new developments are to have upon the *ex parte* relief. Thus the general principle on the *ex parte* application is that an applicant is not entitled to act as a judge in his own cause by selecting the material to be placed before the court.[58] This would appear to apply with equal force in relation to new developments in the case at least whilst the defendant is under a continuing disability in relation to protecting his own interests.[59]

Thus in *Commercial Bank of the Near East Plc* v *A and others* [1989] 2 Lloyd's Rep 319, Saville J considered the position in relation to Mareva relief when subsequent to the application the plaintiffs had obtained leave to register cautions over property belonging to the defendants in Greece in relation to their claim. Although the case was not one in which the court had been misled or incomplete information had been given on the

---

56 Mareva relief often prevents a defendant from dealing with his assets at all, except for very limited purposes, and is liable to damage his standing with third parties who are notified of the order. It is also liable to cause serious complications for third parties concerned with assets covered by the order. As for the possible consequences of Anton Piller relief, see the observations of Scott J in *Columbia Pictures* v *Robinson* [1987] Ch 38 at pp 69–74.

57 Thus in *Republic of Haiti* v *Duvalier* [1989] 2 WLR 261 at pp 265–266, the defendants were not notified of the existence of the *ex parte* relief until a week after it had originally been granted. In the interim parties required to give information about the defendants' assets to the plaintiffs had already taken the case to the Court of Appeal: Court of Appeal (Civil Division) 7 June 1988.

58 See under General Principles (above) at p 80.

59 The position is not at all analogous to that following placement of a contract of insurance where the insurer has taken the risk of new developments.

initial *ex parte* application, Saville J held that 'while the proceedings remain on an *ex parte* basis', the applicant has a duty to the court to bring to its attention any subsequent material changes in the situation, ie any new or altered facts or matters which, had they existed at the time of the application, should have been disclosed to the court.

In *O'Regan* v *Iambic Productions* (1989) 139 NLJ 1378, the applicant who had been granted Anton Piller relief received a letter from the defendant offering to allow the plaintiff access to premises for the purpose of searching for certain items. Other items were returned to the plaintiff and an explanation was given that there had been an unsuccessful attempt to return items a short time earlier. The applicant then executed the Anton Piller order without having first informed the court of the new developments. Sir Peter Pain held that the applicant and the solicitor involved were in breach of their duties to the court in failing to return to the court before executing the order, and he followed the approach which had been adopted by Saville J. Similarly, if it comes to light that certain evidence placed before the court on the *ex parte* application was false, misleading or incomplete then the applicant has a duty to inform the court of the position as soon as possible.[60] If a plaintiff has obtained *ex parte* relief on a basis which he knows he can no longer support, he should apply to the court either to discharge the order, or to continue the order on a new basis.

Thus it may be that certain material has been placed before the court which the plaintiff discovers to be misleading, but there is other material in the affidavit evidence from which he feels he can still draw a sufficiently adverse conclusion to enable him to maintain the order. In those circumstances, the correct approach is to tell the court and the defendant why the material in question has been discovered to be misleading, and to disclaim any further reliance on it, leaving the court to consider the merits of the continuation of the injunction on the material remaining before it. A variant of this situation is where the fresh information obtained by the plaintiff is given to his legal advisers in circumstances which would attract a claim for privilege, or (perhaps less frequently), where a third party claims the fresh information is confidential and prohibits its disclosure or use in the litigation, so the plaintiff may not wish to state what it is unless the court orders him to do so. It is impossible to lay down any specific rules which the practitioner should observe in those circumstances, as the proper course of action will depend upon the facts in each case. However, one possible approach would be for the plaintiff to swear an affidavit, identifying the material in question and stating that since the *ex parte* hearing he has obtained further information, under circumstances attracting a claim for privilege or confidentiality, which shows the material to be false or

---

60 This was common ground between the parties in argument before Saville J in *Commercial Bank of the Near East plc* v *A and Others* (above).

misleading and consequently he disclaims all further reliance upon it. The plaintiff then applies to the court to reconsider the order.

In *Commercial Bank of the Near East plc* v *A and Others* (above), Saville J said that the duty continued whilst the proceedings remained on an *ex parte* basis. However, the circumstances there in question were also known to the defendants, so that once the defendants had been fully apprised of what had occurred on the *ex parte* application, they would have been in a position themselves to make an application to the court to discharge or vary the order in the light of the change of circumstances. The situation could arise where new information became available only to the applicant, or there was a new development, which became known only to the applicant, after the defendant had been fully apprised of what had occurred *ex parte* when:

(1) the defendant did not know or have full information of the new development or fresh information; and

(2) the new development or fresh information meant either that the information given to the court on the *ex parte* application was misleading, or that the basis on which the relief had been granted *ex parte* could no longer be supported or had been substantially impugned.

If the position was that the applicant still had the benefit of the *ex parte* relief which had been obtained then it is thought that in such circumstances the applicant would have a duty either to consent to the discharge of the order, or alternatively the applicant would have a duty to disclose to the court the new position, so that the court could consider what to do in the changed circumstances of the case.

(5) The timing of the application to discharge Anton Piller or Mareva relief for material non-disclosure

If an application to discharge Anton Piller relief for material non-disclosure is made after the order has already been fully executed, the position may be that the only real question between the parties is whether the order should be discharged so as to give rise to a possible claim on the cross-undertaking as to damages. Thus, if the material obtained by the plaintiff under the order would in any event be covered by the defendant's obligations as to discovery, the defendant will not be in a position to contend that it is necessary for the court to entertain an immediate application to discharge the order so that the relevant material can be retrieved from the plaintiff under an order of the court providing for this to occur.

In *Dormeuil Frères SA* v *Nicolian Ltd* [1988] 1 WLR 1362, the court was concerned with an application to discharge Anton Piller relief which had already been fully executed together with an issue as to what were to be the exact terms of an interim injunction, it being common ground that an injunction should be made until the trial. The application to discharge the Anton Piller relief for non-disclosure gave rise to questions which involved detailed consideration of the voluminous evidence and which would be best determined at the trial of the action in the light of cross-examination of the witnesses. In these circumstances Sir Nicolas Browne-Wilkinson VC decided that there was no urgency to determine the application which should be adjourned to be dealt with at the trial. However, in doing so, the Vice-Chancellor observed that in his judgment:

save in exceptional cases, it is not the correct procedure to apply to discharge an *ex parte* injunction on the grounds of lack of full disclosure at the interlocutory stage of the proceedings. The purpose of interlocutory proceedings is to regulate the future of the case until trial. Where an Anton Piller order has been made *ex parte*, in the vast majority of cases, the order has been executed before the *inter partes* hearing. Setting aside the *Anton Piller* order cannot undo what has already been done . . . The sole relevance of the question 'Should the *ex parte* order be set aside?' is, so far as I can see, to determine the question whether the plaintiff is liable on the cross-undertaking in damages given on the *ex parte* hearing. That is not an urgent matter. It is normally much better dealt with at the trial by the trial judge who knows all the circumstances of the case and is able, after cross-examination, to test the veracity of the witnesses (at pp 1369–1370).

The Vice-Chancellor also said that similar considerations applied in the case of Mareva relief.

These observations need to be viewed in the factual context of that case, because there are circumstances in which an application should be dealt with at the interlocutory stage. Often Anton Piller relief is granted in conjunction with Mareva or other injunctive relief, and the non-disclosure question will go to the issue whether or not the Mareva or other injunctive relief should continue in place until trial. In these circumstances plainly the non-disclosure question must be addressed at the interlocutory stage, and ordinarily is to be resolved at that time.[61] In *Lloyd's Bowmaker* v *Britannia Arrow Holdings plc* [1988] 1 WLR 1337, such an interlocutory application was made successfully two years after the grant of the *ex parte* Mareva relief.

Similarly, if the execution of the Anton Piller relief has not been completed, then the court will entertain the application to discharge the order on the grounds of non-disclosure, because then the relevant consequences are not confined to the liability of the plaintiff on the cross-undertaking as to damages.[62]

Even if the position is that the Anton Piller relief has been fully executed and the non-disclosure question does not go to whether or not interlocutory relief is to be continued until trial, then it is still a matter of discretion for the court to decide whether or not to deal with the non-disclosure

---

61 *Ali and Fahd Shobokshi Group* v *Moneim* [1989] 1 WLR 710 at pp 721–722 citing *Bank Mellat* v *Nikpour* [1985] FSR 87, and see generally the cases cited above on the effects of material non-disclosure or misrepresentation, and *Arab Monetary Fund* v *Hashim* [1989] 1 WLR 565 at pp 569–570 distinguishing *Dormeuil Frères SA* v *Nicolian Ltd* (above).
62 *Arab Monetary Fund* v *Hashim* [1989] 1 WLR 565 at pp 569–570.

tion at the interlocutory stage. In *Dormeuil Frères SA* v *Nicolian Ltd* there were good grounds for postponing consideration of the issue until trial. But this is not always the case. It is clear that in appropriate cases the court will discharge Anton Piller relief which has been fully executed and will do so even on an interlocutory application.[63] Thus, for example, a defendant may wish to seek to remove the stigma which has arisen from the granting of the *ex parte* Anton Piller relief, and the court may consider that it is in the interests of justice that the defendant is afforded that opportunity as soon as possible.[64] It is also thought that if the issue which arises is a clear one and can be dealt with conveniently at an interlocutory stage, then the court ought in general to entertain the application. Thus in New Zealand it has been said that the fact that an application to discharge an order which has been fully executed is made on the grounds of non-disclosure, in itself provides a good reason for dealing with the application at an interlocutory stage.[65] There is an element of public policy in entertaining such applications at the interlocutory stage so as to deter future would-be applicants for Anton Piller relief from failing to make full disclosure of material facts to the court. Furthermore, it would be inappropriate to allow an applicant who has obtained the relief through culpable misconduct to retain the benefits of that misconduct.

In the event that leave to serve a foreign defendant out of the jurisdiction is set aside, then any Mareva or Anton Piller relief will be set aside at the same time.[66] Similarly, if an action is struck out under an interlocutory order, any Mareva or Anton Piller relief granted in that action will be set aside.[67] The observation of the Vice-Chancellor in *Dormeuil Frères SA* v *Nicolian Ltd* are not directed to either of those situations.

Accordingly, it is considered that whilst it may be appropriate to adjourn an application to discharge fully executed Anton Piller relief on the grounds of non-disclosure until the trial, there is no general rule of practice for this procedure to be adopted, and whether or not this is done must depend upon the circumstances of the particular case. The relevant factors to be taken into account will include the following.

(1) Whether the defendant is likely to suffer continuing prejudice to his reputation or commercial standing by reason of the making of the Anton Piller order, or there is some other good reason for the application being dealt with promptly.

---

63 *Booker McConnell plc* v *Plasgow* [1985] RPC 425 at pp 434–435, and 442–443, *Randolph M Fields* v *Alison Watts* (1985) 129 SJ 67 (a case against certain members of the Bar); *Jeffrey Rogers Ltd* v *Vinola* [1985] FSR 184.

64 *Booker McConnell* v *Plasgow* (above) involved as defendants two public companies, and *Randolph M Fields* v *Alison Watts* (above) concerned defendants who were barristers and barristers' clerks, and who were therefore unlikely to destroy or conceal documents, so that it was unnecessary and inappropriate to make an Anton Piller order.

65 *DB Baverstock Lord* v *Haycock* [1986] 1 NZLR 342 at p 345; *Anvil Jewellery Ltd* v *River Ridge Holdings Ltd* [1987] 1 NZLR 35 at p 43.

66 *Siskina* v *Distos SA* [1979] AC 210 is an illustration.

67 *Swedac Ltd* v *Magnet & Southerns plc* [1989] FSR 243 at p 253.

(2) Whether the issue involves questions as to the credibility of witnesses or otherwise is likely to require cross-examination of witnesses.

(3) Whether the issue will involve a detailed review of voluminous evidence.

(4) Whether the issue can conveniently be dealt with at an interlocutory hearing and will not be likely to involve the incurring of unnecessary costs.

(5) Whether the issue arises in connection with another application before the court, such as an application to set aside leave granted to serve a defendant with proceedings out of the jurisdiction, or an application to discharge injunctive relief.

If a plaintiff has obtained injunctive relief *ex parte* which has since been discharged or expired, and the defendant wishes to claim damages on the cross-undertaking it is still open to the defendant to apply to the court either to assess damages summarily or to order an inquiry as to damages on the grounds that the *ex parte* order was obtained by non-disclosure.

Chapter 9

The undertaking in damages

(1) Provision of the undertaking

The almost invariable practice of the court is to require the applicant for a Mareva injunction (or indeed, any other form of interlocutory injunction) or Anton Pillar relief to give the court an undertaking to abide by any order of the court as to damages, should the defendant suffer any by reason of the order which, in the opinion of the court, the applicant ought to pay.[1] The undertaking is given to the court,[2] and not to the defendant concerned, and any breach of the undertaking would be a contempt of court. The undertaking is obtained by the court from the applicant as part of the price for granting the *ex parte* relief.[3] The purpose of the undertaking is to enable the court to award damages against the provider of the under-taking in respect of any loss suffered by reason of the order by the party or parties identified in the undertaking. Unless the undertaking is provided the defendant will not be able to obtain compensation for loss caused by the court order,[4] unless perhaps the defendant can show that the order was obtained by the plaintiff maliciously and in abuse of the process of the court.[5]

In *Smith* v *Day* (1882) 21 ChD 421 at p 424, Sir George Jessel MR said that the undertaking in damages had been invented by Knight-Bruce LJ when he was Vice-Chancellor, and had originally only been inserted in *ex parte* orders for injunctions. This was subsequently repeated by Lord Dip-lock in his speech in *F Hoffman-La Roche* v *Secretary of State* [1975] AC 295 at p 360. However, it appears that the practice of requiring an undertak-ing in damages or making express provision in an order for a defendant to

---

1 *Smith* v *Day* (1882) 21 ChD 421; *Attorney-General* v *Albany Hotel Co* [1896] 2 Ch 696; *F Hoff-man-La Roche & Co AG* v *Secretary of State* [1975] AC 295; *Air Express Ltd* v *Ansett Transport Industries (Operations) Pty Ltd* (1981) 146 CLR 249 esp at pp 260–261 and 311.
2 *F Hoffman-La Roche & Co AG* v *Secretary of State* [1975] AC 295 at p 361.
3 *Tucker* v *New Brunswick Trading Co* (1890) 44 ChD 249; *Commodity Ocean Transport* v *Basford Unicorn* [1987] 2 Lloyd's Rep 197 at p 200; *Fletcher Sutcliffe Wild Ltd* v *Burch* [1982] FSR 64 at p 69.
4 *Chisholm* v *Rieff* (1953) 2 FLR 211 (Supreme Court of the Northern Territory of Austra-lia).
5 *Digital Equipment Corporation* v *Darkcrest Ltd* [1984] Ch 512.

be protected from loss caused by the making of an interlocutory injunction which was subsequently found to be unjustified pre-dates 1841, when Knight-Bruce LJ became Vice-Chancellor, and therefore was not originated by him.[6] The practice has been adopted in common law jurisdictions throughout the world.

Exceptionally the court may not insist on an undertaking from the Crown when bringing proceedings to enforce the law, as opposed to bringing proceedings for its own financial benefit.[7] It is thought that in principle the court would be prepared to consider not insisting upon an undertaking in like proceedings brought to enforce the law by a plaintiff other than the Crown. If a plaintiff may not be good for damages on the undertaking this is a material fact which must be disclosed to the court on the *ex parte* application (see pp 82–83). Even though the plaintiff is impecunious, the court may, in rare cases where the merits are strongly in favour of the plaintiff, in the exercise of its discretion, still decide to grant the relief sought, accepting the risk that the undertaking may not be honoured if called upon in due course.[8] Alternatively, the court may require the undertaking to be fortified[9] by the provision either of an unlimited undertaking given by someone other than the plaintiff, or a limited undertaking, the amount of the limit being in the discretion of the court. Ordinarily that limit would be fixed by reference to a reasonable estimate of what losses might be suffered by reason of the order by the party or parties covered by the undertaking.[10]

Although no general rule can be stated as to when the court would order fortification of the cross-undertaking, it is likely that some security would be ordered in circumstances where the defendant could make a successful application for security for costs; the plaintiff's financial position, his domicile or place of business and the strength of his case are among the relevant factors normally considered by the court.

It is entirely a matter for the court's discretion whether it will require the plaintiff to put up security to back his undertaking in damages (usually in the form of a bank guarantee, or payment of a specified sum into a joint account in the names of the parties' solicitors). It is more usual for the court to decide whether security should be provided at the *inter*

---

6 *Chisholm* v *Rieff* (1953) 2 FLR 211 at p 214 (Supreme Court of the Northern Territory of Australia); *Southern Tableland* v *Schomberg* (1986) 11 ACLR 337 at p 340 (Supreme Court of New South Wales).

7 *F Hoffman-La Roche & Co AG* v *Secretary of State* (above).

8 *Allen* v *Jambo Holdings* [1980] 1 WLR 1252. In *Szentessy* v *Woo Ran* (1985) 64 ACTR 98 at p 104 (Supreme Court of the Australian Capital Territory) the court dispensed with the undertaking, but this was in altogether exceptional circumstances.

9 *Baxter* v *Claydon* [1952] WN 376; *Harman Pictures NV* v *Osborne* [1967] 1 WLR 723 at p 739; *Commodity Ocean Transport* v *Basford Unicorn* [1987] 2 Lloyd's Rep 197 at p 198; *Re DPR Futures Ltd* [1989] 1 WLR 778; *Select Personnel Pty Ltd* v *Morgan & Banks Pty Ltd* (1988) 12 IPR 167 (Supreme Court of New South Wales).

10 *Re DPR Futures Ltd* [1989] 1 WLR 778 at p 786.

partes hearing, because that is normally the time at which the court is in the best position to assess the merits and make an estimate of the nature and extent of the damage which the defendant may suffer if it later appears that the injunction should not have been granted, so that security can be ordered for a realistic amount. However, the court may require security to be provided even at the *ex parte* stage, if the circumstances so warrant, and may make the provision of such security a condition precedent to the granting of the injunction.

The usual practice of the court is to require an undertaking in damages in favour of all the defendants in the action even though only one or some of them may be enjoined in the relevant injunction.[11] This is because it may not be clear which of the defendants are liable to suffer loss as a result of the injunction being granted, particularly in complicated cases. It may be the case that a defendant may suffer loss as a result of an injunction being granted against another defendant, and in such circumstances the court has jurisdiction under the cross-undertaking in damages in the usual form, to require the plaintiff to pay compensation to that defendant.

The decision whether or not to provide the required undertaking to the court is that of the applicant, and the provision of it is by the voluntary act of the applicant.[12] If a party who is not included within the scope of an undertaking wishes to be included within it, then it will be necessary for that party to apply to the court for the relevant relief which has been granted, to be discharged unless the applicant provides a widened undertaking. In such circumstances it may be that the applicant chooses not to provide a widened undertaking even though the court seeks it from him, and in consequence the relief granted is discharged. If the position is that the relief granted has already lapsed or been discharged, or if in the case of Anton Piller relief, it has already been fully executed, then the court will not be in a position to stipulate for a widened undertaking as the price for continuance of the relief which has been granted.[13]

It may occur that the applicant is willing to furnish an undertaking in favour of the party applying, but wishes to restrict the scope of the undertaking to loss suffered by that party from the date of that application, as opposed to the date of the original application. It will be a matter for the discretion of the court to consider whether or not to accept the restricted undertaking as the price for continuance of the relief. In principle it is thought that the undertaking ought not to be so restricted unless there is some good reason for such a course being adopted. Thus the court might

11 *Dubai Bank Ltd* v *Galadari (No 2)* (1989) *The Times*, 11 October. *Tucker* v *New Brunswick Trading Co* (1890) 44 ChD 249.
12 *Commodity Ocean Transport* v *Basford* [1987] 2 Lloyd's Rep 197; *F Hoffman-La Roche & Co AG* v *Secretary of State* at p 361.
13 *Deutsche Schachtbau-und Tiefbohrgesellschaft GmbH* v *Ras Al Khaimah National Oil Company* [1988] 3 WLR 230 at pp 263–264, per Lord Goff; *Commodity Ocean Transport* v *Basford* (above). Contrast *Marc Rich* v *Oroleum International* noted in 197 LMLN (21 May 1987) which was a decision from Singapore.

have stipulated for the requisite undertaking at the time of the original application had the court known of the possibility of parties not covered by the existing undertaking as to damages, being subjected to loss. The general principle is that innocent third parties caught up in the granting of Mareva relief ought not to be left to suffer loss caused by the order, but ought to be held harmless from that loss.[14] Thus if on an application made within a reasonable period it appears that some innocent third party may be, or has been, prejudiced by the relief granted, and the court is minded to obtain an undertaking in damages in favour of that third party, then in principle this should be regarded as being by way of an adjustment of the original order in the light of further information becoming available, which, had that information been available to the court originally, would have resulted in the court stipulating for an undertaking in damages to cover the third party at the *ex parte* application. Furthermore, consistently with the general principle that innocent third parties should not be required themselves to suffer loss as a result of finding themselves involved in abiding by a Mareva injunction, it is appropriate that they should not be left to bear losses incurred by them in the period up to their application to the court. Of course if there has been unnecessary delay by the third party in making his application for the undertaking to be widened then the court may, in the exercise of its discretion, decide that it is appropriate for the third party to be confined to a narrower undertaking, or not to be given the benefit of an undertaking at all.

(2) Inadvertent omission of an undertaking in damages

Whenever the court grants an Anton Piller order or an interlocutory injunction, unless the contrary is expressly said, the plaintiff will be taken to have given the usual undertaking in damages by implication.[15] In the Queen's Bench Division it is usually the responsibility of the plaintiff to provide a draft order to the court. That order ought to contain the usual undertaking in damages. If through inadvertence it is not included, the plaintiff could not resist a subsequent application by the defendant to rectify the order either under RSC Order 20, r 11[16] or under the inherent jurisdiction of the court.

In the Chancery Division there are standard draft orders (see Appendix 2) for Mareva and Anton Piller relief which contain an undertaking in damages. The order as drawn up should always include the undertaking in damages unless there is an express contrary direction by the court and a mistake in this respect ought to be rectified. If it is desired to seek rectification of the order either under RSC Order 20, r 11 or under the

14 *Project Development Co SA* v *KMK Securities* [1982] 1 WLR 1470; *Galaxia Maritime SA* v *Mineral-importexport* [1982] 1 WLR 539.
15 *Spanish General Agency Corporation* v *Spanish Corporation* (1890) 63 LT 161; *Colledge* v *Crossley* (1975) *The Times*, 18 March.
16 *Colledge* v *Crossley* (above).

inherent jurisdiction, the application should be made to the court of first instance and not to the Court of Appeal.[17] Alternatively the defendant could invite the court to proceed as if the undertaking in damages was expressly set out in the order.[18]

There are other undertakings besides the undertaking in damages which it has become standard practice to include in an Anton Piller or a Mareva order (as the case may be). It is thought that if one of these standard undertakings is inadvertently omitted from the order, whether or not by virtue of the fault of the plaintiff, then in principle the court would be able to rectify the order.

If a defendant proffers an undertaking to the court to stand in the place of an injunction then the defendant would be prudent to ensure that the plaintiff expressly provides an undertaking in damages in respect of loss caused by the provision of the defendant's undertaking. This is particularly so outside the Chancery Division. In the Chancery Division the practice is to include an undertaking in damages in this situation unless the contrary is expressly stated *Practice Note* [1904] WN 203, at p 208. This came about as a result of a direction by the judges of the Chancery Division subsequent to the decision of the Court of Appeal in *Howard* v *Press Printers Ltd* (1904) 91 LT 718, refusing to include an undertaking in damages when this had not been expressly given by the plaintiff in return for the defendant's undertaking.

If the position is that relief is made or continued *inter partes* when a third party or defendant not covered by an undertaking in damages expressly given by the plaintiff was present in court and made no objection to the form of undertaking proferred, then the court will not subsequently rectify its order to include a wider undertaking. So to act would be to impose an undertaking on the plaintiff inconsistent with the terms of the undertaking voluntarily given by him,[19] and accepted by the court.

(3) Effect of the undertaking in damages

The undertaking in damages is an undertaking given to the court and not directly to the party or parties identified in the undertaking. That party is not entitled to sue on the undertaking by way of a claim in contract.[20] Nor will that party or any other party be able to sue in tort for damages caused by the court order, unless perhaps the order was obtained maliciously, and in abuse of the process of the court.[21] Thus to make good an action in tort, the party injured would need to sue for malicious prosecution (*Speed Seal Ltd* v *Paddington* [1985] 1 WLR 1327 at pp 1333–1334) or, perhaps

---

17 *Tucker* v *New Brunswick Trading Co* (1890) 44 ChD 249.
18 *Oberrheinische Metallwerke GmbH* v *Cocks* [1906] WN 127.
19 *Tucker* v *New Brunswick Trading Co* (above); *Commodity Ocean Transport Corpn* v *Basford Unicorn Industries Ltd* [1987] 2 Lloyd's Rep 197.
20 *Fletcher Sutcliffe Wild Ltd* v *Burch* [1982] FSR 64.
21 *Digital Equipment Corporation* v *Darkcrest Ltd* (above). See also p 253 below.

for the tort of abuse of the process of the court.[22] However, a party covered by the undertaking will have the right at the appropriate stage to ask the court to enforce the undertaking against the plaintiff, and the court can do so, either assessing the damages summarily[23] or, more usually, by directing that the plaintiff do pay the damages awarded on an inquiry as to damages. The question whether or not the injunction had been rightly granted is to be decided by the court and has to be dealt with before any inquiry as to damages is directed. Such an inquiry will only be concerned with the quantum of damages to be awarded to the defendant pursuant to the jurisdiction conferred on the court by the undertaking in damages which has been provided to it. The inquiry is not concerned with any issue as to whether the injunction was justified.[24] Nor in principle should it be concerned with whether the court, in the exercise of its discretion (see pp 104–105), should decide to decline to award damages either wholly or in part. Thus once an inquiry has been directed it is concerned only with matters concerning the quantification of damages.

In Seton's *Chancery Forms*, the draft order directing an inquiry contains provision for the plaintiff to recover the costs of the inquiry. However, this is not the modern practice. Costs of the inquiry remain in the discretion of the court and the plaintiff may choose to protect his position on costs by making a payment into court or, if appropriate, an offer marked without prejudice save as to costs.

In *Smith* v *Day* (1882) 21 ChD 421, Sir George Jessel MR expressed the view that no inquiry as to damages would be directed if the court had made an error in law in granting the original relief. This was expressly dissented from by Cotton LJ, and it was subsequently established that an inquiry would be directed whenever an injunction was subsequently found not to have been justified, and even if the plaintiff could not be said to have been at fault in any respect in obtaining the interlocutory relief. Thus, for example, if the plaintiff fails on a point of law the defendant will be entitled to an inquiry as to damages.[25]

The ordinary practice on interlocutory injunctions is not to order an inquiry into damages on the cross-undertaking unless and until the plaintiff has failed on the merits of the action: *Ushers Brewery Ltd* v *King (PS) & Co (Finance) Ltd* [1972] Ch 148. However, in a case involving a Mareva injunction, a defendant may obtain an inquiry into damages once it is apparent that the injunction was obtained wrongly or without jurisdiction

---

22 *Metall & Rohstoff AG* v *Donaldson Lufkin & Jenrette Inc* [1989] 3 WLR 563; *Speed Seal Ltd* v *Paddington* (above); *Grainger* v *Hill* (1838) 4 Bing NC 212.

23 As in *Columbia Picture Industries Inc* v *Robinson* [1987] Ch 38.

24 *Norwest Holst Civil Engineering Limited* v *Polysius Limited* (1987) *The Times*, 23 July, disapproving of an observation to the contrary made in *Barclays Bank Ltd* v *Rosenberg* (1985) *The Times*, 9 May.

25 *Griffith* v *Blake* (1884) 27 ChD 474; *Vieweger Construction Co Ltd* v *Rush & Tompkins* (1964) 48 DLR (2d) 509 at pp 518–519 (Supreme Court of Canada); *Nelson Burns & Co* v *Grantham Industries* 19 CPR (3d) 71 (Ontario Court of Appeal).

Thus in cases involving non-disclosure the courts have ordered inquiries as to damages once it is clear that the injunction should not have been granted[26] and even though the plaintiff has obtained a substantial judgment against the defendant or may do so. The position is the same for Anton Piller orders. This is because in a Mareva case the question of whether there should be an award of damages on the cross-undertaking is tangential to the main merits of the action. Before directing an inquiry, the court will require to be satisfied that the defendant has a reasonably arguable case that he has suffered loss by reason of the granting of the injunction, for which the plaintiff ought to compensate him. Once an inquiry has been ordered then it is usually just and convenient that the inquiry is held at the same time as the plaintiff's claim is tried.[27] If the plaintiff has already obtained judgment then the defendant may be able to obtain a stay of execution on the judgment pending the outcome of the inquiry as to damages. If an inquiry is ordered and the plaintiff has not yet obtained judgment, then the question is liable to arise whether the plaintiff should obtain judgment, possibly subject to a stay of execution, or whether the defendant's claim on the cross-undertaking is available as a defence (by way of set-off) on the grounds that the plaintiff ought not to be allowed to insist on his claim without the defendant's cross-claim being taking into account. So far this point has not been decided.

It would appear that a claim in the inquiry as to damages is capable of being available as a set-off and the judgments in *Barclays Bank* v *Illingworth* and *Barclays Bank* v *Rosenberg* are consistent with this approach. However, this would not be the position if the plaintiff's claim is one which would ordinarily entitle him to summary judgment without even a stay of execution (eg a claim on a bill of exchange or for freight).

(4) 'Special circumstances' justifying the refusal of an inquiry as to damages

Once it is established that the plaintiff obtained the injunction without justification, even though without fault on his part, the court will almost invariably order an inquiry as to damages. In *Graham* v *Campbell* (1877) 7 ChD 490 at p 494, James LJ delivering the judgment of the Court of Appeal said that the undertaking ought to be given effect to by the court except 'under special circumstances'.

The mere fact that the defendant has broken his contract with the plaintiff or has been guilty of tortious conduct,[28] even deliberate tortious conduct,[29] has not resulted in a refusal by the court to enforce the undertaking.

26 *Barclays Bank Ltd* v *Rosenberg* (1985) *Financial Times*, 12 June; *Barclays Bank plc* v *Illingworth* Court of Appeal (Civil Division) Transcript No 304 of 1985 (10 May).

27 *Barclays Bank Plc* v *Illingworth* Court of Appeal (Civil Division) Transcript No 304 of 1985 (10 May) per Kerr LJ (obiter).

28 *Nelson Burns & Co* v *Grantham Industries* (above) (Ontario Court of Appeal).

29 *Columbia Picture Industries* v *Robinson* [1987] Ch 37.

However, the residual discretion to refuse an inquiry remains, and has been exercised in Canada to refuse an inquiry in a case when the plaintiff was acting in the public interest and the defendant's conduct leading to the institution of the proceedings was viewed with disfavour.[30]

In *F Hoffmann-La Roche & Co AG* v *Secretary of State* [1975] AC 295 at p 361, Lord Diplock said that the discretion not to enforce the undertaking could be exercised if the court considered that the conduct of the defendant in relation to the obtaining or continuing of the injunction, or the enforcement of the undertaking makes it inequitable to do so. Unnecessary delay in making an application to the court to enforce the undertaking can result in the court declining to enforce it.[31]

(5) Measure of damages available under an inquiry as to damages

In *F Hoffmann-La Roche & Co AG* v *Secretary of State* [1975] AC 295, at p 361, Lord Diplock said that if an inquiry as to damages is ordered the 'principles to be applied are fixed and clear. The assessment is made upon the same basis as that upon which damages for breach of contract would be assessed if the undertaking had been a contract between the plaintiff and the defendant that the plaintiff would *not* prevent the defendant from doing that which he was restrained from doing by the terms of the injunction.'

The defendant is only entitled to recover for loss caused by the making of the order. It is not sufficient that the order provided the factual context within which the loss occurred.[32] Thus if the loss would have been suffered because of the bringing of the proceedings regardless of the granting of the order, then this is not covered by the undertaking.[33] The burden of proof is upon the defendant to prove that the loss was suffered as the result of the order. However, once the defendant shows that he has suffered loss subsequent to the order which *prima facie* was caused by the order, then the evidential burden is liable to pass to the plaintiff in respect of any contention that the relevant loss would have been suffered in any event regardless of the making or continuance of the order.[34]

The defendant must have taken all reasonable steps to avoid altogether or mitigate his loss. This will include taking steps to apply for a variation of the injunction in appropriate circumstances, eg so as to enable business debts to be paid and to allow a business to continue to be conducted.[35] The damages to be awarded are not to be artificially restricted to losses suffered during the period for which the order was in force. The losses to

---

30 *Attorney-General for Ontario* v *Harry* 25 CPC 67 (Ontario Supreme Court).
31 *Ex parte Hall* (1883) 23 ChD 644.
32 *Schlesinger* v *Bedford* (1893) 9 TLR 370.
33 *Air Express Limited* v *Ansett Transport Industries* (1981) 146 CLR 249 (High Court of Australia), especially at pp 262–268, 312–313, 323–324.
34 *Financiera Avenida SA* v *Shiblaq* (1988) *The Times*, 21 November (Saville J).
35 *Re DPR Futures Ltd* [1989] 1 WLR 778 at pp 786–787.

be taken into account will include losses suffered as a result of the order even though the losses were not in fact suffered or incurred until after the order had been discharged.[36]

Furthermore, the principles of remoteness of damage apply.[37] Accordingly the plaintiff will not be held liable for a type of loss which is too remote, taking into account what losses could reasonably have been contemplated by him as not unlikely to result from the order at the time he furnished the relevant undertaking, or at any renewal of the undertaking voluntarily entered into by him.

The defendant will not be able to recover compensation for the loss of a business which it was illegal for him to conduct, eg a business selling video tapes or computer software in breach of copyright.[38] However, if the order effectively causes a legitimate business to cease, it is thought that the court could award damages for the loss of that business which would take into account loss of goodwill.

It has been said that exemplary damages can be awarded by the court.[39] However, the wording of the undertaking only obliges the plaintiff to pay damages in respect of losses suffered by reason of the order, and therefore appears to be restricted to damages awarded so as to compensate the defendant for those losses. In principle the court could award aggravated damages when the effect of making and implementing the order has been made more severe for the defendant by the high-handedness or misconduct of the plaintiff or his agents.

Once it is apparent that the defendant will be entitled to recover damages on the undertaking it is thought that the court could grant Mareva relief against the plaintiff in respect of the undertaking.[40] In this respect the position would seem to be analogous to that where there is an untaxed order for costs.[41] Thus if the court is satisfied that damages will be awarded either summarily or on an inquiry as to damages, then in principle Mareva relief is available in respect of the claim. If, on the other hand, it is not clear that an injunction was obtained without justification then it would be premature to grant Mareva relief in respect of a possible claim which might be entertained in due course under the undertaking in damages subsequently should it appear that the injunction was unjustified.

When damages are awarded under the undertaking, an order is made by the court directing the plaintiff to pay those damages. In principle the court can award interest on those damages under s 35A of the Supreme

---

36 *Algonquin Mercantile Group* v *Dart Industries* (1986) 12 CPR (3d) (Federal Court of Canada).
37 *Smith* v *Day* (above); *Air Express Limited* v *Ansett Transport Industries* (above).
38 *Colombia Picture Industries* v *Robinson* (above).
39 *Columbia Picture Industries* v *Robinson* (above) at p 87; *Smith* v *Day* (above) at pp 427–428 per Brett LJ.
40 *Commodity Ocean Transport* v *Basford Corporation* [1987] 2 Lloyd's Rep 197 at p 200.
41 *Faith Panton Property Plan* v *Hodgetts* [1981] 1 WLR 927.

Court Act 1981. In Canada interest has been awarded on damages awarded on the undertaking.[42]

(6) Security for costs of application to set aside Mareva relief

The undertaking in damages does not entitle a defendant who has successfully set aside an injunction to recover the difference between the costs awarded to the defendant on the application, and costs on an indemnity basis.[43] This reflects the general principle that the costs on an application to discharge an injunction do not fall within the ambit of the undertaking in damages, but fall to be dealt with under the court's ordinary jurisdiction concerning costs. This jurisdiction is conferred by s 51 of the Supreme Court Act 1981, which provides:

Subject to the provisions of this or any other Act and to rules of court, the costs of and incidental to all proceedings in the civil division of the Court of Appeal and in the High Court including the administration of estates and trusts shall be in the discretion of the court, and the court shall have full power to determine by whom and to what extent the costs are to be paid.

The exercise of the court's discretion is made subject to rules of court both by the section and by RSC Order 62, r 2(4).[44] Accordingly it follows that:

(1) the court has a wide statutory jurisdiction for dealing with costs, and there is no need in this area for the plaintiff to provide an undertaking to abide by orders of the court. In particular there is no need for such an undertaking in order to confer jurisdiction on the court;[45]

(2) any restricted order for costs or refusal of costs will arise from the exercise by the court of its discretion pursuant to the statutory jurisdiction. This will be the effective cause of any shortfall in costs, and not the making or continuance of the injunction. Thus, any shortfall does not fall within the ambit of loss or damage suffered by reason of the order.[46]

---

42 *Algonquin Mercantile Group* v *Dart Industries* (above).

43 In *Harrison* v *McSheehan* [1885] WN 207, there was an inquiry as to damages ordered by consent in relation to what damages had been caused to a plaintiff by certain acts of a defendant. The court refused to include in those damages the difference between the costs recoverable under a court order and the costs incurred as between solicitor and client, Pearson J observing that this was 'contrary to the practice of the court'.

44 See also *Aiden Shipping Ltd* v *Interbulk* [1986] AC 965 at p 975, per Lord Goff.

45 Contrast the *raison d'être* for the requirement of an undertaking in damages: pp 98 and 102–103, above.

46 This is to be contrasted with the position of a third party who has the benefit of an undertaking by the plaintiff to pay the reasonable costs of complying with the order and to indemnify the third party against liabilities incurred by reason of such compliance. It is considered that such an undertaking would in principle extend to the reasonable costs incurred by a third party in making a justifiable application to the court in connection with compliance with the order: see also *Project Development Co Ltd SA* v *KMK Securities Ltd* [1982] 1 WLR 1470 at p 1473, which was a case concerning the exercise of discretion under the rules of court.

Accordingly even if there is an order for fortification of the undertaking in damages, the quantum of the security so ordered will not take into account security for the defendant's costs.

However, a defendant subject to Mareva relief who intends to make an application to have the relief set aside or who intends to oppose the renewal of the relief, can apply for security for costs in cases where security can be ordered, and the timely provision of the requisite security ordered can be made a condition of the continuance of the Mareva relief pending determination of the application to discharge the injunction or the determination of the application to renew the relief. In *Ali and Fahd Shobokshi Group Limited* v *Moneim*, an application was made to Hoffmann J (unreported, 6 February 1989)[47] for security for costs prior to the hearing of a motion[48] by the plaintiffs to renew Mareva relief which had been granted *ex parte*. The judge made an order for security in an amount which took 'into account the possibility that the defendant may be given an order for costs on an indemnity basis'. In so doing the judge declined to go into the merits of the pending motion because there was no evidence before the court that if ordered to provide security for costs, the plaintiffs would be unable to comply with the order. Hoffmann J made the timely provision of the security a condition for the continuance of the Mareva relief saying that:

I will deal firstly with the point of principle, whether it would be right that the continuance of the Mareva should be conditional not only on the cross-undertaking in damages but also as to there being security for costs. The normal way in which security for costs is required to be provided by a foreign plaintiff is pursuant to an application under Order 23. If the court decides that security is appropriate it will order that in default of security, proceedings shall be stayed. Such an order would not be sufficient to do justice in this case because it would leave the plaintiff in possession of its Mareva without the defendant having any assurance that if he successfully moves to discharge it, the costs of his doing so would be covered. Accordingly it would seem to me appropriate in such a case for the court to use its general discretion which derives from s 37 of the Supreme Court Act 1981 to ensure that the continuance of the Mareva will not cause injustice to the defendant. In principle therefore I see no reason why the Mareva should not be made conditional not only on the cross-undertaking for damages but also for costs.

[Counsel for the defendant] submits that in this case it would be inappropriate to make such an order at this stage of the proceedings. He points out that an application in ordinary form under Order 23 was made on 27 October and is due to come on with other motions on 20 February. This he says would be the appropriate time for the whole question of security for costs to be considered. The court would then be seized of the merits of the action as emerge from the interlocutory evidence and the merits are matters which the court can take into account in exercising its discretion whether to grant an order for security for costs. If I were to make such an order today I would be deprived of an opportunity to consider the merits.

---

47 A transcript of the judgment has been kindly furnished to the author by Mr Richard Slowe, who was counsel for the defendant.
48 By Mervyn Davies J, reported at [1989] 1 WLR 710.

Now I accept that there are occasions when the courts do take the merits into account. The reason why they do so is because it could be unjust to deprive a meritorious plaintiff of the opportunity to litigate in this country by making his action subject to providing security for costs which in practice he could not provide. That would amount to a summary denial of justice. In this case however there is no suggestion that the plaintiff would be unable to provide the amount of security for which the defendant asks. No doubt it is always inconvenient to have to put up security, but there is no question of the plaintiff being deprived of the opportunity to present his case. On the other hand, if no security is given at this stage there must be a real possibility that the plaintiff, if defeated on the motions later this month, would be tempted to abandon the proceedings here and leave the defendant with an unsatisfied claim for costs.

It seems to me therefore that without investigating the merits further than to acknowledge the possibility that the motions could go either way, the balance of convenience is strongly in favour of giving the defendant reasonable security in respect of his costs as a condition of continuing the Mareva.

In principle it is also considered that the court has jurisdiction to order that Mareva or Anton Piller relief is only to be granted or continued provided provision is made for security for costs for the defendant, regardless as to whether security would otherwise be available under statute or the rules of court. However, as a matter of discretion, it is ordinarily to be expected that the court will only order security for costs in cases in which security for costs may be ordered under statute or the rules of court.

Chapter 10

The granting of Mareva relief

(1) Need for an underlying 'actual or potential action'

In *Siskina* v *Distos SA (The 'Siskina')* [1979] AC 210 at p 254, Lord Diplock
(with whom Lords Russell and Keith agreed) stated that s 45(1) of the
Supreme Court of Judicature (Consolidation) Act 1925, from which the
power of the court to grant Mareva injunctions was derived, 'presupposes
the existence of an action, actual or potential, claiming substantive relief
which the High Court has jurisdiction to grant and to which the interlocutory orders referred to are but ancillary.'

The authorities show that there is a rule of general application that
Mareva relief will only by granted in support of an *existing* cause of
action.[1]

In *Chief Constable of Kent* v *V* [1983] QB 34, Lord Denning MR said that
under s 37(1) of the Supreme Court Act 1981, it was not essential for an
injunction to be ancillary to an action claiming a legal or equitable right.
However, his approach was not adopted by Donaldson LJ, and Slade LJ
dissented. The view of Lord Denning MR has not subsequently been
accepted.[2]

In Australia, the courts have, whilst accepting the existence of the
general rule, recognised that the requirement should be approached flexi-
bly, and that Mareva relief may be available in cases not falling within the
general rule.

In *Construction Engineering (Australia) Pty Ltd* v *Tamber* [1984] 1 NSWLR
274, the Supreme Court of New South Wales granted Mareva relief in substantive proceedings where the claim was subject to an arbitration clause in
the *Scott* v *Avery* form, whilst in *Vereker* v *Choi* [1985] 4 NSWLR 277 (see

---

1 *Steamship Mutual Underwriting Association (Bermuda)* v *Thakur Shipping* [1986] 2 Lloyd's Rep
439; *Siporex Trade SA* v *Comdel Commodities* [1986] 2 Lloyd's Rep 428 at pp 436–437; *Ninemia Maritime Corporation* v *Trave Schiffahrtsgesellschaft GmbH (The 'Niedersachsen')* [1983] 2
Lloyd's Rep 600 at p 602. See also pp 57–59 above on buyer's claims on contracts for the
sale of a ship. Compare *Re Oriental Credit Ltd* [1988] Ch 204 at p 208, where the applicant
liquidators had no legal or equitable right, but an order was made under s 37 of the
Supreme Court Act 1981 in aid of a subsisting court order.
2 *Chief Constable of Leicestershire* v *M* [1989] 1 WLR 20 at p 22, per Hoffmann J; *South Carolina Co* v *Assurantie NV* [1987] AC 24 at pp 39–40 per Lord Brandon.

also p 127, below), the court granted an injunction against the wife of the defendant although there was no cause of action against her, justifying the injunction on the grounds that the case should be regarded as an exception to the general rule.[3] In *Deputy Commissioner of Taxation* v *Sharp* (1988) 82 ACTR 1 (Australian Capital Territory), the plaintiff had issued tax assessments to the defendant, and had an existing debt which was not immediately payable. This was held to be sufficient to justify the granting of Mareva relief in that case.

The present position is to be contrasted with the power of the court to grant final relief *quia timet*, and the jurisdiction to make interlocutory orders, including the granting of an injunction, in proceedings seeking such relief. The jurisdiction to grant *quia timet* relief is exercisable even though the plaintiff does not have a right to be paid immediately,[4] or, in the case of suretyship, the creditor has no immediate right to be paid by the surety.[5] Relief is granted *quia timet* when the court refuses to stand aside and allow a position to arise such that when the relevant damage has been suffered or contract broken, the court is powerless to grant effective relief. The jurisdiction of the court to grant *quia timet* relief is not directly applicable to the granting of a Mareva injunction, because *quia timet* relief is granted by the court as final relief, or, in the case of an interlocutory injunction, as ancillary to proceedings in which such final relief is sought. However, it is difficult to see why in principle such a distinction should result in a rigid rule that for the purposes of an application for Mareva relief the plaintiff must have an existing cause of action. This is particularly so when it is borne in mind that a rigid requirement would be likely to give rise to cases of injustice, whilst a flexible approach would leave matters to the discretion of the court. In *Steamship Mutual Underwriting Association (Bermuda) Ltd* v *Thakur Shipping* (above), Sir John Donaldson MR said that in the context of s 37(1) of the Supreme Court Act 1981:

Justice and convenience in this context is not an abstract conception. It predicates that there is a cause of action in respect of which the court may make an order and the court will be unable to enforce its order unless there is security provided by a Mareva injunction.

Section 37(1) is also the statutory provision which gives jurisdiction to the court to grant interlocutory or final injunctive relief *quia timet*. In such cases relief is granted without there being any requirement that the plaintiff has a subsisting entitlement to some final relief independently of the injunction sought *quia timet*. The justification for the present rule in

---

3 See also the remarks of Rogers J in his contribution to Hetherington's *Mareva Injunctions* (1983) at p 29. The general rule was also recognised in *Bank of Queensland Ltd* v *Grant* [1984] 1 NSWLR 409 and *Hortico (Australia)* v *Energy Equipment Co* [1985] 1 NSWLR 545 at p 557.

4 *Flight* v *Cook* (1755) 2 Ves Sen 619, where the plaintiff had a contingent entitlement to be paid out of certain designated assets.

5 *Re Anderson-Berry* [1928] Ch 290 at pp 307–308, per Sargant LJ, referring to *Ascherson* v *Tredegar Dry Dock and Wharf Co* [1909] 2 Ch 401.

Mareva cases rests on the classification of a Mareva injunction as being necessarily only 'interlocutory' and not 'final' relief. If the availability of Mareva relief had been by way of extension of the jurisdiction of the court to grant relief *quia timet*, then the matter could have been approached as one going to the discretion of the court. However, the general rule in England is well established in the case law.

If the plaintiff has not yet acquired a cause of action, but expects soon to do so, the court may, consistently with the rule, grant an injunction which is to take effect only upon the cause of action being acquired.[6]

The enactment of ss 423 to 425 of the Insolvency Act 1986 is likely to be of substantial importance in this area (see pp 132–134). It is considered that the court has jurisdiction under these provisions (see pp 15–16 and 67–69), or alternatively *quia timet* to restrain a disposal of property by an intending transfer or for the purpose of defeating or prejudicing any creditors or persons who may in the future have claims against him. *Locus standi* under the statutory provisions is not restricted to 'victims' who have an existing cause of action. Accordingly, in cases falling within s 423, or where the applicant is applying *quia timet* to prevent a transfer of assets which he fears is intended to be carried out in circumstances falling within the section, the applicant is to be regarded as having a substantive cause of action which is capable of justifying the granting of an injunction.

If Mareva relief is granted in respect of a claim then the practice of the court is to make allowance for interest and costs in calculating the sum in respect of which the injunction is to be granted. Although the plaintiff has no 'cause of action' for interest or costs, these form part of the final relief sought in the action, and, provided that the action can be brought, there is no difficulty in principle in granting Mareva relief by reference to the final relief sought to be obtained in the action. The extent of the allowance to be made is a matter for the discretion of the court. Usually it is comparatively modest.

(2) Good arguable case

It was established early in the emergence of the Mareva jurisdiction that the plaintiff need not show that his case on the merits against the defendant is so strong that he is likely to obtain summary judgment.[7] The test which has been laid down is that the plaintiff must have a 'good arguable case'.[8] In *Rasu Maritima* v *Perusahaan Pertambangan* (at p 661), Lord Denning MR observed that this test was applicable in the context of the granting of leave to serve out of the jurisdiction, and was in 'conformity with' the test as to the granting of injunctions laid down by the House of Lords in *American Cyanamid Co* v *Ethicon Ltd* [1975] AC 396.

---

6 *A* v *B* [1989] 2 Lloyd's Rep 423.
7 *Rasu Maritima SA* v *Perusahaan Pertambangan* [1978] QB 644.
8 *Ninemia Corporation* v *Trave GmbH* (*The 'Niedersachsen'*) [1983] 1 WLR 1412 at pp 1415–1417.

In *Derby & Co Ltd* v *Weldon* [1989] 2 WLR 276, Parker LJ[9] said that the court must not try to resolve conflicts of evidence on affidavit, or to decide difficult questions of law which call for detailed argument and mature consideration.[10] Thus, cases concerning Mareva injunctions fall to be dealt with in accordance with the *approach* laid down in the *American Cyanamid* case, but with the special feature that the test to be satisfied is that of a 'good arguable case' as compared with the test ordinarily applicable to injunction cases, namely that there is a serious question to be tried.

In *Ninemia Maritime Corporation* v *Trave Schiffahrtsgesellschaft GmbH (The 'Niedersachsen')* [1983] 2 Lloyd's Rep 600, at p 605, Mustill J described a good arguable case as 'one which is more than barely capable of serious argument, but not necessarily one which the judge considers would have a better than 50 per cent chance of success'.[11]

This conclusion was reached earlier by Mustill J in relation to the meaning of 'good arguable case' on an application for leave to serve a writ out of jurisdiction under RSC Order 11, r 1, in which there was a dispute on the facts. In *Orri* v *Moundreas* [1981] Com LR 168, Mustill J had said:

The judge is not required to apply the standard of proof which must be attained at the trial . . . Since this standard is one of the balance of probabilities it must follow that the plaintiff does not fail under Order 11 just because he cannot demonstrate a better than even chance that the qualifying condition is satisfied.

This still leaves open the question how far short of an even chance the prospects are allowed to fall before the court should refuse leave under Order 11. Here the words 'strong' and 'good' do become material. It is not enough to show an arguable case, namely, one which a competent advocate can get on its feet. Something markedly better than that is required, even if it cannot be said with confidence that the plaintiff is more likely to be right than wrong.

In *Attock Cement Ltd* v *Romanian Bank* [1989] 1 WLR 1147 the question arose in the context of RSC Order 11, r 1, precisely what standard the plaintiff must satisfy when the disputed facts went to whether the case fell within that rule, and those facts would not arise for re-examination at a trial. The test adopted was that 'the judge must reach a provisional or tentative conclusion that the plaintiff is probably right on it before he allows service to stand. The nettle must be grasped, and that is what I take to be meant by a good arguable case.'[12] In the *Attock Cement* case, the jurisdiction of the court to grant leave to serve out of the jurisdiction was restricted to cases falling within RSC Order 11, r 1. In a matter going to its jurisdiction, the court has to reach at least a provisional view that the

---

9 May LJ agreed with these views at p 282 and Nicholls LJ at p 289.

10 Citing from the speech of Lord Diplock in *American Cyanamid* [1975] AC 396 at pp 407–408. See also *Allied Trust Bank* v *Shukri* (1989) *The Financial Times*, 14 November and *Frogmore Estates plc* v *Berger* (1989) 139 NLJ 1560 at p 1561.

11 This test was applied in relation to a disputed question of law by Bingham J in *Siporex Trade SA* v *Comdel Commodities* [1986] 2 Lloyd's Rep 428 at pp 438–439.

12 Above at p 1197, per Staughton LJ. The analysis of Mustill J in *Ninemia Corporation* [1983] 2 Lloyd's Rep at pp 604–605 was not cited to the court.

case falls within a category for which leave could be granted. In contrast, in the context of Mareva cases this factor does not arise and the all important question is whether, in the circumstances of the case, it is 'just and convenient'[13] to grant the injunction. A requirement that the court must form the provisional view that the plaintiff will probably succeed at trial would be plainly inconsistent with an approach which enables the court to achieve 'its great object viz abstaining from expressing any opinion upon the merits of the case until the hearing'.[14] Nevertheless, the court considering the case will take into account the apparent strength or weakness of the respective cases in order to decide whether the plaintiff's case on the merits is sufficiently strong to reach the threshold,[15] and this can include assessing the apparent plausibility of statements in affidavits.[16] However, the test is not a particularly onerous one.

Although a good arguable case remains the minimum requirement, the judge's view of the merits of the plaintiff's case and his chances of ultimate success is obviously an important factor in the exercise of his discretion. Sufficient of the facts giving rise to the claim should be set out in the affidavit in order to enable the judge to make a realistic assessment of the merits. On an *ex parte* application the plaintiff is expected to place before the court the results of inquiries conducted by him or on his behalf into the claim and into defences or partial defences which may be raised by the defendant, even though the legal burden of proof in relation to those possible defences lies upon the defendant. Thus, for example, in a cargo claim the plaintiff should draw attention in his affidavit to any exclusion clause in the contract of carriage which is liable to be relevant; similarly if s 502 or s 503 of the Merchant Shipping Act 1894 could be relevant then the plaintiff should refer to those statutory provisions in his affidavit. The plaintiff must disclose all defences to the claim which the defendant has already raised, or which are obviously open to him though he need not indulge in speculation.[17]

The fact the plaintiff may have a claim which is unanswerable or virtually incapable of being defended, may be a powerful factor in favour of granting the Mareva injunction though it cannot be decisive in itself. The court may infer the necessary risk of the judgment going unsatisfied from the behaviour of the defendant if he kept promising to honour a bill of exchange but persistently defaulted with implausible excuses, or if the defendant, after a lengthy period of silence, or after admitting liability,

---

13 Section 37(1) of the Supreme Court Act 1981.
14 *Derby & Co Ltd* v *Weldon* [1989] 2 WLR 276 at p 283.
15 In *Allied Trust Bank* v *Shukri* (1989) *The Financial Times*, 14 November, Lloyd LJ reiterated the observations of Parker LJ that the time taken in arguing Mareva case should be ' . . . measured in hours, not days . . .' and that appeals should be 'rare', and in general confined to matters of principle. See also *Frogmore Estates plc* v *Berger* (1989) 139 NLJ 1560 at p 1561 and *Bakarim* v *Victoria P Shipping Co* [1980] 2 Lloyd's Rep 192 at p 198.
16 *Eng Mee Yong* v *Letchumanan* [1980] AC 331 at p 341.
17 See generally on the duty of disclosure: Chapter 8.

raised extremely thin defences once the matter became the subject of litigation.

The plaintiff may have an independent right to proceed on his claim against some other party as well as against the defendant in question. In such circumstances the fact that the plaintiff has such an entitlement is likely to be a material matter to be taken into account by the court in the exercise of its discretion, and will fall to be dealt with in the context of the circumstances of the particular case.[18] Thus for example it may be the case that the plaintiff could fail at trial against the other party but succeed against the defendant in question or it may be that there is reason to doubt whether the other party would satisfy a judgment against him.

A situation which may cause problems is where the plaintiff's claim may be met by a time-bar defence, which in turn may be defeated if the plaintiff obtains leave to prosecute the claim out of time (eg under s 27 of the Arbitration Act 1950). In such circumstances the court should take into account the merits of the plaintiff's application for leave to prosecute the claim out of time together with all the other relevant factors, and grant a Mareva injunction, if appropriate, pending the determination of the plaintiff's application for an extension of time. If that application is successful, and a Mareva injunction would still be appropriate, the court could then extend the order. If the application for an extension of time fails, the plaintiff will almost certainly have to bear the costs of the initial application for the injunction, but his exposure to liability under the cross-undertaking in damages would have been of relatively short duration, and his position would have been adequately safeguarded pending the determination of the application for an extension of time.

(3) Counterclaims and the obtaining of Mareva relief

In most cases where the counterclaim only arises if the claim fails (eg if each party alleges that the other wrongfully terminated a contract) the court will assess the merits of the claim in the usual way. In such circumstances the court may grant a Mareva injunction for the full amount of the claim (eg as in *Avant Petroleum Inc* v *Gatoil Overseas Inc* [1986] 2 Lloyd's Rep 236). Alternatively the court may only be willing to grant a Mareva injunction on terms whereby the plaintiff makes available a fund within the jurisdiction upon which the defendant could execute a judgment should he succeed on the counterclaim. In cases in which both the claim and the counterclaim could succeed, the court has to go through the more complex exercise of assessing the relative merits of each claim, and assessing how much (if anything) the applicant is likely to recover at the end of the day. In such cases the court might decide to limit the amount of the injunction to the sum by which the claim exceeds the counterclaim (or vice versa if the defendant is seeking the injunction). However, there are

---

18 See for example *A* v *C (No 1)* [1981] QB 956 at p 961.

cases where the claim and counterclaim effectively cancel each other out. This was the position in *Barry (JD) Pty Ltd* v *M&E Constructions Pty Ltd* [1978] VR 185 at p 187. One of the factors which the court may take into account is the likelihood that the claim or counterclaim will be extinguished (eg by payment of the sum claimed by a third party).

A further variant arises in cases in which the plaintiff is to obtain summary judgment against the defendant on the claim, leaving the defendant seeking Mareva relief on the counterclaim: eg, if the plaintiff's claim is a dishonoured bill of exchange or a claim for freight and the defendant has a good counterclaim (eg for rescission of the sale contract in respect of which the bill of exchange was given, or for damages for its breach, or a claim for cargo damage). Can the defendant obtain a Mareva injunction on the counterclaim? In such circumstances the position appears to be as follows:

(1) The existence of the plaintiff's claim is an important factor to be taken into account in deciding whether to grant Mareva relief and, if so, upon what terms.

(2) The court may grant an immediate Mareva injunction against the plaintiff restraining him from disposing of the claim (eg by assigning the proceeds of the claim). The granting of a Mareva injunction preventing the plaintiff from disposing of the claim would not be inconsistent with the principle that the plaintiff's claim is one on which he is entitled to payment free of any claim of set off or stay of execution. Thus it is clear that if the plaintiff had already obtained judgment on the claim, the defendant could obtain Mareva relief in respect of the plaintiff dealing with the proceeds of the judgment: *Montecchi* v *Shimco (UK)* [1979] 1 WLR 1180 at pp 1183–1184; *Intraco Ltd* v *Notis Shipping Corporation* [1981] 2 Lloyd's Rep 256 at p 258. This is because an injunction restraining the plaintiff from disposing of the fruits of his judgment is not the same as taking action (eg by staying execution) which will prevent the plaintiff from obtaining the cash. Accordingly, if the plaintiff has not yet obtained judgment, an injunction restraining him from disposing of the claim is not the same as preventing him from prosecuting his claim to judgment and obtaining cash under that judgment.

(3) As a matter of discretion, the court may not be prepared to grant the defendant Mareva relief in respect of the counterclaim unless he undertakes to secure the plaintiff's claims together with interest and costs (eg by providing a bank guarantee or making a payment into court).

(4) If the counterclaim exceeds the plaintiff's claim, then the court may grant the defendant Mareva relief over the plaintiff's claim together with further Mareva relief over other assets of the plaintiff, in respect of the amount by which the counterclaim exceeds the plaintiff's claim. Again the granting of such relief may be made conditional upon the plaintiff's claim being secured.

In circumstances in which the plaintiff succeeds in obtaining a Mareva injunction on a claim and there is a counterclaim, the question may arise as to whether the plaintiff can obtain security for costs in respect of the defendant's counterclaim in addition to the Mareva injunction. If the Mareva injunction has succeeded in trapping substantial assets of the defendant within the jurisdiction then no order will be made in favour of the plaintiff for security for costs to be provided on the counterclaim. This may also be the position if the Mareva injunction has meanwhile been varied with the defendant providing the plaintiff with partial security for the claim: *Hitachi Shipbuilding & Engineering Co Ltd* v *Viafel Compania Naviera SA* [1981] 2 Lloyd's Rep 498 at pp 508–509.

(4) A real risk that a judgment or award may go unsatisfied

The early authorities in which the principles governing the exercise of the Mareva jurisdiction were first laid down tended to suggest that the plaintiff would have to satisfy the court that the defendant would remove his assets from the jurisdiction *for the purpose* of defeating any judgment which the plaintiff might obtain against him. This was interpreted in at least one case as meaning that the plaintiff must show 'nefarious intent'.[19] Of course, this would be an extremely difficult test to satisfy, for however unreliable a defendant may have been in the past, it is nevertheless far from easy to prove what objective there might be behind the dealings with assets in the future.

In *Ninemia Maritime Corporation* v *Trave GmbH* (*The 'Niedersachsen'*) [1983] 1 WLR 1412, (CA) (affirming Mustill J, reported at [1983] 2 Lloyd's Rep 600 at pp 601–602), Mustill J at first instance set out a series of citations ([1983] 2 Lloyd's Rep at pp 605–606) from Mareva cases[20] directed to what risk the plaintiff had to show, and invited the Court of Appeal, if the case should go further, to give guidance. In the Court of Appeal, the applicable test was formulated as being [1983] 1 WLR at p 1422:

. . . whether, on the assumption that the plaintiffs have shown 'a good arguable case', the court concludes, on the whole of the evidence then before it, that the refusal of a Mareva injunction would involve a real risk that a judgment or award in favour of the plaintiffs would remain unsatisfied.

It is now clear that in order to justify the granting of Mareva relief, there is no requirement that a plaintiff must show that the defendant

---

19 *Home Insurance Co* v *Administration Asigurarilor de Stat* (unreported) referred to by Kerr LJ at [1983] 1 WLR at p 1422.
20 *Mareva Compania Naviera SA* v *International Bulkcarriers Ltd* [1975] 2 Lloyd's Rep 509; *Rasu Maritima SA* v *Perusahaan* [1978] QB 644; *Iraqi Ministry of Defence* v *Arcepey Shipping* [1981] QB 65; *Third Chandris Shipping Corporation* v *Unimarine SA* [1979] QB 645 at p 669 (per Lord Denning MR) and p 672 (per Lawton LJ); *Montecchi* v *Shimco (UK) Ltd* [1979] 1 WLR 1180 at pp 1183–1184; *Barclay-Johnson* v *Yuill* [1980] 1 WLR 1259; *Rahman* v *Abu-Taha* [1980] 1 WLR 1268; *Z Ltd* v *A-Z and AA-LL* [1982] QB 558 at p 571 (Lord Denning MR) and pp 585–586 (per Kerr LJ).

intends to deal with his assets with the *objective* of ensuring that any judgment will not be met. This approach has also been adopted in other common law jurisdictions.[21] In Ontario, In *Chitel* v *Rothbart* (1982) 39 OR (2d) 513 at pp 532–533,[22] the Court of Appeal referring to the judgment of Lord Denning MR in *Third Chandris Shipping Corporation* v *Unimarine* [1979] QB 645 at p 669, said:

Turning finally to item (iv) of Lord Denning's guidelines—the risk of removal of these assets before judgment—once again the material must be persuasive to the court. The applicant must persuade the court by his material that the defendant is removing or there is a real risk that he is about to remove his assets from the jurisdiction to avoid the possibility of a judgment, or that the defendant is otherwise dissipating or disposing of his assets, in a manner clearly distinct from his usual or ordinary course of business or living, so as to render the possibility of future tracing of the assets remote, if not impossible in fact or in law.

This formulation of the test must now be read in the context of the Mareva jurisdiction having developed to encompass dissipation of assets whether inside or outside of the jurisdiction. Removal of assets from the jurisdiction merely represents a possible way in which assets may be dealt with so as to give rise to the risk that a judgment may go unsatisfied.

Consistently with this approach, in *Felixstowe Dock & Railway Co* v *United States Lines Inc* [1989] QB 360, the defendant was an insolvent company incorporated in the United States which was the subject of proceedings in New York under Chapter 11 of the United States Federal Bankruptcy Code. If the English assets of the defendant were repatriated to New York, the consequence would have been to prejudice the English claimants (who intended to apply for summary judgment on their claims) because they would have been unlikely to obtain even *pro rata* payment with the creditors in the United States. Although the purpose of the intended transfer was to advance the commercial interests of the defendants, nevertheless Mareva relief was granted because, in the circumstances of the case, the balance of convenience strongly favoured the assets remaining in England, where in due course they could be the subject of ancillary winding-up proceedings as a result of which they would be fairly distributed among the relevant creditors. Hirst J declined to treat the existence of the Chapter 11 proceedings in New York and the wish of the defendants to make the English assets available to be dealt with under the provisions of Chapter 11, as a paramount or overriding factor, inconsistent with the granting of Mareva relief.

In *Derby & Co Ltd* v *Weldon* [1989] 2 WLR 276, the submission was made that in regard to Mareva relief in respect of assets situated outside of

---

21 Eg in New South Wales: see *Hortico (Australia) Pty Ltd* v *Energy Equipment Co (Australia) Pty Ltd* (1985) 1 NSWLR 545 at pp 557-558; *Ausbro Ferex Pty Ltd* v *Mare* (1986) 4 NSWLR 419 at pp 423-424.
22 See also *Di Menza* v *Richardson Greenshields of Canada Ltd* (1988) 65 OR (2d) 225 and *Price* v *CIBC* (1987) 19 CPC (2d) 13 (New Brunswick Court of Appeal).

the jurisdiction there was a requirement that the plaintiff produce evidence of 'previous malpractice or nefarious intent'. However, this was not accepted by the court, even in the context of the wide relief (described by May LJ as 'draconian') sought in that case.

It is not every risk of a judgment being unsatisfied which can justify Mareva relief. Thus for example:

(1) A company may be faced with insolvency if it loses the case. However, in the meantime it is entitled to carry on its business,[23] and it would be contrary to principle for Mareva relief to be granted for the purpose either of preventing it from doing so, or preserving some assets for the plaintiff in case he succeeds at trial.[24]

(2) An individual is entitled to pay his ordinary[25] living expenses. Mareva relief will not be granted so as to prevent him using his assets to pay such expenses.[26]

(3) A defendant may have some pre-existing legal or moral obligation to a third party which it is appropriated for him to satisfy (eg repayment of a loan). Mareva relief should not be granted for the purpose of preventing the defendant from honouring the obligation even though in consequence the risk of an eventual judgment going unsatisfied is substantially increased.[27]

It may be that the defendant would in the ordinary course expect to receive payment of a debt out of the jurisdiction from his debtor within the jurisdiction. The fact that such remittance would not be *designed* to prejudice enforcement in due course of a future judgment, does not preclude the granting of Mareva relief. Nor does the fact that such a remittance would be an ordinary commercial transaction confer immunity. In such circumstances, Mareva relief can be granted, and the plaintiff would be prudent[28] to seek an order which expressly restrains the defendant from taking steps to obtain or accept payment of the debt, except payment into a designated account.

The plaintiff must adduce 'solid evidence' to support his assertion that there is a real risk of the judgment or award going unsatisfied.[29] Since each case depends on its own facts it is impossible to lay down any general

---

23 *Normid Housing Association Ltd* v *Ralphs and Mansell (No 2)* [1989] 1 Lloyd's Rep 275; *Avant Petroleum Inc* v *Gatoil Overseas Inc* [1986] 2 Lloyd's Rep 236; *Iraqi Ministry of Defence* v *Arcepey Shipping* [1981] QB 65; *Hortico (Australia) Pty Ltd* v *Energy Equipment Co (Australia) Pty Ltd* (1985) 1 NSWLR 545 at p 558.

24 *K/S A/S Admiral Shipping* v *Portlink Ferries* [1984] 2 Lloyd's Rep 166.

25 Ie 'ordinary, recurrent expenses in maintaining the subject of the injunction in the style of life to which he is reasonably accustomed': *TDK Tape Distributor* v *Videochoice Ltd* [1986] 1 WLR 141 at p 146.

26 *Law Society* v *Shanks* [1988] FLR 504; *PCW (Underwriting Agencies) Ltd* v *Dixon* [1983] 2 Lloyd's Rep 197.

27 *Iraqi Ministry of Defence* v *Arcepey Shipping* (above).

28 In view of *Bank Mellat* v *Kazmi* [1989] QB 541; see generally pp 11–14.

29 *Ninemia Corporation* v *Trave GmbH (The 'Niedersachsen')* [1983] 2 Lloyd's Rep at pp 606–607 per Mustill J.

guidelines as to how and when this evidential burden will be satisfied. However, some of the factors which may be relevant are the following.[30]

(1) The nature of the assets which are the proposed subject of the injunction, and the ease or difficulty with which they could be disposed of or dissipated. The plaintiff may find it easier to establish the risk of dissipation of a bank account, or of moveable chattels, than the risk of the defendant disposing of real estate, eg his house or office. Nevertheless, in appropriate cases Mareva injunctions can be, and have been, granted where the defendant's only known asset within the jurisdiction is his house (for example, if he has put it up for sale and has evinced an intention to go and live abroad).

(2) The nature and financial standing of the defendant's business: see Lord Denning's remarks about certain types of offshore company in *Third Chandris Shipping Corporation* v *Unimarine* [1979] QB 645, and Lawton LJ, ibid, at p 672 and *Siporex Trade SA* v *Comdel Commodities Ltd* [1986] 2 Lloyd's Rep at p 439. Contrast, however, *The 'Niedersachsen'* [1983] 1 WLR 1412: even a 'one-ship' company incorporated in Panama or Liberia may be a subsidiary of a wealthy company incorporated elsewhere, and would be likely to honour its debts.

(3) The length of the defendant's establishment in business. Stronger evidence of potential dissipation will be needed where the defendant is a long-established company with a reasonable market reputation than where little or nothing is known or can be ascertained about it.

(4) The domicile or residence of the defendant. At one time, Mareva injunctions were only granted to prevent foreign defendants from removing their assets from the jurisdiction to defeat a judgment or arbitration award. While the jurisdiction has widened to include domestic defendants, the court will be less ready to infer that a defendant who is based in England, and has a home or established business here, will remove or dissipate his assets. On the other hand, if the defendant company, though English, is controlled by an offshore company of the kind described by Lord Denning in *Third Chandris Shipping Corporation* v *Unimarine*, the inference may be drawn more readily that there is a real risk that a judgment or an award may go unsatisfied.

(5) If the defendant is a foreign company, partnership, or trader, the country in which it has been registered or has its main business address, and the availability or non-availability of any machinery

---

30 In *O'Regan and Others* v *Iambic Productions* (1989) 139 NLJ 1378 at p 1379, Sir Peter Pain approved these factors as a 'very useful check list . . . as to the sort of factors about which the court should have information before it decides to grant an application for a Mareva injunction.'

for reciprocal enforcement of English judgments or arbitration awards in that country. If such machinery does exist, the length of time which it would take to implement it may be an important factor. See *Montecchi* v *Shimco (UK) Ltd* [1979] 1 WLR 1180, per Bridge LJ at pp 1183–1184; *Third Chandris Shipping Corporation* v *Unimarine* (above) per Lawton LJ at p 672; and *The 'Niedersachsen'* (above).

(6) The defendant's past or existing credit record. A history of default in honouring other debts may be a powerful factor in the plaintiff's favour—on the other hand, persistent default in honouring debts, if it occurs in a period shortly before the plaintiff commences his action, may signify nothing more than the fact that the defendant has fallen upon hard times and has cash-flow difficulties, or is about to become insolvent. The possibility of insolvency, as such, is usually a neutral factor: it may even weigh against the grant of Mareva relief, on the grounds that an injunction would be oppressive because it might deprive the defendant of a last opportunity to put his business affairs in good order again. The fact that a Mareva injunction has been granted over the defendant's assets may well discourage a bank or another company from lending him money or otherwise coming to his aid.

(7) Any expressed intention on the part of the defendant as to his future dealings with his English assets, or assets outside the jurisdiction.[31]

(8) Connections between a defendant company and other companies which have defaulted on arbitration awards or judgments. If the defendant company is the subsidiary of a foreign company which has allowed other subsidiaries to default on awards or judgments or go into liquidation owing large sums of money to trade creditors, this may be a powerful factor in favour of granting an injunction.

(9) The defendant's behaviour in response to the plaintiff's claims: a pattern of evasiveness, or unwillingness to participate in the litigation or arbitration, or raising thin defences after admitting liability, or total silence, may be factors which assist the plaintiff.

Mere unsupported statements to the effect that the deponent to an affidavit fears that assets may be dissipated do not comply with the requirements of RSC Order 41, r 5(2) and can be of no evidential weight.[32]

---

31 These words have been added to take into account the fact that Mareva relief can be granted in respect of assets abroad as well as assets within the jurisdiction.

32 *Third Chandris Shipping Corporation* v *Unimarine SA* [1979] QB 645 at p 672, per Lawton LJ; *Ninemia Corporation* v *Trave GmbH (The 'Niedersachsen')* [1983] 1 WLR 1412 at p 1419 ('bare assertions . . . are clearly not enough'); *O'Regan and Others* v *Iambic Productions*, above, per Sir Peter Pain: 'unsupported statements and expressions of fear, carry very little, if any, weight. The court needs to act on objective facts.'

(5) Assets inside or outside of the jurisdiction

The original basis upon which Mareva relief was granted was to restrain a foreigner from removing his assets from the jurisdiction, and there was a requirement placed on the plaintiff of producing clear evidence[33] of assets within the jurisdiction which were liable to be removed. However in *Third Chandris Shipping Corporation* v *Unimarine SA* [1979] QB 645, it was held that this requirement had been put too high, and that it could suffice even to have evidence of a bank account in overdraft, situated within the jurisdiction. It was thought that the Mareva jurisdiction was only available to prevent threatened dissipation of assets within the jurisdiction.[34] But it is now clearly established that Mareva relief can be granted whether before or after judgment in relation to assets of the defendant wherever situated.[35] This presupposes that the defendant can be served with the originating process, if necessary under the provision of RSC Order 11, r 1(1) or (2). In the case of proceedings on the merits which are not to take place in England, but which are within the ambit of s 25(1) of the Civil Jurisdiction and Judgments Act 1982, Mareva relief can still be granted under that section, which applies to assets wherever situated.[36]

The jurisdiction to grant Mareva relief is an *in personam* jurisdiction against the defendant. However, it is well established that the granting of an injunction may have an impact on third parties. Special consideration needs to be given to this aspect of the matter when the court considers granting relief over assets abroad, and the practice has been adopted of inserting a proviso in the order which is intended to circumscribe its effect on third parties who are outside of the jurisdiction. The proviso adopted in *Derby & Co Ltd* v *Weldon (Nos 3 and 4)* (above) read as follows:

PROVIDED THAT, insofar as this order purports to have any extraterritorial effect, no person shall be affected thereby or concerned with the terms thereof until it shall be declared enforceable or be enforced by a foreign court and then it shall only effect them to the extent of such declaration or enforcement UNLESS they are:
  (a) a person to whom this order is addressed or an officer or an agent appointed by a power of attorney of such a person or
  (b) persons who are subject to the jurisdiction of this court and
     (i) have been given written notice of this order at their residence or place of business within the jurisdiction, and
     (ii) are able to prevent acts or omissions outside the jurisdiction of this court which assist in the breach of the terms of this order."[36A]

---

33 *MBPXL Corporation* v *International Banking Corporation Ltd* Court of Appeal (Civil Division) Transcript No 411 of 1975 (28 August 1975).
34 *Ashtiani* v *Kashi* [1987] QB 888; *Intraco Ltd* v *Notis* [1981] Lloyd's Rep 256.
35 *Babanaft Co SA* v *Bassatne* [1989] 2 WLR 232; *Republic of Haiti* v *Duvalier* [1989] 2 WLR 261; *Derby & Co Ltd* v *Weldon* [1989] 2 WLR 276; *Derby & Co Ltd* v *Weldon (Nos 3 and 4)* [1989] 2 WLR 412. See also: 'The Territorial Reach of Mareva Injunctions' by Lawrence Collins, (1989) 105 LQR 262.
36 *Republic of Haiti* v *Duvalier*, above.
36A See also *Securities and Investments Board* v *Pantell SA* [1989] 3 WLR 698.

The position of third parties in relation to extra-territorial Mareva relief is considered at p 175, below.

Although Neill LJ in *Derby & Co Ltd v Weldon (Nos 3 and 4)* envisaged that cases in which Mareva relief would be granted in respect of foreign assets would be unusual, the Court of Appeal has declined to impose any restrictions on the availability of the relief, eg that the plaintiff has to have a case of a special strength or that the defendant has to be shown to be intent on transferring and hiding assets so as to defeat enforcement of a possible future judgment.

In cases before judgment, the defendant may be ordered to disclose information, including documents, relating to the whereabouts and details of his assets by way of ancillary order made in aid of the Mareva relief. After judgment, disclosure of such information may also be ordered under the provisions of RSC Order 48.[37] Ordinarily Mareva relief and disclosure orders in relation to assets abroad will only be made provided that the plaintiff gives an undertaking to the court not to pursue any foreign proceedings to enforce the Mareva relief without the leave of the court, and an undertaking not to use any information obtained by virtue of the disclosure order in proceedings abroad without the leave of the court. These undertakings are required so that the court can retain sufficient control of matters so as to prevent the plaintiff acting oppressively by forcing the defendant 'to face litigation, brought by financially more powerful parties, in overseas courts throughout the world.'[38]

The granting of Mareva relief over assets abroad is likely to involve a substantial expenditure of costs for the parties and may lead to protracted interlocutory proceedings in England or abroad. It is also liable to deflect the efforts of the parties from the resolution of the substantive merits of the litigation. Furthermore it is undesirable that litigation should be made more complex and onerous than is necessary for doing justice between the parties, and the defendant to a disputed claim is not be treated on the same basis as if he were a judgment debtor. These considerations are particularly important when the court is considering the granting of Mareva relief over assets abroad.

If it appears that the assets within the jurisdiction are likely to suffice for the purposes of enforcement of an eventual judgment then the court will not as a matter of discretion grant relief over assets abroad.[39] If, on the other hand, the assets within the jurisdiction may well not suffice, then the court will consider granting extra-territorial relief.

If Mareva relief is granted, restricted to assets within the jurisdiction then the injunction will apply to any assets which are subsequently

---

37 *Interpool* v *Galani* [1988] QB 738.
38 *Derby & Co Ltd* v *Weldon* [1989] 2 WLR 276 at p 285 per Nicholls LJ.
39 *Derby & Co Ltd* v *Weldon (Nos 3 and 4)* [1989] 2 WLR 412 at p 422, per Lord Donaldson MR.

acquired by the defendant within the jurisdiction or brought into the jurisdiction by the defendant.[40]

In cases in which the plaintiff makes a proprietary claim to an asset outside the jurisdiction, the court may grant interlocutory relief, independently of the Mareva jurisdiction, in respect of assets abroad. Thus in an
action in which the plaintiff is seeking to trace property which in equity
belongs to him, the courts are anxious 'to see that the stable door is locked
before the horse has gone.'[41] In the context of such claims, the courts have
granted interlocutory relief by injunction or the appointment of a receiver
over assets abroad in support of the plaintiff's claim against the defendant
in respect of the asset itself. With the recognition that Mareva relief can be
granted over assets abroad, it is no longer necessary for a court considering an application for interlocutory relief over assets abroad to consider in
detail the strength of the plaintiff's claim on the merits to proprietary
relief.[42] Nevertheless, where it is clear that the plaintiff has an apparently
well-founded proprietary claim this will be an important factor in favour
of the granting of an injunction or the appointment of a receiver over
assets abroad.

40 *TDK Tape Distributor (UK) Ltd* v *Videochoice Ltd* [1986] 1 WLR 141 at p 145.
41 *Mediterranea Raffineria Siciliana Petroli Spa* v *Mabanaft GmbH* Court of Appeal (Civil Div-
    ision) Transcript No 816 of 1978 (1 December 1978) per Templeman LJ; *A* v *C* [1981]
    QB 956 at pp 958–959; *Bankers Trust* v *Shapira* [1980] 1 WLR 1274 at pp 1280–1281.
42 *Republic of Haiti* v *Duvalier*, above.

Chapter 11

Mareva relief against assets in the name of or claimed by a third party

(1) General principles

The usual rule is that an injunction will only be granted against a party to an action. As Lord Eldon LC said in *Iveson v Harris* (1802) 7 Ves 251 'you cannot have an injunction except against a party to the suit'.[1] In consequence of this rule an injunction should always be addressed to a party or an intended party to an action, who, if not joined as a party is about to be joined. Furthermore, the injunction should be addressed to the named party 'by himself his servants or agents or otherwise howsoever', or equivalent wording which makes it clear that the injunction does not enjoin the party's servants or agents, but has effect against the named party and restrains him from doing the prohibited acts, whether by his own act or by that of others acting as his servants or agents.[2] This rule of practice has been applied to the drafting Mareva relief.[3]

However, occasionally the courts have granted injunctions against persons who were not named as parties to an action. Thus for example, an injunction was granted against a person threatening to aid and abet a contempt of court,[4] and similarly, an injunction was granted against trustees of a will who held a legacy for a man who had absconded from the jurisdiction and who had appointed an agent to receive the legacy.[5] In a decision of the Supreme Court of the Capital Territory of Australia Mareva relief was granted against the defendants to an action and also against a third party who had received a transfer of land from the defendants but was a person who appeared to have no substantial assets or income of his own.[6] The injunction was granted directly against the third party in that case enjoining him 'whether as trustee or agent for the defendants or

---

1 See also *Brydges v Brydges* [1909] P 187; *Royal Bank of Canada v Canstar Sports Group Inc* [1989] 1 WWR 662 (Manitoba Court of Appeal); *Elliott v Klinger* [1967] 1 WLR 1165.
2 *Marengo v Daily Sketch* [1948] 1 All ER 406 at p 407.
3 *Abella v Anderson* [1987] 2 Qd R 1 (Supreme Court of Queensland).
4 *Hubbard v Woodfield* (1913) 57 SJ 729, see also Halsbury's Laws of England (4th edition) Vol 24 para 1045.
5 *Bullus v Bullus* (1910) 102 LT 399. Kerr on *Injunctions* (6th ed) at p 614.
6 *Basiric v Topic* (1981) 37 ACTR 1.

otherwise'. These cases are to be regarded as exceptional to the general rule. In *SCF Finance Co* v *Masri* [1985] 1 WLR 876, *ex parte* relief was granted against a defendant's accounts at three named London banks. Subsequently the plaintiffs became aware of certain matters which showed that the defendant might be using the bank accounts of his wife for his business, and as a result she was added as a defendant and the injunction was extended so as to include accounts held by or on behalf of the husband in the name of the wife. This procedure was therefore in accordance with the general rule stated above.

Thus the appropriate practice in Mareva cases is for the plaintiff to seek an injunction against the named defendant to restrain the defendant, whether by himself, his servants or agents, or otherwise from dealing with such assets as may be specified in the order. If certain assets are thought to be in the name of a nominee then those assets should be specifically designated in the order. If the name of the nominee is known, then the order should be expressed to restrain 'the defendant whether by himself his servants or agents or by [the named nominee] or otherwise howsoever from'. If it is believed that the defendant may exercise control of the assets through a nominee but the name of the nominee is not known then the plaintiff may wish to seek an order which applies to specified assets 'held by or on behalf of the defendant jointly with any other persons or by nominees or otherwise howsoever'. This practice was adopted by the Commercial Court in *SCF* v *Masri* [1985] 1 WLR 876.[7]

(2) Mareva relief against an alleged nominee

The question arose in *SCF* v *Masri* whether it was right in principle for the court to grant or continue Mareva relief in respect of assets which were in the name of and claimed by a third party, in that case the wife of the defendant to the substantive claim. The husband had used a cheque to complete a substantial exchange transaction, which was a cheque that was drawn on a bank account in the name of his wife and had been pre-signed in blank by his wife in her maiden name. On the application by the wife to discharge the injunction which had been granted in respect of bank accounts in her name, a preliminary point was taken by her to the effect that when there is an issue as to whether or not particular assets truly belong to the defendant to the substantive claim or to the third party, the court should always discharge or vary the Mareva relief so as to enable the third party to deal with the assets in question. The Court of Appeal rejected the contention and summarised the applicable principles as follows (at p 884):

(i) Where a plaintiff invites the court to include within the scope of a Mareva injunction assets which appear on their face to belong to a third party, the court should not accede to the invitation without good reason for supposing that the assets are in truth the assets of the defendants.

---

7 At p 878 where the relevant extract from the order of Webster J is set out.

(ii) Where the defendant asserts that the assets belong to a third party, the court is not obliged to accept that assertion without inquiry, but may do so depending on the circumstances. The same applies where it is the third party who makes the assertion, on an application to intervene.

(iii) In deciding whether to accept the assertion of a defendant or a third party, without further inquiry, the court will be guided by what is just and convenient, not only between the plaintiff and the defendant, but also between the plaintiff, the defendant and the third party.

(iv) Where the court decides not to accept the assertion without further inquiry, it may order an issue to be tried between the plaintiff and the third party in advance of the main action, or it may order that the issue await the outcome of the main action, again depending in each case on what is just and convenient.

The Court of Appeal also held that the judge had been 'plainly right' to hold that he could not decide the matter without further inquiry.[8]

In England it is an established principle that Mareva relief will only be granted in relation to an accrued cause of action against the defendant.[9] In Australia the question whether the availability of Mareva relief was so limited was raised but not decided by the Court of Appeal of New South Wales in *Riley McKay Pty Ltd* v *McKay* [1982] 1 NSWLR 264 at p 277. However, the Supreme Court of Australian Capital Territory has decided that Mareva relief is available at least when there is an existing debt owed by the defendant, albeit a debt which is not payable until some time in the future.[10] The granting of Mareva relief against an alleged nominee who is said to hold or control assets for the defendant to the substantive claim but against whom there is no substantive claim might be viewed as an infringement of this principle. Thus in *Vereker* v *Choi* [1985] 4 NSWLR 277, the Supreme Court of New South Wales granted Mareva relief against a wife on the basis that the facts in question were such that it was appropriate to grant Mareva relief as 'an exception to the general rule' namely that 'it was necessary for an applicant for a Mareva injunction to establish the existence of [an existing] cause of action' [1985] 4 NSWLR.[11]

However, it is thought that the position is not to be so analysed. The cause of action lies against the defendant to the substantive proceedings. Mareva relief can properly be granted enjoining that defendant from dealing with his assets. A question has arisen as to whether particular assets are properly to be regarded as assets of the defendant to the substantive claim. The existence of that question and the need for its resolution before it can be unequivocally stated that the assets in question fall within the

---

8 For subsequent proceedings in the action see *SCF* v *Masri (No 2) and (No 3)* [1987] QB 1002 and 1028.

9 *Siporex Trade SA* v *Comdel Commodities* [1986] 2 Lloyd's Rep 428; *Steamship Mutual Underwriting Association (Bermuda)* v *Thakur Shipping* [1986] 2 Lloyd's Rep 439. This is a legacy of the decision of the House of Lords in *Siskina* v *Distos SA* [1979] AC 210. See also pp 110–112, above.

10 *DCT* v *Sharp* (1988) 82 ACTR 1.

11 At p 283 citing the judge's own previous decision in *Bank of Queensland Ltd* v *Grant* [1984] 1 NSWLR 409.

Mareva relief granted as against the defendant to the substantive claim makes it inappropriate to limit the injunction to the defendant to the substantive claims. Thus, first, until the matter is resolved, third parties such as banks will be left in the position that they do not know in practice what acts are prohibited by the injunction. Secondly, the defendant to the substantive claim and the claimant to the asset would be in the same position. Thirdly, whether the assets in question are to be maintained intact should not be left to the interpretation which may be placed on the injunction by the defendant and third parties as to its scope and effect in the circumstances in question. Fourthly, if the assets are to be maintained in fact under an injunction it is appropriate that a third party claimant to the assets should have the benefit of an undertaking in damages and should be made a party to an issue to be resolved in relation to the ownership of the assets in question.

These considerations show that the injunction granted against the third party is in effect ancillary relief granted by the court in aid of and as part of the Mareva relief granted against the defendant to the substantive claim. In effect, it is relief granted in respect of the substantive claim against that defendant, albeit that the injunction has had to be directed to the third party, because of the rule of practice that an injunction only enjoins the person or persons to whom it is directed. Accordingly the granting of Mareva relief against a third party pending resolution of an issue as to the scope and effect of Mareva relief granted against the defendant to the substantive claim, is to be distinguished from the category of case in which an applicant is seeking Mareva relief without any existing cause of action at all, and, perhaps, without even an existing chose in action against the prospective respondent or respondents to the relief.

(3) The principles as applied in practice

In *SCF* v *Masri*, the Court of Appeal did not seek to elucidate upon the general principle that Mareva relief should not be granted in relation to assets which appear on their face to belong to a third party 'without good reason' for supposing that the assets ' are in truth assets of the defendants'. In *Coxton Pty Ltd* v *Milne*,[12] a decision of the Court of Appeal of New South Wales, Hope JA in a judgment with which Glass JA and Priestly J agreed, specified a number of conditions which, if met, would make it appropriate to grant Mareva relief against a third party, in respect of whom no principal relief was claimed as follows:

Without attempting to define or to limit the extent of the exception, the necessary circumstances will exist when [1] the affairs of a defendant sued by a creditor for

---

12 Unreported, 20 December 1985, referred to in *Sterling* v *NIM* (1986) 66 ALR 657 at p 673; *Winter* v *Marac Australia* (1986) 6 NSWLR 11 at p 12; and *DCT* v *Winter* (1988) 19 ATR 827 at pp 829–830.

an alleged debt and of the third party against whom the injunction is sought are intermingled, [2] the alleged debtor and the disposition of his assets are effectively controlled, *de jure* or *de facto*, by the third party, [3] the debtor's assets will be insufficient to meet the debt, [4] the creditor, although having no vested or accrued cause of action against the third party, may become entitled to have recourse to the third party or his assets to meet his debt, and [5] there is a danger that the third party will send his assets abroad or otherwise dispose of them.

(The numbers in square brackets have been inserted into the text for the purpose of identifying separately each of the five factual requirements.)

This statement provides a description of circumstances which if they exist would be sufficient to justify the granting of Mareva relief, without laying down that the existence of those circumstances or any of them is a necessary pre-condition. In relation to requirement [4] this was further explained by Hope JA in *Winter* v *Marac Australia* (above) at pp 12–13: it is not sufficient for the plaintiff to satisfy the court that the defendant to the substantive claim could persuade the third party to accede to any request by him in relation to the assets in question. Thus: 'It must be shown that the person against whom judgment may be obtained has some right in respect of or control over or other access direct or indirect, to the relevant assets so that they or the proceeds of their sale or other disposition could be required to be applied in discharge of the judgment debt'.

In relation to the position of a wife, it is clearly not a sufficient basis for the granting of Mareva relief that a substantive claim is made against the husband, and the wife owns property which she could be persuaded by the husband to use to satisfy a judgment against him.[13] Facts must be proved establishing that the assets in the hands of the wife could be *required* to be applied directly or indirectly in satisfaction of the judgment debt.[14]

Requirement [2] stated by Hope JA includes a situation in which the defendant to the substantive claim is a company which is controlled by a third party either *de jure* or *de facto*. However, it is considered that it would be sufficient to show that the defendant to the substantive claim has caused assets to be held by or vested in a third party which, or who, is effectively acting as a banker for the defendant[15] or as a nominee for the defendant.[16] Alternatively it will be sufficient to show that although the defendant to the substantive claim has no legal or equitable right to the assets in question he has some right in respect of, control over, or other right of access to the assets.[17] Thus for example if a defendant has set up a

---

13 *Allied Arab Bank* v *Hajjas* (1988) *The Times*, 18 January; *Winter* v *Marac Australia* (above) at pp 12–13.

14 These can include facts which enable a claim to be made against the wife under statutory provisions to set aside one or more prior transfers of assets to the wife by her husband: see pp 132–134, below.

15 As did the wife in *SCR* v *Masri* (above): see *SCF* v *Masri (No 3)* [1987] QB 1028.

16 This appears to have been the position in relation to the eighth and ninth respondents in *Jackson* v *NIM* (1986) 66 ALR 657 at p 673. This point was not affected by the subsequent appeal to the Court of Appeal and then the High Court of Australia sub nom *Jackson* v *Sterling Industries* 69 ALR 92, and 71 ALR 457.

17 *Winter* v *Marac Australia*.

network of trusts and companies to hold assets over which he has control, and he has apparently done this for the purpose of making himself judg-ment-proof, then this would be an appropriate case for the granting of Mareva relief against the relevant third parties.

In *Re A Company* [1985] BCLC 333,[18] the plaintiffs (which were com-panies in liquidation), brought an action against the defendant alleging deceit and for breach of trust and fiduciary duty. The evidence disclosed 'an elaborate and most ingenious scheme brought into operation at the instance of the . . . defendant, whereby his personal assets were organised in such a way that they were held by foreign and English corporations and trusts in a manner that effectively conceals his true beneficial interest in English assets'. There was strong evidence to the effect that the defendant had deliberately set up this network of companies and trusts so as to defeat the defendant's creditors, and those with claims against him. In these circumstances the Court of Appeal upheld orders which had been made requiring disclosure of information of 'an unusually extensive and detailed character' and imposing injunctions restraining him from dispos-ing of his shares in companies or his rights under the trusts, and from causing the companies or the trusts to dispose of those assets, and did so on the ground that the court would use its powers 'to pierce the corporate veil if it is necessary to achieve justice irrespective of the legal efficacy of the corporate structure under consideration'. At that time the courts were restricting Mareva relief to assets within the jurisdiction, and accordingly the relief granted by the court was directed to restraining dealings with assets located within the jurisdiction, albeit that, the assets were held by a foreign company or trust. Also at that time s 423 of the Insolvency Act 1986 had not been enacted. These considerations indicate that relief could be granted in even wider terms in a comparable case. As for the possibility that third parties might be entitled to, or claim, an interest in the relevant assets, Cumming-Bruce LJ said:

If there are other genuine interests vested in third parties beneficially, the first defendant can state the facts in his answer to the interrogatories, and the notice of the injunctions can be served on the parties alleged to be beneficially interested, and their objection can be made to the court and its validity upheld. When there is such massive evidence of nominees, and puppet directors dancing to the first defendant's tune, it is for him to state on oath his belief, if he holds it, that one or more persons implicated in the silken skein of his spider's web has a genuine bene-ficial interest.

Similarly in *DCT* v *Winter* (1987) 19 ATR 827 (Supreme Court of New South Wales), summary judgment had been obtained by the Deputy Commissioner of Taxation against the same Mr Winter as featured in *Winter* v *Marac Australia*. His sister, mother, and companies which he con-trolled were co-defendants, and it appeared well arguable that Mr Winter

---

18 Also reported as *X Bank* v *G* (1985) *The Times*, 13 April. See also *Bank Bumiputra Malaysia Bhd* v *Lorrain Osman* [1985] 2 MLJ 236 (Malaysia).

had used the various co-defendants to hold assets so that they would not be available to pay his debts. In these circumstances Mareva relief was continued against the co-defendants in contemplation of bankruptcy proceedings being brought against Mr Winter.

In contrast in *Allied Arab Bank Ltd* v *Hajjas* (1988) *The Times*, 18 January, the wife of one of the defendants, who was being sued on his personal guarantee by the plaintiff bank for a substantial sum, had two bank accounts against which the defendant husband had authority to draw. Hirst J refused to direct an issue as to whether money in those two accounts was owned by the husband, and his decision was upheld by the Court of Appeal. Thus the existence of material on which an issue could be raised as to whether the accounts belonged beneficially to the husband was insufficient to justify extending the Mareva injunction which had been granted to include the bank accounts in the name of the wife. There had to be 'good reason to suppose' that the bank accounts were owned beneficially by the husband before such a course could be taken. This formulation was taken from principle (i) (quoted at p 126 above) stated by the Court of Appeal in *SCF* v *Masri* [1985] 1 WLR 876. In that case the evidence before the court had been such that there was 'good reason to suppose' that the wife's accounts belonged beneficially to the husband, albeit that further evidence might have shown that this was not the case.

In *Uttamchandai* v *Central Bank of India* (1989) 139 NLJ 222, the defendant bank refused payment of a credit balance on the basis that there were strong grounds for believing that another customer of the bank had an equitable interest in the account, and that that other customer owed substantial sums to the bank, which sought to justify the non-payment on the grounds that it could exercise a right of set off. The Court of Appeal held that the defence of equitable set off was not available in circumstances where it was it was not clear beyond argument that the third party was entitled to the money due on the account. However, it is considered that in such circumstances, provided that there is good reason to believe that the third party was so entitled, Mareva relief can be granted over the proceeds of the account. As with bills of exchange and letters of credit (see pp 23–26, above), the fact that there is no set off available does not preclude the granting of relief in respect of the proceeds.

When the facts are such that Mareva relief should be granted against assets in the name of third parties (eg a wife of a defendant), the appropriate procedure is that if an issue is to be directed to be tried as between the plaintiff and the third party, this will be dealt with in the existing action in which the Mareva relief has been granted and not in separate proceedings,[19] and it will ordinarily be appropriate for the court to direct pleadings in the issue and to give directions for discovery to take place.

---

19 *McIntyre* v *Pettit* (1988) 90 FLR 196 (Supreme Court of New South Wales), implementing the procedure envisaged in *SCF* v *Masri* (above).

(4) Claims involving setting aside under statutory provisions prior transfers of assets

Section 172 of the Law of Property Act 1925 re-enacted a provision in para 31 of Part II of Sched 3 of the Law of Property (Amendment) Act 1924, and replaced in different terms ss 1 and 5 contained in the statute of Elizabeth I (13 Eliz I, c5). That section made provision that every conveyance of property made 'with intent to defraud creditors' should be voidable at the instance of 'any person thereby prejudiced'. That s 172 has been repealed[20] and transactions defrauding creditors are now dealt with by s 423 of the Insolvency Act 1986. In the case of individuals who have been adjudged bankrupt, provisions for dealing with transactions at an undervalue and transactions entered into by way of preference are set out in ss 339 and 340 of the Insolvency Act 1986, and the corresponding provisions for a company subject to an administration order or which has gone into liquidation are set out in ss 238 and 239 of the Act. In cases falling within their ambit, ss 339 and 340 enable the trustee of the bankrupt's estate, and ss 238 and 239 enable the liquidator or administrator of the company to apply to the court for relief to reverse the effect of transactions entered into at an undervalue or preferences. In contrast ss 423, 424 and 425 of the Act (set out in Appendix 1 below):

(1) apply to transactions entered into at an undervalue for the purpose of 'putting assets beyond the reach of a person who is making, or may at some time make, a claim against him' or 'of otherwise prejudicing the interests of such a person in relation to the claim which he is making, or may make';

(2) confer a direct cause of action on a plaintiff regardless of whether or not he has obtained judgment, and regardless of whether, in the case of an individual, the defendant has been adjudged bankrupt, and in the case of a company, the defendant has been put into liquidation or made the subject of an administration order;

(3) allow transactions to be impeached which have been entered into before proceedings were commenced by the plaintiff on his claim against the defendant;

(4) allow transactions to be impeached which have been entered into by the defendant before the plaintiff acquired a cause of action against the defendant provided that, as a result of the transaction, the plaintiff either has been prejudiced by it or may be prejudiced by it, and thus has become, in the words of the statute, 'a victim'.

It would appear to be the case that a plaintiff can seek relief based on the sections even though the transaction sought to be impugned was not entered into for the purpose of defeating enforcement of his particular claim or potential claim, provided that in consequence of the transaction he is a victim. The sections enable direct claims to be made against third

---

20 By s 235(3) and Sched 10, Part IV of the Insolvency Act 1985.

parties who have benefited from the impugned transaction, and an application made for relief by a victim is treated as made on behalf of every victim of the transaction. A consequence of this is that the relief sought is not restricted to the prejudice suffered by the applicant and accordingly Mareva relief would ordinarily be granted by reference to the cumulative prejudice caused or liable to be caused by the impugned transaction to the victims.

For the purpose of obtaining immediate Mareva relief against a third party it is thought that it would not ordinarily be sufficient for a plaintiff to contend that if his substantive claim succeeds against a defendant, he will then be in a position to have the defendant adjudged bankrupt, and to cause relief to be sought by the trustee in bankruptcy against the third party under ss 339 or 340 of the Insolvency Act 1986 in respect of a prior transaction as a result of which the third party has obtained benefit. Thus in *Bank of Queensland* v *Grant* (above), the Supreme Court of New South Wales declined to grant Mareva relief against an estranged wife when this was sought on the basis that the plaintiff could, in due course, seek to make the husband bankrupt, and the trustee in bankruptcy might be able to set aside a maintenance agreement under which the husband had transferred to the wife his interest in the jointly owned matrimonial home. On the other hand the position would be different in a case in which the plaintiff claimed to impeach a prior transaction under ss 423, 424 and 425 of the Insolvency Act 1986 on the grounds that the transaction was entered into by the husband for the purpose of putting assets beyond the reach of a person 'who is making, or may at some time make, a claim against him'. Those sections give a direct cause of action to the plaintiff against the wife which is available in the circumstances set out above, regardless of whether the plaintiff has obtained judgment against the husband or has made the husband bankrupt.

Accordingly, in *DCT* v *Ahern* [1986] 2 Qd R 342 (Supreme Court of Queensland), summary judgment had been obtained against the first defendant, and the plaintiff sought Mareva relief against the third and fourth defendants which were companies incorporated and resident outside the jurisdiction of the court. These companies were alleged to have assets within the jurisdiction, but otherwise had no connection with the jurisdiction. The plaintiffs originally sought leave to serve a writ out of the jurisdiction on these companies in respect of the Mareva relief, but without alleging a cause of action directly against either company. This was refused on the grounds that, under the Queensland rules of court, leave could only be granted for a claim based on a cause of action and since the claim for Mareva relief was not an assertion of a cause of action, then, following *Siskina* v *Distos SA* [1979] AC 210,[21] no leave could be granted.

---

21 For the current position in England, see pp 134–138, below.

However, the plaintiff also put forward a claim based on s 228 of the Property Law 1974 of Queensland which provided:

Save as provided in this section, every alienation of property . . . with intent to defraud creditors shall be voidable at the instance of any person thereby prejudiced.
(ie the same wording as s 172(1) of the Law of Property Act 1925.)

The court granted leave to serve out of the jurisdiction in respect of a writ against the companies seeking relief setting aside prior transfers of the relevant assets from the first defendant, based on s 228, and granted Mareva relief, in respect of that claim, against the two companies. Similarly in *FCT* v *Goldspink* (1985) 17 ATR 290 at pp 297–298 (Supreme Court of New South Wales), the court granted Mareva relief against the wife of a judgment debtor in contemplation of proceedings seeking relief setting aside prior transfers by the husband to the wife which were said to be voidable dispositions under the relevant statutory provisions.

Accordingly once the plaintiff is in a position to commence proceedings against a third party to set aside a transfer, Mareva relief can be granted against the third party[22] in support of the cause of action conferred by statute. Anton Piller relief can also be granted in these circumstances[23] against the transferor and the third party.

If the defendant is already subject to Mareva relief and wishes to have the injunction varied so as to enable a transfer to proceed, the court is not obliged to refuse the application simply because there is the possibility that once the plaintiff has obtained judgment he will take steps to have the transfer impeached on the grounds that it was carried out at an under-value or constituted a preference falling within the statutory provisions.[24] Whether the intended transfer is to be allowed is a matter of discretion for the court.

(5) Service out of the jurisdiction of proceedings against a third party in respect of assets in the name of and held by the third party

For the purposes of service out of the jurisdiction, a distinction needs to be drawn between four categories of case as follows.
  (i) Cases in which a direct cause of action is asserted in England against the third party, eg in respect of assets within the jurisdiction which are the subject of a claim to relief under ss 423, 424 and 425 of the Insolvency Act 1986, or in respect of which the plaintiff asserts a tracing claim.
 (ii) Cases in which a direct cause of action is asserted against the third party where proceedings on the merits have been or are to be com-

---

22 Also see *Reiser (Robert) and Co Inc* v *Nadorfe Food Processing Equipment Ltd* (1977) 81 DLR (3rd) 278 referring to *Toronto Carpet Co* v *Wright* (1912) 3 DLR 725.
23 *Cook Industries* v *Galliher* [1979] Ch 439.
24 *Iraqi Ministry of Defence* v *Arcepey Shipping Co (The 'Angel Bell')* [1981] QB 65 at p 72.

menced otherwise than in England, and the application falls within s 25 of the Civil Jurisdiction and Judgments Act 1982.

(iii) Cases in which a cause of action is asserted only against a defendant to a substantive claim on the merits in England and the involvement of the third party arises as ancillary relief against the third party ancillary to Mareva relief against the defendant to the substantive claim.

(iv) Cases in which a cause of action is asserted only against a defendant to a substantive claim on the merits otherwise than in England, who is subject to interim relief granted against that defendant under the provisions of s 25, and the involvement of the third party arises as ancillary relief against the third party in respect of Mareva relief granted against the defendant to the substantive claim.

Category (i)

The plaintiff is asserting a substantive claim against the third party which the plaintiff may proceed with provided that he can satisfy one of the requirements of RSC Order 11, r 1(1), or can bring within the ambit of RSC Order 11, r 1(2). If the claim is in respect of assets within the jurisdiction then in principle the substantive claim will fall within RSC Order 11, r 1(1)(*b*); the injunction is claimed as part of the substantive relief consequential upon a cause of action and thus satisfies the test which was appropriate under the former RSC Order 11, r 1(1)(i) considered by the House of Lords in *Siskina* v *Distos SA* [1979] AC 210.[25]

Category (ii)

If the third party cannot be served within the jurisdiction, the plaintiff will either have to show a case falling within RSC Order 11, r 1(2)[26] or obtain leave for service of proceedings out of the jurisdiction under RSC Order 11, r 1(1). In *Siskina* v *Distos SA* [1979] AC 210, the House of Lords decided that a bare claim to Mareva relief did not amount to the assertion of a substantive cause of action for an injunction and therefore did not fall within the ambit of RSC Order 11, r 1(1)(i), as it then was. Since then the rules have been redrafted to take into account the coming into force of the Civil Jurisdiction and Judgments Act 1982, which in s 25 confers jurisdiction on the High Court to grant interim relief where 'proceedings have been or are to be commenced in a contracting state other than the United Kingdom'. The wording of RSC Order 11, r 1(1)(i) has now been transposed to RSC Order 11, r 1(1)(*b*), but otherwise remains the same.

In *Republic of Haiti* v *Duvalier* (above), the plaintiffs argued that s 25 conferred by statute a cause of action for interlocutory relief and that therefore a claim falling within s 25 came within RSC Order 11, r 1(1)(*b*). This submission was the subject of a concession by counsel who argued

---

25 Also see *DCT* v *Ahern* [1986] 2 Qd R 342 (Supreme Court of Queensland).
26 *Republic of Haiti* v *Duvalier* [1989] 2 WLR 261.

the case before Leggatt J, which was withdrawn before the Court of Appeal. That court did not decide the point because it did not arise in view of their decision that the case came within RSC Order 11, r 1(2). Although the subject of a concession before him, Leggatt J said in his judgment at first instance in *Republic of Haiti* v *Duvalier* (unreported (22 June 1988)) that leave to serve out of the jurisdiction was available in respect of the application for interim relief under s 25 because the section gave what the judge described as 'a cause of action for interim relief'. In *X* v *Y* [1989] 3 WLR 910,[27] it was held that an application under s 25 did come within RSC Order 11, r 1(1)(*b*) on the grounds that the wording now had to be construed in the context of a redrafted RSC Order 11, r 1 which was intended to be in effect together with that section. To give RSC Order 11, r 1(1)(*b*) the limited scope applicable to the former RSC Order 11, r 1(i) would mean that there would be frustration of the bringing of proceedings under s 25 when the intended respondent to the application was a foreigner who had to be served out of the jurisdiction and could not be served under the provisions of RSC Order 11, r 1(2). In these circumstances the court gave RSC Order 11, r 1(1)(*b*) a purposive construction so that applications under s 25, although only seeking interim relief, came within its ambit.

Category (iii)

In these circumstances there is a bare claim to Mareva relief against the third party which is ancillary to Mareva relief granted against the defendant to the substantive claim. Two paragraphs of RSC Order 11, r 1 fall for particular consideration, namely RSC Order 11, r 1(1)(*b*) and (*c*).

One possible view in relation to (*b*) is that since there is no claim to substantive relief against the third party, the case cannot be brought within (*b*) for the reasons given by the House of Lords in *Siskina* v *Distos SA* [1979] AC 210. This view is supported by a decision of the Supreme Court of Queensland[28] in relation to Order 11, r 1(4) of the Rules of the Supreme Court in Queensland which reads:

1. An originating proceeding, or notice thereof, . . . may be served out of the jurisdiction in any of the following cases, that is to say: . . .
    (4) When any act . . . sought to be restrained . . . is to be done . . . within the jurisdiction.

The court held, applying the *Siskina* decision, that a bare claim for Mareva relief against a third party did not come within the rule. On this view, the decision in *X* v *Y* (above) does not assist because that was a category (ii) case.

However, once it is accepted that Mareva relief comes with the term 'an

---

27 Mr Anthony Diamond QC sitting as a deputy judge of the High Court.
28 *DCT* v *Ahern* [1986] 2 Qd R 342.

injunction' in RSC Order 11, r 1(1)(*b*),[29] then on the basis of the wording of the rule it would appear to include within its ambit a bare claim to Mareva relief in relation to conduct within the jurisdiction, where that Mareva relief is granted in relation to a substantive claim on the merits otherwise properly before the court. The view to the contrary would unnecessarily limit the availability of effective Mareva relief in relation to assets within the jurisdiction, for a substantive claim properly before the court.

As for RSC Order 11, r 1(1)(*c*) this is appropriate to cover cases where the plaintiff does not as such have a cause of action against the intended foreign defendant, but that defendant must be joined so as to ensure that the substantive claim against the primary defendant can be properly adjudicated upon and determined, eg where the intended foreign defendant has given a good equitable assignment to the plaintiff of a chose in action against the primary defendant. It might be said that in order to come within the scope of the rule the intended defendant must be a person who is a 'necessary or proper party' to the substantive claim on the merits and that the intended foreign defendant is only a 'necessary or proper party' to the Mareva relief. However, that argument restricts the scope of the words 'the claim' to covering the prosecution of the claim up until judgment, and excludes steps taken to obtain satisfaction of the claim. Thus if for example 'the claim' on the merits is for damages, interest and costs on certain grounds, the plaintiff seeks not merely a judicial determination that he is entitled to that relief, but also the granting and enforcement of that relief in 'the action begun by the writ'. That is all part of his 'claim'. So analysed, category (iii) can be brought within RSC Order 11, r 1(1)(*c*).

If the third party is domiciled in a contracting state as defined in s 1 of the Civil Jurisdiction and Judgments Act 1982, then the question arises whether the claim for Mareva relief comes within RSC Order 11, r 1(2). It is thought that it will do so on the grounds that the Mareva relief constitutes provisional measures being granted by a court which is seized with jurisdiction on the substantial merits of the case. That court necessarily has jurisdiction to grant 'provisional measures' (see Art 24 of the Convention which is drafted on this premise). If the Mareva relief is being granted in contemplation of possible enforcement of a judgment in England against assets situated here, then the case can also be brought within Art 16(5) of the Convention.

Category (iv)

In the case of a third party domiciled in a contracting state, this category appears to come within Art 24 of the Convention since the Mareva relief sought against the third party is part of the 'provisional measures' envisaged by that Article. RSC Order 11, r 1(2) is capable of applying to a bare claim for Mareva relief and the wording of s 25 of the Civil Jurisdiction

---

29 This necessarily follows from the decision in *X* v *Y* (above).

and Judgments Act 1982 is sufficient to encompass a claim for interim relief addressed to the third party. Again if the Mareva relief is sought in contemplation of enforcement of a judgment in England, the case might also be brought within Art 16(5) of the Convention.

In the case of third parties domiciled elsewhere, in principle RSC Order 11, r 1(1)(*b*) and (*c*) are capable of being applied. Paragraph (*c*) would fall to be applied in the context of the third party being a proper or necessary party to Mareva relief granted against the defendant to the substantive claim, who can be served with proceedings out of the jurisdiction if this is necessary (eg under RSC Order 11, r 1(1)(*b*) or RSC Order 11, r 1(2)).

(6) Cases in which the third party does not claim to own the assets outright

It may be the case that the third party does not claim that he owns the assets outright, only that he has an existing right to possess or to sell them: for example because he has a charge or lien over them. Mortgagees and debenture-holders are among the most common types of third party affected by Mareva injunctions falling within this category—frequently they are also banks. A Mareva injunction will not normally be allowed to interfere with the exercise by a mortgagee of his powers of sale.[30] Similarly, if the assets are clearly subject to a pre-existing lien or other charge, the court will usually exclude them from the terms of the Mareva injunction, or else the third party will be granted a specific variation enabling him to exercise his rights in respect of those assets.

---

30 For an example of a case where an injunction specifically aimed at preventing the sale of two mortgaged vessels was discharged, see *The 'Arietta' and 'Julia'* [1985] 2 Lloyd's Rep 50.

Chapter 12

Appointment of a receiver

(1) General principles

The jurisdiction of the court to appoint a receiver is contained in s 37(1) of the Supreme Court Act 1989 which provides that:

(1) The High Court may by order (whether interlocutory or final) grant an injunction or appoint a receiver in all cases in which it appears to the court to be just and convenient to do so.

The section also provides the court with jurisdiction to grant relief by way of injunction, including Mareva relief. Section 37(1) is the successor to s 45 of the Supreme Court of Judicature (Consolidation) Act 1925, which in turn replaced s 25(8) of the Judicature Act 1873.

Despite the apparent breadth of the statutory jurisdiction it has been said that its exercise is governed by the principles which were applied by the Court of Chancery prior to the coming into force of the Judicature Act of 1873,[1] although it has also been said that 'to some extent' the statutory jurisdiction had enlarged the powers of the court.[2] However, it is now clear that with the emergence of the Mareva jurisdiction, the power of the court to appoint a receiver *pre-judgment* by interlocutory order is exercisable whenever it is 'right or just' to do so,[3] and in particular that power is exercisable even when the plaintiff does not claim any proprietary interest in the relevant assets nor any legal or equitable entitlement to have the

---

1 *North London Railway Co* v *Great Northern Railway Co* (1883) 11 QBD 30; *Holmes* v *Millage* [1893] 1 QB 551 at p 557; *Anglo-Italian Bank* v *Davies* (1878) 9 ChD 275; *Manchester & Liverpool District Banking Co* v *Parkinson* (1888) 22 QBD 173; *Harris* v *Beauchamp* [1894] 1 QB 801.
2 *Cummins* v *Perkins* [1899] 1 Ch 16 at p 20, per Chitty LJ.
3 *Derby & Co Ltd* v *Weldon (Nos 3 and 4)* [1989] 2 WLR 412. See also *Ballabil Holdings Pty Ltd* v *Hospital Products* [1985] 1 NSWLR 155, in which a receiver was appointed over assets outside the jurisdiction of the courts of New South Wales, and *Ka Wah International Merchant Finance Ltd* v *Asean Resources* 8 IPR 241 in which the High Court in Hong Kong appointed a receiver over shares in a Singapore company with the intent that the receiver would use the voting rights so as to secure the underlying assets.

assets dealt with in a particular way.[4] Thus it is sufficient that the plaintiff has a claim against the defendant, even though that claim is unrelated to the assets sought to be made subject to the appointment of a receiver, provided that in all the circumstances of the cases it is 'right or just' to appoint a receiver. These circumstances could be, for example, that the defendant may deal with the assets so as to frustrate enforcement of an eventual judgment against him. In such circumstances the appointment of a receiver may be made either in support of a Mareva injunction or independently of the granting of Mareva relief. That it is not necessary for the plaintiff to claim some interest in or right over or in respect of the relevant assets, in order to justify the appointment of a receiver has been put beyond doubt by the decision of the Court of Appeal in *Derby & Co Ltd* v *Weldon (Nos 3 and 4)* (above) in which the Court of Appeal upheld (with certain variations) an order made by Sir Nicholas Browne-Wilkinson V-C appointing a receiver over a corporate defendant's assets wherever situated and requiring disclosure of information about the relevant assets. The receivership applied to assets situated outside of the jurisdiction. The Court of Appeal varied the order made by the Vice-Chancellor by deleting a proviso inserted by him to the effect that the defendants to the action should only become bound to vest the foreign assets in the receiver if the order was recognised by the Luxembourg courts. It was contemplated that such recognition would be accorded to the order in Luxembourg by virtue of Art 25 of the European Judgments Convention. The Court of Appeal held that it was inappropriate to insert such a proviso in relation to the effect of the order on the parties to the action.[5] This is to be contrasted with the position of third parties either in relation to Mareva relief granted in respect of assets abroad,[6] or on the appointment of a receiver by the court over assets abroad.[7] Thus when the court appoints a receiver over assets abroad, it does not automatically put him in possession of foreign assets.[8] To do this the court recognises that something more must be done so as to put the receiver into possession under the law of the country where the assets are situated. Accordingly the court will not hold a third party (whether or not resident in this country) liable for contempt in refusing to deliver up foreign assets to the receiver or taking steps to obtain those assets for himself. In contrast, parties to the action in which the receiver has been appointed would be liable for contempt in such circumstances.

---

4 As in *Cummins* v *Perkins* [1899] 1 Ch 16 (right to be paid out of the separate estate of a married woman).
5 *Langford* v *Langford* (1835) 5 LJ Ch 60.
6 *Derby & Co Ltd* v *Weldon (Nos 3 & 4)* (above) at p 426; *Babanaft International Co SA* v *Bassatne* [1989] 2 WLR 232; *Republic of Haiti* v *Duvalier* [1989] 2 WLR 261; *Derby & Co Ltd* v *Weldon (No 1)* [1989] 2 WLR 276 at p 285.
7 *Re Maudsley Sons & Field* [1900] 1 Ch 602.
8 *Re Huinac Copper Mines Limited* [1910] WN 218; *Re Maudsley Sons & Field* (above) at pp 611–612.

The power of the court to appoint a receiver *pre-judgment* when the plaintiff does not claim any interest in the relevant assets or any right over or in respect of them has been exercised in a series of landlord and tenant cases.[9] In *Parker* v *Camden London Borough Council* [1986] Ch 162 the question arose as to whether a receiver should be appointed to manage certain housing estates when the local Council was not providing various services, and the Court of Appeal only declined to appoint a receiver on discretionary grounds, namely that the power of management of the estates had been vested in the Council by statute.[10] Sir John Donaldson MR expressly rejected the contention that the statutory power to appoint a receiver was only to be exercised in accordance with 'the pre-Judicature Act practices of the Court of Chancery or any other court' [1986] Ch 162 at p 173. This line of authority has been criticised on the ground that the plaintiff in each case had 'no conceivable claim' to the rents payable to the landlord and no interest in them, and that therefore there was no basis for the appointment of a receiver.[11] But it is thought that the criticism is misplaced, and that consistently with the recognition of the existence of the Mareva jurisdiction[12] it is now the law that the plaintiff does not have to show a claim to an interest in the rent or right over, or in respect of, the rent in order to justify the appointment of a receiver under s 37(1) of the Supreme Court Act 1981.

The appointment of a receiver is a discretionary remedy as is the granting of an interlocutory injunction. If the circumstances are such that it would not be just and convenient to grant a remedy by way of injunction, then equally a receiver will not be appointed. Thus, for example, Mareva relief pre-judgment will not be granted in a form which has the effect of preventing the defendant from carrying out ordinary transactions in the course of business,[13] and similarly a receiver will not be appointed so as to prevent such transactions being done.

---

9 *Hart* v *Emelkirk Ltd* [1983] 1 WLR 1289; *Daiches* v *Bluelake Investments Ltd* (1986) 51 P&CR 51; *Blawdziewicz* v *Diadon* [1988] 2 EG 52. See also the appointment by the master in *Clayhope Properties* v *Evans* [1986] 1 WLR 1223 at p 1225.

10 Applying the principle that it is improper for the court to appoint its own officer to exercise powers of management and to discharge duties which have been respectively vested in or imposed upon the Council by Statute. See also *Gardner* v *London Chatham and Dover Railway Co (No 1)* (1867) LR 2 Ch App 201.

11 Kerr on *Receivers* (17th edition) at pp 76–77.

12 That the same principles must be applied to the appointment of receivers as to the granting of injunctions was expressly recognised in *Holmes* v *Millage* [1893] 1 QB 551 at p 557. Both are now dealt with in the same terms in the single statutory sub-section, and are types of relief which are closely related. The appointment of a receiver is liable to involve greater interference with the status quo, and more expense and complexity than the granting of an injunction, and this falls to be taken into account on the exercise of the discretion.

13 *Normid Housing Association Ltd* v *Ralphs and Mansell (No 2)* [1989] 2 Lloyd's Rep 274; *Avant Petroleum Inc* v *Gatoil Overseas Inc* [1986] 2 Lloyd's Rep 236; *Iraqi Ministry of Defence* v *Arcepey Shipping (The 'Angel Bell')* [1981] QB 65.

(2) Appointment of a receiver by way of equitable execution

The court has jurisdiction under s 37(1) of the Supreme Court Act 1981 to appoint a receiver post-judgment in aid of enforcement or execution of the judgment.[14] An order granted in these circumstances is referred to as the appointment of a receiver by way of 'equitable execution', although it would be more appropriate to refer to the procedure as being the granting of equitable relief in order to enable enforcement of the judgment to proceed.[15] The general principle is that the appointment of a receiver will only be made if the plaintiff shows that it would be right or just to make the order, and it is thought that with the emergence of the Mareva jurisdiction the court will adopt a more flexible approach than previously,[16] so as to achieve a just result taking into account all the circumstances of the case including practical convenience,[17] avoiding unnecessary delay, cost or expense,[18] and allowing the plaintiff to adopt a procedure which is likely to be effective in obtaining the fruits of a judgment. Thus there is an inconsistency between the broad, flexible approach now taken in the *pre-judgment* case law, and the more restrictive *post-judgment* case law, which is now ripe for reconsideration by the courts. If the circumstances are appropriate for the appointment of a receiver pre-judgment then it cannot be said that by obtaining judgment the plaintiff has thereby disqualified himself from inviting the court to exercise its discretion under s 37(1) of the Supreme Court Act 1981 to appoint or to continue the appointment of a receiver.

Accordingly, the appointment of a receiver by way of equitable execution is not restricted to cases in which there is no other way to obtain execution. On the other hand, if execution can be obtained without difficulty or risk of prejudice to the judgment creditor by another route then the court would decline to appoint a receiver in the exercise of its discretion.[19] The fact that the judgment debtor is liable to dissipate his assets is plainly a material factor to be taken into account in exercising the discretion in favour of the appointment of a receiver rather than leaving the judgment creditor to pursue another route which might not be effective. Thus in *Goldschmidt* v *Oberrheinische Metalwerke* [1906] 1 KB 373, the judgment debtors had no place of business in England, and their own assets in England consisted of money which was due or would become due from purchasers of goods from them. The judgment creditors did not know the

---

14 *Maclaine Watson & Co* v *ITC* [1988] Ch 1 at pp 17–21, per Millett J. The appointment is ordinarily made by a master under RSC Order 51, r 2.
15 *Re Shephard, Atkins* v *Shephard* (1889) 43 ChD 131; *Morgan* v *Hart* [1914] 2 KB 183; *Re A Company* [1915] 1 Ch 520; *Norburn* v *Norburn* [1894] 1 QB 448.
16 Under which practical convenience provided no basis for the exercise of the jurisdiction: *Re Shephard, Atkins* v *Shephard* (above); *Harris* v *Beauchamp Brothers* (above) at pp 806–807.
17 *Levermore* v *Levermore* [1979] 1 WLR 1277 is an example of this approach.
18 An inquiry can be directed on the likely costs before the court decides whether or not to make the appointment, under RSC Order 51, r 1.
19 *Manchester and Liverpool District Banking Co* v *Parkinson* (1888) 22 QBD 173.

amount of the debts due or accruing due and were not in a position to take garnishee proceedings because they could not depose to an affidavit in a form required by the rules of court, as a result of the lack of information available to them. The Court of Appeal appointed a receiver on the grounds that there were 'special circumstances . . . rendering it just or convenient to make the order' and in particular, first, because the appointment was 'a more convenient mode of procuring satisfaction of the judgment than garnishee proceedings' and secondly, on the separate ground of preventing 'someone from making away with property liable to execution'.

The court in dealing with an application to appoint a receiver will take into consideration the nature of the asset over which the appointment is sought. In particular, if the position is that the appointment of a receiver would not result in the receiver having any legal right or entitlement to convert or to seek to convert the asset into money with which the judgment can be satisfied, then no appointment will be made. Thus a receiver was not appointed over a patent which had not been exploited,[20] because there was no property for the receiver to receive. In *Maclaine Watson Ltd* v *International Tin Council* [1989] Ch 253 affirming [1988] Ch 1 (the House of Lords upheld the decision of the Court of Appeal on the same grounds: [1989] 3 WLR 969, no receiver was appointed because the rights which the judgment creditors claimed existed as between the judgment debtor, the International Tin Council, and its members which included sovereign states were not justiciable before the courts, because such rights (if any) were based upon or were to be derived from international treaty obligations which had not been the subject of an enactment so as to incorporate them into English law; the rights arose, if at all, by reason of the express words of an international treaty or by implication into that treaty. The contention that a receiver could only be appointed over an asset which was an equitable interest which, if it had been a legal interest could have been reached by execution in law, was rejected by Millett J [1988] Ch 1 and not renewed on appeal.

(3) Effect of appointment of a receiver over assets in England

A receiver is an officer of the court.[21] He is not an agent or trustee for the party on whose application he has been appointed or any of the other parties.[22] The receiver does not have any title or interest in the assets by vir-

---

20 *Edwards & Co* v *Picard* [1909] 2 KB 903; 'a case where there was a hindrance which even equity could not remove', per Millett J in *Maclaine Watson & Co* v *ITC* [1988] Ch 1 at p 26.
21 *Evans* v *Clayhope Properties* [1988] 1 WLR 358, at p 362.
22 *Boehm* v *Goodall* [1911] 1 Ch 155.

tue of his appointment.[23] On the other hand he may as a result of his appointment acquire a chose in action which he can enforce personally, eg if he becomes the holder of a bill of exchange.[24] The order appointing the receiver has effect as an injunction[25] restraining the parties to the action from receiving any part of the property, and commonly[26] the order expressly provides for any party who has possession of a relevant asset to surrender that possession to the receiver. If the order makes provision for the appointment of the receiver upon the provision of security then ordinarily the order will be construed as providing for the appointment to take effect only once the security has been provided.[27] The appointment of a receiver over assets does not create any charge or lien over the assets.[28] Interference by a party to the action with the performance by the receiver of his duties under the order appointing him will constitute a contempt of court. Furthermore, if a third party with knowledge of the order and without the leave of the court takes steps which will interfere with the receiver getting in the assets, or which constitute an interference with the possession by the receiver of the assets, this will constitute a contempt.[29]

(4) Effect of appointment over assets abroad

If an order is made appointing a receiver over assets abroad on the grounds that the defendant may otherwise dissipate the assets, then the order will ordinarily contain an express provision directed to the defendant to give up possession of the assets to the receiver or his agent. The court has power under s 37(1) of the Supreme Court Act 1981 to order the defendant to deliver up specified chattels to the receiver or to provide the receiver with particular funds or their proceeds which are held by the defendant. The court will however not make an order the effect of which is

---

23 *Vine* v *Raleigh* (1883) 24 ChD 238 at p 243, per Chitty J; *Re Muirhead, ex parte Muirhead* (1876) 2 ChD 22; *Re Sacker, ex parte Sacker* (1888) 22 QBD 179; *Stevens* v *Hutchinson* [1953] Ch 299; *Levermore* v *Levermore* [1979] 1 WLR 1277 at p 1281; *Clayhope Properties Ltd* v *Evans* [1986] 1 WLR 1223 at pp 1227–1228.
24 *Ex parte Harris* (1876) 2 Ch D 423 as explained in *Re Sacker* (above).
25 *Re Sartoris's Estate* [1892] 1 Ch 11; *Tyrell* v *Painton* [1895] 1 QB 202; *Re Marquis of Anglesey* [1903] 2 Ch 727.
26 When the ground upon which the appointment is made is that the assets are in jeopardy of being dissipated, there will be an express direction in the order requiring the defendant to give up possession of the assets to the officer of the court. In contrast, if the appointment is simply to safeguard the interim profits to be made from land in a mortgagee's action for foreclosure or sale, the court might in the exercise of its discretion allow the mortgagor to stay in possession subject to his paying rent to the receiver: *Pratchett* v *Drew* [1924] 1 Ch 280 at p 286.
27 *Ridout* v *Fowler* [1904] 1 Ch 658 at p 662.
28 *Re Potts* [1893] 1 QB 648; *Stevens* v *Hutchinson* (above) at p 305; *Re Whiteheart, ex parte Trustee in Bankruptcy* v *John A Clark & Co* (1971) 116 SJ 75; *Clayhope Properties* v *Evans* [1986] 1 WLR 1223 at p 1229.
29 *Ames* v *Birkenhead Docks Trustees* (1855) 20 Beav 332; *Royal Bank of Canada* v *Canstar Sports Group Inc* [1989] 1 WWR 662 (Manitoba Court of Appeal).

to require the defendant to provide the plaintiff with security for his claim.[30]

An order may be made for the appointment of a receiver over assets abroad even though the defendant is a foreigner with no presence in England, provided that the defendant can be served with proceedings out of the jurisdiction.[31] That order will be effective upon the parties to the action, although in relation to third parties they will not be affected unless and until the order is enforced by the courts of the place where the assets are situated (see p 140, above).

(5) Appointment of a receiver over a chose in action

The court may authorise a receiver to take proceedings in respect of a chose in action over which he has been appointed as receiver.[32] Ordinarily such proceedings will be brought in the name of the party to the action who has title to the chose in action.[33] The court may order the party to assign to the receiver the chose in action so that the receiver can take proceedings in his own name in respect of the chose in action. Thus, for example, if a judgment debtor has a right to an indemnity against a third party, or at least may have such a right, then the court may appoint a receiver over that entitlement and authorise him to make a call or claim on the indemnity in the name of and on behalf of the judgment debtor.[34] Thus jurisdiction to appoint a receiver before trial could provide an important interlocutory remedy in relation to the preservation of 'disappearing assets'. Thus, for example, a receiver could be appointed for the purpose of selling perishable assets and receiving the proceeds of sale. Similarly, a receiver could protect time limits in relation to a defendant's potential claims against third parties.[35]

(6) Costs of a receiver

A receiver is an officer of the court and not an agent for the parties, and accordingly in the absence of a special arrangement with one or more of the parties, his only entitlement is to look to the court to see that he is paid out of the assets which are the subject of the appointment. If those assets

---

30 *Jackson* v *Sterling Industries* 71 ALR 457 (The High Court of Australia). On this point *Lister & Co* v *Stubbs* (1890) 45 ChD 1 is still to be regarded as good law. Otherwise the court would be in effect threatening the defendant with being in contempt of court unless he provided security for the plaintiff's claim.

31 *Duder* v *Amsterdamsch Trustees Kantoor* [1902] 2 Ch 132; *Republic of Haiti* v *Duvalier* [1989] 2 WLR 261 at p 273 applying *In Re Liddell's Settlement Trusts* [1936] Ch 365 at p 374.

32 *Levermore* v *Levermore* [1979] 1 WLR 1277 at p 1283.

33 *Re Sacker* (1888) 22 QBD 179.

34 *Bourne* v *Colodense Ltd* [1985] ICR 291; *Maclaine Watson & Co* v *ITC* [1988] Ch 1 at p 17 per Millett J (affirmed at [1989] Ch 253) (CA) and [1989] 3 WLR 969 (HL).

35 Eg by giving notice of claim to an insurer—see the facts in *The 'Vainqueur José'* [1979] 1 Lloyd's Rep 557.

are insufficient the court has no jurisdiction to order any of the parties to the action to pay the remuneration, costs or expenses of the receiver.[36] If a fund over which a receiver has been appointed is to be distributed, then the distribution of the fund will be made first to meet the costs and expenses of realising the fund, secondly to pay the receiver his remuneration and expenses, and thirdly as between the parties to the action.[37] Because the receiver has to look to the assets over which he has been appointed in order to obtain his remuneration and expenses, it is the ordinary practice of the court not to make an order for distribution of part of those assets without first being satisfied that the receiver's position is adequately safeguarded. Thus if the defendant seeks an order releasing funds to him to pay legal costs or his living expenses, the court will not usually grant such an application, if to do so would prejudice the receiver's claim for remuneration to which he is entitled: *Clark Equipment Credit of Australia Limited* v *Como Factors* (1988) 14 NSWLR 552 at p 568, per Powell J (New South Wales Supreme Court). The court will not make an order against a party for interim payment of a receiver's fees and expenses (see footnote 36). At the end of the proceedings the question may arise as to whether a successful plaintiff could seek an order against the defendant requiring him to pay the receiver's fees and expenses. In principle it is thought that the receiver's fees and expenses will in effect represent a cost of safeguarding assets and realising them as part of execution of a judgment. Thus the fees and expenses go to reduce the amount available to be paid to a judgment creditor, who will be entitled to look to the judgment debtor for any shortfall in relation to discharge of the judgment debt. If, on the other hand, the fund is insufficient to meet the fees and expenses of the receiver and the plaintiff has to pay the shortfall under a special arrangement which he has entered into with the receiver in order to induce him to accept or continue with the appointment, then the better view is that the amount which the plaintiff has to pay to the receiver forms part of the costs of the proceedings within the scope of costs as set out in RSC Order 62, r 1(4).[38]

If an order appointing a receiver has been discharged, then the successful defendant will ordinarily be entitled to an inquiry on the undertaking in damages and, if he can show loss arising from the assets having had to bear the costs and expenses of the receiver, then it is considered that this would fall within the scope of the undertaking. In such circumstances the costs and expenses of the receiver do not form part of the defendant's costs of the action because he has not incurred them and nor is he liable for them (see generally pp 105–107).

---

36 *Boehm* v *Goodall* [1911] 1 Ch 155; *Evans* v *Clayhope Ltd* [1988] 1 WLR 358.

37 *Batten* v *Wedgwood Coal and Iron Co* (1884) 28 ChD 317.

38 *Evans* v *Clayhope Ltd* (above) at pp 362–363. If this view is incorrect then the plaintiff would have to seek to recover the shortfall by reference to a cause of action. Thus, for example, if he succeeded on a claim for damages for fraud against the defendant, then the shortfall, if reasonably incurred, could form part of the damages (see also *Maritime Transport* v *Unitramp* [1981] 2 Lloyd's Rep 284).

(7) Receiver appointed over land

Unlike the position in relation to a Mareva injunction (see p 20), if an order is made appointing a receiver over land then this will be registrable[39] as a land charge or a caution, according to whether or not the land is registered. This is the case even though the order appointing the receiver does not have the effect of giving the applicant an interest in the land, and even though the applicant has no interest in the land over which the appointment has been made.

(8) Recognition of an order appointing a receiver

Provided an order is made *inter partes*,[40] or at least upon notice having been given of the application, it will be capable of being enforced in the courts of a contracting state to the European Judgments Convention under Art 25 of the Convention.[41] In the case of a receiver appointed by a foreign court when the order does not fall within the European Judgments Convention, the order may still be recognised in this country provided that there is sufficient connection between the relevant defendant whose assets have been made the subject of the appointment and the jurisdiction in which the appointment was made.[42]

(9) Practice and procedure

An order appointing a receiver may in cases of extreme urgency (eg when assets are in immediate jeopardy) be made *ex parte*. Ordinarily, however, the court will only appoint a receiver upon a hearing *inter partes* of an application made by summons or motion (under RSC Order 30, r 1(1)), and an injunction may be granted *ex parte* restraining the defendant from dealing with the assets pending the hearing of the application for the appointment (under RSC Order 30, r 1(3)). The court has a discretion whether or not to require the person appointed to give security, which, unless the court otherwise directs, has to be by way of guarantee (RSC Order 30, r 2). The receiver can at any time (RSC Order 30, r 3) request the court to give him directions in connection with his appointment, and this may be done informally by letter. A master has the power to appoint a receiver by way of equitable execution and to grant an ancillary injunction (RSC Order 51, r 2).

---

39 *Clayhope Properties Ltd* v *Evans* [1986] 1 WLR 1223.
40 *Denilauler* v *Snc Couchet Frères* [1980] ECR 1553; *Babanaft International Co SA* v *Bassatne* [1989] 3 WLR 232 at pp 245–246.
41 *Derby* v *Weldon (Nos 3 and 4)* [1989] 2 WLR 412.
42 *Schemmer* v *Property Resources Ltd* [1975] Ch 273.

If security is not to be required from the receiver before he takes up his appointment then ordinarily the applicant will be required to furnish an undertaking to the court to be answerable for all the funds or other assets obtained or collected by the receiver. The applicant will in any event be required to furnish an undertaking in damages.

Chapter 13

The granting of Anton Piller relief, and execution of the order

(1) Introduction

An Anton Piller order requires the defendant to give permission to the plaintiff's representatives to enter the premises of the defendant for the purpose of searching for and removing into safe custody, articles, documents, evidence, assets or other material (eg information stored on a computer), as specified in the order. Almost invariably the order includes other mandatory orders directed to the defendant requiring him to inform the plaintiff's representatives of where documents or articles are to be found, and it may include orders requiring the surrender of keys, the printing out of information held on computer[1] or other assistance to be given[2] which will enable the search to be effective and the subject matter designated in the order to be obtained and removed from the premises. Anton Piller relief usually includes an order requiring the defendant to provide certain specified information either forthwith or within a very short time and it may also include provision for the defendant to verify that information on affidavit. The order often also contains a prohibitory injunction restraining the defendant from destroying or damaging evidence or documents described in the order. In certain cases it may also be necessary for an injunction to be granted preventing those served with the order from informing third parties of the existence of the proceedings or the fact that an order has been made. It has been described as one of the law's two nuclear weapons,[3] the other being Mareva relief. The nature of the jurisdiction has been described in Chapter 1, and the limits to the jurisdiction of the court to grant Anton Piller relief (including the position under the Civil Jurisdiction and Judgments Act 1982) are set out in

---

1 *Gates* v *Swift* [1982] RPC 339.
2 The jurisdiction to require the defendant to provide assistance in connection with the carrying out of the order can be justified by reference to s 37 of the Supreme Court Act 1981, see generally *Bayer AG* v *Winter* [1986] 1 WLR 497. Furthermore, assistance may be required from a defendant by an order made under an applicable rule of court (eg for delivery up of certain goods under RSC Order 29, r 2A).
3 *Bank Mellat* v *Nikpour* [1985] FSR 87, at p 92, per Donaldson LJ.

Chapter 5. The application is almost invariably made *ex parte* (for the procedure, see Chapter 7).

The plaintiff on such an application has a duty to the court to make full disclosure of all material facts and circumstances, and if he fails to comply with this duty, the order may be discharged on this ground (see Chapter 8). After an opportunity to take legal advice, the defendant comes under an immediate obligation to comply with the order, and failure to comply will place him in contempt of court (see Chapter 14). The plaintiff on the *ex parte* application is required to furnish to the court various undertakings which include an undertaking in damages (see Chapter 9).

Often Anton Piller orders are made for the purpose of preserving evidence (eg documents or articles which are being 'passed off' as being manufactured by the plaintiff), which the plaintiff needs in order to prove his claim against the defendant.[4] The order may also be made so as to enable the plaintiff to obtain evidence and information so as to enable him to proceed against third party wrongdoers under the principle in *Norwich Pharmacal Co* v *Customs and Excise Commissioners* [1974] AC 133 ie, from a person who has been 'mixed up' in the wrongdoing. These principles apply regardless of whether or not the defendant is himself alleged to be a wrongdoer. Cases involving intellectual property rights are a classic example of a type of case in which Anton Piller relief may be appropriate.[5]

Anton Piller relief may also be appropriate in order to obtain information about assets held by the defendant and to preserve such assets. Thus the court may order the defendant to deliver up to the plaintiff's representatives assets of a specified type,[6] as part of an order granting Anton Piller relief. Anton Piller relief directed to preserving assets can be granted by way of interlocutory order granted before the trial[7] or in aid of execution of a judgment.[8]

In cases involving a tracing or proprietary claim, an Anton Piller order may be granted in order to assist the plaintiff to locate the assets in question or their proceeds.[9] Thus, in *Rank Film Ltd* v *Video Information Centre* [1982] AC 380 at p 417, Templeman LJ said that a court of equity has jurisdiction to make mandatory and other peremptory and penal orders at any stage of any proceedings or in contemplation of proceedings where damages will not be an adequate remedy, and where rights, properties or remedies claimed by the plaintiff are in jeopardy.

---

4 Eg as in *Yousif* v *Salama* [1980] 1 WLR 1540 and *Emanuel* v *Emanuel* [1982] 1 WLR 669.
5 Eg *Rank Film Ltd* v *Video Information Centre* [1982] AC 380 and *Columbia Pictures Inc* v *Robinson* [1987] Ch 37.
6 *CBS United Kingdom Ltd* v *Lambert* [1983] Ch 37. In *Johnson* v *L&A Philatelics Ltd* [1981] FSR 286, an order for delivery up was made in conjunction with Mareva relief.
7 As in *CBS United Kingdom Ltd* v *Lambert*, above.
8 *Distributori Automatici* v *Holford Trading Co* [1985] 1 WLR 1066.
9 See generally the statement of Templeman LJ in *Mediterranea Raffineria Siciliana Petroli SpA* v *Mabanaft GmbH* Court of Appeal (Civil Division) Transcript No 816 of 1978 (1 December) cited by Lord Denning MR in *Bankers Trust Co* v *Shapira* [1980] 1 WLR 1274 at pp 1280–1281; *Cook Industries* v *Galliher* [1979] Ch 439.

(2) The circumstances in which Anton Piller relief may be granted

The relief is an exceptional remedy for use to enable a plaintiff to preserve articles, documents, evidence, assets or other material held by or under the control of the defendant when there is a serious risk that unless the relief is granted, the relevant subject matter will be destroyed, damaged, hidden or otherwise not made available, and in consequence the ends of justice are liable to be defeated. In *Anton Piller KG* v *Manufacturing Processes Ltd* [1976] Ch 55 at p 62, Ormrod LJ specified what he described as 'three essential pre-conditions' for the making of the order, namely:

(1) there must be 'an extremely strong *prima facie* case';

(2) the damage, 'potential or actual', must be 'very serious' for the applicant;

(3) there must be 'clear evidence' that the defendants have in their possession 'incriminating documents or things' (which was the subject matter sought to be preserved in that case) and that there is a 'real possibility' that the defendants may destroy such material before any application *inter partes* can be made.

In practice, Anton Piller orders have become established 'as part of the tools of the administration of justice in civil cases',[10] and the question whether or not to grant an order is a matter of discretion for the court.

In relation to pre-condition (1) laid down by Ormrod LJ, this should not be interpreted as a requirement that the plaintiff make out 'an extremely strong *prima facie* case' on the merits of his claim, but that the plaintiff should only be granted the order if there is a very clear *prima facie* case that the ends of justice are otherwise liable to be defeated. The whole purpose of an order may be to preserve evidence which the plaintiff needs. In *Yousif* v *Salama* [1980] 1 WLR 1540, the Court of Appeal granted Anton Piller relief directed to preserving documents on two files and a desk diary which were described by Lord Denning MR as 'the best possible evidence to prove the plaintiff's case'. Although Donaldson LJ dissented, in the course of his judgment he envisaged the relief as being available to preserve evidence even when otherwise the 'plaintiff will be left without any evidence to enable him to put forward his claim' (at p 1543). Accordingly it may be the case that Anton Piller relief is sought because otherwise the plaintiff may have insufficient evidence in support of his claim.

It has been pointed out that the granting of Anton Piller relief potentially involves serious inroads being made on what are regarded as ordinary civil liberties,[11] such as the right of a defendant to be heard in his own defence before an adverse order is made against him,[12] the right to be fully protected against unjustified and arbitrary searches and seizures,[13] and

---

10 *Columbia Pictures Inc* v *Robinson* [1987] Ch 37 at p 70, per Scott J.

11 *Lock International plc* v *Beswick* [1989] 1 WLR 1268 at p 1279.

12 *Jeffrey Rogers Knitwear Productions Ltd* v *Vinola (Knitwear) Manufacturing Co* [1985] FSR 184 at p 187; *Columbia Pictures Inc* v *Robinson* [1987] Ch 37 at pp 73–74.

13 *Lock International plc* v *Beswick*, above.

the right to privacy in one's own home.[14] Whilst there are cases in which it is appropriate that the relief should be granted because of the risk of the interests of justice otherwise being defeated, the possible alternatives to granting such relief and the extent of the risk, if the relief is not granted, need to be considered on each application. In *Lock International plc v Beswick*, Anton Piller relief had been granted to a former employer of the defendant who had gone into competition with him. The order had been made ostensibly for the purpose of protecting trade secrets and other information which was said to be confidential to the employer.[15] After observing that a lack of particularity in the applicant's evidence about the precise nature of the trade secrets sought to be protected is often 'a symptom of an attempt to prevent the employees from making legitimate use of the knowledge and skills gained in the plaintiff's service', Hoffmann J said ([1989] 1 WLR 1268 at p 1281):

Even in cases in which the plaintiff has strong evidence that an employee has taken what is undoubtedly specific confidential information, such as a list of customers, the court must employ a graduated response. To borrow a useful concept from the jurisprudence of the European Community, there must be *proportionality* between the perceived threat to the plaintiff's rights and the remedy granted. The fact that there is overwhelming evidence that the defendant has behaved wrongfully in his commercial relationships does not necessarily justify an *Anton Piller* order. People whose commercial morality allows them to take a list of the customers with whom they were in contact while employed will not necessarily disobey an order of the court requiring them to deliver it up. Not everyone who is misusing confidential information will destroy documents in the face of a court order requiring him to preserve them.

In many cases it will therefore be sufficient to make an order for delivery up of the plaintiff's documents to his solicitor or, in cases in which the documents belong to the defendant but may provide evidence against him, an order that he preserve the documents pending further order, or allow the plaintiff's solicitor to make copies. The more intrusive orders allowing searches of premises or vehicles require a careful balancing of, on the one hand, the plaintiff's right to recover his property or to preserve important evidence against, on the other hand, violation of the privacy of a defendant who has had no opportunity to put his side of the case. It is not merely that the defendant may be innocent. The making of an intrusive order *ex parte* even against a guilty defendant is contrary to normal principles of justice and can only be done when there is a paramount need to prevent a denial of justice to the plaintiff. The absolute extremity of the court's powers is to permit a search of a defendant's dwelling house, with the humiliation and family distress which that frequently involves.

In the case of the granting of an injunction *ex parte* by way of Mareva relief, it is open to the defendant or a third party to apply to discharge or vary the order on short notice or even, in cases of absolute urgency, *ex parte*.[16] Although this is equally true of Anton Piller relief, by its nature it

---

14 *Columbia Pictures Inc v Robinson*, above, at p 73.
15 See generally *Faccenda Chicken Ltd v Fowler* [1987] Ch 117.
16 *London City Agency (JCD) Ltd v Lee* [1970] Ch 597.

is intended to be acted upon immediately and the defendant will not have the opportunity to assemble evidence or even to apply to the court for its discharge before being in contempt for non-compliance. Even if an urgent application were to be made for discharge of the order or a stay of execution, it is not the usual practice of the court to alter its order, at least not without good reason supported by sworn evidence. Also, once the order has been acted upon, the plaintiff's representatives will have had access to the premises in question and will have at least commenced a search, and this is in itself liable to expose the defendant to stigma, and loss of business and goodwill. These considerations show that at the *ex parte* stage the plaintiff must be scrupulous in placing all material facts before the court (see Chapter 8), including what investigations have been made, and with what results, into the question whether or not in the absence of Anton Piller relief the proposed subject matter of the order would be done away with,[17] even in the face of an injunction restraining the defendant from so acting, and whether the plaintiff is likely to be good for damages if these are awarded in due course under the undertaking in damages.[18] Furthermore these considerations show that at the *ex parte* stage the court will require to be satisfied with clear evidence that in the circumstances the interests of justice require that the order be made and implemented before the defendant is afforded a proper opportunity to present his side of the case.[19] Thus, for example, an order will not be made against persons of good standing who are unlikely to disobey an order of the court.[20]

In *Ex parte Matshini and Others* [1986] 3 SALR 605; [1986] FSR 454, the Eastern Cape Division of the Supreme Court of South Africa held in a case seeking preservation of evidence, in respect of intended claims for assault against the police, that Anton Piller relief would not be granted because the evidence in question was not 'essential or absolutely necessary' in order for the applicants to prove their claims. In reaching this decision the court cited passages from the judgments of the majority of the Court of Appeal in *Yousif v Salama* [1980] 1 WLR 1540. It is considered, however, that this imposes a requirement which is inconsistent with English law and practice. Thus in *Yousif v Salama*, even if the two files in question and the desk diary had been destroyed or were not available at the trial, the plaintiff would still have been able to proceed with his claim, albeit that in

17 *Jeffrey Rogers Ltd* v *Vinola (Knitwear) Manufacturing Co*, above; *Columbia Pictures Inc* v *Robinson* [1987] Ch 37 at pp 77–81.

18 *Manor Electronics* v *Dickson* [1988] RPC 618; *Jeffrey Rogers Ltd* v *Vinola (Knitwear) Manufacturing Co*, above; *Intercontex* v *Schmidt* [1988] FSR 575; *Vapormatic Co* v *Sparex Ltd* [1976] 1 WLR 939 at pp 940–941 (where a bond was provided in support of the undertaking in damages).

19 *Columbia Pictures Inc* v *Robinson*, above, at p 76.

20 *Randolph M Fields* v *Watts* (1985) 129 SJ 67 (a case concerning barristers and barristers' clerks); *Booker McConnell plc* v *Plasgow* [1985] RPC 425 at pp 438–439, in relation to the second and third defendants who were 'highly reputable public companies'. The risk of disobedience may be inferred from clear evidence of dishonesty, see *Dunlop Holdings Ltd* v *Staravia Ltd* [1982] Com LR 3 and *Yousif v Salama*, above.

the view of the majority of the court, the evidence in support would not have been as strong.

(3) Matrimonial proceedings and Anton Piller relief

Anton relief may be appropriate in the context of matrimonial proceedings. In *Emanuel* v *Emanuel* [1982] 1 WLR 669, relief was granted in proceedings for ancillary relief brought by a wife following a divorce, when the husband had clearly been shown as ready to flout the authority of the court and to mislead the court if he considered it to be in his interests to do so. The husband in that case had acted in breach of previous court orders, had been committed to prison for six weeks for contempt, and there was *prima facie* evidence that the husband had previously lied to the court on two occasions. In the course of his judgment Wood J referred to the relief as being granted 'only very rarely'. Although such relief is available in the context of matrimonial proceedings,[21] it is appropriate for it to be borne in mind that 'family feelings are well known to be very strong at times, and in a family environment suspicion can grow out of all reason',[22] and that this might colour the evidence presented to the court, particularly when spouses or former spouses are in contention over financial provision. Thus strong evidence in support of the *ex parte* application is insisted upon in the context of matrimonial proceedings.[23]

(4) Class actions and Anton Piller relief

The situation may arise where the plaintiff is confronted with a number of persons who are infringing his rights but whose identity is unknown to him. In *EMI Records Ltd* v *Kudhail* [1985] FSR 36, the plaintiffs wished to obtain relief against street traders who were dealing in pirated cassette tapes which had been recorded illegally and which were being sold to the public under the name 'Oak Records'. In Canada, the courts have permitted proceedings to be brought against unnamed defendants (commonly called 'John Doe') and have granted relief in those proceedings.[24] However, in England there is a firmly established rule of practice that, save in accordance with special provisions in the rules of court,[25] the defendants must be named in the proceedings and that even a description of them will

---

21 See also *K* v *K* (1982) 13 Fam Law 46; *Kepa* v *Kepa* (1982) 4 FLR 515.
22 *Yousif* v *Salama* [1980] 1 WLR 1541 at p 1543, per Donaldson LJ (albeit in the course of a dissenting judgment, but neither of the other members of the court expressed a view inconsistent with this observation).
23 *Francis* v *Francis* Court of Appeal (Civil Division) Transcript 197 of 1986.
24 See 'Ex Parte Anton Piller orders with John Doe Defendants' by Gordon Hayhurst in [1987] 9 EIPR 257.
25 RSC Order 113 permits summary proceedings for the possession of land against unnamed defendants.

not suffice.[26] Nevertheless, under RSC Order 15, r 12, provision is made for the bringing of proceedings against named defendants who represent a class consisting of numerous persons who 'have the same interest in any proceedings'. In cases falling within the rule the plaintiff is not required to name members of the class other than those who are the representative defendants, and an injunction can be granted against the whole class. Thus in *EMI Records Ltd* v *Kudhail* injunctive relief was granted by the Court of Appeal against the persons who sold the pirated cassettes,[27] and Anton Piller relief was also granted against certain named individuals.[28]

An injunction granted in representative proceedings is binding on the entire class (RSC Order 15, r 12(3)), but can only be *enforced* (eg under RSC Order 45, r 5(1)) against a member of the class who is not a representative defendant, with the leave of the court which must be obtained on an application made by summons, which has been personally served on the person in question. Since the injunction is binding from when it is granted by the court, it is considered that a represented member of the class would be in contempt of court if he acted contrary to its terms having been notified of the making of the order. In such circumstances, before bringing contempt proceedings against the person in question, the plaintiff would first need to seek and obtain leave from the court to enforce the order.

(5) Duty to the court of legal advisers of the plaintiff

In *Booker McConnell plc* v *Plasgow* [1985] RPC 425, Dillon LJ observed that there was a responsibility in each case on the plaintiff's advisers to consider seriously whether it is justifiable to seek an Anton Piller order against the particular defendant concerned and if so the width of the order to be sought. This observation has been criticised by Scott J in *Columbia Pictures Inc* v *Robinson* [1987] Ch 37 at pp 78 and 82, on the ground that the responsibility for deciding what order is to be made (if any) lies with the judge and not with the legal advisers to the plaintiff. However, Scott J expressly said that 'solicitors and counsel must obviously accept the duty of ensuring that full disclosure of all relevant material is made to the court'[29] and plainly that personal duty can only be properly discharged if the legal advisers of the plaintiff do consider the matters referred to by Dillon LJ.

---

26 *Friern Barnet Urban District Council* v *Adams* [1927] 2 Ch 25; *Re Wykeham Terrace* [1970] Ch 204 at pp 213–214.
27 Applying *Kennaway* v *Thompson* [1981] QB 88. See also *M Michaels (Furriers) Ltd* v *Askew* (1983) *The Times*, 25 June.
28 The headnote at [1985] FSR 36 is misleading on this point. However, in principle it is considered that Anton Piller relief could be granted against the whole class in respect of particular premises.
29 [1987] Ch 37 at p 82; see also p 84, above.

(6) An order for disclosure of a list of customers, or names of third parties

The question may arise in proceedings, particularly those concerned with breach of copyright, passing-off or trademark infringement, whether or not the defendant should be ordered to disclose documents or answer interrogatories relating to the names and addresses of his customers. Such information could result in considerable damage being done to the defendant's business as a result of the customers being informed of the plaintiff's claim, and any further steps which might be taken against the customers themselves by the plaintiff. In these circumstances, even in the context of the usual discovery procedures of the court, disclosure of the names and addresses of customers involves an exercise of discretion by the court, taking into account on the one hand the likely prejudice to the defendant by way of damage to his business, and on the other hand whether the discovery is material for the purpose of enabling the plaintiff to prove his claim, and not merely the quantum of his damages, which can be assessed in a subsequent inquiry following the trial.[30] It is well established that the court has jurisdiction to require disclosure of names and addresses of customers and other information to enable the plaintiff to bring proceedings or take other action against the customers concerned.[31] This can be done by interlocutory order on motion[32] or summons, or even *ex parte*. However, because the making of such an order is particularly liable to cause damage to a defendant, the jurisdiction to grant relief *ex parte* should be exercised with great caution, particularly in circumstances when the defendant may suffer substantial prejudice in the conduct of his business as a result. In *Sega Enterprises Ltd* v *Alca Electronics* [1982] FSR 516, an order for disclosure had been granted *ex parte* in conjunction with Anton Piller relief. The defendants hired out the video games in question in the proceedings to public houses, and there was 'a serious issue to be tried with regard to copyright' (at p 521, per Lawton LJ). In these circumstances, the Court of Appeal held that the order should be discharged. The discovery was not necessary for determining the plaintiff's claim (as opposed to the quantum of damages if the plaintiff succeeded at trial), and in the circumstances of the case it could not be said that there was any serious risk of prejudice to the plaintiff if the discovery was not ordered pending the outcome of the trial on liability. The public houses were apparently responsible third parties, and if the plaintiff succeeded at trial, the discovery could be ordered for the purposes of quantifying the damages against the defendant, and enabling the plaintiff to take steps against the public houses concerned.

---

30 *Carver* v *Pinto Leite* (1871) 7 LR Ch App 90.
31 *Norwich Pharmacal Co* v *Customs and Excise Commissioners* [1974] AC 133; *British Steel* v *Grenada* [1981] AC 1096.
32 *RCA Corporation* v *Reddingtons Rare Records* [1974] 1 WLR 1445; *Loose* v *Williamson* [1978] 1 WLR 639.

On the other hand, there can be circumstances where the balance of convenience is such that immediate disclosure should be ordered *ex parte*. In particular this may be the case if, in the absence of an order made *ex parte*, the defendant may destroy or hide the information, or if the plaintiff's rights can only be adequately safeguarded if he is able to take immediate steps against the third parties concerned, for example because on the evidence the customers are likely themselves to be 'irresponsible wrongdoers who will seek to evade their responsibilities or conceal their activities' (at p 525, per Templeman LJ). But such relief should not be granted simply as part and parcel of Anton Piller relief without investigation of the particular circumstances of the case, and the court 'coming to the conclusion that it is necessary for the long-term protection of the plaintiff that such a draconian course should be taken.'

If *ex parte* relief is sought either by way of disclosure order or by way of Anton Piller relief which will have the effect of providing to the plaintiff names and addresses of customers, then if the court is minded to grant the relief it may be appropriate to require the plaintiff to furnish an undertaking to the court not to use or act upon the information without the leave of the court.

The same principles will be involved whenever a plaintiff seeks disclosure under *ex parte* relief of information which will enable him to proceed against third parties in circumstances where, as a result, substantial damage or prejudice may be unfairly caused to the defendant. In the case of *suppliers* of alleged infringing articles to the defendant different considerations arise than those applicable to customers. It is one matter to allow a defendant to continue to deal with his customers and not to ruin the goodwill of his business pending trial, it is another when considering whether or not the plaintiff should be informed of the sources of the articles in question so that he can bring proceedings or take other steps against persons directly responsible for putting the articles into circulation. Relief is often granted in Anton Piller cases for this purpose.[33]

(7) Privilege against self-incrimination

Under s 14(1) of the Civil Evidence Act 1968 it is provided that:

14 Privilege against incrimination of self or spouse

(1) The right of a person in any legal proceedings other than criminal proceedings to refuse to answer any question or produce any document or thing if to do so would tend to expose that person to proceedings for an offence or for the recovery of a penalty—

  (a) shall apply only as regards criminal offences under the law of any part of the United Kingdom and penalties provided for by such law; and

---

33 *Rank Film Ltd* v *Video Information Centre* [1982] AC 380 at p 444, per Lord Fraser; *EMI Ltd* v *Sarwar* [1977] FSR 146; *Golf Lynx* v *Golf Scene* (1984) 59 ALR 343 (Supreme Court of South Australia), where an order was made in respect of suppliers, after considering *Sega Enterprises Ltd* v *Alca Electronics*, above.

(*b*) shall include a like right to refuse to answer any question or produce any document or thing if to do so would tend to expose the husband or wife of that person to proceedings for any such criminal offence or for the recovery of any such penalty.

This section is declaratory of the privilege at common law,[34] which is available both to individuals and to companies.[35] But the section also limits the ambit of the privilege,[36] and there is no room for the assertion of a privilege in circumstances falling outside s 14(1), to be permitted at the discretion of the court.[37] Thus, the privilege does not extend to protection in relation to a criminal offence or the recovery of a penalty under foreign law.[38] Furthermore, since proceedings for contempt of court in respect of breach of a court order are not proceedings for a *criminal* offence, the privilege does not extend to protection in relation to such proceedings.[39] The privilege is personal to the individual or company liable to be proceeded against, and does not extend to protect third parties (other than spouses), who may be concerned at the risk of incriminating the defendant. It appears that the privilege will not be available to be invoked in relation to oral evidence or information which may be available to be given by a servant or agent of that individual or company.[40] This view accords with the wording of s 14(1) of the Act. On the other hand, if documents are held by a person on behalf of the individual or company, then it is very doubtful whether those documents would be made the subject of a mandatory order directed to the servant or agent concerned. In such circumstances it is considered that as a general rule the servant or agent should not be ordered to produce documents without the permission of his principal,[41] because to produce them would be inconsistent with his duty to the principal, and the principal cannot be required to give that permission when there is a risk of self-incrimination.

An Anton Piller order as such merely requires the defendant to give permission for entry and search by the plaintiff's representatives. As such the granting of an order will not involve an infringement of the privilege.[42] However, the privilege is capable of applying to orders commonly made in conjunction with Anton Piller or Mareva relief, such as orders for disclosure of documents or the supplying of information. Orders of this kind

---

34 *Re Westinghouse Uranium Contract* [1978] AC 547 at p 637, per Lord Diplock.

35 *Triplex Safety Glass Company Ltd* v *Lancegaye Safety Glass (1934) Ltd* [1939] 2 KB 395.

36 *Garvin* v *Domus Publishing Ltd* [1989] Ch 335, at p 345.

37 *Arab Monetary Fund* v *Hashim* [1989] 1 WLR 565 at pp 573–574.

38 *Arab Monetary Fund* v *Hashim*, above.

39 *Garvin* v *Domus Publishing Ltd*, above (not following the dicta of Lord Denning MR in *Comet Products UK Ltd* v *Hawkex Plastics Ltd* [1971] 2 QB 67 at pp 73–74).

40 *Re Westinghouse Uranium Contract* [1978] AC 547 at pp 637–638, per Lord Diplock. (The other members of the House of Lords expressed no view on the point, but see the contrary argument referred to at p 617, per Lord Wilberforce, and at pp 651–652, per Lord Fraser.)

41 *B* v *B (Matrimonial Proceedings: Discovery)* [1978] Fam 181 at pp 186–187.

42 *Rank Film Ltd* v *Video Information Centre* [1982] AC 380 at p 441.

will not be made in circumstances where, if the defendant complied with the order, there would be a real and appreciable risk that in consequence the defendant would be exposed to criminal proceedings or proceedings for a penalty. Furthermore in *Rank Film Ltd* v *Video Information Centre*, the House of Lords rejected the suggestion that in such circumstances an order could be made provided that the plaintiff furnished to the court an undertaking not to use the information disclosed in criminal proceedings.[43] Accordingly, for the purposes of considering whether or not such orders can be made, when there may be a risk of self-incrimination it is important to take into account the precise ambit of the protection capable of being afforded by it.

The privilege can only be invoked if the risk of exposure to proceedings is not 'remote and fanciful' and therefore cannot be disregarded.[44] Furthermore the court must conclude that as a consequence of supplying the information or otherwise complying with the order, there would be a tendency 'to incriminate [the defendant] either in the sense of setting up a case against him or strengthening an already existing case'.[45]

Following the decision of the House of Lords in *Rank Film Ltd* v *Video Information Centre*, s 72 of the Supreme Court Act 1981[46] has been enacted which withdraws the benefit of the privilege in civil proceedings concerning passing off or for the infringement of 'intellectual property' rights, which are defined as meaning rights in 'any patent, trade mark, copyright, registered design, technical or commercial information or other intellectual property'. There is also removal of the privilege in respect of the risk of criminal proceedings under the Theft Acts 1968 and 1978 by reason of s 31 of the Theft Act 1968 and s 5(2) of the Theft Act 1978. In *Khan* v *Khan*, the defendant sought to suggest that proceedings might be brought against him not only under the Theft Act 1968 but also under the Forgery Act 1913 and that since s 31 did not apply in relation to proceedings under the latter, the privilege applied. However, the Court of Appeal as one of the grounds for the decision held that proceedings under the Forgery Act 1913, if instituted, would simply be a contrivance to circumvent the effect of s 31, and the criminal court would not permit evidence to be adduced by means of such a contrivance. Accordingly, the claim to privilege failed.

It is also the case that a defendant will not be entitled to invoke the privilege simply on the grounds that compliance with an order may tend to show that he has already perjured himself in evidence given in the proceedings about his assets. Thus, in *Emanuel* v *Emanuel* [1982] 1 WLR 669,

---

43 The decision on this point was not followed by the majority of the full court of the Supreme Court of New Zealand in *Busby* v *Thorn EMI Video Programmes Ltd* [1984] 1 NZLR 461, but has been followed in New South Wales in *BPA Industries* v *Black* (1987) 11 NSWLR 609.

44 *Khan* v *Khan* [1982] 1 WLR 513 at p 519.

45 *Khan* v *Khan*, above, at p 521, per Griffiths LJ.

46 See Appendix 1. For the meaning of s 72(5)(*b*), see *United City Studios* v *Hubbard* [1984] Ch 225.

there was an issue in divorce proceedings as to what assets a husband owned which was relevant to the question of what orders should be made in favour of his ex-wife for financial relief ancillary to the divorce. It appeared that the husband might have committed perjury in the course of the proceedings about his assets. Nevertheless, Wood J granted an *ex parte* application for Anton Piller relief which included a mandatory order that the ex-husband produce documents in relation to his assets. The judge considered that there should not be any provision in the order to protect the ex-husband against self-incrimination in relation to perjury. In his view the privilege would not be available because the perjury would have been in the course of the proceedings themselves. If perjury could be invoked then there would be an inducement to a defendant to commit perjury at an early stage and then to seek to hide behind the privilege in an attempt to prevent the court from establishing the true position. The view of Wood J was adopted by Leggatt J in *Distributori Automatici* v *Holford Trading Co* [1985] 1 WLR 1066 at p 1073, in which it appeared that the defendant might have perjured himself in relation to the existence of assets upon which a judgment could be enforced. The judge granted Anton Piller relief (including mandatory orders requiring the defendant to disclose information and documents) notwithstanding the risk of self-incrimination in respect of perjury.

Whilst it is wrong in principle for the court to grant *ex parte* a mandatory order which is inconsistent with maintaining the privilege, this does not preclude the court from considering the relevant evidence and reaching a judgment at the *ex parte* stage as to whether the privilege would be available to be invoked where otherwise there would be a risk of self-incrimination. If the court concludes that the privilege would not be available in the circumstances of the case, then the risk of self-incrimination on the part of the defendant does not preclude the making of the contemplated order.

In cases falling outside of the scope of the privilege the court may, in the exercise of its discretion, under s 37(1) of the Supreme Court Act 1981 or otherwise, take into account the risk of adverse consequences befalling the defendant or third parties if there is compliance with the relief sought. In *Arab Monetary Fund* v *Hashim* (above) there was a concern that third parties might be exposed to criminal proceedings in Iraq as a result of disclosure of information and in consequence part of the order was limited to disclosure of information to the solicitors acting for the plaintiff, and not to the plaintiff itself. This was an exceptional form of limitation, the general rule being that disclosure will be ordered to be made to the other party to the litigation.

(8) Undertakings by the plaintiffs in the order

If, as is often the case, the plaintiff has not yet issued his proceedings, he will be required to undertake to issue and serve the writ or other originating process forthwith (see pp 231–232). As a matter of practice the writ is usually not issued before the Anton Piller order is executed but it should be issued immediately after the commencement of execution.[47] It is often the case that the application is made on the basis of a draft affidavit, in which case there must be an undertaking to swear or have sworn the affidavit. If information is given to the court which is not included in the draft affidavit, then the undertaking should be expressed in terms which cover all the evidence and information relied upon in the application before the court, including that contained in the draft affidavit. Depending upon the circumstances, it may be convenient to deal with the matter by an undertaking to swear the draft affidavit, and a supplementary affidavit to incorporate the further material. If further information is provided to the court then this should be recorded either at the time of the application or shortly thereafter. The undertaking should also require the sworn affidavit to be filed with the court.

The order should include an undertaking to serve the defendant with a copy of the sworn affidavit and copies of the exhibits, except in so far as the exhibits are not capable of being copied. The undertaking ordinarily requires service of the copy affidavit and exhibits to be made by a solicitor.

Because of the nature of Anton Piller relief it has become part of the standard practice of the court to require an undertaking that service of the order and its execution should be effected by a qualified solicitor,[48] and the solicitor or solicitors concerned (who almost invariably are the plaintiff's solicitors) are themselves required to provide undertakings to the court as to how service and execution will be performed.

If, as is almost invariably the case, the order contains prohibitory injunctions, it it usual in the Chancery Division to require the plaintiff to undertake to serve a Notice of Motion for renewal of the injunctions. Delay in compliance with such an undertaking may lead to the court declining to renew the relief on the hearing of the motion.[49] The plaintiff is required to give the usual undertaking in damages, and may be required to give an undertaking designed to protect the position of third parties who may be affected by implementation of the order. This latter undertaking is not a standard undertaking invariably required by the court in the context of an Anton Piller order.

(9) Undertakings by the plaintiff's solicitors, and service and execution of the order

Service of an Anton Piller order is a delicate matter requiring tactful handling and due regard for the rights of the defendant. To this end the

---

47 *VDU Installations Ltd* v *Integrated Computer Systems and Cybernetics Ltd* [1989] FSR 378.
48 *Vapormatic Co* v *Sparex Ltd* [1976] 1 WLR 939 at p 940; *Protector Alarms Ltd* v *Maxim Alarms Ltd* [1978] FSR 442 at p 444.
49 *Intercontex* v *Schmidt* [1988] FSR 575, where the delay in question was a factor taken into account by the court in declining to grant the relief sought.

solicitors intended to implement the order are themselves required to give certain undertakings to the court. The order itself will make provision limiting the times when it can be served and executed. An undertaking is required to ensure that, on service of the order, the solicitor will give an explanation to the person served of its meaning and effect, 'fairly in every-day language', and will advise the person of his right to obtain legal advice before complying with the order, provided that the advice is sought and obtained 'forthwith'. Under this undertaking it is essential that the solicitor gives a fair and accurate explanation of the order in simple language, including what acts are required to be done and what acts are prohibited, and says that if the person in question wishes to seek immediate legal advice then he is at liberty to do so without there being any breach of the mandatory terms of the order, including those which require permission to be given for the entry and search. The liberty to seek such legal advice is usually subject to a requirement that it is obtained 'forthwith'. This does not entitle a person served with the order to insist on obtaining advice from a particular individual if that individual happens not to be available, and competent professional advice is available to be given by someone else (eg by another partner in the same firm of solicitors).

In *VDU Installations Ltd* v *Integrated Computer Systems and Cybernetics Ltd* (above), there was reference in the order to another document, which in that case was a draft affidavit. This was inconsistent with the principle that a person should be able to read an order of the court and know from that document alone what he is and is not precluded from doing, and what the order requires to be done (see p 178). This defect resulted in the solicitor serving the order failing to comply with his obligation to give true and accurate answers in response to questions from the person served, and an accurate explanation of the order. It was held that the solicitor had acted without proper care, and that there had been a contempt of court by virtue of the breach of the undertaking. As a matter of good practice the solicitor should prepare in advance of service his intended explanation of the order, and it may be helpful for a note expressed in informal terms to be handed over at the same time as the oral explanation is given. The solicitor may also include in the explanation a statement to the effect that he will not enter the premises without permission being given, or if he is already on the premises having been invited in, that he will immediately leave the premises if asked to do so.

It is envisaged that the order will be served at the premises in question on the person appearing to be in charge of the premises. That person may be the defendant in question or, if the defendant is a company, a director or other officer of the company. But if the person is a third party, then it should be borne in mind that if effective contempt proceedings are to be taken against the defendant in respect of non-compliance with mandatory orders of the court, then it will be necessary to effect personal service of the order on the defendant. The usual form of undertakings do not require personal service to be effected first upon the defendant in question, before service at the specified premises on the person appearing to be in charge there. Nor, as a matter of practice, is this course ordinarily adopted.

Often Anton Piller relief is granted without there being any undertaking required from the plaintiff or his solicitors that service of the copy affidavit and exhibits is made at the same time as the order is itself served. Failure to provide the copy evidence at that time will not constitute a breach of the undertaking to give an explanation of the order.[50] However, it is expected as a matter of practice that this will be done.[51] First, the making of the order in the absence of the defendant is in itself a strong step for the court to take and, as a matter of fairness to the defendant, he should be given full information as soon as practicable of what has occurred, including what evidence was placed before the court. Secondly, the defendant has the right to apply to the court for the order to be discharged or varied. It is both unnecessary and unjust that the defendant should be hindered in his consideration of whether or not to make the application, by being deprived of material which is plainly important to the decision. Thirdly, if the right to obtain legal advice is to be properly respected, it is necessary to give the defendant's legal advisers the material they need in order to give adequate advice. Fourthly, there is a substantial difference between an application to discharge an order which has not yet been fully executed and one that has. In the case of the latter, the application to discharge may well not be dealt with on an interlocutory hearing, but be stood over to be dealt with at the trial. It is unjust that the plaintiff through delaying service of the evidence should procure this situation to arise. Fifthly, the court will not ordinarily favourably entertain an application to stay the order or to discharge it, without sworn evidence from the defendant. It is wrong in principle that the defendant should have to prepare such evidence without sight of the plaintiff's evidence. Sixthly, no consideration can be given by the defendant and his advisers to the question whether or not full disclosure has been made on the *ex parte* application, until the plaintiff's evidence has been served. Yet material non-disclosure might provide an important justification for applying immediately to the court for a stay of execution or discharge of the order. Seventhly, it is highly desirable that the court order is respected. This is more likely to occur if the evidence has been provided.

The plaintiff's solicitors are also required to furnish undertakings to the court regarding the implementation of the order once permission has been given for entry and search. The precise form of the undertakings required will depend upon the purpose for which the Anton Piller order has been granted, and the circumstances of the particular case. If documents or articles are to be removed then it is a standard requirement that there should be an undertaking that the documents and articles be listed, and

---

50 *VDU Installations Ltd* v *Integrated Computer Systems and Cybernetics Ltd,* above, at p 393.
51 *Booker McConnell plc* v *Plasgow* (above) at p 442, per Dillon LJ; *AB* v *CDE* [1982] RPC 509 at p 510; *International Electronics Ltd* v *Weight Data Ltd* [1980] FSR 423.

that a copy of the list be provided to the defendant or the person served with the order, prior to any removal. This undertaking is required so that, so far as possible, disputes as to what material is being or has been removed, are avoided.[52] The defendant or the person in charge of the premises, or their representatives ought to be allowed a full opportunity to see what is intended to be removed before removal so that they can check the list as it is being prepared. The solicitors executing the order are usually required to furnish an undertaking to the court to answer questions directed to them as to whether documents or articles are said to be within the scope of the order, and this includes providing a reasonable justification as to why any documents or articles not self-evidently within the scope of the order are said to be so. If large numbers of documents are intended to be removed then it will not be reasonable for there to be a requirement that the solicitors give a detailed justification document by document. However, the solicitors should usually be prepared, in response to appropriate questions, to say why particular categories or classes of documents are considered to be within the order. If a justification cannot be provided, the solicitors in question should give careful thought to whether the particular categories or classes should be removed at all, given the terms of the order. Unless they are able to justify removal at the time it would usually be improper to remove the documents in question at all, without a variation first having been obtained to the existing order, so as expressly to include those documents. Furthermore, it should be borne in mind that it is not good practice for the plaintiff's solicitors to seek to obtain agreement from the defendant or the person in charge of the premises to the removal of documents or articles additional to those specified in the order. In *Columbia Pictures Inc* v *Robinson* (above, at p 77),[53] Scott J said that he would not be prepared to accept that in the circumstances in which Anton Piller orders are 'customarily executed (the execution is often aptly called 'a raid')', apparent consent to additional material being removed had been 'freely and effectively given unless the respondent's solicitor had been present to confirm and ensure that the consent was a free and informed one'. The justification for Anton Piller relief being granted is that the defendant is otherwise liable to destroy or hide away the documents, even in the face of less Draconian relief such as an injunction prohibiting destruction, or a mandatory order requiring delivery up of the documents in question.[54] It is unlikely that such a defendant would voluntarily agree to additional material being removed. But, in any case, it is unfair that the defendant should be both subjected to

---

52 *Columbia Pictures Inc* v *Robinson* [1987] Ch 37 at p 76.

53 See also *VDU Installations Ltd* v *Integrated Computer Systems and Cybernetics Ltd* [1989] FSR 378.

54 A mandatory order requiring delivery up of articles was made in preference to Anton Piller relief in *Universal Studios* v *Mukhtar & Sons* [1976] 1 WLR 568, where there was merely suspicion that the defendants were not acting in good faith.

the pressures of complying with an Anton Piller order, and also be required to deal with a request for additional material, outside of the scope of the order.

If articles are removed for evidential purposes, which either belong to the defendants or in respect of which there is a dispute as to ownership, the court ordinarily requires those articles to be lodged with the defendant's solicitors subject to their undertaking for safe custody and production if required in court.[55] An undertaking to this effect is usually to be given by the plaintiff's solicitors on the *ex parte* application for the relief.

It is undesirable that the solicitor having conduct of the service and execution of the Anton Piller order should be personally related to the plaintiff or should have any personal as opposed to professional connection with the parties.[56]

It is the usual practice for the solicitor to swear an affidavit shortly after completion of the search, which deposes to what has occurred during execution of the order and what material has been obtained.

(10) Presence of the police

An Anton Piller order is relief granted in civil litigation, and it is undesirable that the police should be involved save in so far as their presence is necessary to prevent a breach of the peace. If police are present this may give rise to the impression that they are there to enforce the order of the court, and that the entry and search will be made regardless of whether permission is given by the defendant. This is not the effect of the order, and it is not appropriate that such an impression should be given.[57]

As a general rule an Anton Piller order should not be served and executed so as to coincide with a police raid on the premises. In *ITC Films Distributors Ltd* v *Video Exchange (No 2)* (1982) 126 SJ 672, an Anton Piller order was executed on premises simultaneously with a police search carried out under a warrant to search for and seize any pornographic video films. The judge on the *ex parte* application had not apparently been informed of any intention to execute the order in this way. The Court of Appeal upheld the original Anton Piller order, but nevertheless criticised the manner in which the order had been implemented, Lawton LJ observing that it was most undesirable that solicitors executing an Anton Piller order should be 'seen to be hangers-on of a squad of police carrying out a warrant'. In subsequent proceedings the European Court of Human Rights[58] held that the mode of execution of the order had not resulted in a violation of Art 8 of the European Convention on Human Rights, but

---

55 *Columbia Pictures Inc* v *Robinson*, above, at p 77.
56 *Manor Electronics Ltd* v *Dickson* [1988] RPC 618 at p 622 (the solicitor was the daughter of the chief executive of the plaintiff company).
57 *Manor Electronics Ltd* v *Dickson*, above at pp 621–622.
58 *Chappell* v *United Kingdom* (Case No 17/1987/140/194); (1989) *The Times*, 6 April.

agreed with the criticisms made by the Court of Appeal of the mode of obtaining entry to the premises and of the carrying out of the search.

If a policeman is present when an Anton Piller order is served, it is considered that ordinarily the person served should be told that the policeman is only present in case there might be a breach of the peace.

(11) Substituted service

It is considered that as a general rule it is not desirable that an order for substituted service be made in respect of an Anton Piller order. The nature of the relief requires immediate compliance backed up with the possibility of the imposition of sanctions for contempt of court. In relation to mandatory orders, RSC Order 45, r 7 only permits enforcement pursuant to RSC Order 45, r 5, if there has been non-compliance following personal service of the order endorsed with a penal notice. A defendant is not then able to say that he did not know of the order or that he did not understand the possible consequences of not complying with the order. Substituted service should not be employed simply as a procedural device to strip the defendant of this safeguard. In *Gates* v *Swift* [1982] RPC 339, an order was made providing that service of the order on 'any apparently responsible person appearing to be in charge of the . . . premises shall be deemed good service of this order'; the report does not set out the evidence before the court, which resulted in this order being made.

(12) Privileged documents

The purpose of Anton Piller relief is to enable material to be preserved. It is not intended to, nor does it have the effect of depriving a defendant of his rights to insist upon a claim for privilege in relation to disclosure of documents or information. If documents are found which are clearly privileged, they should not be removed from the premises. If documents are found which might or might not be privileged, there can be no objection in principle to the documents being preserved pending resolution of the matter. However, the plaintiff's solicitors, as a matter of good practice, ought to separate out documents which may be the subject of a claim for privilege, and should as far as possible seek to respect the fact that the documents may be privileged. It is considered that such documents should be made available without copying to the defendant's solicitors, when appointed, subject to their undertaking to preserve them and hold them in safe custody, and to produce them to the court when required. If this is acceptable, the defendant's solicitors can then deal in an orderly manner with any claim to privilege, and the matter can, if necessary, be resolved by the court. If the plaintiff's solicitors removed privileged documents and then sought to use them in the proceedings, relief could be granted by the court directed to preserving the privilege.[59]

---

59 *English and American Insurance Co Ltd* v *Herbert Smith* [1988] FSR 232.

Chapter 14

Contempt of court: the position of the defendant and third parties

(1) Introduction

The law of contempt of court is both of ancient origin and fundamental contemporary importance.[1] It has been described as 'the Proteus of the legal world, assuming an almost infinite diversity of forms'.[2] For the purpose of considering its effect in the context of Mareva and Anton Piller relief it is necessary to distinguish between the position of the defendant and that of third parties, such as, for example, a bank. It is well established that an injunction is addressed to the party enjoined, who must be a party to the action.[3] Whilst it is possible that there may be power in the court to grant an injunction *contra mundum*,[4] this is only liable to arise in very exceptional circumstances such as in connection with wardship proceedings or preserving confidential or secret information. Accordingly, third parties are not themselves enjoined by a Mareva injunction or by an Anton Piller order. They may, however, be liable for contempt of court. This can arise when the third party knowingly aids and abets a breach of an injunction.[5] It can also arise independently of there being any breach of the injunction when the third party with knowledge of the order does 'something which disables the court from conducting the case in the

---

1 Borrie and Lowe's *Law of Contempt* (2nd ed, 1983) at p 1. The present chapter considers the law of contempt in the particular context of Anton Piller orders and Mareva relief. For works devoted to the law of contempt see Borrie and Lowe's *Law of Contempt* (2nd ed, 1983); Arlidge and Eady, *The Law of Contempt*, and CJ Miller, *The Law of Contempt* (2nd ed, 1989).
2 'Contempt of Injunctions, Civil and Criminal' by Joseph Moskovitz (1943) 43 Col LR 780. This statement is referred to in a passage from Borrie and Lowe's *Law of Contempt* (2nd ed, 1983) cited by Sir John Donaldson MR, in *A-G v Newspaper Publishing Plc* [1988] Ch 333 at pp 361–362.
3 *Iveson v Harris* (1802) 7 Ves Jun 251; *Brydges v Brydges* [1909] P 187; *Marengo v Daily Sketch* [1948] 1 All ER 406 at p 407; *A-G v Newspaper Publishing plc*, above; *Royal Bank of Canada v Canstar Sports Group Inc* [1989] 1 WWR 662 (Manitoba Court of Appeal).
4 *Re X (A Minor) (Wardship: Injunction)* [1984] 1 WLR 1422; *A-G v Newspaper Publishing plc* (above).
5 *Lord Wellesley v Earl of Mornington* (1848) 11 Beav 180; *Lord Wellesley v Earl of Mornington (No 2)* 11 Beav 181; *Seaward v Paterson* [1897] 1 Ch 545; *Acrow Automation Ltd v Rex Chainbelt Inc* [1971] 1 WLR 1676; *Z Ltd v A-Z and AA-LL* [1982] QB 558.

intended manner' and thereby interferes with the due administration of justice.[6]

(2) Mareva relief: the position of the defendant

The defendant is personally enjoined by the injunction. Precisely what he is enjoined from doing will depend upon the precise wording of the injunction. Thus, for example, under a Mareva injunction restraining the defendant from 'dealing with' or 'disposing of' his assets, the defendant is not apparently prevented from receiving payment of a debt due to him.[7]

The injunction takes effect at the moment it is pronounced.[8] Contempt proceedings seeking a writ of sequestration or committal pursuant to RSC Order 45, r 5, can only be taken in respect of disobedience to the injunction if the defendant has been served personally with a copy of the injunction endorsed with a penal notice, pursuant to RSC Order 45, r 7. However, under RSC Order 45, r 7(6) a prohibitory injunction, such as a Mareva injunction in the usual form, may be enforced notwithstanding absence of personal service, if the defendant was present when the order was made or if he had been notified of the terms of the order (eg by telephone, telex, facsimile or telegram).

It is entirely discretionary whether the court will enforce the injunction pursuant to these provisions. In *Hill Samuel & Co* v *Littaur* Court of Appeal (Civil Division) Transcript No 126 of 1985 (3 April), Parker LJ said that RSC Order 45, r 7(6) was to be regarded as applicable only to cases of emergency which arose pending personal service of a copy of the injunction upon the defendant. However, RSC Order 45, r 7(7) allows the court to dispense entirely with the need for personal service before seeking to enforce a Mareva injunction by committal or sequestration, and this would appear appropriate to cover any case in which a defendant has knowingly acted in breach of the injunction (*Hill Samuel & Co* v *Littaur*, above).

The injunction restrains the defendant by himself 'his servants, his agents or otherwise howsoever'. Thus the defendant must not do the prohibited acts either himself or through others. This has the consequence that upon obtaining notice of the injunction the defendant must take immediate steps to countermand instructions already given which are inconsistent with the order.[9] It is also clear that if a servant or agent commits a prohibited act in the course of his employment or within the scope of his authority this will place the defendant in breach of the injunction.[10] In the case of an agent, he may have a limited authority confined to a

---

6 *A-G* v *Newspaper Publishing Plc* (above).
7 See pp 11–14 above. *Bank Mellat* v *Kazmi* [1989] QB 541.
8 *Z Ltd* v *A-Z and AA-LL* [1982] QB at p 572; RSC Order 42, r 3(1).
9 *Hone* v *Page* [1980] FSR 500.
10 *Heatons Transport* v *TGWU* [1973] AC 15 at pp 99–100, per Lord Wilberforce delivering the joint opinion of their Lordships.

particular task or he may have a more general authority to act for his principal. The scope of his authority will depend upon the facts of the case.

In the case of corporate defendants provision is made in RSC Order 45, rr 5 and 7 for enforcement by sequestration or committal against a director or other officer of the company, provided that the officer in question had been served personally with a copy of the order endorsed with a penal notice, or the court could proceed under RSC Order 45, r 7(6).

The mere fact that the corporate defendant acts in breach of a Mareva injunction does not have the consequence that any director or other officer who has been personally served with an order endorsed with a penal notice, is placed in contempt of court. Thus, if no allegation is made against such a director of a failure to supervise or investigate, or of wilful blindness, his mere passivity will not amount to a contempt (see *Director-General of Fair Trading* v *Buckland* (1989) *The Independent*, 20 July). It appears that a director will be liable for contempt if either he knowingly participates in the breach of the order (*Re Galvanized Tank Manufacturers' Association's Agreement* [1965] 1 WLR 1074 at p 1092), or if he 'wilfully' fails to take reasonable steps to ensure that there is compliance with the order by the corporation, and is as a result guilty of 'culpable conduct': *Attorney-General for Tuvalu* v *Philatelic Distribution Corporation Ltd* (1989) *The Times* 24 October. But he is not to be made vicariously liable for the conduct of others. This is to be contrasted with the positioin of an individual who is personally enjoined by an injunction and may be placed in contempt of court as a result of the conduct of his servants or agents.

A Mareva injunction has the effect of revoking the authority of a bank to pay banker's orders, and operates so as to countermand the payment of cheques.[11] It does not affect payment by a bank under a letter of credit or performance guarantee, because the bank is under a personal contractual duty to make payment under such an instrument. Similarly, charge card companies must still pay third parties under credit card transactions. In such circumstances the credit card company undertakes a personal commitment. As between the user of the card and the supplier, acceptance by the supplier of payment by credit card may constitute absolute payment,[12] but whether or not this is the case, the credit company must still pay.

A Mareva injunction restrains the defendant from writing cheques addressed to his bank drawn on an account which is in credit, because in consequence one of his assets, namely the account in question, will be disposed of to the extent of the amount of the cheque. However, a Mareva injunction does not prevent the defendant from incurring liabilities as such, and accordingly it is considered that the defendant is free to write cheques to be debited to an account in overdraft, or to use a credit card, thereby committing the credit card company to pay the supplier. The position, however, will be different if the bank or credit card company has

---

11 *Z Ltd* v *A-Z and AA-LL* (above).
12 *Re Charge Card Services Ltd* [1988] 3 WLR 764.

security over an asset belonging to the defendant, and the consequence of the transaction will be to increase the burden of the encumbrance on the asset in question, thereby diminishing its value to the defendant.

There is an exception from liability for contempt when the act in question has been 'casual or accidental and unintentional'. This does not have the consequence that the defendant will only be in contempt of court if there has been deliberate or wilful contumacy. The exception only applies if the relevant act was itself accidental and unintentional, and occurred despite the exercise of proper care by the defendant, and his servants or agents.[13] Originally the rules of court required the conduct in question to have been carried out 'wilfully' and it was in that context that Warrington LJ in *Stancomb* v *Trowbridge UDC* [1910] 2 Ch 190 at p 194,[14] referred to this exception, which also applies in the context of the present rules. Accordingly, as soon as the defendant is notified of the injunction he must take immediate steps to ensure that assets covered by the order are preserved and that no servant, employee or person acting on his behalf or with his authority commits an act contrary to the terms of the injunction. Thus, for example, the defendant should notify his bank and stop payment of cheques.

An undertaking by a defendant given to the court has the same effect as an injunction.[15]

The fact that a defendant obtained and acted on professional advice provides him with no defence, even if he believed that what he was doing did not infringe the requirements of the injunction.[16] Nor is it a defence for a defendant to contend that a variation to the injunction would have been granted, had one been sought, which would have permitted the act in question (eg to enable him to pay legal costs).[17] However, the 'technicality' of the contempt and the absence of any serious fault will mitigate the position, and may lead to no penalty being imposed by the court.

(3) Anton Piller relief: the position of the defendant

Anton Piller relief usually includes both mandatory and prohibitive orders. As for prohibitory orders, the principles to be applied are set out in section (2) of this chapter. As for mandatory orders, it is not sufficient for the purposes of enforcement by committal or sequestration that the court

---

13 *Heatons Transport* v *TGWU* [1973] AC 15; *Steiner Products Ltd* v *Willy Steiner Ltd* [1966] 1 WLR 986; *Re The Agreement of the Mileage Conference Group of the Tyre Manufacturers' Conference Ltd* [1966] 2 All ER 849; *Knight* v *Clifton* [1971] Ch 700; *Hone* v *Page* [1980] FSR 500 at pp 507–509; *VDU Installations Ltd* v *Integrated Computer and Cybernetics Systems Ltd* [1989] FSR 378.

14 Referring to *Fairclough* v *Manchester Ship Canal Co* [1897] WN 7.

15 *Biba Ltd* v *Stratford Investments* [1973] Ch 281 at p 287.

16 *Re The Agreement of the Mileage Conference Group of the Tyre Manufacturers' Conference Ltd* [1966] 2 All ER 849.

17 *TDK Tape Distributor (UK) Ltd* v *Videochoice Ltd* [1986] 1 WLR 141.

is satisfied that the defendant in question had notice of the order.[18] Under RSC Order 45, r 7, the defendant must have been served personally with a copy of the order endorsed with a penal notice. Under RSC Order 65, r 4 the court can make an order for substituted service of the Anton Piller order. Also under the concluding provision of RSC Order 45, r 7(6) there is power in the court to dispense with the service of the order, but this power would only be exercised in circumstances where the defendant was deliberately evading service of the order.[19] Accordingly, if the plaintiff wishes to be in a position to take contempt proceedings against the defendant for breach of the court order requiring permission to be given for entry on to the premises, it is necessary for personal service to have been effected on the defendant. In practice this is also the case in relation to mandatory orders for disclosure of documents and provision of information, subject to the unlikely possibility, in the context of Anton Piller procedure, of the plaintiff seeking to proceed under RSC Order 24, r 16 or RSC Order 26, r 6, by service on the defendant's solicitor. These are by their nature inappropriate to be invoked in relation to orders which require immediate compliance on the part of the defendant.

In relation to the prohibitory orders, it is incumbent upon the defendant on obtaining notice that the order has been made to take immediate steps to ensure that the documents or articles specified or described in the order are preserved. This is because of the principles applicable to prohibitory orders set out in section (2) of this chapter. Thus, for example, if a defendant is contacted by telephone by an employee at the premises in question, who has been served with a copy of the order, the defendant ought to instruct the employee to ensure that the relevant subject matter of the order is preserved. If he fails to do this, and the material is subsequently destroyed or damaged by one of his servants or agents, or with his permission, the defendant will be liable for contempt of the order.

In addition, if subsequently, after service of the order upon him, the defendant failed to provide documents or information as ordered by the court because he had in the meantime, prior to service of the order disabled himself from complying with its requirements then, it is considered that he would plainly be liable to be proceeded against for contempt of court in respect of the non-compliance.[20] This is not inconsistent with the principle which enables a party in breach of a mandatory order to raise the defence that he was genuinely unable to comply with the order. In such circumstances in the proceedings for contempt it must be proved beyond reasonable doubt that the defendant could have complied with the

---

18 RSC Order 45, r 7(6); *Re Tuck: Murch* v *Loosemoore* [1906] 1 Ch 692.
19 *Re Tuck: Murch* v *Loosemoore*, above at p 696.
20 *Lewis* v *Pontypridd, Caerphilly and Newport Railway Co* (1895) 11 TLR 203.

order.[21] However, wilful disablement caused by the defendant after he knows of the existence of the order takes the case outside of this category.

In relation to mandatory orders, a telephone conversation with an employee is not sufficient to ground contempt proceedings simply for non-compliance with the mandatory requirements of the order. However, this rule does not preclude contempt proceedings if the defendant is guilty of conduct with knowledge of the order, which has the effect of frustrating, and is intended to frustrate, the successful implementation of the order in due course. Thus, for example, if the defendant, knowing of the order, was to cause documents to be destroyed which were documents falling within the ambit of the search to be permitted under its terms, then this would clearly constitute a contempt of court. Although the search could still proceed the documents would no longer be there to be found the defendant having destroyed part of what was intended to be preserved pursuant to the court order. Even if a third party with knowledge of the court order destroyed the documents so as to frustrate the intended search, he would be guilty of contempt.[22]

Once the defendant has been personally served with the order, then subject to an opportunity to take legal advice, he becomes under an immediate obligation to comply with its mandatory terms. A refusal or failure to do so will constitute contempt. This is so even if he applies to the court to discharge the order, and even if that application is successful.[23]

(4) Mareva injunction: the position of third parties

A third party is not personally enjoined by the injunction. However, a third party who has been notified of a Mareva injunction is bound not to take any steps which would constitute a breach of the order made. This is regardless of whether the defendant has been served with or knows of the order. Thus for example, a bank once served with notice of the order must not wilfully assist in the disposal of funds by honouring cheques drawn by the defendant. The third party will be liable in contempt of court, if with knowledge of the order, he aids and abets a breach of the order by the party enjoined,[24] and this is so regardless of whether the party enjoined would himself be liable in contempt or not. The third party will only be responsible if he has the necessary *mens rea*. In the case of a bank it will not be sufficient to constitute contempt that a clerk in the bank made a payment without knowing of the order, albeit that another department of the

---

21 *Re Bramblevale Ltd* [1970] Ch 129.
22 *A-G v Newspaper Publishing plc* [1988] Ch 333 at pp 372 and 379–390.
23 *Wardle Fabrics Ltd v G Myristis Ltd* [1984] FSR 263; *Columbia Pictures Inc v Robinson* [1987] Ch 38 at pp 71–72.
24 *Lord Wellesley v Earl of Mornington (No 2)* (1848) 11 Beav 181; *Seaward v Paterson* [1897] Ch 545; *Acrow (Automation) Ltd v Rex Chainbelt Inc* [1971] 1 WLR 1676; *Z Ltd v A-Z and AA-LL* [1982] QB 558.

bank did have such knowledge. Thus it is not possible to add together the act of the clerk and the knowledge of the other department in order to constitute contempt by the bank.[25] If, on the other hand, the payment was made because there had been a deliberate failure on the part of the relevant department to stop transactions, then there would be a contempt. It is not clear whether recklessness as such would suffice. In *Z Ltd v A-Z and AA-LL*, Eveleigh LJ stated the necessary test as being that there had been a 'deliberate' failure to stop a payment either when the payment was authorised by the department in question or 'knowing that the payment was likely to be made under a general authority derived from' that department. If a payment is requested which could be consistent with compliance with the injunction, and the bank makes that payment, then it will be extremely difficult to make good a case of contempt of court against the bank. Thus, with an injunction limited to a maximum sum, if the bank has knowledge that the provision does not apply, then plainly the mere existence of that provision can provide no justification for making the payment. Eveleigh LJ said that carelessness 'or even recklessness on the part of the banks' would not make them liable for contempt 'unless it can be shown that there was indifference to such a degree that was contumacious'. This may be putting the test too high, and it may be the case that, contrary to the views of Eveleigh LJ, recklessness could suffice. Under a Mareva injunction in the usual form, which restrains the defendant from 'dealing with' or 'disposing of' his assets, the defendant is apparently not precluded from drawing sums out of his bank.[26] However, if the withdrawal is preparatory to a transaction which will be in breach of the order, the bank will be held liable for contempt of court if it knew that this was the case. Again it is not clear what degree of knowledge, short of actual knowledge of the intended transaction could suffice to expose the bank to liability for contempt.

It is now clear that there is also another principle under which a third party could be held liable for contempt, even though there was no breach of the injunction on the part of the defendant. If, for example, a Mareva injunction restrains the defendant from dealing with or disposing of a certain asset or allowing it to be removed from the jurisdiction, the question may arise whether a third party with knowledge of the injunction, could himself cause the asset to be dealt with or disposed of, or removed from the jurisdiction. In such a case, if the third party was not acting as the servant or agent of the defendant, nor on his behalf, there would not be even a breach of the terms of the injunction, because necessarily it is only addressed to the defendant. The third party might be seeking to act so as to advance his own personal interests. Nevertheless, the third party will be

---

25 *Z Ltd v A-Z and AA-LL* [1982] QB 558 at pp 581–582, per Eveleigh LJ.
26 *Bank Mellat v Kazmi* [1989] QB 541. See further pp 11–14 above.

in contempt of court if, with knowledge of the order, he intentionally frustrates its objective. In *A-G* v *Newspaper Publishing plc* [1988] Ch 333 an injunction had been granted against certain newspapers prohibiting them from publishing allegedly confidential information. Other newspapers which were not enjoined published extracts from the information. This did not constitute a breach of the injunction which had been granted. But it resulted in partial frustration of the objective sought to be achieved by the injunction in that information which was intended to be preserved as confidential, had been published. The Court of Appeal held that such conduct by the third parties was *capable of* constituting a contempt of court, provided it was done with the requisite intent. In that case the requisite intent fell to be decided in the context of the Contempt of Court Act 1981, since it involved a publication.[27] Had it not been so, it may have been the case that recklessness might have sufficed ([1988] Ch at pp 381–382) or even possibly that there would be strict liability ([1988] Ch at pp 373–374 and 381). The third party does not have to *desire* to bring about a contempt of court: *Attorney-General* v *Newspaper Publishing plc (No 2)* [1989] FSR 457 (Morritt J) applying *Reg* v *Moloney* [1985] AC 905 at p 926. In *Re Lonrho* [1989] 3 WLR 535, Lord Goff assumed that the case had been correctly decided, but left the matter open, it being contemplated that an appeal was likely to be brought challenging it.

In the context of Mareva relief, an injunction may have been granted restraining a defendant from disposing of a particular bank account. A third party might claim the right to deal with the account, for example the wife of the defendant. It is considered that the wife would not be free in such circumstances to deal with the account, even though it was in her own name, until the matter had been considered by the court and a decision taken as to whether the wife should be free to deal with the account.[28] Similarly, an injunction might restrain a defendant from removing certain specified cargo from the jurisdiction. The shipowners could not allow their ship to proceed out of the jurisdiction with the cargo on board ([1988] Ch at p 367, per Sir John Donaldson MR).

For a third party to be liable for contempt under this principle, it is not sufficient that he has failed to take steps to prevent the destruction of the subject matter of the injunction or the frustration of its objective. The third party either himself or through those for whom he is responsible must have acted in some way which has had this consequence, despite knowing of the injunction.[29]

---

27 See also *A-G* v *News Group Newspapers Plc* [1989] QB 110.
28 Compare the facts in *SCF* v *Masri* [1985] 1 WLR 876, before the injunction was expressly extended to the wife who was joined as a co-defendant, and see the observations of Lloyd LJ in *A-G* v *Newspaper Publishing plc* [1988] Ch 333 at pp 378–380.
29 *A-G* v *Observer Ltd* [1988] 1 All ER 385.

(5) Extra-territorial Mareva injunctions and third parties

In relation to a defendant the fact that a Mareva injunction or the appointment of a receiver, relates to assets abroad, makes no difference to his potential liability for contempt of court. Similarly, this is the case in relation to an Anton Piller order in respect of premises abroad. However, the position in relation to third parties and extra-territorial Mareva injunctions has attracted special attention from the courts, and has resulted in the practice of inserting a 'proviso' to the order which restricts the extent of the effect of the order on third parties.[30] It is clearly established that the injunction is not intended to have an effect on third parties who are resident abroad, and who are in no sense subject to the court's jurisdiction. As Nicholls LJ said in *Babanaft International Co* v *Bassatne* [1989] 2 WLR 232 at p 257:

It would be wrong for an English court, by making an order in respect of overseas assets against a defendant amenable to its jurisdiction, to impose or attempt to impose obligations on persons not before the court in respect of acts to be done by them abroad regarding property outside the jurisdiction. That self-evidently would be for the English court to claim an altogether exorbitant, extra-territorial jurisdiction.

However, in the context of contempt of court it is clear that a party to the proceedings can be held in contempt in respect of actions abroad, and it is difficult to see why in principle a third party who is *not* resident or carrying on business abroad, should not equally be bound to respect the order of the court in relation to his conduct abroad. The proviso takes this into account.

More difficult is the position of third parties who are either resident or carry on business abroad, but also have a presence within the jurisdiction. For example, is a distinction to be made between a third party bank which has no branch within the jurisdiction and one which happens to have a branch within the jurisdiction? As the proviso is presently formulated such a distinction is made. Thus a bank which is locally resident in England is required to observe the effect of the injunction in relation to a bank account at a branch abroad.[31] However, this approach does not give effect to the consideration that although the third party may have a presence within the jurisdiction there may be excellent reasons for the English court not to make an order in relation to that party's conduct abroad. Thus in the context of granting a subpoena or making an order for inspection and taking copies of extracts in a banker's book under s 7 of the Bankers' Books Evidence Act 1879, the court has, as a general rule, declined to exercise jurisdiction to grant such relief against a bank in respect of an account held at a foreign branch.[32] The justified restraint exercised by the

---

30 *Derby & Co Ltd* v *Weldon (Nos 3 and 4)* [1989] 2 WLR 412. The text of the proviso is set out at p 122 above.
31 *Securities and Investments Board and Pantell SA* [1989] 3 WLR 698.
32 *Mackinnon* v *Donaldson Lufkin and Jenrette* [1986] Ch 482.

court in this area, is to be contrasted with the position under the proviso in use for extra-territorial Mareva orders.[33]

(6) Anton Piller relief and third parties

An Anton Piller order is often served on a person other than the defendant who is at the premises in question at the relevant time, and appears to be the person in charge of the premises. Provided that the order has been drafted in the appropriate form, it should require the defendant by himself or by any person appearing to be in control of the premises to give the permission needed for the entry on to the premises and for the search to take place.[34] Accordingly, a person, who is not the defendant enjoined under the order, is not himself ordered by the terms of the order, to give the relevant permission.

The principles applicable to the personal position of such an individual are set out in section (4) of this chapter (p 172, above). For example, if that individual, knowing of the order, deliberately destroyed documents which fell within the scope of the order so as to prevent them being found by the representatives of the plaintiff, and preserved, then this would constitute a contempt of court.

But is the individual on being served with the order obliged, after an opportunity to take legal advice, to give permission for the entry and the search? Obviously if the individual does not have the authority so to act, he can be under no obligation personally to purport to give such permission. But is he then obliged to seek such permission from the defendant? Although in practice the individual concerned might well be prepared to contact his principal for instructions, it is considered that as a general rule he would not be in contempt of court if he chose not to do so. The order is not addressed to him personally. Furthermore, whilst seeking instructions would tend to progress matters more rapidly, it could not usually be said that the mere failure to seek instructions constituted a deliberate interference with the administration of justice.[35] If, however, the individual does seek instructions, he must do nothing to influence the defendant to refuse permission for the entry and search.

If the individual concerned does have the authority to give permission for the entry and search, what is then the position? Would the failure to give permission constitute a contempt of court? It might be suggested that

---

33 See further 'The Territorial Reach of Mareva Injunctions' by Lawrence Collins (1989) 105 LQR 262 at pp 281–286.

34 *Manor Electronics* v *Dickson* [1988] RPC 618. Contrast the irregular form of order made in *VDU Installations Ltd* v *Integrated Computer Systems and Cybernetics Ltd* [1989] FSR 378 at p 383 which provided that: 'the defendant or any person appearing to be in control of the premises hereinafter mentioned do permit.'

35 See also *Eccles & Co* v *Louisville and Nashville Railroad Company* [1912] 1 KB 135, in which a servant who had been ordered to produce documents which he held for his master, was held not to be in contempt when he did not produce them and had not sought permission from his master to produce them.

a mere omission by a third party cannot constitute a contempt of court.[36] Thus, it might be said that the third party can only be liable for contempt if he *actively* participates in a breach of the court order or deliberately *interferes* with the administration of justice. As a general proposition this is no doubt correct. But is a refusal to give permission to be viewed as a mere omission, and can the applicable principles apply to such a refusal? In *Acrow (Automation) Ltd* v *Rex Chainbelt Inc* [1971] 1 WLR 1676, the defendant, in breach of an injunction, instructed a third party not to continue to supply certain machinery parts to the plaintiff, and the third party knowing of the injunction, acted on the instruction and refused to continue to supply the plaintiff. The Court of Appeal held that the third party by acting on the instruction had committed a contempt of court, even though in one view of the matter it might have been said that the third party had simply 'omitted' to supply the parts.

It is considered that even if the individual has authority to give the permission required by the order, he will as a general rule be entitled not to give that permission. He is not personally subject to the order of the court and the result of declining to give permission will not usually be to frustrate the eventual implementation of a search. However, if the refusal is simply part of a plan to delay the search so as to enable documents to be removed from the premises, or hidden, or destroyed by others, then it is considered that the individual would plainly be in contempt of court.

(7) Irregular or unjustified orders

It is established that a defendant, or for that matter a third party, cannot justify contempt on the grounds that the order should never have been made, or was irregular. If an order has been made, it must be obeyed until it is set aside.[37]

(8) Proof of breach of the order

If proceedings are to be taken for contempt it is essential that there is strict observance of the procedural requirements. Committal proceedings are regulated by RSC Order 52. In the case of Anton Piller or Mareva relief contempt proceedings are held in open court before a single judge and are made by notice of motion, supported by affidavit. The notice of motion must clearly state the grounds of the application and specify with particulars precisely what it is that the alleged contemnor is said to have done.[38] The notice of motion and a copy of the affidavit in support must be served personally on the alleged contemnor although there is power to dispense

---

36 *Seaward* v *Paterson* [1897] 1 Ch 545 at p 557; *Thorne Rural District Council* v *Bunting (No 2)* [1972] 3 All ER 1084; *A-G* v *Observer Ltd* [1988] 1 All ER 385 at p 399.
37 *Isaacs* v *Robertson* [1985] AC 97; *Hadkinson* v *Hadkinson* [1952] P 285.
38 *Chiltern District Council* v *Keane* [1985] 1 WLR 619; *Churchman* v *Joint Shop Stewards' Committee* [1972] 1 WLR 1094.

with this requirement.[39] Although the proceedings are civil and not criminal, the burden of proof is equivalent to the criminal burden.[40] Furthermore, since contempt proceedings although not in fact criminal proceedings, partake of a criminal nature, the alleged contemnor is permitted to make a submission of no case to answer, without being put to his election whether or not he chooses to call evidence: *Attorney-General for Tuvalu* v *Philatelic Distribution Corporation Ltd* (above). This is in contrast with the usual position in civil proceedings: *Alexander* v *Rayson* [1936] 1 KB 169.

When preparing a draft order at the *ex parte* stage of proceedings it is essential that it is as definite, clear and precise in its terms as possible, so that there will be no excuse to a defendant for misunderstanding it or failing to obey it. The court will not make a finding of contempt if the relevant part of the order or undertaking in question is vague or is imprecise in a material respect. An order should be clear on its face and should not require the defendant to cross-refer to other documents in order to ascertain the full extent of his obligations: *Rudkin-Jones* v *Trustee of the Property of the Bankrupt* (1965) 109 SJ 334. The person to whom the order is directed should be able, by reading it and without more, to know at once what it is that he must do, or refrain from doing in order to comply with its terms. For this reason, an order which refers to another document (eg a contract, another order of the court or an affidavit) and grants relief by reference to what is set out in that document is defective and may result in contempt proceedings founded upon it being unsuccessful.[41]

(9) Penalties for contempt

If the court makes a finding of contempt, the nature of the penalty to be imposed will depend upon the circumstances of the case. The relevant considerations include the following:

(1) Whether the plaintiff has been prejudiced by virtue of the contempt, and if so whether that prejudice can be rectified and how. For example, if money which ought to have been preserved under a Mareva injunction has been paid to a third party, the third party might be required to reconstitute the fund.[42] If the defendant has hidden away assets which are the subject of a Mareva injunction,

---

39 RSC Order 52, r 4(3); *Mansour* v *Mansour* (1989) *The Times*, 2 January.

40 *Re Bramblevale* [1970] Ch 128; *The Commissioner of Water Resources* v *Federated Engine Drivers' and Firemen's Association of Australasia* [1988] 2 Qd R 385 (Supreme Court of Queensland); *Attorney-General for Tuvalu* v *Philatelic Distribution Corporation Ltd* (1989) *The Times*, 24 October; *Attorney-General* v *Newspaper Publishing plc (No 2)* [1989] FSR 457.

41 *The Commissioner of Water Resources* v *Federated Engine Drivers' and Firemen's Association of Australasia*, above at p 390.

42 *TDK Tape Distributor (UK) Ltd* v *Videochoice Ltd* [1986] 1 WLR 141.

then the court may decide to seek to compel the defendant to restore the position.[43]

(2) The extent to which the contemnor has acted under pressure. In the context of Anton Piller relief, a defendant is liable to act under the pressure of the moment rather than by the way of deliberate misconduct. If a defendant has so acted this provides good reason for not making a committal order.[44]

(3) If there has been a deliberate and contumacious breach of a court order then the court has to bear in mind the public interest in ensuring that court orders are obeyed. Thus a committal order may be fully appropriate when there has been a deliberate breach of a Mareva injunction,[45] even if in the meantime the defendant has sought to rectify the prejudice suffered by the plaintiff.

(4) Whether the contemnor has been placed in breach of the court order by reason of the conduct of others, and if so the extent to which he is personally at fault.

(5) Whether the contemnor has acted on mistaken legal advice.

(10) Refusal to hear a party in contempt

If a defendant is in contempt of court in respect of compliance with an order the question may arise as to whether the court will refuse to hear the party in contempt until after he has purged that contempt. The general principles which apply in such circumstances are as follows:

(1) The contemnor may be precluded from making applications in the same action as that in which the order was made in respect of which he is in contempt, but he will not be prevented from making applications in other actions.[46]

(2) The contemnor is not precluded from defending himself in the action (eg by appearing to resist an interlocutory application made by another party or by defending himself at the trial).[47]

(3) The contemnor is not precluded from making an application or advancing an appeal in the action for the purpose of seeking to set aside the very order in respect of which he is in contempt.[48] This principle applies regardless of whether the grounds of the application or appeal contend that the order was itself irregular or was

---

43 *Enfield London Borough Council* v *Mahoney* [1983] 1 WLR 749.
44 *HPSI Ltd* v *Thomas and Williams* (1983) 133 NLJ 598.
45 *Popischil* v *Philips* (1988) *The Times*, 19 January; Court of Appeal (Civil Division) Transcript No 31 of 1988.
46 *Hadkinson* v *Hadkinson* [1952] P 285 at p 296.
47 *Hadkinson* v *Hadkinson*, above, at pp 289–290, and p 296; *Parry* v *Perryman* (MR July 1838) referred to in the notes to *Chuck* v *Cremer* (1846) 1 Coop temp Cott 205; *Midland Bank* v *Green (No 3)* [1979] Ch 496 at p 506.
48 *Chuck* v *Cremer*, above; *Hadkinson* v *Hadkinson*, above; *Astro Exito Navegacion SA* v *Southland Enterprise Co Ltd* [1981] 2 Lloyd's Rep 595 at pp 601–602, per Brandon LJ.

made as a result of irregular proceedings.[49] In the context of Anton Piller relief this principle has the effect that a defendant who is in breach of the provisions of the order is not precluded by reason of his contempt from seeking to have the order discharged, either by interlocutory application or at the trial. But he may still be penalised for contempt.[50]

(4) The contemnor is not precluded from making an application or advancing an appeal for the purpose of setting aside subsequent proceedings in the action on the grounds that an order has been made without jurisdiction or there has been some other irregularity.[51]

(5) Where a contemnor seeks to make a voluntary application in the action which does not fall within (3) or (4) above, then the court has a discretion whether or not to refuse to hear the contemnor until he has purged his contempt, which will be exercised taking into account the nature of the application sought to be made and the circumstances of the particular case.[52] In the context of Mareva relief, in *National Bank of Greece v Constantinos Dimitriou* (1987) *The Times*, 16 November, the defendant who was subject to a Mareva injunction, was in contempt of court in failing to disclose details of his assets and their whereabouts pursuant to a disclosure order which had been made against him. The defendant applied to the court for a variation to be made to the injunction to enable him to use assets subject to the injunction to pay his solicitors. The Court of Appeal refused to make the proposed variation, and said that the court would not assist the defendant who was abusing the process of the court and in contempt of court.

(11) Ordering a defence to be struck out on the grounds that the defendant is in contempt of court

A different but related question which may arise is whether the court will make an order striking out the defence of a contemnor when there has been a breach of a court order granting Anton Piller or Mareva relief. If the breach is of an order requiring discovery of documents or the answering of interrogatories there is express provision under RSC Order 24, r 16 and RSC Order 26, r 6, empowering the court to strike out a defence and to enter judgment against the defendant. What of breaches which do not fall within either of these categories? It is considered that the court has jurisdiction in such circumstances to order that a defence be struck out

---

49 *Astro Exito Navegacion SA v Southland Enterprise Co Ltd*, above, at p 602.
50 *Wardle Fabrics Ltd v G Myristis Ltd* [1984] FSR 264; *Columbia Pictures Inc v Robinson* [1987] Ch 38 at pp 71–72.
51 *Gordon v Gordon* [1904] P 163.
52 *Hadkinson v Hadkinson*, above; *Garstin v Garstin* [1865] 4 Sw & Tr 73; *Cavendish v Cavendish and Rochefoucauld* (1866) 15 WR 182.

under the inherent jurisdiction of the court to regulate its own proceedings. In *Derby & Co Ltd v Weldon (Nos 3 and 4)* [1989] 2 WLR 412 at p 428, Lord Donaldson MR referred to the possibility of not allowing a defendant to defend the action if there was a failure to co-operate with the receiver appointed over its assets. Furthermore, in *Richo International Ltd v International Industrial Food Co SAL* [1989] 1 Lloyd's Rep 106, the plaintiffs had a very strong proprietary claim advanced in arbitration proceedings and an order was made by the court under s 12(6)(*f*) of the Arbitration Act 1950 for payment of the fund in dispute into court, and that in default the contemnor be debarred from defending the arbitration. Hirst, LJ held that there would have been jurisdiction to debar a defendant from defending High Court proceedings on the merits if an order had been made for the preservation of the fund in those proceedings and that there was an equivalent jurisdiction to prevent the defendant defending arbitration proceedings in such circumstances.[53] In the course of the judgment the judge said that the sanction was 'undoubtedly a severe one' but on the facts of the case, there was no other practicable way in which the preservation order could be enforced and in calculating the sum to be preserved under the order, the court excluded any amount in respect of which the defendants in question might conceivably have had a viable defence.

Accordingly, it is considered that it will only be in extreme circumstances that this inherent jurisdiction will be exercised by the court, when the contempt does not involve prejudicing the plaintiff in relation to advancing his case on the merits. Thus, when a defendant within the jurisdiction was in breach of an order requiring an interim payment to be made, the Court of Appeal set aside an order striking out the defence in the action,[54] Lawton LJ observing that there were other ways in which the order could be enforced, and that the provisions regulating the making of interim payment orders left 'no room' for invoking the inherent jurisdiction of the court.

The result of exercising the jurisdiction in any particular case will be to confer upon the plaintiff a judgment in default of defence, or the benefit of an arbitration award obtained in circumstances where the defendant has been prevented from defending himself. The plaintiff may well have difficulties in seeking to enforce such a judgment or award abroad. If the position is that the plaintiff is entitled to succeed in full on the merits of his claim, the invoking of the inherent jurisdiction of the court will be liable to leave him in a substantially worse position (save in relation to the incurring of legal costs) than would otherwise be the case. This is particularly likely to be so in cases where there is no other way to enforce the relevant

---

53 Reasoning by analogy with the power of the court to strike out a *claim* made in arbitration proceedings when there was a failure to comply with an order for security for costs made under s 12(6)(*a*) of the Arbitration Act 1950; and applying *The Argenpuma* [1984] 2 Lloyd's Rep 563.
54 *HH Property Co Ltd v Rahim* [1987] 1 EGLR 52.

court order in respect of which the defendant is in breach. If, on the other hand, the true position is that the plaintiff would not be found entitled to succeed in full on his claim on the merits, then it must be seriously open to doubt whether striking out the defence is in accordance with the justice of the case. Furthermore, there is the apparent injustice in preventing a defendant from putting forward his defence, when the relevant contempt has not given rise to any prejudice to the innocent party in relation to advancing the claim on the merits. In *Richo International Ltd* v *International Industrial Food SAL* (above), Hirst J sought to negative this apparent injustice by limiting the preservation order to a sum in respect of which the defendants had no conceivable viable defence. However, if striking out is only to be ordered in such circumstances then the threatened sanction is unlikely to achieve the aim of procuring the defendant to comply with the order of the court. If, on the other hand, striking out is sought when the defendant may have a defence to the claim, the granting of the application may well result in substantial injustice being done. This consideration may also explain why the striking out of a defence is not available as a sanction when there is a failure by a defendant to comply with an interim payment order.

Chapter 15

Mareva injunctions and third parties

(1) Introduction

A Mareva injunction is liable to have important practical consequences for third parties. Thus, for example, banks need to protect themselves against the risk of finding themselves participating in a breach of the order, and a creditor of the defendant may find that the injunction is preventing payment being made to him. Third parties are entitled to apply to the court either to vary or to discharge the order, or to seek directions as to its effect.[1] Such applications are common, and provided that the application has been made reasonably, it is standard practice to order the plaintiff to pay the costs of the third party on an indemnity basis subject to the third party proving that the particular costs in question were reasonably incurred (see p 186, below).

(2) Effect of notification of the injunction to third parties

Once a third party has been notified of the making of an injunction, he would be prudent to examine its precise terms and to regard himself as bound not to take any steps inconsistent with the preservation of the assets covered by the injunction, subject to the liberties contained within the order (eg for the defendant to pay his ordinary living expenses). Otherwise if the third party assists in the disposal of the assets in question then he may find himself being made subject to proceedings for contempt of court.

Thus, for example, a bank should not honour cheques drawn by the defendant even though such cheques were issued before the Mareva injunction was granted,[2] if the effect of honouring the cheques would be to diminish the defendant's credit balance at the bank, or increase the level of indebtedness secured by mortgages or charge over assets of the

---

1 *A-G v Newspaper Publishing plc* [1988] Ch 333 at p 375; *Harbottle Ltd v National Westminster Bank* [1978] QB 146 at p 157; *Cretanor Maritime Co Ltd v Irish Marine Ltd* [1978] 1 WLR 966 at p 978; *Galaxia Maritime v Mineralimportexport* [1982] 1 WLR 539; *Z Ltd v A-Z and AA-LL* [1982] QB 558 at p 588 per Kerr LJ.
2 *Z Ltd v A-Z and AA-LL* [1982] QB 558.

defendant covered by the injunction. If a third party has issued a cheque to the defendant, the position appears to be that there is no objection in principle to the cheque being presented for payment, and the proceeds obtained for the defendant.[3] That transaction simply involves obtaining the proceeds of the cheque and although the cheque has been dealt with, the defendant's overall asset position remains the same. However, the bank is not at liberty to credit the proceeds against an account which is in overdraft,[4] unless the bank has a right of set off which it is permitted to exercise under the order. It is standard form for a liberty to be given by the order for the bank to exercise any set off it might have in respect of facilities granted by the bank to the defendant prior to the granting of the injunction.[5]

The liberty does not extend automatically to cover loans made after the date of the injunction because a new loan might otherwise be used as a device on the part of the defendant to defeat the effect of the injunction. Therefore, set off in regard to such loans will not be sanctioned as a matter of course. If the defendant enjoys a good relationship with his bank, he might consider that he would rather try to obtain a large enough loan to enable him to continue trading with unaffected assets, than go back to court to seek a variation of the original order. However, if the only security he can offer the bank happens to be assets subject to the injunction, he would have to go to court to seek a variation because the creation of an encumbrance over those assets would otherwise amount to a breach of the injunction. The court would undoubtedly sanction a bona fide loan transaction and vary the injunction to enable it to be carried out.

Normally, the third party is notified of the existence and terms of the injunction by the plaintiff. The defendant has an independent obligation to comply with the terms of the order whether or not those in control of his assets know about it. The risk of a third party committing a contempt of court exists even if he acquires his knowledge from a source other than the plaintiff. It should be stressed that there is no legal duty on a third party to make inquiries or to go to any expense when it is uncertain whether assets in his possession are subject to a Mareva injunction. However, if he knows that a Mareva injunction has been granted and if there is a likelihood that those assets are caught by the terms of that injunction, the third party remains inactive at his peril.

It is often in the plaintiff's best interests that he should give prompt notice of the injunction to as many as possible of the third parties (such as banks) whom he believes to be holding assets belonging to the defendant. This reduces the risk that a defendant who is prepared to break the injunction will succeed in removing his assets. The form of notification

3 *Bank Mellat* v *Kazmi* [1989] QB 541 and pp 11–14, above.
4 *Re Gray's Inn Construction Co Ltd* [1980] 1 WLR 711 and see p 13, above.
5 *Oceanica Castelana Armadora SA* v *Mineralimportexport Ataka Navigation Inc* [1983] 1 WLR 1294.

usually does not matter (it is quite common for the plaintiff's solicitor to read the terms of the order to the bank over the telephone), but it is advisable to follow up any such communication by delivery of a copy of the stamped order when it has been drawn up, so that the bank is fully aware of the exact terms of the injunction with which it must comply. In accordance with his undertaking to the court, the plaintiff must notify each third party whom he has notified of the Mareva injunction that the third party has the right to apply to the court to vary or set aside the injunction. Even if this is self-evident from the terms of the copy of the order when it is delivered to the third party, it is necessary to give separate notification in order to comply with the undertaking. It is quite common for the undertaking to provide that the plaintiff will do this at the same time as he gives notice of the injunction to the third party.

(3) Third parties have no obligation to disclose information about assets unless the court so orders

The plaintiff may believe that there are sufficient assets in one bank account to satisfy his claim. In those circumstances, he may not wish to risk exposing himself to wider liability under his cross-undertaking by notifying more banks (and thus potentially widening the damage to the defendant). It is inadvisable to serve notice indiscriminately, because of the impact which this may have on the plaintiff's future liability in damages, and also because of the plaintiff's potential liability to third parties. On the other hand, the plaintiff may wish to safeguard against the possibility that the account, contrary to his belief, has no money in it or has money which is subject to a prior claim by the bank. Unfortunately, from the plaintiff's point of view, there is no obligation on a third party served with notice of a Mareva injunction to tell the plaintiff how much, if anything, he has 'caught'. Banks almost invariably refuse to do so because otherwise they would be in breach of the obligation of confidentiality which they owe to their customer. The plaintiff may apply to the court for discovery or for an order under the Bankers' Books Evidence Act 1879. However, such orders will only be granted in aid of the injunction so as to render it effective. Furthermore, a bank or other third party which seeks a variation of the Mareva injunction is under no duty to disclose information about the defendant's assets to the plaintiff as a precondition of obtaining such relief: *Oceanica Castelana Armadora SA* v *Mineralimportexport* [1983] 1 WLR 1294.

(4) Third parties and notification of the defendant

The defendant should always receive separate notification by the plaintiff of the terms of the Mareva injunction. However, a third party served with notice of the injunction will usually tell the defendant about it. Indeed, he may be under contractual obligation to do so; for example, if the third party is a bank and the injunction prohibits it from honouring cheques drawn on the defendant's account. However, the third party cannot delay his compliance with the terms of the injunction pending the receipt of instructions from the defendant. He is bound to obey its terms from the moment at which he becomes aware of them. Furthermore, if the third party receives instructions from the defendant to deal with the assets in question he should not do so without the sanction of the court unless it is plain that there are sufficient other assets available to enable the dealings to take place without breaching the terms of the order. If the third party is in any doubt he should apply to court himself for an order sanctioning the transactions which the defendant has instructed him to carry out.

(5) Rights of third parties to an indemnity

An innocent third party who has been notified of an injunction and has incurred expense in complying with its terms is entitled to recover those expenses (provided that they have been reasonably incurred) from the plaintiff under the standard form undertaken by the plaintiff furnished to the court and recorded in the order.[6] If the plaintiff has to pay such expenses, it is considered that such a payment would be a disbursement or expense falling within the definition of 'costs' in RSC Order 62, r 1(4), and would form part of the plaintiff's costs of the action.[7]

If a third party applies to the court in relation to the injunction (for example, if he seeks a variation of the injunction) then, provided that he acts reasonably, he is entitled to recover from the plaintiff his reasonable costs in respect of the application. Prior to the revision of RSC Order 62 this was achieved by directing that the costs should be taxed on a solicitor and own client basis, but with a special direction that notwithstanding the terms of r 29(1), the burden of establishing the reasonableness of the amount should be upon the third party to whom the costs were awarded: *Project Development Co Ltd SA* v *KMK Securities Ltd* [1982] 1 WLR 1470 at p 1472. The third party will now normally be granted an equivalent order under the new rules.

Persons affected by Mareva injunctions normally fall within one or more of the following categories:

    (*a*) persons holding the defendant's assets as bailees or trustees;

    (*b*) debtors of the defendant;

    (*c*) creditors of the defendant;

---

6 *Z Ltd* v *A-Z and AA-LL* [1982] QB 558 at p 575; *Searose Ltd* v *Seatrain UK Ltd* [1981] 1 WLR 894; *Clipper Maritime Co Ltd* v *Mineralimportexport* [1981] 1 WLR 1262.

7 *Searose* v *Seatrain UK Ltd* [1981] 1 WLR 894 at p 896 (see further the argument put forward in relation to the remuneration of a receiver and manager appointed by the court in *Evans* v *Clayhope Properties Ltd* [1988] 1 WLR 358 at pp 362–363).

(*d*) persons who claim that they own, or have a charge over, assets which *prima facie* appear to belong to the defendant.

(6) Bailees, trustees and debtors

Persons who are looking after the defendant's chattels or other assets normally find that the practical effect of the Mareva injunction is to make them liable to keep the assets in question (and maintain them in a reasonable condition) until further order. If the third party is unwilling to incur the expenditure of looking after the assets for any length of time (for example because his bailment was supposed to be temporary, or he cannot afford the costs of so doing), or if he distrusts the plaintiff's ability to reimburse him, he can apply to court for relief. The court may make such directions as may be appropriate for the preservation of the assets—for example, the court may, as the price for continuance of the injunction, require an undertaking from the plaintiff to pay the storage costs to the third party at a given rate in advance, or it may require the plaintiff's solicitors to look after the assets instead of the third party.

The question might arise as to whether the court has power to order a sale of assets caught by a Mareva injunction. It is thought that RSC Order 29, r 4 is too narrow in its terms to provide jurisdiction to order such a sale. The rule only applies to 'any property which is the subject matter of the cause or matter or as to which any question may arise therein' and thus appears only to cover property which is the actual subject of the litigation (eg a case in which the buyer claims to reject goods which have been sold and delivered to him), or property as to which an issue arises in the litigation itself. However, it is considered that a sale may be ordered by granting a mandatory injunction pursuant to s 37(1) of the Supreme Court Act 1981 requiring the defendant to sell the asset or to consent to a sale arranged by the plaintiff's solicitors. Thus, the case law on the scope of s 37(1) would appear to provide ample warrant for the court having jurisdiction to do this (*Bekhor* v *Bilton* [1981] QB 923; *House of Spring Garden Ltd* v *Waite* [1985] FSR 173; and *Bayer* v *Winter (No 1)* [1986] 1 WLR 497). Alternatively, it seems that the court could appoint a receiver under s 37(1) with power to take possession of the goods and effect a sale even though the goods are not part of the subject matter of the action: *Hart* v *Emelkirk Ltd* 1 WLR 1289 and see Chapter 12, at pp 139–141. As a matter of discretion, particularly before the plaintiff has obtained judgment in the action, the courts would be most reluctant to make an order requiring assets of the defendant to be sold; thus 'the courts must be vigilant to ensure that the Mareva defendant is not treated like a judgment debtor': *Bekhor* v *Bilton* [1981] QB 923 at p 942, per Ackner LJ. The position is entirely different to that which arises when the Admiralty Court decides whether to sell an arrested ship *pendente lite* (*The 'Myrto'* [1977] 2 Lloyd's Rep 243) because in that situation the ship has become effectively encumbered with the plaintiff's claim.

Mareva relief in standard form does not prevent third parties paying their debts to the defendant or returning goods to him. If the plaintiff wishes to obtain an injunction which has this effect then he will need to seek special wording (see p 13, above) or alternatively he will need to seek the appointment of a receiver by the court. Ordinarily, before judgment the court will not interfere with the way in which the defendant carries on his business, and if he uses one account to receive payments from trade debtors and to pay his trade creditors that pattern will not be disturbed without very good reason.[8]

If the defendant has a claim against a third party (eg an insurer) and wishes to enter into a bona fide settlement of that claim, the Mareva injunction will ordinarily be varied so as to enable this to occur.[9] Furthermore, as a matter of practice, on such an application the court usually will not be concerned with any investigation as to the merits and demerits of any proposed settlement, unless there is clear *prima facie* evidence that the settlement would be in bad faith or collusive ([1989] 1 Lloyd's Rep at p 279, per Slade LJ).

Occasionally a third party bailee may be under an obligation to deliver the goods to someone else—for example, he may be carrying the goods to a purchaser from the defendant to whom the property has not yet passed, or he may be a freight forwarder who is about to ship them on a vessel which is due to depart imminently. That is a situation which almost invariably results in an urgent application by the third party (independently or together with the defendant), for a variation of the original Mareva injunction to enable shipment or delivery to be made. If the contract of sale or supply can be proved, and it is clear that the transaction is a legitimate business transaction, such a variation will almost invariably be made.

(7) Operation of 'maximum sum' orders

Another problem which frequently faces third parties (especially banks) holding assets belonging to the defendant is how to comply with the terms of an injunction which limits the defendant's dealings with assets up to a specified sum. The defendant may have accounts at various banks, but each bank may not know how much money the other banks are holding— indeed, they may be unaware of the existence of the accounts with other banks. If the bank is holding assets which exceed the 'maximum sum' the operation of the order is fairly straightforward so far as it is concerned. It will simply permit the defendant to draw down to the maximum sum and no further. If the bank becomes aware that there are other assets which, together with the assets which it is holding, exceed the maximum sum, the prudent course of action is to make an application to the court for a

---

8 *Avant Petroleum Inc* v *Gatoil Overseas Inc* [1986] 2 Lloyd's Rep 236.
9 *Normid Housing Association Ltd* v *Ralph A Mansell (No 2)* [1989] 1 Lloyd's Rep 274 and see p 14, above.

variation of the original order to limit it to specific assets so that the account in question is freed.

In *Z Ltd* v *A-Z and AA-LL* [1982] QB 558 at p 576, Lord Denning MR suggested that in some cases the best course could be for the injunction to omit a maximum sum altogether because of the difficulty that a maximum sum order is liable to cause to a bank—the bank should not be expected to monitor what other assets a defendant has within the jurisdiction and what the value is of those assets. An alternative suggestion was that the injunction should be subject to a maximum sum and that there should be a special injunction in respect of assets held or controlled by each bank or other third party served with a copy of the order so as to 'freeze' the assets of the defendant held by each third party up to the maximum sum (per Kerr LJ at p 589; see also the judgment of Lord Denning MR at p 576). However, in practice the courts have simply granted injunctions in forms limited to a single maximum sum (which makes an allowance for interest and costs), leaving it to banks or other third parties to apply to the court for a variation in case there is any difficulty in any particular case. If an injunction was granted in the form contemplated by Kerr LJ this would be liable to leave the plaintiff with a greater exposure on his cross-under-taking as to damages.

In deciding what was to be the value of assets to be retained, subject to the injunction, the courts might have taken the view that it would be appropriate to retain sufficient assets to satisfy the claim (with interest and costs) together with an additional amount to meet ongoing commit-ments of the defendant. This approach would have had the merit of pre-serving extra funds to be available to the defendant to make bona fide payments. However, the courts have refused to allow Mareva injunctions to be used in this way on the grounds that it would in effect involve a rewriting of the established law of insolvency: *K/S A/S Admiral Shipping* v *Portlink Ferries Ltd* [1984] 2 Lloyd's Rep 166, at p 168. Thus the maximum sum to be retained under a Mareva injunction is calculated solely by refer-ence to the claim, interest and costs, and the value of the assets of the defendant subject to the injunction at any one time is assessed subject to existing mortgages but not subject to future set offs which have not yet arisen. It is true that the assets actually caught by the Mareva are then subject to reduction (eg as future set offs arise on a bank account in respect of loan interest on an outstanding overdraft), but this has been said to be 'an inevitable consequence of a defendant who is subject to a "maximum sum" Mareva—and who has no other free assets, being allowed to pay his debts as they fall due' per Lloyd J in *Oceanica Castlelana Armadora SA* v *Mineralimportexport* [1983] 1 WLR 1294 at p 1301.

A question which could arise is whether it is necessary to take into account existing rights of set off against choses in action belonging to the defendant in calculating the value of assets of the defendant subject to the injunction. If the set off has already been asserted by the third party then it must be right to take it into account as reducing the value of the chose in action against which the set off has been asserted. If, on the other hand, the set off has not yet been asserted by the third party, then it might be said that it was entirely a matter for the third party to decide whether or not to exercise a set off and that he is not obliged to do so, see *Davis* v *Hedges* (1871) LR 6 QB 687, which is a case on the entitlement of the defendant to abate the price on a building contract at common law—the same principles would appear to apply to the entitlement of the third party to assert a set off. However, it is thought that the entitlement to claim a set off on the value of a chose in action should be taken into account once this entitlement had arisen and provided that, applying good accountancy practice, the existence of the entitlement to assert a set off should be taken into account in placing a value on the particular chose in action.

(8) Notice of more than one injunction

If the plaintiff knows of another Mareva injunction against the defendant then *prima facie* he will be entitled to obtain a Mareva injunction which is intended to be cumulative in its effect with the other injunction. In such circumstances it is desirable for the plaintiff to apply for express words to be inserted into the injunction to the effect that the defendant is restrained from dealing with his assets within the jurisdiction save in so far as these exceed the aggregate of the maximum sum and the sum which the defendant is enjoined from dealing with under the other injunction. (For the purposes of any contempt proceedings which might subsequently be taken it is essential to have an injunction which is clear and precise in its terms and effect.) On the other hand, a defendant or a third party such as a bank faced with two orders which appear to have been obtained independently of each other and which are not expressed to be cumulative may be faced with the question of whether to treat the orders as being cumulative. Ordinarily third parties should proceed on the assumption that the intention of the court is to preserve assets in respect of each of the claims. Thus, the injunctions should be treated as each having effect on the defendant with the maximum sum provisos only becoming relevant when there are sufficient assets covered by the combination of the maximum sums. This would be in accordance with the objective to be imputed to the court in granting each injunction, since it should be borne in mind that it is often the case that *ex parte* Mareva relief is granted without it being known that relief has already been granted in other proceedings. This should be the approach of third parties even when, on the literal wording of each injunction, it only enjoins dealings with assets 'up to an unencumbered value of' a specified maximum sum. This wording on a literal reading in itself would not be sufficient to make the maximum sums cumulative, because the Mareva injunctions do not have the effect of creating any encumbrance on the assets of the defendant.[10]

---

10 *Cretanor Maritime Co Ltd* v *Irish Marine Management Ltd* [1978] 1 WLR 966.

It is open to the defendant or to the third party to apply to the court for the injunctions to be discharged or varied.[11] As a matter of prudence the third party should normally apply for variation of the injunctions so as to make the position absolutely clear rather than risk subsequently being made a party to proceedings for contempt. On such an application the court will ordinarily grant a variation to each injunction so as to make them each subject to a maximum sum calculated by reference to the total claims against the defendant.

(9) The defendant's creditors

The court will always be concerned to ensure that a Mareva injunction does not operate oppressively and that a defendant will not be hampered in his ordinary business dealings any more than is absolutely necessary to protect the plaintiff from the risk of *mala fide* dissipation. Since the plaintiff is not in the position of a secured creditor, and has no proprietary claim to the assets subject to the injunction, there can be no objection in principle to the defendant dealing in the ordinary way with his business and with his other creditors, even if the effect of such dealings is to render the injunction of no practical value.

Upon the application of the defendant or an interested third party with notice of the injunction (usually, but not invariably, a third party creditor or a bank), the court may make an order varying the terms of the injunction enabling payment to be made of bona fide business debts or commitments, or other expenses (eg living expenses). These may include expenses such as staff salaries, normal office expenses, payments due to trade creditors, and legal fees. Of course, the type of expenses in respect of which such a variation will be ordered depends upon the circumstances of each particular case. Such an order has become known as an 'Angel Bell' order—a term derived from the leading case, *Iraqi Ministry of Defence* v *Arcepey Shipping Company SA (The 'Angel Bell')* [1981] QB 65. Of course, a defendant may be well aware of the possibility of rendering a Mareva injunction worthless by obtaining variations and then making sufficient payments out of his funds within the jurisdiction to exhaust them. The court will seek to hold a balance between on the one hand allowing the defendant to abuse his position in seeking variations designed for the sole purpose of depriving the injunction of practical effect, and on the other hand allowing the plaintiff to use the injunction as an instrument of oppression preventing the defendant from honouring his commitments to third parties, from discharging his living expenses or from running his business.

The general principle is that where a party seeks a variation to the

11 On the third party's *locus standi* to do this: see *Harbottle Ltd* v *National Westminster Bank* [1978] QB 146 at p 157; *Cretanor Maritime Co Ltd* v *Irish Marine Ltd* [1978] 1 WLR 966 at p 978; *Galaxia Maritime* v *Mineralimportexport* [1982] 1 WLR 539.

injunction to enable a payment to be made, it is incumbent upon that party to satisfy the court that the proposed payment would not be in conflict with the policy underlying the Mareva jurisdiction.[12] Where the defendant is seeking the variation, it is usual for him to satisfy this requirement by swearing an affidavit deposing to the amount of the proposed payment, and why the defendant wishes to make the payment. If there are a number of items included within the proposed payment, then these should be identified, and if the payment concerns a particular transaction between the defendant and a third party, then ordinarily the defendant will give some details of that transaction and exhibit any appropriate documents so as to negative any suggestion that the relevant transaction is otherwise than a bona fide one. Often the defendant will also disclose in his affidavit what assets he has subject to the injunction, although this is not invariably necessary.

In *A* v *C (No 2)*, Robert Goff J declined to grant an application by certain defendants for a variation to enable them to make a payment in respect of legal costs likely to be incurred in the defence of the proceedings. In that case Mareva relief had been granted restricted to assets within the jurisdiction and the defendants placed no evidence at all before the court concerning any other assets of the defendants, besides those covered by the injunction. In these circumstances, on the facts of that case which concerned a substantial claim for fraud, the judge held that the evidence had not satisfied him that the proposed payment out of the assets subject to the injunction would not conflict with the principle underlying the Mareva jurisdiction.

The decision of Robert Goff J, in *A* v *C (No 2)* might have resulted in the courts refusing to allow the defendant to use assets within the jurisdiction to make payments unless the defendant proved that there were no other assets readily available to him from which he could make such payments. However, this is not the approach which has been adopted. Thus, for example, a foreign defendant has been permitted to use his assets within the jurisdiction to discharge certain personal expenses incurred within the jurisdiction regardless of the absence of any information about the extent and nature of his assets outside the jurisdiction—those expenses would normally have been paid out of assets within the jurisdiction, and consequently the proposed payments did not conflict with the purpose of the Mareva injunction: *Campbell Mussells and Others* v *Thompson* (1984) *The Times*, 30 May (and see also the report in (1985) 135 NLJ 1012). In that case Sir John Donaldson MR went on to observe that *A* v *C (No 2)* illustrated that judges should have a very healthy scepticism when they are dealing with parties to whom Mareva injunctions apply.

Similarly, in *Kea Corporation* v *Parrott Corporation Ltd* Court of Appeal

---

12 *A* v *C (No 2)* [1981] QB 961.

(Civil Division) Transcript No 808 of 1986 (24 September 1986), Mareva relief had been obtained against a foreigner in respect of assets within the jurisdiction, and he was allowed to use those assets to pay his legal expenses in respect of the proceedings brought against him in England. The plaintiffs contended that it was likely that the defendant had assets abroad which could be used to pay his legal costs, and that the English assets should be preserved subject to the injunction so as to be available to pay a future judgment. The Court of Appeal rejected this contention, Sir John Donaldson MR observing that on the facts of the case, it could not 'possibly be said that [the defendant's] purpose [was] to ensure that assets are not available to satisfy a judgment'. The *prima facie* principle is that a defendant is entitled to use his own assets within the jurisdiction for a purpose for which they would ordinarily have been used if the proceedings had not been brought: for example, for purpose of payment of the expenses of living in England, or financing the defence of proceedings brought against the defendant in England.

Accordingly, it is not the practice of the courts to allow the use of the Mareva jurisdiction so as to bring pressure on the defendant to use assets outside the jurisdiction of the court in preference to assets within the jurisdiction, to meet expenses which ordinarily would not have been paid from outside of the jurisdiction. With the recognition of the availability of Mareva relief in respect of assets abroad, there is now even less justification for a plaintiff seeking to put such pressure on the defendant.

However, in exercising discretion whether or not to grant a variation to an injunction the court acts in accordance with what is just and convenient, and there may be circumstances which clearly make it unjust that the defendant should be able to use English assets to pay English living expenses or legal costs. Thus, for example, if the evidence indicates that the defendant has apparently already hidden away substantial assets abroad, it would be unjust to permit the defendant to use what may be left of the depleted English assets to make such a payment. Similarly, in *National Bank of Greece v Constantinos Dimitriou* (1987) *The Times*, 16 November, Mareva relief had been granted against a defendant in respect of assets within the jurisdiction, and a disclosure order had been made in respect of all assets. A variation had been granted to the injunction for legal costs, when on the evidence it appeared that the defendant did not have available assets outside the jurisdiction. Subsequently it emerged that contrary to the defendant's sworn evidence, there were substantial funds abroad from which the payments could be made. The defendant had given false evidence and was in contempt of court in respect of the disclosure order, and it appeared from the evidence that he was doing everything he could to preserve and keep secret his assets abroad. In these circumstances the Court of Appeal refused to sanction a variation to enable assets subject to the injunction to be used to pay the legal expenses. If an injunction is granted in terms which are sufficiently wide to apply *prima facie* to all of the defendant's assets (eg an unlimited Mareva when there is no reason to believe that the defendant has assets outside of the jurisdiction) then it will usually be inappropriate for the court to insist on evidence concerning the particular assets of the defendant, on an application for a variation to the injunction to permit payment of legal costs or living expenses: *Clark Equipment Credit of Australia Ltd* v *Como Factors* (1988) 14 NSWLR 552 at p 569.

In the case of business accounts of a trading company the Court of Appeal has held that it would be a misuse of the Mareva jurisdiction to require the defendant to change his method of trading or to require him, for the purpose of such trading, to use assets presumably designated for some injunction to allow bona fide trading payments to be made from the accounts which were payments of a type which, prior to the granting of the injunction, were normally made from the accounts by the defendant in the ordinary course of trading: *Avant Petroleum Inc* v *Gatoil Overseas Inc* [1986] 2 Lloyd's Rep 236. The court did not inquire into what assets might be available to the defendant to enable such payments to be made.

A question sometimes arises as to whether as a term of the variation of the injunction, the defendant should be required to bring into the jurisdiction future business proceeds. Although the court undoubtedly has jurisdiction to impose such a term, it would only be in exceptional circumstances that this would be appropriate. Thus, ordinarily, the court will not seek pursuant to the Mareva jurisdiction to supervise the operation of the defendant's ongoing business activities. Nor will the defendant be required to conduct those activities in a particular manner so as to facilitate the enforcement of a possible future judgment.

In the case of payment of business debts and expenses, it is often not appropriate or practicable for the defendant to be required to justify to the court each proposed payment. In such circumstances it is usual for the court to grant a variation to the injunction expressed in general terms to enable business payments to be made subject to the safeguard that the plaintiff in advance of the payments which he intends to make, and supply the plaintiff with sufficient information to enable him to investigate whether they are genuine and reasonable in amount. The terms of the Angel Bell variation can be expressed so as to permit the defendant to make payments out of assets caught by the injunction, provided that the plaintiff has been informed of the intended payment and supplied with supporting documents, and has not within a specified period after notification objected to the proposed payment. In practice, this notification may operate by means of a weekly list supplied by the defendant's solicitors to the plaintiff's solicitors supported by copy invoices, vouchers and other relevant documentation.

Sometimes, however, the advance notification procedure described above is too cumbersome and would place the defendant in real business difficulties. If, for example, he is in a business such as insurance, where brokers operate a complex system of set offs with insurers regarding moneys due in respect of premiums, commission and claims, prior notification to a plaintiff of every set off transaction or claim payment would be impracticable. In that situation, the variation may provide instead for subsequent notification of all relevant transactions with sufficient details to enable the plaintiff to check that they were genuine. Subsequent notification may be small consolation to the plaintiff. On the other hand, the defendant should not be prejudiced in the conduct of his ordinary business affairs by a procedure which would or could work oppressively. The plaintiff's cross-undertaking is not sufficient ground for inflicting on a defendant a notification procedure which could halt or hinder the carrying out of ordinary business transactions.

A further safeguard, which is sometimes combined with prior or subsequent notification, is to place a financial limit on the payments which may be made by the defendant during a certain period, so that if he wishes to make larger payments he must apply to the court. The sum may be fixed by reference to the defendant's normal business expenditure each week or month on the basis of affidavit evidence showing a pattern of payments; or if this is impossible because an average sum cannot be ascertained, the court may decide on an appropriate figure by reference to the size and nature of the defendant's business and turnover.

(10) The defendant's creditors and tracing claims

If the relevant assets are subject to a tracing or other proprietary claim by the plaintiff, then ordinarily it will be inappropriate to allow the defendant to spend what may be the plaintiff's money.[13] However, the plaintiff has no absolute entitlement to an injunction and it is a question of discretion whether or not the injunction will be varied and if so subject to what terms, if any. Thus, in connection with living expenses it may be unjust to prevent the defendant from maintaining his ordinary living standards out of assets which may in fact be his own. Thus, as a matter of discretion, the court may vary the injunction to allow the defendant to use the disputed assets, see *PCW (Underwriting Agencies) Ltd* v *Dixon* [1983] 2 Lloyd's Rep 197 (Lloyd J), and [1983] 2 All ER 697 (CA). Nevertheless, the court will usually require the defendant to use first what are indisputably his own assets. In the *PCW* case the injunction was varied by the Court of Appeal so as to provide that the defendant was first to draw against any funds which were indisputably his own. Then he could draw against funds which he reasonably believed to be free from any equitable interests, and next against funds which he did not know to be subject to such an interest. To the extent that funds withdrawn were later held by the court or agreed to be subject to an equitable interest, the defendant was to replace the sums withdrawn out of his own funds. The Court of Appeal ordered that a schedule of assets should be prepared to assist in this task. In a tracing case it is thought that the court might well impose as a term of a variation permitting the defendant to use

---

13 See: *Investors and Pensions Advisory Service Ltd* v *Gray* (1989) 139 NLJ 1415 at p 1416, per Morritt J (obiter).

disputed assets, a requirement that the defendant furnish an undertaking to bring into the jurisdiction assets presently located abroad.

(11) Ordinary living expenses

Mareva relief granted against an individual defendant must always make suitable provision for the defendant to pay his ordinary living expenses, unless there is reason to believe that the defendant has other assets to which the injunction does not apply and which would be available for that purpose. This is so even in the context of relief granted or continued post-judgment.[14] Ordinary living expenses in this context have been described as 'ordinary recurrent expenses involved in maintaining the subject of the injunction in the style of life to which he is reasonably accustomed. It does not include exceptional expenses like the purchase of a Rolls-Royce or the equivalent in legal terms of the private employment of Queen's Counsel to defend you against a serious criminal charge'.[15] However, this is not intended to be a comprehensive definition and it is considered that in deciding whether or not an intended payment is such an expense, all the surrounding circumstances concerning the payment and the ordinary lifestyle of the individual would fall to be taken into account. Thus, for example, a comparatively modest bill for private medical treatment might be unusual for the particular defendant, but be in accordance with his usual lifestyle. The defendant is of course entitled to carry on maintaining his family as well as himself if this has been his practice before the granting of the injunction.

The plaintiff must make provision for ordinary living expenses, where appropriate, in the draft order on the *ex parte* application. If the figure provided for is not sufficient, the defendant can apply to the court to increase the amount.[16]

(12) Applications by third party creditors for variations

A third party with notice of the Mareva injunction will have liberty to apply to have the order set aside or varied on notice, but it is usual for him to proceed by issuing a summons in the action. If the third party is a trade creditor whom the defendant wishes to pay, it is likely that the defendant will make the application for a variation himself, or at least lend his support to it, and will provide the third party with evidence capable of satisfying the court that it is appropriate to grant a variation of the injunction. If the defendant is unsympathetic, the third party may find that without the assistance of evidence from the defendant there is little if any evidence upon which he can rely to satisfy the court that it is appropriate to vary

---

14 *Law Society* v *Shanks* [1988] FLR 504.
15 *TDK Tape Distributor (UK) Ltd* [1986] 1 WLR 141 at p 146, per Skinner J.
16 *PCW (Underwriting) Agencies Ltd* v *Dixon and another* [1983] 2 Lloyd's Rep 197; *House of Spring Gardens* v *Waite* [1984] FSR 173 at p 284.

the injunction, and even if he does succeed, the fact that the defendant has the liberty to make payment without breaching the injunction, does not mean that he will do so. The third party creditor will not be able to obtain a variation simply on the ground that the debt was incurred prior to the injunction. However, he may obtain the variation if he shows that the debt relates specifically to the frozen assets and that, at the date of the injunction, he had an existing right to payment from that particular source: see generally *A* v *B* *(X intervening)* [1983] 2 Lloyd's Rep 532. It is also thought that the creditor will obtain a variation if he can show that it would be entirely usual for the debt to be paid from assets within the jurisdiction (eg the debt is an ordinary living expense of a defendant resident within the jurisdiction).

(13) Application by a judgment creditor for a variation

There remains some uncertainty as to the precise position of judgment creditors. If a judgment is to be enforced against assets of the defendant which are subject to a Mareva injunction, then:

(*a*) such enforcement would simply be carrying out an order of the court; and

(*b*) the enforcement would not involve any dealing with the relevant assets by or on behalf of the defendant.

Thus in principle it seems that the enforcement of the judgment would not involve any breach of the injunction. Support for this view is to be found in *Iraqi Ministry of Defence* v *Arcepey Shipping (The 'Angel Bell')* [1981] QB 65 at p 72 and *A* v *B* *(X intervening)*, above, at p 534. Furthermore, in so far as there might be any practical difficulty encountered by the judgment creditor arising from the existence of the injunction, then in principle it can be said that the court should vary the injunction as a matter of course, because the plaintiff should not be permitted to use the Mareva injunction so as to give his claim priority or even so as to ensure that a reserve is made for his claim from the defendant's assets.

However, the practicality is that a third party creditor could obtain judgment by default or even simply by formal consent of the defendant. In these circumstances, if obtaining a judgment enabled the third party to circumvent the Mareva injunction as a matter of course, then this could be open to abuse. In particular, the defendant could incur liabilities, consent to judgment on those liabilities and then leave the third party free to enforce the judgment on assets within the jurisdiction. Alternatively, the defendant could simply allow judgment to go by default on a claim brought against him, and then leave it to the third party to decide whether to seek to execute on assets within the jurisdiction. These considerations show that there could be cases in which it would be entirely inappropriate to allow the judgment creditor to enforce his judgment on the defendant's assets, for example if the judgment is the product of a collusive plan aimed at circumventing the Mareva injunction. In such circumstances it would appear that to allow enforcement of the judgment would conflict with the underlying purpose of the Mareva injunction.

When the third party has obtained a judgment, the question arises as to how he can enforce the judgment. If the relevant asset of the defendant is a bank account then the judgment creditor may seek to proceed by way of garnishee procedure pursuant to RSC Order 49. However, it is a matter of discretion for the court whether or not a garnishee order should be granted (see generally *Roberts Petroleum Ltd* v *Bernard Kenney Ltd* [1983] 2 AC 192). It is thought that the court would decline to grant a garnishee order if it was satisfied that the granting of the order would result in the injunction being improperly circumvented—it could then be said that it would be inequitable for the order to be made absolute. The position would be the same in relation to an application for a charging order (eg on land or shares).

However, there are circumstances in which the judgment creditor can execute the judgment by way of writ of *fieri facias* without the leave of the court. The plaintiff could not apply under RSC Order 47, r 1 for an order staying execution by writ of *fieri facias* because he is not 'the judgment debtor or other party liable to execution'. It is thought that the existence of the Mareva injunction in itself would not prevent the judgment creditor from executing judgment in this way, and if the plaintiff wished to seek to prevent execution by writ of *fieri facias* then an application would have to be made to the court. There is some doubt as to whether the proper course would be to seek a stay of further proceedings in the action in which the judgment has been obtained or to seek an injunction restraining the judgment creditor from executing the judgment by writ of *fieri facias*. A stay is clearly the correct course in cases in which the judgment creditor has to apply to the court for leave to execute.[17] However, in a case where the writ of *fieri facias* is available as of right then the stay procedure would probably not be available: *TC Trustees Ltd* v *Darwen* (below) and *Llewellyn* v *Carrickford* [1970] 1 WLR 1124, at p 1128. The plaintiff's remedy, if any, would be by way of injunction against the judgment creditor. Whichever course is correct in the particular case, the same principles would apply. Thus, in order to obtain a stay or an injunction the plaintiff would need to show some legitimate interest which should be protected by the court: *European Asian Bank AG* v *Punjab & Sind Bank* [1982] 2 Lloyd's Rep 356 at p 369. If the plaintiff claims an interest in the relevant assets (eg in a tracing claim) then he would have a legitimate interest in preventing execution. However, in an ordinary Mareva case it is thought that the mere existence of a claim by the plaintiff against the defendant would not in itself suffice. But, if the conduct of the defendant and the third party amounted to an abuse of the process of the court, then it is considered that the court could

17 *Artistic Colour Printing Company, Re* (1880) 14 ChD 502; *Wright* v *Redgrave* (1879) 11 ChD 24; *TC Trustees Ltd* v *Darwen* [1969] 2 QB 295 at p 303.

intervene by granting a stay or an injunction.[18] Furthermore, in cases where the defendant is seeking to transfer assets for the purpose of defeating his creditors or prejudicing claimants then the plaintiff may be able to obtain relief preventing enforcement or execution of the judgment, or successfully resist such enforcement or execution by reference to ss 423, 424 and 425 of the Insolvency Act 1986 (see pp 67–68 and 132–134, above).

In the case of a tracing or proprietary claim, and an adverse judgment obtained by a third party judgment creditor against the defendant, the court will not take assets which may well belong to the plaintiff by way of enforcement or execution of the judgment. In such circumstances if the judgment creditor wished to enforce his judgment against the assets in question then there would have to be an issue as to the ownership of the assets as between the judgment creditor and the plaintiff. The injunction would ordinarily be maintained pending the determination of such an issue.[19]

(14) Variation of the injunction after the plaintiff has obtained judgment

If the plaintiff has become a judgment creditor then he will be in a much stronger position, as compared with his position pre-judgment, for resisting an application by the defendant or a third party for a variation to the injunction. In considering such an application the court will take into account the plaintiff's status as a judgment creditor, and the other remedies which are or may be available to him, including execution of the judgment or the commencement of bankruptcy or winding-up proceedings. Thus, for example, if the plaintiff could petition to wind up the defendant then it would ordinarily be appropriate to restrain the defendant company from disposing of its property at all save as sanctioned by the court (see pp 51–53). Similarly, if the plaintiff could institute a process of execution or enforcement such as seeking a garnishee order or the appointment of a receiver in aid of execution, then the court ordinarily will maintain the position until the outcome of that procedure is known.

If a default judgment has been obtained which the defendant intends to seek to set aside, the court may well grant a variation to the injunction pending the hearing of that application even though such a variation would not have been permitted after final judgment had been obtained at trial or by way of proceedings for summary judgment. It is common for default judgments to be set aside, albeit occasionally, on terms, and the fact that the judgment is only a default judgment will be taken into account. The court hearing the application for a variation is not obliged to deal in detail with the merits of the application to set aside the judgment,

---

18 See generally *Castanho* v *Brown & Root* [1981] AC 557 at p 571; *South Carolina Co* v *Assurantie NV* [1987] AC 24 at pp 39–40.
19 *Northwest Airlines Inc* v *Shouson Chen* [1989] HKLR 382 (Hong Kong).

but is entitled to take into account the apparent merits or demerits, on the application to vary the injunction. Often it would be entirely premature to treat such a defendant as being in substantially the same position as if judgment had been obtained after the merits of the claim had been determined.

In cases involving the reciprocal enforcement of a judgment by way of registration, the rules of court prohibit execution of the judgment until after the expiry of the period allowed to the defendant to make an application to set aside the registration, and if the application is so made then until after that application has been finally determined.[20] There is a corresponding prohibition which applies when there is registration of a foreign arbitration award (RSC Order 73, r 8) or there is summary enforcement of an arbitration award (RSC Order 73, r 10(6)). If an application is made to vary Mareva relief pending the final determination by the High Court of an application to set aside registration of a judgment or foreign award, or an order giving leave to enforce an award in the same manner as a judgment or order, then it is considered that the court will be reluctant to permit any payment, which would not be permitted if there had not been a stay of enforcement or execution under the rules of court. In such circumstances the plaintiff has already achieved[21] the status of a judgment creditor, and this is to be taken into account in the exercise of the discretion. If the defendant is a company, the plaintiff may in any event be able to petition for winding up of the company in advance of the hearing of the defendant's application to vary the injunction, even though the defendant's application to set aside registration or leave to enforce is still pending.

It is also considered that once the High Court has finally determined the defendant's application to set aside registration or leave to enforce (as the case might be) then the mandatory stay of execution or enforcement under the rules of court ceases to have effect. Thus the application to set aside is made to 'the court'(eg see RSC Order 71, r 9(2) and (3)), which in the context of the rules means the High Court and not the Court of Appeal (RSC Order 1, r 4(2)). Any stay pending appeal would fall to be dealt with as a discretionary matter by the High Court or the Court of Appeal or a single judge of the Court of Appeal, and ordinarily the plaintiff will be allowed to enforce the judgment pending an appeal. If a stay is to be granted the court will usually impose terms on the defendant requiring him to give security.

Even though the plaintiff has become a judgment creditor, the court will not grant or maintain an injunction over assets which will not be

---

20 RSC Order 71, r 10. See also RSC Order 71, r 21 (a Community Judgment), and RSC Order 71, r 34 (a judgment registered under S 4 of the Civil Jurisdiction and Judgments Act 1982).

21 *Deutsche Schachtsbau-und Tiefbohrgesellschaft GmbH* v *R'As al Khaimah* [1987] 3 WLR 1023 (see the judgment of Sir John Donaldson MR in the Court of Appeal), and p 53, above.

available to satisfy the judgment through execution, or through bankruptcy or winding-up proceedings. In *Prekookeanska Plovidba* v *LNT Lines* [1989] 1 WLR 753, the plaintiffs had obtained leave to enforce an arbitration award in the same manner as a judgment or order pursuant to s 26 of the Arbitration Act 1950, and an injunction was granted *ex parte*, which restrained the defendants from dealing with their assets within the jurisdiction, including sums held by their solicitors on client account. Provision was made for the solicitors to be at liberty to exercise any right of set off for bills already delivered to the defendants for past legal services. The solicitors concerned had funds in their client account over which they had a lien, and on the evidence the plaintiffs had no prospect of obtaining any part of those sums for satisfaction of the amounts due to them. The sums could not be attached by means of garnishee proceedings and the solicitors' rights would prevail over any claim by a liquidator. Accordingly, Hirst J varied the injunction in relation to the funds held on client account so as to enable the solicitors to obtain payment. In *Deutsche Schachtsbau-und Tiefbohrgesellschaft GmbH* [1988] 3 WLR 230, the House of Lords declined to maintain in place an injunction in favour of judgment creditors when garnishee proceedings were dismissed even though there remained the theoretical possibility of winding-up proceedings. In that case the reasons that made it inequitable to grant a garnishee order, likewise made it inequitable to maintain the injunction.

There could be circumstances in which a judgment creditor has taken a deliberate decision not to commence bankruptcy or winding-up proceedings and is permitting the judgment debtor to continue trade in the hope of obtaining satisfaction of the judgment in due course. In such circumstances the court might decline to allow garnishee proceedings to be taken against the defendant's solicitors' client account because it would be unfair in the particular circumstances to deprive the judgment debtor of the benefit of continuing legal advice and representation. In those circumstances the court would also ensure that any injunction granted in aid of execution did not prevent the solicitors paying themselves out of the client account.

(15) Mareva relief and insolvent defendants

If the defendant is a company which is in the process of liquidation, the liquidator will take over the conduct of all of the defendant's affairs including the conduct of any litigation to which the company is a party. Once a liquidator or provisional liquidator has obtained control of the defendant's assets there will be no justification for the continuance of Mareva relief. If a winding-up petition has been presented, the company, or any creditor or contributory may apply for a stay of court proceedings brought against the company (s 126 of the Insolvency Act 1986). In the event of a winding-up order being made or a provisional liquidator being appointed, no action or proceedings against the company can be commenced or continued without the leave of the court (s 130 of the Insolvency Act 1986). These provisions also apply in the case of winding-up proceedings against an unregistered company under Part V of the Insolvency Act 1986 (s 221(1)), in which case they are extended so as also to apply to proceedings brought against a contributory of the company (ss 227 and 228). An unregistered foreign company which has been carrying on business in Great Britain and has ceased to carry on business in Great Britain may be wound up under Part V of the Act notwithstanding the fact that it has been dissolved or otherwise ceased to exist under the laws of the place of incorporation (s 225).[22] If an action has been brought against a company which has ceased to exist under the laws of the place of its incorporation then any judgment obtained will be a nullity and no process of execution will be permitted.[23]

If bankruptcy proceedings against an individual are pending, or a bankruptcy adjudication has been made the court may stay proceedings against that individual (s 285). In the event of control of an individual's property being obtained by an interim receiver appointed under s 286 of the Insolvency Act 1986 or by the trustee in bankruptcy, there will be no basis for continuing Mareva relief granted against the defendant, and ordinarily the action will be stayed.

In the case of the judgment debtor being a company which is the subject of a winding-up order, or an individual who has been adjudged bankrupt, a judgment creditor will not be able to execute or enforce his judgment against the assets of the judgment debtor, nor will the judgment creditor be entitled to retain the benefit of execution or attachment, unless the execution or attachment in question had been completed before the commencement of the winding-up or bankruptcy proceedings (ss 183 and 346).

Under s 1 of the Third Parties (Rights Against Insurers) Act 1930, if there is insurance covering a liability then, on the insured becoming bankrupt or making an arrangement or composition or arrangement with his creditors, or (in the case of the insured being a company) the insured being the subject of a winding-up order, the rights against the insurer are transferred to and vest in the person to whom the insured is liable. It is thought that the court would be prepared to make a winding-up order even in respect of a foreign unregistered company which has no assets within the jurisdiction, where as a result of the order the petitioner will acquire rights under the Act. Thus in *Re Eloc Electro-Optiek and Communicate BV* [1982] Ch 43, a foreign company was ordered to be wound up when it had no assets or place of business within the jurisdiction, in order to enable the petitioning creditors to make an application to the Secretary of State for Employment for payment out of a redundancy fund established

---

22 See further on winding up foreign companies, pp 52–53, above. Section 225 does not limit the jurisdiction to wind up foreign companies including those which have ceased to exist.
23 *Lazard Brothers* v *Midland Bank* [1933] AC 289 at pp 296–297.

under statute, and there was a reasonable possibility of the petitioners obtaining payment out of the fund. A plaintiff may contemplate in due course being in a position after obtaining judgment to bring bankruptcy or winding-up proceedings with a view to obtaining rights under a contract of insurance, pursuant to the Act. However, this in itself does not entitle the plaintiff to obtain an injunction preventing a defendant from settling with the insurers (see pp 14–16, above).

(16) The plaintiff's undertaking to protect third parties

It has become a standard undertaking[24] on the part of the plaintiff to be included in an order granting Mareva relief to pay the reasonable costs and expenses of third parties incurred in coupling with the order, and to indemnify them against liabilities arising from such compliance. Different forms of the undertaking are to be found used in practice.[25] It is not standard practice to include in an order granting a Mareva injunction an undertaking by the plaintiff in damages in favour of third parties, and covering them against losses caused by the order, although such an undertaking may be required by the court in the particular circumstances of a case. In *Deutsche Schachtsbau-und Tiefbohrgesellschaft GmbH* v *R'as Al Khaimah* [1988] 3 WLR 230 at pp 262–263, an attempt was made by Shell International, who were third parties, to contend that there was an 'implied undertaking' by the plaintiff in damages in favour of Shell. In that case the contention was put upon the basis that although there was no such 'implied obligation' in every case, there was such an implied undertaking in the circumstances of that case. The House of Lords did not find it necessary to decide the point raised; however, it is considered that the correct analysis is that no such undertaking is given by 'implication' and that if a third party wishes to obtain such protection in any particular case then in the absence of an express undertaking having been provided, he must apply to the court for an order making the continuance of the injunction conditional upon the provision of an undertaking formulated in appropriate terms.[26]

Unlike the plaintiff's undertaking in damages in favour of a defendant, the standard undertaking given to the court to protect third parties does not cover loss or damage caused by the order to a third party. It is limited to costs and expenses, and liabilities incurred as a result of compliance with the order. Thus, for example, it would cover the costs involved for a bank in finding out whether it had accounts or held assets covered by an injunction, or in ensuring that assets subject to the injunction were

---

24 *Z Ltd* v *A-Z and AA-LL* [1982] QB 558 at p 575, per Lord Denning MR; *Searose Ltd* v *Seatrain UK Ltd* [1981] 1 WLR 894; *Clipper Maritime Co Ltd of Monrovia* v *Mineralimportexport* [1981] 1 WLR 1262.

25 See the precedents in Appendices 2 and 3.

26 See also *Commodity Ocean Transport Corporation* v *Basford Unicorn Industries Ltd* [1987] 2 Lloyd's Rep 197.

preserved in accordance with its terms. If a third party held valuables subject to an injunction, and as a result of the order incurred insurance charges or safety deposit fees, in relation to preserving the valuables, then these would fall within the undertaking. On the other hand, the undertaking would not cover loss suffered by the third party as a result of the defendant not doing business with the third party following the granting of the injunction.

The standard undertaking enables a third party to send a demand to the plaintiff for payment of costs or expenses, or an indemnity against a liability incurred without the need to obtain a specific order of the court requiring the plaintiff to pay the particular sums involved. If the plaintiff fails to pay the demand then he may, as a result, be in breach of his undertaking and in contempt of court. In contrast, an undertaking in damages only applies to a relevant order of the court made in relation to specific loss or damage, requiring payment by the plaintiff under the undertaking.

The standard undertaking applies in favour of third parties to whom notice of the order is given. It is envisaged that this notice will be given to the third party by the plaintiff,[27] but the forms of the undertaking do not provide a specific limitation that the notice to the third party of the order must have been so given. Thus it may be that notice is given to a bank which passes it on to another branch where an account with a subsidiary or associated company of the bank is blocked as a result of the order. Although the subsidiary or associated company had not itself been given notice directly by the plaintiff, nevertheless the plaintiff's act in giving notice to the bank resulted, as one might have expected, in the subsidiary or associated company obtaining notice. In these circumstances it is considered that the subsidiary or associated company could itself claim the benefit of the undertaking, because in effect notice has been given to them by the plaintiff through the bank. However, if a third party has obtained knowledge of the injunction entirely fortuitously then, even though that party incurs a cost as a result of complying with the order, he will not be able to claim the benefit of undertaking because he is not a third party to whom notice of the order has been given within the meaning of the undertaking. It is considered that this wording applies to third parties given notice by the plaintiff either directly or indirectly, but would not include a third party who obtained knowledge of the order, purely accidentally, in circumstances where it could not have been foreseen by the plaintiff that the third party would obtain knowledge of the order in question.

(17) Substantial interference with business or other rights of third parties

The court will protect third parties against exposure to unacceptable levels of interference by an injunction with their business or other

---

27 See *Z Ltd* v *A-Z and AA-LL*, above, at p 575.

activities. This may be capable of being done by modifying the injunction. In *Galaxia Maritime SA* v *Mineralimportexport* [1982] 1 WLR 539, an injunction had been obtained restraining the defendant cargo owners from removing the cargo out of the jurisdiction. The shipowners had been given notice of the injunction and faced possible contempt proceedings if they allowed the vessel to sail.[28] The vessel was on voyage charter to the defendants, and therefore *prima facie* the shipowners would not be paid extra money by the defendants for the delay. The plaintiffs had given an undertaking to the court to pay the reasonable costs of third parties, such as the shipowners, in complying with the order. The shipowners applied to the judge to discharge the injunction and he ordered the injunction to be maintained on terms that the plaintiffs provided a first class bank guarantee against the shipowners' loss and expense. However, on appeal the injunction was discharged on the grounds that it constituted too great an interference with the freedom of action of third parties, and the plaintiff had no entitlement or justification to effect a 'compulsory purchase' by means of the guarantee (at p 541, per Eveleigh LJ). It was also unfair to the crew to require the vessel to be detained subject to the injunction, because it interfered with their personal arrangements. Even if the vessel had been on time charter, so that the defendants had to pay hire during the delay, this would not have materially altered the position. In substance it would merely have affected who had the responsibility to pay the shipowners for the period of the detention, but it would not have lessened the degree of interference with the shipowners' freedom of action or with the crew. Even if a defendant is poised ready to provide security, an injunction may still be discharged.[29] This principle has also resulted in the refusal of Mareva relief in respect of bunkers on board a trading vessel, being bunkers alleged to belong to the defendant charterers of the vessel.[30]

In *Clipper Maritime* v *Mineralimportexport*, an injunction was granted *ex parte* over cargo and bunkers belonging to the defendants, who were the time charterers of the vessel, which prevented removal of these assets from the jurisdiction. The shipowners in that case did not apparently appear before the court to object to the injunction. This may have been because the vessel was on time charter to the defendants who were presumably still liable for time charter hire on the vessel notwithstanding the existence of the injunction. If an objection had been made then it would have fallen to be dealt with in accordance with the principles set out above.

---

28 See Chapter 14, and *Attorney-General* v *Newspaper Publishing plc* [1988] Ch 333 at p 367 and at p 380.

29 *Zephros Maritime* v *Mineralimportexport* (1981) 133 NLJ 234.

30 *Unicorn Shipping Ltd* v *Demet Navy Shipping Co Ltd* [1987] FTLR 109; *Gilfoyle Shipping* v *Binosi Pty* [1984] NZLR 742.

Chapter 16

The writ *ne exeat regno* and s 6 of the Debtors Act 1869

(1) Introduction

The historical origins of the writ *ne exeat regno* are to be found in the exercise by the crown of its prerogative power to prevent individuals from leaving the realm. It was used from the thirteenth century by the crown for 'great political objects and purposes of state, for the safety and benefit of the realm'.[1] The writ came to be used in cases between individuals. This development started during the reign of Elizabeth I and had become 'well established by the reign of James I'.[2] In 1820, Lord Eldon LC observed:[3]

This writ was originally issued in attempts against the safety of the state. . . How it happened that this great prerogative writ, intended by the laws for great political purposes and the safety of the country, came to be applied between subject and subject, I cannot conjecture. Where Courts on this side of the Hall[4] have held debtors to bail by analogy, though it is a very imperfect one, to what is done on the other side, they have said they could give this equitable bail in equitable cases; but they do not grant it where you can arrest at law, except in this particular case,[5] in which being matter of account, they have concurrent jurisdiction.

As a result of dissatisfaction with the process whereby claimants before obtaining judgment could have defendants imprisoned, the Debtors Act 1869 was enacted, which abolished the power of arrest save with certain limited exceptions, one of which was contained in s 6 of the Act.[6] This section as amended is still in force and provides:

Where the plaintiff in any action . . . in which . . . the defendant would have been

---

1 Story's *Commentaries on Equity Jurisprudence*, 3rd English edition pp 620–624. See also generally *A Brief View of the Writ Ne Exeat Regno* (1812) by Beames.
2 *Felton* v *Callis* [1969] 1 QB 200 at p 205; *Ne Exeat Regno* Toth 136.
3 *Flack* v *Holm* (1820) 1 Jac & W 405 at p 414.
4 Ie in the High Court of Chancery.
5 There came to be two recognised exceptions to the general rule that the writ was only available in respect of equitable debts and claims, namely a claim on an account where the debtor admitted some but not all of the claim, and a claim for alimony: *Felton* v *Callis* [1969] 2 QB at p 215, per Megarry J.
6 Subsequently this was amended by s 1 and Sched I of the Statute Law Revision (No 2) Act 1893.

liable to arrest, proves at any time before final judgment by evidence on oath, to the satisfaction of a judge . . . that the plaintiff has good cause of action against the defendant to the amount of £50 or upwards, and that there is probable cause for believing that the defendant is about to quit England unless he apprehended, and that the absence of the defendant from England will materially prejudice the plaintiff in the prosecution of his action, such judge may . . . order such defendant to be arrested.

Since the Court of Chancery in exercising the jurisdiction to issue the writ of *ne exeat regno* acted by analogy to the procedure for arrest available at common law, a consequence of the enactment of the Debtors Act 1869 was that the courts by analogy to the statutory provisions limited the circumstances in which the writ of *ne exeat regno* could be issued.[7]

(2) Section 6 of the Debtors Act 1869

This section only enables an order to be made against a defendant requiring his arrest at 'any time before final judgment', when the absence of the defendant would 'materially prejudice the plaintiff in the prosecution of his action'. Thus in *Yorkshire Engine Co* v *Wright* (1872) 21 WR 15,[8] the Court of Appeal held that once final judgment had been obtained against the defendant, the section did not apply, and security which had been obtained from the defendant in return for his release from arrest under the section had to be returned to him. This is because the purpose of the section was to ensure the presence of the defendant so that the judgment could be obtained. At that stage the section ceased to be applicable. If the defendant had been under arrest under s 6, then once final judgment had been obtained he would have been entitled to be released, because 'the prosecution of the action' within the meaning of the section ended with final judgment.[9] At that stage, s 4 of the Act would have been applicable, which prohibits arrest or imprisonment. Section 6 does not apply post-judgment, nor is it possible for its power of arrest to be invoked for the purpose of assisting the plaintiff in connection with the contemplated enforcement of a possible future judgment.

Section 6 is also limited by the requirements that:
(1) the claim must be one which prior to the enactment of the statute would have rendered the defendant liable to arrest in an action brought in one of the 'superior courts of law' (eg a claim for debt);
(2) the plaintiff has clearly to show a strong claim for at least £50;
(3) the evidence shows 'probable cause' for believing that the defendant is about to leave the country;

---

7 *Drover* v *Beyer* (1879) 13 ChD 242 at p 243, per Sir George Jessel MR; *Felton* v *Callis* [1969] 2 QB at pp 208–210.
8 See also *Felton* v *Callis* [1969] 1 QB 200 at pp 212–213.
9 *Hume* v *Druyff* (1873) LR 8 Exch 214.

(4) the plaintiff has an existing cause of action;[10]

(5) as a matter of discretion it is appropriate to make the order.[11]

(3) The writ of *ne exeat regno*

The Debtors Act 1869 severely restricted the jurisdiction of the common law courts to order the arrest of a defendant on *mesne* process (ie in proceedings prior to judgment). Since the courts of equity proceeded by analogy with the common law courts in relation to arrest, the process of *ne exeat regno* could be no wider. Following the passing of the Judicature Acts, the administration of common law and equity was done by the same courts, and the consequence of allowing the writ to issue in circumstances outside the audit of s 6, would have been to restore the availability of arrest as *mesne* process to what it had been prior to the Debtors Act 1869. In *Drover* v *Beyer* (1879) 13 ChD 242, Sir George Jessel MR held that the availability of the writ of *ne exeat regno* was limited by analogy with s 6 of the Act. In the Court of Appeal it was held that since the claim in question was for a debt due under the mortgage of a ship, it was not an equitable claim but a claim which prior to the Judicature Acts would have been dealt with in the common law courts. Accordingly, the case was directly governed by s 6, and the Court of Appeal did not address the question whether by analogy the availability of the writ of *ne exeat regno* was also limited by the requirements of the section. Nevertheless, it subsequently became clear that this was the case.[12]

Prior to 1985, the last successful application for the writ had been in 1893 and subsequently there had only been four applications for the writ.[13] In *Yiu Wing Construction Company (Overseas)* v *Ghosh*,[14] Anthony Evans J declined to allow the writ to be issued in the circumstances of that case but observed, in the course of a judgment given in chambers, that the writ could be issued for the purpose of ensuring that the defendant did not leave the jurisdiction so as to defeat the effect of a Mareva injunction.

In *Al Nahkel Trading Ltd* v *Lowe* (below), an *ex parte* application was made for the issue of the writ against a former employee of the plaintiff. The defendant was suspected by his employers of corruption, and in the circumstances he left Saudi Arabia, where he had been employed, having first travelled to Mecca and collected from third parties considerable sums of money owed to his employers. He had also managed 'by an admitted ruse' to recover his passport, which had been held by his employers. At London airport he was met by representatives of the plaintiffs and the

---

10 *Colverson* v *Bloomfield* (1885) 29 ChD 341 at p 342.

11 *Hasluck* v *Lehman* (1890) 6 TLR 376; *Felton* v *Callis* [1969] 1 QB 200 at p 211.

12 *Colverson* v *Bloomfield* (1885) 29 ChD 341; *Felton* v *Callis* [1969] 1 QB 200 at pp 208–210; *Allied Bank* v *Hajjar* [1988] QB 787 at p 792.

13 'Antiquity in Action—Ne Exeat Regno Revived' (1987) 103 LQR 246 at p 249, by Lesley J Anderson.

14 21 February 1985 in Chambers, referred to in *Al Nahkel for Contracting and Trading Ltd* v *Lowe* [1986] QB 235 at pp 238–239.

police. He surrendered certain cheques which were payable to his employers but declined to hand over the large sums of cash which he held. The view was apparently taken that the police could not intervene in the matter because the alleged thefts had taken place in Saudi Arabia. The defendant intended to leave the jurisdiction on the next day for Manila.

In these circumstances Tudor Price J granted the application for a writ of *ne exeat regno* and gave his reasons in open court. In *Felton* v *Callis* [1969] 1 QB at p 211, Megarry J had set out the four requirements before an order could be made for the arrest of a defendant pursuant to s 6 of the Debtors Act 1869 as follows:

(1) the action is one in which the defendant, prior to the coming into force of the 1869 Act, would have been liable to arrest at law;

(2) a good cause of action for at least £50 is established;

(3) there is 'probable cause' for believing that the defendant is 'about to quit England' unless he is arrested; and

(4) 'the absence of the defendant will materially prejudice the plaintiff in the prosecution of the action.'

These were cited by Tudor Price J, and it appears that he considered that these requirements were met in the circumstances of the case before him. The decision has been the subject of criticism.[15] The purpose for which the writ was issued was said to be in aid of Mareva relief, namely to preserve the cash assets held by the defendant. However, this purpose does not satisfy the statutory requirement that the plaintiff must prove 'that the absence of the defendant from England will materially prejudice the plaintiff in the prosecution of his action'. A clear distinction has been drawn between on the one hand prosecuting the action up until final judgment and on the other hand, the execution of that judgment. It is for the purpose of enabling the plaintiff to obtain final judgment[16] that arrest can be justified under s 6 of the Act, or in the case of equitable claims,[17] or a claim on an account[18] which has been partially but not wholly admitted, that the writ *ne exeat regno* can be issued. The remedies are not available on the ground that the absence of the defendant 'may be very embarrassing to the plaintiff in regard to obtaining the fruit of his action'.[19] The same criticism is to be made of the decision of Wood J in *Thaha* v *Thaha* [1987] 2 FLR 142,[20] when he granted an *ex parte* application to issue the writ in aid

---

15 See the excellent analysis by Lesley J Anderson in (1987) 103 LQR 246 at pp 257–259.

16 *Felton* v *Callis* [1969] 1 QB at pp 212–214; *Hume* v *Druyff* (1873) LR 8 Exch 214; *Lipkin Gorman* v *Cass* (1985) *The Times*, 29 May; *Allied Bank* v *Hajjar* [1988] QB 787 at p 793.

17 *Glover* v *Waters* (1950) 80 CLR 172 at p 173, per Dixon J; *Felton* v *Callis* [1969] 1 QB 200 at pp 215–216, per Megarry J; *Drover* v *Beyer* (1879) 13 ChD 242; 28 WR 89 at p 110, per James LJ; *Allied Arab Bank* v *Hajjar* [1988] QB 787 at p 794, per Leggatt J.

18 This, historically, was a claim which could be dealt with by the High Court of Chancery or in the common law courts and is therefore referred to as falling within the 'concurrent jurisdiction' of equity and common law: [1969] 1 QB at p 216.

19 *Felton* v *Callis* [1969] 1 QB at p 214 citing from the report of the judgment of James LJ in *Drover* v *Beyer* at 49 LJ Ch 37 at p 38.

20 The text of the writ issued in that case is set out at pp 144–145 of the report.

of enforcement of a periodic payments order. However, in *Allied Arab Bank* v *Hajjar* [1988] QB 787, in a judgment given after a hearing *inter partes*, Leggatt J held that an *ex parte* order for the writ should be discharged, and directed an inquiry as to damages on the undertaking in damages given by the plaintiff on the *ex parte* application, when the purpose for which the writ had been sought was to enforce Mareva relief and an order for disclosure of information concerning assets. Such a purpose did not fall within s 6 of the Debtors Act 1869 because it was not for the purpose of advancing 'the *prosecution* of the action' as required by the section. This decision is in accordance with the principles laid down in the applicable case law. In an appropriate case this requirement would not preclude the granting of the writ as part of an order which included Anton Piller relief, directed to obtaining discovery of documents or information, designed to assist the plaintiff in respect of proving his claim and obtaining the appropriate final relief in the action.

The Mareva jurisdiction has now evolved its own ancillary remedy[21] to prevent a defendant from leaving the jurisdiction, based upon s 37(1) of the Supreme Court Act 1981. As for the writ of *ne exeat regno*, its availability is defined by the case law,[22] and the restrictions imposed by s 6 of the Debtors Act 1869 apply by analogy. It appears only to be available:

(1) when there is an equitable claim or demand, or a demand in respect of a partially admitted account;[23]

(2) the claim or demand is presently payable,[24] and not merely a claim or demand in respect of a sum to become due in the future;

(3) a good cause of action is clearly established for at least £50;

(4) there is probable cause for believing that the defendant is about to leave the jurisdiction;

(5) the absence of the defendant will materially prejudice the plaintiff in the *prosecution* of the action. Prejudice in relation to obtaining fruits of a possible future judgment does not qualify under this requirement;

(6) the application is made before judgment. The defendant must be released after judgment is obtained;

(7) as a matter of discretion it is appropriate to issue the writ.

The Final Report of the Committee on Supreme Court Practice and Procedure (1953: Cmd 8878) considered the writ[25] and observed that the writ is 'useless in its present application'. It is thought that the availability

---

21 *Bayer AG* v *Winter* [1986] 1 WLR 497; *Re Oriental Credit Ltd* [1988] Ch 204.

22 In *Bayer AG* v *Winter* [1986] 1 WLR 497, at p 501, the plaintiffs accepted that the case was not one in which a writ of *ne exeat regno* could be granted, but nevertheless were granted an injunction restraining the first defendant from leaving the jurisdiction and an order requiring him to deliver up his passports to the person serving the order upon him.

23 In *Felton* v *Callis*, Megarry J doubted when a claim in the nature of *quia timet* proceedings was sufficient.

24 *Colverson* v *Bloomfield* (1885) 29 ChD 341.

25 At paras 455 and 456. See also [1969] 1 QB at pp 213–214.

of the writ is limited in the respects set out above, by virtue of the case law, and that any judicial consideration for its enlargement should take into account that:

(1) sections 4 and 6 of the Debtors Act 1869 are still in force, and were enacted in pursuance of a deliberate policy to restrict judicial powers of arrest;

(2) the Insolvency Act 1986 contains specific powers of arrest in relation to certain cases in which a person is threatening to abscond.[26] The powers of arrest in the context of civil litigation are pre-eminently a matter to be dealt with by statute, and indeed restricted powers are conferred on the courts by the Act;

(3) the courts have evolved a separate jurisdiction in aid of Mareva relief for preventing a defendant from leaving the jurisdiction, based on s 37(1) of the Supreme Court Act 1981 by the granting of an injunction.

(4) Procedure

The application is made *ex parte*, with evidence by affidavit. The plaintiff is required to provide an undertaking in damages. A form of order is set out in Daniell's *Chancery Forms* (7th ed 1932) at pp 756–758 and this was modified in *Al Nahkel Trading Ltd* v *Lowe* so that:

(1) the writ was addressed to the tipstaff and not to the sheriff;

(2) the writ required the tipstaff to bring the defendant before the judge forthwith or as soon as possible, so that he can make the appropriate order.

The order made in *Thaha* v *Thaha* [1987] 2 FLR 142 at pp 144–145, is set out in full in the report and follows the modified form adopted in *Al Nahkel Trading Ltd* v *Lowe*. The writ is marked with a specified sum which the defendant is able to pay in order to avoid arrest pursuant to the order.

---

26 Section 158 (power to arrest absconding contributory) and s 364 (power of arrest of a debtor to whom a bankruptcy petition relates, an undischarged bankrupt or a discharged bankrupt whose estate is still being administered under the Act).

Chapter 17

Ancillary orders

(1) Introduction

With the emergence of the Mareva jurisdiction the courts have found justification in s 37(1) of the Supreme Court Act 1987, not only for the granting of Mareva relief itself, but also for the granting of relief ancillary to the injunction so as to ensure that it is effective. This ancillary jurisdiction is now well established, and includes power to make orders under the section:

(1) requiring the defendant to give discovery of documents or provide information about his assets,[1] wherever situated;[2]

(2) requiring the defendant not to leave the jurisdiction, and to deliver up his passport;[3]

(3) requiring the defendant to attend the court for immediate cross-examination about his assets;[4]

(4) requiring the defendant to deliver up forthwith certain of his assets into the custody of the plaintiff's solicitors;[5]

(5) requiring the defendant to sign a document directing his bank to disclose information to the plaintiff.[6] If the defendant failed to comply with the order, the court could nominate a person to sign the necessary document in the name of the defendant pursuant to

---

1 *Maclaine Watson & Co Ltd* v *International Tin Council (No 2)* [1989] Ch 286; *A* v *C* [1981] QB 956; *Bekhor Ltd* v *Bilton* [1981] QB 923; *CBS United Kingdom Ltd* v *Lambert* [1983] Ch 37 at pp 42–43.

2 *Babanaft International Co SA* v *Bassatne* [1989] 2 WLR 232; *Republic of Haiti* v *Duvalier* [1989] 2 WLR 261; *Derby & Co Ltd* v *Weldon (No 1)* [1989] 2 WLR 276.

3 *Bayer AG* v *Winter* [1986] 1 WLR 497. See also *Re Oriental Credit* [1988] Ch 204 (relief granted in aid of an order made for the private examination of a person in connection with the affairs of a company in liquidation).

4 *House of Spring Gardens Ltd* v *Waite* [1985] FSR 173; *Bayer AG* v *Winter (No 2)* [1986] 1 WLR 540.

5 *CBS United Kingdom Ltd* v *Lambert* [1983] Ch 37; *Johnson* v *L&A Philatelics Ltd* [1981] FSR 286.

6 *Bayer AG* v *Winter (No 3)* reported sub nom *Bayer AG* v *Winter (No 2)* [1986] FSR 357 at p 365. Hoffmann J's view that disclosure orders should not be limited to assets within the jurisdiction, was rejected in *Ashtiani* v *Kashi* [1987] QB 888 at p 898, but was expressly approved by Kerr LJ in *Babanaft Co SA* v *Bassatne*, above.

s 39 of the Supreme Court Act 1981. The bank would then be bound to treat the document for all purposes as if it had been signed by the defendant;[7]

(6) by way of Anton Piller relief in aid of the injunction.[8]

In *Bayer AG v Winter* (above), Fox LJ said in relation to s 37(1):

Bearing in mind we are exercising a jurisdiction which is statutory, and which is expressed in terms of considerable width, it seems to me that the court should not shrink, if it is of opinion that an injunction is necessary for the proper protection of a party to the action, from granting relief, notwithstanding it may, in its terms be of a novel character.

This principle appears to apply equally to the granting of relief ancillary to an Anton Piller Order. Whether or not an ancillary order is to be granted in any particular case is a question of discretion.

(2) Ancillary orders in aid of Mareva relief to obtain disclosure of documents or information by a defendant concerning his assets

The plaintiff will often be concerned to find out as much information as he can about the defendant's assets so that steps can be taken to preserve those assets. These steps may be by way of giving notice of a Mareva injunction to third parties, or seeking an order for delivery up of specified assets. There are also other possible reasons for it being desirable for information about the defendant's assets to be made available. Thus, for example, in *A v C* [1981] QB 956 at p 959, Robert Goff J said:

The defendant may have more than one asset within the jurisdiction—for example, he may have a number of bank accounts. The plaintiff does not know how much, if anything, is in any of them; nor does each of the defendant's bankers know what is in the other accounts. Without information about the state of each account it is difficult, if not impossible, to operate the Mareva jurisdiction properly: for example, if each banker prevents any drawing from his account to the limit of the sum claimed, the defendant will be treated oppressively, and the plaintiff may be held liable on his undertaking in damages. Again, there may be a single claim against a number of defendants; in that event the same difficulties may arise. Furthermore, the very generality of the order creates difficulties for the defendant's bankers, who may for example be unaware of the existence of other assets of the defendant within the jurisdiction; indeed, if a more specific order is possible, it may give much-needed protection for the defendant's bankers, who are after all simply the innocent holders of one form of the defendant's assets.

However, an order for disclosure of information about the defendant's assets is not made as part and parcel of Mareva relief without there being consideration given as to whether such an order is really necessary. Thus in *Bekhor Ltd v Bilton*, [1981] QB 923 at p 950 Griffiths LJ said:

I agree that the power to order discovery in support of a Mareva injunction should

---

7 *Astro Exito Navegacion SA v Chase Manhattan Bank* [1983] 2 AC 787 at p 802.
8 *Distributori Automatici Italia SpA v Holford General Trading Co Ltd* [1985] 1 WLR 1066; *Emanuel v Emanuel* [1982] 1 WLR 669; *CBS United Kingdom Ltd v Lambert*, above.

be sparingly exercised, and if too readily resorted to could easily become a most oppressive procedure. I am sure that the judges in the commercial court have this well in mind. There should become no question of an order for discovery becoming a usual part of the Mareva relief.

An order for disclosure of information about assets by discovery or affidavit will only be made if the purpose of the order is genuinely ancillary to the effective working of the injunction. Thus, for example, such an order was not granted when it was sought in an attempt to show past dealings with assets within the jurisdiction in order to justify restoration of a Mareva injunction which had been discharged: *Smith* v *Hegard* Court of Appeal (Civil Division) Transcript No 603 of 1980 (7 August). Similarly, such an order will not be made if its purpose is merely to investigate whether an injunction has been broken and (if so) to supply material for contempt proceedings.[9] On the other hand, an order would be made if the purpose is to identify and preserve assets of the defendant which might otherwise be dissipated notwithstanding the existence of the injunction: *House of Spring Gardens Ltd* v *Waite* [1985] FSB 173 at pp 181 and 183.

It is now clearly established that disclosure orders may be made in relation to assets abroad, for the purpose of enabling the plaintiff to identify those assets and take steps to preserve them. In *Bayer AG* v *Winter (No 3)* (above) Hoffmann J observed that to confine disclosure orders to assets within the jurisdiction was 'a pointless insularity', and this view has now been vindicated (see p 212 above). In *Derby & Co Ltd* v *Weldon (Nos 3 & 4)* [1989] 2 WLR 442 at pp 429 and 436, the Court of Appeal left open the question whether a disclosure order can be made with a wider ambit than the Mareva relief granted by the court. When the Mareva jurisdiction had been regarded as limited to assets situated within the jurisdiction, it had been decided that a disclosure order should not be granted with wider ambit than the Mareva relief to which it was ancillary.[10] However, once it became accepted that relief can be granted under s 37(1) of the Supreme Court Act 1981 in relation to assets abroad for the purpose of preserving them, then it is merely a question of machinery whether this is done by Mareva relief combined with a disclosure order, or a disclosure order which is intended to be in aid of steps taken abroad to preserve those assets. It is now established that it is entirely proper to seek information for the purpose of initiating proceedings abroad to preserve assets there[11] or to enforce a judgment.[12] Although a disclosure order can be made

---

9 *Bekhor Ltd* v *Bilton* [1981] QB 923 at p 949, per Griffiths LJ who dissented on the particular facts of the case from the majority, as to whether the discretion had been properly exercised, but whose judgment on this point appears to be plainly correct; *Bayer* v *Winter (No 2)* [1986] 1 WLR 540 at p 544.

10 *Ashtiani* v *Kashi* [1987] QB 888; *Reilly* v *Fryer* (1988) 138 NLJ 134.

11 *Babanaft International Co SA* v *Bassatne* [1989] 2 WLR 232; *Republic of Haiti* v *Duvalier* [1989] 2 WLR 261; *Derby & Co Ltd* v *Weldon* [1989] 2 WLR 276; *Bayer AG* v *Winter (No 3)* reported sub nom; *Bayer AG* v *Winter (No 2)* [1986] FSR 357.

12 *Interpool Ltd* v *Galani* [1988] QB 738 at p 742.

simply as an ancillary measure to Mareva relief, it is considered that it may be made with the objective of enabling proceedings to be initiated abroad to preserve assets or facilitating the conduct of those proceedings, and accordingly a disclosure order can be made for this purpose, regardless of whether or not Mareva relief is granted, or is of narrower ambit.

If a disclosure order is to be made in relation to assets abroad then the court requires an undertaking to be furnished by the plaintiff not to use the information obtained without the leave of the court. This is so that the court will retain a measure of control over the plaintiff using the information to bring foreign proceedings against the defendant, so as to avoid the information being misused and the defendant as a result being subjected to harassment or oppression abroad.[13]

If an order is to be made for disclosure of information about bank accounts, it is desirable that it should require the defendant to specify in relation to each account, the name or names in which the account is held, the number of the account, the branch of the bank at which the account is held and the account's balance. In New South Wales it has been held that a disclosure order expressed in general terms in relation to bank accounts requires these particulars to be furnished.[14] In that case the court construed the order as requiring disclosure of the balance as at the date of service of the information order on the defendant. However, it is thought that an order requiring disclosure of information within a particular period, to be made by letter or affidavit, requires the letter or affidavit to set out the up-to-date information available when it is finalised. If there is a material change in the position prior to service of the letter or affidavit, then this should be disclosed pursuant to the order so that the plaintiff is provided with a true and accurate picture of the up-to-date position. The objective of the disclosure order must be to provide to the plaintiff up-to-date information, and not information which has become out of date and irrelevant.

(3) Cross-examination of a defendant about his assets

The question whether an order should be made for the defendant to be cross-examined about his assets can arise in a number of different situations.

(1) The plaintiff may make such an application so as to obtain information which can then be used to make the injunction effective. Such an order may be made even if the defendant has not yet been ordered to make an affidavit or has not made an affidavit as to his assets (*House of Spring Gardens Ltd* v *Waite* [1985] FSR 173), but normally would only be contemplated if the defendant has already made an affidavit. In this situation the

---

13 *Derby & Co Ltd* v *Weldon (No 1)* [1989] 2 WLR 276 at pp 281 and 285. See also: 'The Territorial Reach of Mareva Injunctions' by Lawrence Collins (1989) 105 LQR 262 at pp 286–288.
14 *Ausbro Forex Pty Ltd* v *Mare* (1986) 4 NSWLR 419.

order is made in aid of the Mareva injunction: *Bekhor Ltd* v *Bilton* (above) at pp 944, 950 and 955. An order for cross-examination may also be made in aid of execution of a judgment. In cases falling within RSC Order 48, an examination of a judgment debtor is not limited to assets (including debts owed to him) within the jurisdiction,[15] and can include questions directed to obtaining information which will enable the judgment in question to be enforced abroad (above, at p 742). There is also jurisdiction under s 37(1) of the Supreme Court Act 1981 to order such an examination.[16]

(2) The plaintiff may make such an application in relation to an affidavit which has been made by the defendant in support of a pending application for a variation of the Mareva injunction under Angel Bell principles. The application is made pursuant to RSC Order 38, r 2. Whether the application is to be granted is a matter of discretion but in general a bona fide application to cross-examine should normally be granted: *Comet Products* v *Hawkex Plastics* [1971] 2 QB 67 at pp 76 and 77.

(3) An application to cross-examine might be made in order to find out whether there has been any breach of the injunction or orders for disclosure of information and to obtain material for possible contempt proceedings. In *Bayer* v *Winter (No 2)* [1986] 1 WLR 540, the plaintiff applied for an order to be made for cross-examination to establish whether the defendant had complied properly with a mandatory order for disclosure of information. In the course of dismissing the application Scott J said:

Star Chamber interrogatory procedure has formed no part of judicial process in this country for several centuries. The proper function of a judge in civil litigation is to decide issues between parties. It is not, in my opinion, to preside over an interrogation. The police, charged with upholding of the public law, cannot subject a citizen to cross-examination before a judge in order to discover the truth about the citizen's misdeeds. How then, as a matter of discretion, can it be right in a civil case, in aid of rights which, however important, are merely private rights, to subject a citizen to such a cross-examination? *A fortiori* it cannot be right to do so in a case where the plaintiff seeking cross-examination of the defendant is holding itself free to use the defendant's answers for the purpose of an application to commit him to prison for contempt.

In *House of Spring Gardens Ltd* v *Waite* [1985] FSR 173, the Court of Appeal was concerned with the existence of jurisdiction in the court to order cross-examination of the defendant, and not directly with the question of how any discretion should be exercised. At first instance, Scott J (whose judgment was summarised by Slade LJ at p 178) had held that cross-examination could not take place *in vacuo*, ie in the absence of it being directed towards the decision of particular issues between the parties. However, the Court of Appeal rejected this view, and held that cross-examination could be ordered notwithstanding that such cross-

---

15 *Interpool Ltd* v *Galani* [1988] QB 738.
16 *Maclaine Watson & Co Ltd* v *International Tin Council (No 2)* [1989] Ch 286 at pp 305–306.

examination would be purely interrogatory in nature and not directly relevant to the determination of any issues between the parties; for another example of purely interrogatory proceedings not directed to the determination of issues between the parties see RSC Order 48: Examination of Judgment Debtors. The circumstance that the proceedings are purely investigative may make it appropriate that the cross-examination is not conducted before a judge but instead is conducted before an examiner of the court pursuant to RSC Order 39, r 1.

In view of the decision of the Court of Appeal in *House of Spring Gardens Ltd* v *Waite*, the part of Scott J's reasoning in *Bayer* v *Winter (No 2)* which proceeds upon the grounds that there was no relevant issue pending for determination by the court to which the cross-examination would be directed cannot be supported. However, the other part of the reasoning is cogent. The plaintiff may be able to obtain an order for cross-examination if the purpose of such cross-examination is to make the injunction effective. If the plaintiff wishes to bring proceedings for contempt of court then again he may be able to obtain an order that the defendant be cross-examined (see situation (4) below). If, on the other hand, the plaintiff does not have sufficient material to justify the bringing of contempt proceedings then it is inappropriate that he should be afforded the opportunity of using a purely investigative procedure in order to seek to establish that a contempt has been committed.

(4) In the context of subsisting contempt proceedings, the plaintiff may wish to cross-examine on an affidavit (which may or may not have been served in relation to the particular contempt motion) so as to prove contempt of court. The question whether an order should be made for the cross-examination of the defendant is a matter of discretion. In exercising that discretion the court will take into account the proposed width of the cross-examination. Thus, for example in *Comet Products* v *Hawkex Plastics* [1971] 2 QB 67, the defendant in a passing-off action filed an affidavit in relation to the plaintiff's motion to commit the defendant to prison for contempt of court. The plaintiff wished to conduct a wide-ranging cross-examination going beyond the particular events relied upon as constituting contempt, and including previous events said to be relevant to the defendant's state of mind. The Court of Appeal refused to grant the application as a matter of discretion. However, the judgments recognised that cross-examination could be ordered on a contempt motion even though the defendant is liable to be asked questions the answers to which could prejudice him.[17] Privilege against self-incrimination does not extend to affording protection to a person who is at risk of prejudicing himself in

---

17 See also *Bekhor Ltd* v *Bilton* [1981] QB 923 at p 946 (per Ackner LJ) and at p 955 (per Stephenson LJ), and the dicta of Scott J at first instance in *House of Spring Gardens Ltd* v *Waite* [1985] FSR 173 referred to by Slade LJ at p 178 and Cumming-Bruce LJ at p 182 without disapproval on this point.

relation to contempt proceedings,[18] whether or not those proceedings have already been commenced.

(4) An order for the delivery up of the defendant's assets

The power of the court to make ancillary orders in aid of a Mareva injunction extends to making orders for the delivery up of assets belonging to the defendant, and their safe preservation pending trial. This jurisdiction is independent of the court's powers under the Torts (Interference with Goods) Act 1977, and its powers under RSC Order 29, r 2, to make interlocutory orders for the preservation of property forming the subject matter of the action. The power to order the delivery up of assets where it is 'just and convenient' to do so, in order to enforce or make effective a Mareva injunction, may be exercised even in circumstances where the plaintiff has no proprietary claim in respect of the assets.

In *CBS United Kingdom Ltd* v *Lambert* [1983] Ch 37, the Court of Appeal made an order for the delivery up into safe custody of certain assets (motor cars) which it was alleged had been purchased by the defendants with the proceeds of sale of 'pirated' cassettes infringing the plaintiffs' copyright. The order for discovery which was made by the Court of Appeal directed the defendants to disclose the full value and whereabouts of their assets, and an order was made for the delivery up of the motor cars into the custody of the plaintiffs' solicitors. Lawton LJ, who delivered the judgment of the court, considered the principles governing the exercise of the court's power to order delivery up of assets. He pointed out that such an order could cause a defendant extreme hardship if the assets were used in his business:

Even if a plaintiff has good reason for thinking that a defendant intends to dispose of assets so as to deprive him of his anticipated judgment, the court must always remember that rogues have to live and that all orders, particularly interlocutory ones, should as far as possible do justice to all parties.

The nature of the assets (which were easily and quickly disposable) and the fact that they were not used in the defendants' business were clearly factors which significantly influenced the decision of the Court of Appeal in that case.

Lawton LJ went on to lay down guidelines for the making of ancillary orders for the delivery of chattels. The first prerequisite is that the plaintiff must show, by clear evidence, that the defendant is likely, unless restrained by order, to dispose of or otherwise deal with his assets so as to deprive the plaintiff of the fruits of any judgment he may obtain. The remaining guidelines are as follows:

    (1) the court should be slow to order the delivery up of property
        belonging to the defendant unless there is some evidence or an

---

18 *Garvin* v *Domus Publishing Ltd* [1989] Ch 335. On privilege against self-incrimination, see pp 157–160, above.

inference that the property was acquired by the defendant as a result of his alleged wrongdoing;

(2) no order should be made for the delivery up of a defendant's wearing apparel, bedding, furnishing, tools of his trade, farm implements, livestock or any machines (including motor vehicles) or other goods such as materials or stock in trade, which it is likely he uses for the purposes of lawful business. (However, if there is strong evidence that the defendant has purchased antique furniture or valuable paintings for the purposes of frustrating judgment creditors, these may be included in the order, notwithstanding the fact that they might fall within the broad description 'furnishings'.);

(3) the order should specify as clearly as possible what chattels or classes of chattels are to be delivered up. (If the plaintiff is unable to identify the chattels which he wishes to be delivered up, or to state clearly his reasons for the application, the court should refuse to make the order.);

(4) the order must not authorise the plaintiff to enter on the defendant's premises or to seize the defendant's property save by permission of the defendant. (In practice, the order will take broadly the same form as an Anton Piller order, and is likely to be subject to the same safeguards.);

(5) no order should be made for delivery up to anyone other than the plaintiff's solicitor or a receiver appointed by the High Court. The court should appoint a receiver unless it is satisfied that the plaintiff's solicitor has, or can arrange, suitable safe custody for what is delivered to him;

(6) the court should follow the guidelines in *Z Ltd v A-Z and AA-LL* [1982] QB 558, in so far as they apply to chattels in the possession, custody or control of third parties;

(7) provision should always be made for liberty to apply to stay, vary or discharge the order.[19]

(5) Orders against third parties leading to the disclosure of information about assets

In ordinary Mareva cases (ie cases not based on a proprietary claim) it is unusual for the plaintiff to need to seek information from third parties for the purpose of the court proceedings concerning the granting or continuation of Mareva relief. However, such situations can occur: for example, there may be an issue as to whether certain assets belong beneficially to the defendant (and therefore should be subject to a Mareva injunction), or

---

19 For an earlier example of a case in which Anton Piller relief was granted so as to enable the plaintiff to procure that certain assets (stamps) of the defendant were placed into safe custody, see *Johnson* v *L&A Philatelics Ltd* [1981] FSR 286.

information may be needed in order to enable the court to formulate injunctions against several defendants in appropriate terms (as in *A* v *C* [1981] QB 956) or in order to make a Mareva injunction fully effective (eg by enabling the court to specify particular assets in the order which can then be notified to third parties holding the defendant's assets).

If circumstances arose in which the plaintiff needed to obtain information for the purpose of the court proceedings by way of an order directed to a third party, then the plaintiff could seek leave *ex parte* under RSC Order 32, r 7 to issue subpoenas returnable on the application to discharge or vary the injunction, or (in the case of a bank) an order under s 7 of the Bankers' Books Evidence Act 1879. Section 7 provides as follows:

On the application of any party to a legal proceeding a court or judge may order that such party be at liberty to inspect and take copies of any entries in a banker's book for any of the purposes of such proceedings. An order under this section may be made either with or without summoning the bank or any other party, and shall be served on the bank three clear days before the same is to be obeyed, unless the court or a judge otherwise directs.

In *A* v *C* [1981] QB 956 at p 960, Robert Goff J referred to the existence of the power of the court under s 7 as follows:

In order to establish his right to relief at all the plaintiff has at least to give grounds for believing that the defendant has assets here, but having established that, it may be necessary for the exercise of the jurisdiction that the defendant should be required to give discovery, or provide information, about a particular asset—though obviously, if the asset is worth more than the plaintiff's claim, he need do no more than establish that fact. But if the asset is a bank balance, the court, if it holds that the plaintiff is entitled to discovery in respect of that balance, may exercise its power under s 7 of the Bankers' Books Evidence Act 1879.

An order under s 7 can be made at any stage of the proceedings and can be granted *ex parte*: *Arnott* v *Hayes* (1887) 36 ChD 731. In *A* v *C* (above) at p 961, Robert Goff J granted relief which included an order under s 7 directed to a bank (who had been joined as sixth defendant) on the grounds that such an order was required for the proper exercise of the Mareva jurisdiction in that case. An order was made in chambers under s 7 of the Bankers' Books Evidence Act 1879 against Williams & Glyn's Bank on 30 November 1976 by Kerr J in *H&H Brothers* v *Astro-Naviero (The 'Calliope L')* (unreported), when the question arose as to whether an injunction should be continued until trial and if so in what form, and it was not known whether or not the defendants had any credit balances at the bank.

(6) Orders for disclosure of information by third parties in tracing actions

If a person through no fault of his own gets 'mixed up' in the tortious acts of others so as to facilitate their wrongdoing, he may not incur any personal liability, but he comes under an obligation to assist the person wronged by giving him full information and disclosing the identity of the wrongdoers, per Lord Reid in *Norwich Pharmacal* v *Customs & Excise Commissioners* [1974] AC 133 at p 175. The courts have adopted and extended this principle in the case of tracing actions so as to grant interlocutory orders at any stage in proceedings requiring those who may have information (including documents) as to what has happened to particular assets, and who has been involved in their disposal, to provide that information to the plaintiff. This has included orders made against banks for disclosure of information about assets.[20] The relief can be granted *ex parte* and may take the form of an Anton Piller order, but more usually is granted *inter partes*. The person from whom information is sought is usually joined as a defendant in the action although this is not essential (see eg *A* v *C* [1981] QB 956 at pp 958 and 959). In suitable cases it appears that the person from whom information is sought may be restrained from communicating with the defendant or other third parties (except for the purpose of seeking legal advice) about what is afoot. An example of such an order is the order granted by Walton J set out in *Rank Film Ltd* v *Video Information Centre* [1982] AC 380 at p 385.

If an order is to be made against a bank or other third party then the plaintiff is required to furnish an undertaking in damages, and must pay the expenses of the innocent third party in complying with the order. The documents or information obtained can only be used for tracing the assets or their proceeds.[21]

(7) Information from a bank relating to an account at a branch abroad

The plaintiff could wish to seek information about a bank account held abroad, from a bank either in the context of a tracing claim or simply to preserve assets of the defendant either pre-judgment or in aid of execution of a judgment. The plaintiff may seek to obtain the relevant information in the following ways.

(1) under RSC Order 39, r 1, the court has power 'where it appears necessary for the purposes of justice' to make an order for the examination on oath of any person. A letter of request can be issued to the judicial authorities of a foreign country to obtain the evidence. The rule is not limited by its terms to obtaining evidence directed to the determination of the substantive claim on the merits. If there is a tracing claim, information about assets subject to the claim may well be relevant evidence in the substantive proceedings. In the context of a non-tracing claim, the information

---

20 See generally *Mediterranea Raffineria Siciliana Petroli SpA* v *Mabanaft GmbH* Court of Appeal (Civil Division) Transcript No 816 of 1978 (1 December 1978); *A* v *C* [1981] QB 956; *Bankers Trust Co* v *Shapira* [1980] 1 WLR 1274; *Mackinnon* v *Donaldson Lufkin and Jenrette Corporation* [1986] Ch 482; and also *London & Counties Securities Ltd (In Liquidation)* v *Caplan* (unreported) 26 May 1978 (Templeman J) which is referred to in the other cases.

21 *Bankers Trust Co* v *Shapira* [1980] 1 WLR 1274 at p 1282.

may still be relevant evidence for the purpose of proceedings concerning Mareva relief, or an injunction granted in aid of execution of the judgment.

(2) An application may be made directly to the foreign court to order disclosure of the information. Such an application would ordinarily be an entirely appropriate way of obtaining the information, and be viewed by the English court as entirely proper. There can be no objection in principle to the plaintiff obtaining information abroad which can be used to preserve the relevant assets either abroad or within the jurisdiction. Thus, in *Republic of Haiti* v *Duvalier* [1989] 2 WLR 261, the English court itself made orders directed to obtaining information about assets, when the proceedings on the merits were in France, and did so regardless of whether the claim on the merits was properly to be regarded as the equivalent of a tracing or proprietary claim (at pp 270–271). The English court would only restrain the application to the foreign court for information, if in the circumstances it would be 'unconscionable' for the plaintiff to make the application.[22]

(3) The plaintiff might seek to serve a subpoena on the English branch of the bank or might seek an order from the court under s 7 of the Bankers' Books Evidence Act 1879. The courts have laid down the principle that in general the foreign branch should be subject to the orders of the foreign court, and that the English court should not seek information from the foreign branch by means of process served on the English branch. Although there is jurisdiction to uphold the subpoena or to make an order under s 7, the English court, as a matter of discretion will, as a general rule, refrain from requiring disclosure of documents or information from the English branch in relation to an account at the foreign branch.[23] In *Mackinnon* v *Donaldson, Lufkin and Jenrette Securities*, a subpoena had been served, and an order obtained *ex parte* under s 7, which had the effect of requiring the production by a non-party of documents outside the jurisdiction, concerning business which it has transacted outside the jurisdiction. Hoffmann J set aside both the subpoena and the order, and in the course of his judgment said [1986] Ch 482 at p 493:

In principle and on authority it seems to me that the court should not, save in exceptional circumstances, impose such a requirement upon a foreigner, and in particular, upon a foreign bank. The principle is that a state should refrain from demanding obedience to its sovereign authority by foreigners in respect of their conduct outside the jurisdiction.

22　*South Carolina Co* v *Assurantie NV* [1987] AC 24 at p 41.
23　*Mackinnon* v *Donaldson, Lufkin and Jenrette Securities Corporation* [1986] Ch 482; *R* v *Grossman* (1981) 73 Cr App R 302; *Power Curber* v *National Bank of Kuwait* [1981] 1 WLR 1233 at p 1241.

In the converse situation, where a foreign court seeks to serve process on a branch abroad compelling disclosure of information concerning transactions or an account at an English branch, the court may grant an injunction to prevent the bank complying with the foreign court order.[24]

(4) In the context of a tracing claim, the plaintiff might seek to obtain relief against the bank on the grounds that the bank had innocently become mixed up in the tortious acts of others so as to facilitate their wrongdoing and had as a result come under a duty to assist the plaintiff by giving him full information about what had happened to certain assets or their proceeds.[25] However, this route is subject to precisely the same discretionary constraint as applies in the case of a subpoena or the exercise of the jurisdiction under s 7 of the Bankers' Books Evidence Act 1879.[26] The fact that under this route discovery is sought by way of substantive relief against the bank does not affect the application of the general principle.

(8) Orders affecting the liberty of the defendant

In *Bayer AG* v *Winter* [1986] 1 WLR 497, relief was granted against the defendants which included mandatory orders for the disclosure of documents and information concerning both the substantive claim on the merits and the defendants' assets, and an Anton Piller order covering both premises and vehicles. The plaintiffs claimed that the defendants were engaged in marketing counterfeit insecticides, which appeared as if they had been manufactured by the plaintiffs. The information and documents would hopefully enable the plaintiffs to identify other parties who were involved in supplying or purchasing the goods. The first defendant appeared to have no permanent residence within the jurisdiction, and it was feared that he might leave the jurisdiction and thus frustrate subsequent enforcement of the orders of the court (eg by means of an order for cross-examination). The Court of Appeal, sitting in camera, granted an injunction of short duration restraining him from leaving the jurisdiction and ordering him to deliver up his passports. If hardship was caused to the defendant, he could apply forthwith to the High Court to vary or discharge the order.

The jurisdiction to grant this relief is derived from s 37(1) of the Supreme Court Act 1981,[27] and is separate from and not subject to the

---

24 *XY and Z* v *B* [1983] 2 Lloyd's Rep 535.
25 *Bankers Trust Co* v *Shapira* [1980] 1 WLR 1274 at pp 1281–1282; *Norwich Pharmacal Co* v *Customs and Excise Commissioners* [1974] AC 133 at p 175, per Lord Reid.
26 *Mackinnon* v *Donaldson, Lufkin and Jenrette Corporation* [1986] Ch 482 at pp 497–499.
27 *Re Oriental Credit* [1988] Ch 204; *Maclaine Watson & Co* v *International Tin Council (No 2)* [1989] Ch 286 at pp 305–306.

limitations of the procedure by way of the writ *ne exeat regno* (Chapter 16). Since this relief constitutes an interference with the liberty of the subject, it should be in force for no longer than is necessary to achieve its purpose,[28] namely to ensure that the orders of the court can be enforced.

---

28 *Allied Arab Bank Ltd* v *Hajjar* [1988] QB 787 at pp 795–796.

Chapter 18

Discharge, variations and appeals

(1) Expiry of Mareva relief by reason of effluxion of time

Mareva injunctions are usually granted 'until trial or further order' or, in the case of Marevas in aid of arbitration proceedings, until a specified time after publication of the final award or further order of the court. The reference to a final award is so that the injunction will not expire following publication of an interim award. If the injunction is expressed to be 'until trial or further order' then as a matter of caution it is prudent to mention the matter to the court prior to the commencement of the trial so that the injunction can be expressed to continue until after judgment has been given in the action. If the plaintiff succeeds in the action he may apply for an extension of the injunction in aid of execution. If the plaintiff fails on all or part of the claim then the court may grant an extension of the injunction pending appeal. The general principle is that the court will seek to preserve the status quo so that the appeal if successful is not rendered nugatory: *Erinford Properties Ltd* v *Cheshire County Council* [1974] Ch 261. Sometimes Mareva relief is granted up until a specified date or further order, in which case if the injunction is not renewed on or before the specified date, it lapses.

(2) Discharge of Mareva relief on settlement

If the plaintiff wishes to conclude a settlement of the claim then, depending on the wording of the proposed settlement, the claim may become extinguished. However, notwithstanding the settlement, an injunction until trial or further order will continue until formally discharged by the court: *Hadkinson* v *Hadkinson* [1952] P 285 at p 288 and *Isaacs* v *Robertson* [1985] AC 97. Such discharge would be granted as a matter of course because the plaintiff no longer has the claim to which the injunction was ancillary.

If the plaintiff wishes to settle the claim but preserve the Mareva injunction pending payment under the settlement then an appropriate procedure is by way of a Tomlin order, with the defendant expressly furnishing to the court an undertaking in appropriate terms corresponding to the Mareva injunction. Such an undertaking should be expressed to continue until after payment under the settlement or further order of the court, and can be enforced by the court without the need to commence a new action.[1]

If an action is settled under a Tomlin order without any such undertaking by the defendant, it is thought that the court would have jurisdiction to grant a new Mareva injunction against the defendant. The injunction would be granted so as to preserve assets of the defendant for the purpose of carrying the terms of the settlement (embodied in the schedule to the order) into effect. However, the general rule is that an injunction will not be granted unless the plaintiff has a cause of action. Accordingly, if the settlement agreement results in an immediate compromise of the cause of action and provides for the defendant to perform certain obligations in due course, this general rule will have the consequence that Mareva relief can only be granted once a cause of action is acquired by the plaintiff, which ordinarily would be on there being default by the defendant under the settlement. If it is desired to maintain Mareva in place pending payment under a settlement agreement scheduled to a Tomlin order, then the settlement agreement should be formulated in terms which leave intact the plaintiff's underlying cause of action until payment has been made.

An alternative to the Tomlin order procedure is for the plaintiff to conclude a settlement which is expressed to come into effect only upon payment being made within a specified time. If payment is made, then an application should be made to the court to discharge the Mareva injunction, which will only cease to have effect upon the order for discharge being granted. This is the case even though the court would have regarded itself as without jurisdiction to continue the injunction following performance of the settlement because the claim had become extinguished. *See Isaacs* v *Robertson* [1985] AC 97, approving the dictum of Romer LJ in *Hadkinson* v *Hadkinson* [1952] P 285 at p 288.

(3) Discharge of Mareva relief by provision of alternative security

Mareva injunctions are commonly discharged by mutual consent, the parties handing the terms of the draft consent order to the judge for initialling. Often the defendant will prefer to put up security in place of the Mareva injunction so that he is free to deal with all his assets as he pleases. The defendant may incur expenses in providing security (eg bank charges), but the plaintiff's cross-undertaking in damage will not protect the defendant unless it is specially extended for that purpose. This is because the charges are not to be regarded as having been incurred by reason of the granting of the injunction. In such circumstances, the defendant should ask the plaintiff to agree to furnish a further undertaking to the court to abide by any order which the court may make as to costs,

---

1 *EF Philips & Sons Ltd* v *Clarke* [1970] Ch 322.

expenses, loss or damage suffered by the defendant by reason of the provision of security. Such an undertaking could then be incorporated in an order of the court discharging the injunction upon the giving of security by the defendant in a designated form. If the plaintiff declined to proffer the further undertaking, it would be open to the defendant to apply to discharge the Mareva injunction, unless such an undertaking was provided.

(4) Discharge of Mareva relief by the provision of an undertaking

Rather than provide the plaintiff with security for the claim, the defendant might wish to provide an undertaking to the court instead of the injunction, but in terms corresponding to those of the injunction. Such an undertaking has the same effect as an injunction and if it is broken by the defendant, he will be in contempt of court. It also has a similar effect as regards third parties who have knowledge of its terms: *Biba Ltd* v *Stratford Instruments* [1973] Ch 281 at p 287. When the defendant proffers an undertaking in lieu of the injunction he should ask the plaintiff to furnish a cross-undertaking to abide by any order the court may subsequently make as to damages should the defendant suffer any damage by reason of the giving of the undertaking which the plaintiff ought to pay. It has been the practice since 1904 in the Chancery Division to require the plaintiff to furnish such a cross-undertaking: *Practice Note* [1904] WN 203 at p 208. Unless the plaintiff agrees to furnish the further undertaking, the court may discharge the injunction. As in the case of the defendant obtaining discharge of the injunction by providing a guarantee or other security, unless such a further undertaking is obtained, the defendant may not be able to recover costs, fees and losses arising from the furnishing of his undertaking: they may not be regarded as having been incurred or suffered by reason of the Mareva injunction (see the reasoning of Evans J in *Barclays Bank* v *Rosenberg* (1985) *Financial Times*, 12 June, in regard to the undertaking furnished by Mr Rosenberg on 11 August 1981).

If an undertaking is furnished the question may arise as to whether the defendant can subsequently apply to have it discharged or modified before the trial and if so, whether the defendant's application will fall to be dealt with in the same way as if he was applying to discharge an interlocutory injunction.

If an undertaking is expressed to be 'until further order' then this necessarily contemplates that it may be discharged by a further order of the court.[2] Even if the relevant order has been 'by consent', the undertaking itself contains provision for it to be discharged or modified (at p 492).

However, a distinction is to be drawn between an undertaking which is given with the intention that it should be binding until trial, and an undertaking given in circumstances where it is in contemplation either that there will or may be a further interlocutory hearing in relation to the

---

2 *Chanel Ltd* v *Woolworth & Co* [1981] 1 WLR 485.

subject matter of the undertaking. If an undertaking is furnished which is expressed to be 'until trial or further order' as part of a consent order which also stands over the interlocutory motion to be dealt with at the trial, then it is contemplated that the undertakings will be binding until trial. The court will only discharge or modify the undertaking prior to trial if good grounds for doing so are shown such as a significant change of circumstances or new facts. A change of heart prompted by recent case law will not be sufficient.[3] In *Pet Plan Ltd* v *Protect-A-Pet Ltd* [1988] FSR 34, an undertaking was given at an *ex parte* application, which was expressed to be 'until trial or further order', and which was embodied in a consent order which included an express liberty to apply to discharge or vary the order on 48 hours' notice. The defendant in the consent order had agreed to comply with various positive obligations to be performed for some time ahead. In the circumstances the Court of Appeal ruled that this was not a case in which the undertaking had been provided as a short-term holding operation until there could be an interlocutory hearing. Accordingly, the defendant had to show good reason for the discharge of the undertaking.[4] In contrast, in *Butt* v *Butt*, an undertaking had been given as part of an order adjourning generally the relevant interlocutory hearing. Furthermore, there had been an express intimation that the defendant was contemplating a possible application to discharge once his evidence was in order. In these circumstances, the defendant was not faced with the burden of showing good reason for re-opening the matter before the trial.

Accordingly, if the defendant wishes to preserve an unfettered right to apply to discharge or modify an undertaking, prior to the trial, it is prudent for him to reserve expressly the right to make such an application preferably by express wording incorporated in the undertaking.

(5) Submission to the jurisdiction and an application to discharge Mareva relief

A defendant outside the jurisdiction who is made subject to a Mareva injunction in proceedings for which leave has been granted to the plaintiff to effect service upon the defendant under RSC Order 11 may combine an application for discharge of the injunction with an application to set aside the leave granted under RSC Order 11, r 1(1) (see RSC Order 12, r 8(1)(*f*)). However, it is not essential for the defendant to adopt this course. If a defendant does seek to discharge a Mareva injunction this will not in itself amount to a submission to the jurisdiction so as to preclude the defendant from challenging the jurisdiction under the procedure laid down in RSC Order 12, r 8(1): *Obikoga* v *Silvernorth Ltd* (1983) *The Times*, 6 July (Parker J). In principle, the defendant must also be entitled to seek variation of the injunction, pending the determination of his application

---

3 *Chanel Ltd* v *Woolworth & Co*, above.
4 See also: *Esal Commodities Ltd* v *Pujara* [1989] 2 Lloyd's Rep 479 at p 484, per Slade, LJ.

challenging the jurisdiction, without thereby submitting to the jurisdiction. However, the defendant should make it clear that he is only seeking a variation of the jurisdiction, pending the determination of his application to challenge the jurisdiction of the court and to discharge the injunction. In such circumstances the application for a variation does not involve the court in making any assumption that it has jurisdiction to determine *the merits* of the plaintiff's claim in the action: *Williams & Glyn's Bank plc* v *Astro Dinamico Compania Naviera SA* [1984] 1 WLR 438. On such an application the defendant should invite the court to maintain the varied injunction until after the determination of his application under RSC Order 12, r 8(1) or further order (the injunction can then subsequently be extended). If the defendant does not make the position clear and invites the court to maintain the varied injunction until trial or further order he may thereby have submitted to the jurisdiction. Thus, in *Esal (Commodities) Ltd* v *Pujara*,[4A] prior to service of the statement of claim, the defendant consented to Mareva relief in '. . . far reaching terms . . .' expressed to be '. . . until after judgment in this action or further order . . .', and which provided for the opening of a deposit account in which moneys were '. . . to abide the outcome of these proceedings . . .' and reserved the costs of the motion '. . . to the trial . . .'. There was an express liberty to apply to discharge or vary the order on 24 hours notice. On these facts, the Court of Appeal held that the defendant had unequivocally submitted to the jurisdiction.

(6) Discharge or variation of Mareva relief by the court

If the defendant wishes to set aside Mareva relief obtained *ex parte* by the plaintiff, his proper course is to apply to the judge, and not to proceed to appeal to the Court of Appeal, without having first been before the court at first instance for reconsideration of the *ex parte* order.[5] An application can be made under the provision in the *ex parte* order granting 'liberty to apply', without the need to serve a summons, though adequate notice should be given to the plaintiff unless the circumstances are such that the application to discharge the injunction can properly be made *ex parte*.

The court has jurisdiction to grant an application made *ex parte* by a defendant to discharge or vary the Mareva injunction; however this power will only be exercised in cases of great urgency: *London City Agency (JCD) Ltd* v *Lee* [1970] Ch 597. Sometimes the period of notice which the defendant should give to the plaintiff is specified in the *ex parte* order, but it is standard practice in the Commercial Court simply to provide for liberty to apply 'on notice'. The court can refuse to hear the application if it considers that the notice which was given was insufficient.

A defendant or third party who wishes to intervene to set aside the *ex parte* injunction may prefer to issue a summons; this is a sensible way to proceed when there are a number of parties involved and where the defendant (or the third party) is seeking to vary the injunction if the application to discharge it is unsuccessful. The precise terms of the variation

4A [1989] 2 Lloyd's Rep 479.
5 *WEA Records Ltd* v *Visions Channel 4 Ltd* [1983] 1 WLR 721. See also RSC Order 32, r 6.

can then be set out in the summons and this may enable the parties to reach agreement. If the defendant wishes to apply to have the order set aside he should make his application expeditiously.

The application takes the form of a complete rehearing of the matter, with each party being at liberty to put in evidence (in the form of affidavits in support of their case). Thus, for example, the defendant may seek to persuade the court that on all the evidence there is insufficient risk of a judgment being unsatisfied to justify the granting of Mareva relief. The court decides the application on all of the evidence before the court: *Ninemia Corporation* v *Trave GmbH (The 'Niedersachsen')* [1983] 1 WLR at pp 1425–1426.

(7) Discharge by the court of Anton Piller relief

An Anton Piller order is intended to be implemented forthwith and a defendant who has been served with an Anton Piller order and refuses to comply with its terms is at risk of being penalised for contempt of court, even if he makes a speedy and successful application to have the order set aside. The fact that an Anton Piller order is subsequently set aside does not prevent any disobedience of that order, while it was in force, from being a contempt of court: *Wardle Fabrics Limited* v *G Myristis Limited* [1983] FSR 263. In *Hallmark Cards Inc* v *Image Arts Ltd and others* [1977] FSR 150 at p 153, Buckley LJ stated that while a defendant who refuses access to his premises pending an application to have the Anton Piller order set aside is technically in contempt of court, he could not conceive of the defendant being liable to any penalties for that contempt if the order was set aside. This approach was approved by Sir John Donaldson MR in *WEA Records Ltd* v *Visions Channel 4 Ltd* [1983] 1 WLR 721. However, in *Wardle Fabrics Limited* v *G Myristis Limited* (above), a case in which an Anton Piller order was set aside for non-disclosure, Goulding J penalised the successful defendants by ordering them to pay the costs of the plaintiff's motion for contempt of an indemnity basis. The court has a discretion to suspend the operation of the Anton Piller order pending an application by the defendant to have it set aside, but that discretion should only be exercised on production of evidence and not simply on the basis of what is said by counsel on behalf of the defendant: *Hallmark Cards Inc* v *Image Arts Ltd and others* [1977] FSR 150. The discretion to suspend the operation of the Anton Piller order is unlikely to be exercised save in special cases. As Scott J pointed out in *Columbia Picture Industries and others* v *Robinson* [1987] Ch 37 at p 72:

if respondents to Anton Piller orders were to be allowed to delay their execution while applications to apply to discharge were being made, the purpose of Anton Piller orders and procedure would be largely lost. Ample time would then be available to those disposed to destroy evidence or to secrete away master tapes to do so.

If an application to discharge Anton Piller relief is not made until after the order has been fully executed, the question is likely to arise as to whether such an application should be stood over until the trial. This question arises particularly in the context of applications to discharge for non-disclosure and it is considered fully in Chapter 8 at pp 94–97, above. The same principles apply even if the grounds for discharge do not include or are not limited to allegations of non-disclosure. The court plainly has jurisdiction to determine at an interlocutory hearing an application to discharge fully executed Anton Piller relief, but may in the exercise of its discretion adjourn the matter to be dealt with at the trial, depending on the nature of the issues involved in the application and whether in the circumstances it would be appropriate to do so.

(8) Discharge of Anton Piller or Mareva relief for failure to comply with an undertaking to commence proceedings forthwith or some other undertaking given to the court by the plaintiff

Under RSC Order 29, r 1(3) there is provision for the court to grant an injunction where the case is one of urgency before the issue of the writ or originating summons, and in such a case 'the injunction applied for may be granted on terms, providing for the issue of the writ or summons, and such other terms as the court thinks fit'. Thus in non-urgent cases the court has no power to grant an injunction before the issuing of the relevant originating process, while in urgent cases a special dispensation is given on the express basis that the applicant will regularise the position without delay. It is common for Mareva and Anton Piller relief to be granted *ex parte* before the writ is issued, the plaintiff providing an undertaking to issue the writ. In the case of an Anton Piller order, the plaintiff often does not issue the writ until the order has been served.[6]

Unless the undertaking is complied with the court may discharge the *ex parte* order, without regard to the question of whose fault it was that the undertaking was not performed, or whether the defendant has been prejudiced by the irregularity, which, being a breach of an undertaking, is a contempt of court.[7] However, in general the court is reluctant to penalise the litigant for the error of his solicitor, where it is the solicitor's fault that the writ or originating summons was not issued timeously.[8] This is particularly so when the solicitor's failure has arisen from an honest oversight or when the client is not personally at fault.[9]

---

6 *VDU Installations Ltd* v *Integrated Computer Systems and Cybernetics Ltd* [1989] FSR 378.

7 *Refson* v *Saggers* [1984] 1 WLR 1025; *Spanish General Agency Corporation* v *Spanish Corporation Limited* (1890) 64 LT 161.

8 An example of a case in which the originating process was not issued for some two months and the injunction was discharged is *Siporex Trade SA* v *Comdel Commodities Ltd* [1986] 2 Lloyd's Rep 428.

9 This approach was adopted by Potter J in *Sabani* v *Economakis* (1988) *The Times*, 17 June, when there had been failure to comply with undertakings concerning notification of the defendant of the terms of the order and his right to apply for its discharge, and service on the defendant of the affidavit relied upon *ex parte*.

There is a clear duty on the solicitor personally to ensure that the undertaking given on behalf of the plaintiff is complied with, and if, as is usually the case, the applicant has given the general conduct of the proceedings to the solicitor, the solicitor will be in breach of his duties owed both to the court and to his own client. This could result in a complaint being made by the court to the Law Society or the court itself dealing with the matters under its own punitive jurisdiction over solicitors.

If the plaintiff fails to comply with an undertaking other than one relating to the commencement of proceedings, such as an undertaking to serve a copy of the evidence on the defendant forthwith or to inform the defendant or a particular third party of his right to apply to discharge or vary the order, the court is reluctant to discharge the order on this ground if the plaintiff was not personally to blame and no serious prejudice has been caused to the relevant defendant or third party.[10]

(9) Delay by the plaintiff in serving a statement of claim or otherwise in the conduct of the proceedings

Anton Piller procedure should not be used for the purpose of enabling a plaintiff to find out whether allegations or charges can be made against the defendant and if so how they might be formulated. Accordingly, it is no justification or excuse for a plaintiff who has obtained Anton Piller relief, but has failed to serve his statement of claim timeously in accordance with the time limits laid down by the rules of court, or any court order extending that time, to say that more time was required to consider the material which became available under the Anton Piller order, so that the statement of claim could be drafted.[11]

Similarly, when a plaintiff has obtained Mareva relief, he is bound to prosecute the action to trial, not simply to 'rest content with the injunction'.[12] Accordingly, if there is unjustified delay, the injunction is liable to be discharged.

The same principles apply to a case in which the defendant is applying to discharge an existing injunction on the grounds of delay,[13] and a case in which the court has already decided to discharge the injunction for some other reason (eg non-disclosure) and is considering whether or not to grant a new injunction, notwithstanding the delay.[14] Whether or not an injunction is to be discharged (or not regranted) is a matter of discretion

---

10 *Sabani* v *Economakis*, above.

11 *Hytrac Conveyors Ltd* v *Conveyors International Ltd* [1983] 1 WLR 44 (where the action was struck out on the grounds of inordinate delay).

12 *Lloyd's Bowmaker Ltd* v *Britannia Arrow Ltd* [1988] 1 WLR 1337 at pp 1349–1350, per Dillon LJ.

13 *Town and Country Building Society* v *Daisystar Limited* (1989) *The Times*, 16 October. *Francesca Blach* v *Mohammed Al Mereikhi*, unreported, Judgment delivered 20 October 1989 (Mr Anthony Colman QC sitting as a Deputy Judge of the High Court).

14 This was the position in *Lloyd's Bowmaker Ltd* v *Britannia Arrow Ltd* [1988] 1 WLR 1337.

for the court to be determined in the light of all the circumstances of the case, but in principle the court will not permit a plaintiff simply to obtain a Mareva injunction and then to rest content with that relief and not to prosecute the proceedings. In *Town and Country Building Society* v *Daisystar* the plaintiff had obtained Mareva relief against an individual defendant in respect of a claim for fraud, but had taken the view that the individual defendant did not have sufficient assets for it to be worthwhile for the plaintiff to pursue the proceedings. Subsequently, after a long delay, the defendant applied to discharge the injunction, and the Court of Appeal (allowing an appeal from the decision of the judge) discharged the Mareva relief, on the grounds that it was an abuse of the Mareva jurisdiction for a plaintiff to obtain Mareva relief but then leave the proceedings in abeyance. Farquharson LJ observed that it was the duty of the plaintiff to press on with the claim so that the defendant was subjected to the Mareva injunction for as little time as possible, and that if the plaintiff wished not to proceed with the claim expeditiously, even temporarily, then it was his duty to apply to the court to discharge the injunction.

However, the court will not always discharge the injunction where there has been delay, even though the delay has been substantial.[15] It is considered that in exercising the discretion the court will take into account all the circumstances of the case including the following:

(1) whether there has been delay as a result of a deliberate decision on the part of the plaintiff;

(2) the length of the delay, and any explanations put forward by the plaintiff for the delay (eg the need to obtain legal aid);

(3) the degree of prejudice liable to be caused to the plaintiff if the injunction is discharged;

(4) whether the plaintiff has sought to rectify the position and proceed with the action or whether the delay is still continuing at the time of the hearing;

(5) the degree of prejudice likely to be caused to the defendant as a result of the delay which has occurred;

(6) whether the defendant has through his conduct either caused the delay or contributed to it.

In the *Francesca Blach* case, there had been a clear failure to prosecute proceedings for 8 months, followed by a further delay attributable to the plaintiff's lack of means whilst she changed solicitors and successfully applied for legal aid. If the injunction were to be discharged, the prospect of the plaintiff recovering anything from the defendant would be 'very substantially diminished'. The fund subject to the injunction had been earning interest on deposit. In these circumstances the judge decided not to discharge the injunction. On the other hand, the *Town and Country*

---

15 The injunction was not discharged in *Francesca Blach* v *Mohammed Al Mereikhi*, above.

Building Society case is one in which the plaintiff had deliberately decided not to continue to prosecute the proceedings, and the injunction was discharged.

(10) Appeals to the Court of Appeal

A defendant subject to a Mareva injunction, or a third party affected by such an injunction can appeal to the Court of Appeal against a refusal to discharge or modify the injunction. Such an appeal is an interlocutory appeal and can be heard by a court of two judges (s 54(4) of the Supreme Court Act 1981), but leave to appeal is not required. This is because of s 18(1)(*h*)(iii) of the Supreme Court Act 1981, which enables an appeal to be brought without leave 'where an injunction or the appointment of a receiver is granted or refused'. However, leave to appeal is required in respect of an order refusing to discharge or modify an undertaking given in place of an injunction.[16]

An Anton Piller order contains a mandatory order requiring the defendants to permit the entry and search of premises for the purposes specified in the order. In *EMI Ltd* v *Pandit* [1975] 1 WLR 302, the purposes of the intended search fell within and were justified by Templeman J by reference to RSC Order 29, rr 2 and 3. The part of the relief requiring the defendant to permit entry was referred to by Templeman J as a mandatory injunction (at p 308). There are also other judicial observations which are consistent with at least that part of Anton Piller relief being an interlocutory injunction granted pursuant to s 37(1) of the Supreme Court Act 1981.[17] Nevertheless, the general practice has been for a defendant who wishes to appeal against a decision declining to set aside Anton Piller relief, to seek leave of appeal.[18] It is considered that if and in so far as an appeal challenges the order requiring the defendant the permit for entry and search for the purposes or any of them specified, then such an appeal falls within s 18(1)(*h*)(iii) of the Supreme Court Act 1981, and no leave is required.

The Court of Appeal has said that it is an abuse of the process of the court for a defendant to seek to challenge Anton Piller relief granted *ex parte* by way of an appeal direct to that court.[19] If a challenge is to be made to relief which has been granted *ex parte*, this should be by way of application to the High Court to discharge or vary the order, and then by way of appeal, which in general should only be brought against a refusal to discharge or vary the order made on an application when the relevant

---

16 *Chanel Ltd* v *Woolworth & Co* [1981] 1 WLR 485.
17 *Distributori Automatici Italia SpA* v *Holford General Trading Co Ltd* [1985] 1 WLR 1066 at p 1073; *Rank Film Ltd* v *Video Information Centre Ltd* [1982] AC 380 at p 417, per Templeman LJ.
18 See for example *WEA Ltd* v *Visions Channel 4 Ltd* [1983] 1 WLR 721 at p 723; *Booker McConnell plc* v *Plasgow* [1985] RPC 425 at p 427.
19 *WEA Ltd* v *Visions Channel 4 Ltd*, above.

evidence is complete.[20] If an application to discharge or vary Mareva relief has been dismissed with the relief being granted or left in place to continue 'until trial or further order', the court still has jurisdiction to entertain a further application to discharge or modify the injunction.[21] However, as a general rule, the court will require good reason to be shown why the injunction should be discharged or varied notwithstanding the previous decision of the court, for example because there has been a significant change of circumstances, or because new evidence has come to light which was not previously available.[22] In such circumstances, it is considered that the application to discharge or vary the injunction should be made to the court of first instance, and not by way of an application for leave to appeal out of time against the previous decision of the court.

In the event of a plaintiff wishing to appeal against a decision declining to continue a Mareva injunction, he may apply to the court of first instance to continue the injunction pending appeal.[23] On such an application the general principle is that the court ought to see that the appeal if successful is not nugatory. If the court of first instance refuses to continue the injunction the plaintiff may make an application to the Court of Appeal to continue the injunction pending appeal. The application can be heard by a single judge of the Court of Appeal pursuant to the jurisdiction conferred by s 58(1) of the Supreme Court Act 1981, and an appeal lies from his decision to the Court of Appeal itself pursuant to RSC Order 59, r 14(12). Even if the court of first instance is not minded to continue the injunction pending appeal, the court will normally maintain the status quo pending the hearing of an application to the single judge or the Court of Appeal (as the case may be) for an injunction to be granted pending appeal.

The principles upon which an appellate court will interfere with the decision of a judge in granting or discharging an interlocutory injunction are stated in *Hadmor Productions Ltd* v *Hamilton* [1983] 1 AC 191 (and see *Garden Cottage Foods Ltd* v *Milk Marketing Board* [1984] AC 130 and *The 'Niedersachsen'* [1983] 1 WLR 1412 at p 1421). The appellate court will not interfere with the exercise by the judge of his discretion merely on the grounds that the members of the appellate court would have exercised their discretion differently. However, it may conclude that the judge exercised his discretion wrongly, by reason of a misunderstanding of the law or the evidence before him, by taking into account irrelevant factors or failing to take into account relevant ones, or that the existence of fresh evidence which has become available subsequent to the hearing at first

---

20 *Hunters & Partners* v *Wellings & Partners* [1987] FSR 83.
21 This is so even if the injunction has been granted or continued by consent, see *Chanel Ltd* v *Woolworth & Co* [1981] 1 WLR 485 at p 492.
22 *Chanel Ltd* v *Woolworth & Co*, above at pp 492–493.
23 *Erinford Properties* v *Cheshire County Council* [1974] Ch 261.

instance shows an inference drawn by the judge to have been wrong, although it may have appeared to be correct at the time of the hearing. The Court of Appeal has emphasised that in general, appeals in Mareva cases should be 'rare' and confined to matters of principle.[23A]

(11) Costs of an application to discharge or vary Mareva or Anton Piller relief

Under s 51(1) of the Supreme Court Act 1981, the court has 'full power to determine by whom and to what extent . . . costs are to be paid'. Ordinarily when an order for costs is made, these are ordered to be taxed on the standard basis (RSC Order 62, r 3(4)).

If a plaintiff has made inadequate inquiries before seeking Anton Piller or Mareva relief this may result in his being deprived of costs relating to the obtaining of such relief in circumstances where otherwise the costs might have been awarded to him.[24] In circumstances where relief is obtained *ex parte* on the basis of false evidence relied upon by the plaintiff, the court may order the defendant's costs to be paid by the plaintiff on an indemnity basis, to be paid and taxed forthwith, regardless of whether or not the false evidence had been fabricated by a third party without the knowledge of the plaintiff.[25] The court may also order costs to be paid on an indemnity basis by the plaintiff if there has been an abuse of the process of the court[26] either in the obtaining of the order or subsequently, in the manner in which the order has been implemented. Although material non-disclosure on the *ex parte* application is a breach of the plaintiff's duty owed to the court there is no general practice of the court that where there has been non-disclosure, and costs are to be awarded against the plaintiff, they ought to be on an indemnity basis.[27] However, the fact that there has been material non-disclosure is plainly a relevant factor to be taken into account on the question of costs and is capable of justifying an award on this basis, particularly if the non-disclosure was deliberate or was seriously culpable.

If an innocent third party affected by a Mareva injunction successfully applies to the court to discharge or vary the injunction so as to protect his interests, he ought as a general rule be awarded his costs on an indemnity basis, but subject to a direction that the burden is upon the third party to justify that the costs had been reasonably incurred and were reasonable in

23A *Derby & Co Ltd* v *Weldon* [1989] 2 WLR 276; *Allied Trust Bank* v *Shukri* (1989) *Financial Times*, 14 November. See also p 113 above.
24 *Systematica Ltd* v *London Computer Centre* [1983] FSR 313.
25 *Bir* v *Sharma* (1988) *The Times*, 7 December.
26 *Granvias Oceanicas Armadora* v *Jibsen Trading Co* [1977] 2 Lloyd's Rep 344 at p 353. See also *NZ Michalos* v *The Food Corporation of India* [1983] 1 Lloyd's Rep 409 at p 416.
27 Eg see *Thermax* v *Schott Industrial Glass* [1981] FSR 289 at p 298; *Lloyd's Bowmaker Ltd* v *Britannia Arrow plc* [1988] 1 WLR 1337 at p 1350; *Bank Mellat* v *Nikpour* [1985] FSR 87 at p 93.

amount.[28] This is because of the principle that innocent third parties ought to be indemnified against costs and expenses, or liabilities incurred, as a result of complying with the order.[29] If an innocent third party reasonably applies to the court for directions concerning an injunction then similarly he should ordinarily be awarded the costs of the application on the same basis.

---

28 *Project Development Co Ltd SA* v *KMK Securities Ltd* [1982] 1 WLR 1470.
29 See p 186, above.

Chapter 19

The uses to which disclosed documents or information may be put

(1) Introduction

Questions are liable to arise about the uses to which documents or information acquired in the course of legal proceedings may be put. Such questions may arise, for example, if the plaintiff is considering commencing new proceedings and making an application in those proceedings supported by documents or information obtained in other proceedings. If the plaintiff has obtained documents or information as a result of an order made ancillary to a Mareva injunction or an Anton Piller order, what use may he make of the documents or information? Is the position different if the documents and information are supplied by the defendant voluntarily in support of an application for a variation of a Mareva injunction?

It is well established that documents obtained by a party by way of discovery under a court order are subject to an implied undertaking by that party to the court to the effect that the documents will only be used for the purpose of the litigation. In Bray on *Discovery* (1st edition (1885)) at p 238, the principle was stated:

A party who has obtained access to his adversary's documents under an order for production has no right to make their contents public or communicate them to any stranger to the suit: . . . nor to use them or copies of them for any collateral object . . . If necessary an undertaking to that effect will be made a condition of granting an order.

Such an undertaking is implied.[1] A party who obtains discovery in proceedings does so on condition that he will make use of the documents for the purposes of that action.[2] This is so as to encourage and ensure full and unreserved discovery of documents,[3] and also because the documents

---

1 *Harman* v *Home Office* [1983] 1 AC 280; *Riddick* v *Thames Board Mills* [1977] QB 881; *Crest Homes Plc* v *Marks* [1987] AC 829; *Alterskye* v *Scott* [1948] 1 All ER 469 at p 470.

2 *Riddick* v *Thames Board Mills*, above at pp 896, 901–902 and 910; *Crest Homes plc* v *Marks* [1987] AC 829 at p 853; *Sybron Corporation* v *Barclays Bank* [1985] Ch 299 at pp 319–321, per Scott J.

3 *Home Office* v *Harman* [1983] 1 AC 280 at pp 306, 308 and 321–322.

belong to the party disclosing them, and use of the documents for some purpose collateral to the action by the other party is an infringement of the disclosing party's rights in the document.[4] The implied undertaking prevents the use of the documents in another action, even though it is based on the same cause of action.[5] However, the documents can be used to obtain further discovery or disclosure of information for use in the action albeit that this is being done by means of a second set of proceedings brought for this purpose.[6] This is because the disclosed documents are still being used solely for the purpose of prosecuting the first action. The implied undertaking takes effect in respect of any documents disclosed as a result of an order of the court, including documents obtained by a party pursuant to Anton Piller relief.[7] It applies so as to prevent the use of the documents in question in a second set of proceedings between the same parties, even when the subject matter of the second set of proceedings is closely related to that of the proceedings in which the discovery has been obtained.[8]

If discovery is ordered by the court under the principle that the defendant, by virtue of becoming innocently mixed up in the wrongdoings of others, has become under a duty to give the plaintiff full information concerning the wrongdoing,[9] then the purpose for which the discovery has been ordered is to enable the plaintiff to identify and sue the wrongdoers. In such circumstances there is no implied undertaking by the plaintiff which precludes him from using the documents or other information obtained for the purpose of suing the third parties.[10] Thus in the context of a tracing claim, if discovery of documents or disclosure of information is ordered to be given by a bank so as to enable the plaintiff to trace assets,[11] there will be no implied undertaking by the plaintiff preventing him from using the documents or information to preserve the relevant assets or their proceeds, or to sue third parties. But the information cannot be used for

---

4 *Halcon International Inc* v *Shell Transport and Trading Co* [1979] RPC 97 at p 121, per Megaw LJ.
5 *Sybron Corporation* v *Barclays Bank*, above.
6 *Wilden Pump* v *Fusfeld* [1985] FSR 581.
7 *Crest Homes plc* v *Marks*, above; *Customs and Excise Commissioners* v *AE Hamlin & Co* [1984] 1 WLR 509 at pp 517–518; *VDU Installations Ltd* v *Integrated Computer Systems and Cybernetics Ltd* [1989] FSR 378 at pp 395–396.
8 *Halcon International Inc* v *Shell Transport and Trading Co* [1979] RPC 97 (discovery by the defendants in English proceedings brought by the plaintiffs to restrain alleged infringements of United Kingdom letters patent could not be used in Dutch proceedings between the same parties concerning applications made by the plaintiffs for patents in The Netherlands); *Riddick* v *Thames Board Mills* [1977] QB 881 (memorandum obtained on discovery in the first action could not be used to launch libel proceedings).
9 Ie, under the principle referred to by Lord Reid in *Norwich Pharmacal* v *Customs & Excise Commissioners* [1974] AC 133 at p 175.
10 *Sony Corporation* v *Anand* [1981] FSR 398; *Rank Film Ltd* v *Video Information Centre* [1982] AC 380 at p 447.
11 Eg as in *Bankers Trust Co* v *Shapira* [1980] 1 WLR 1274.

the purpose of pointing out to a third party some wrongdoing on the part of the defendant.[12]

In *Home Office* v *Harman*, confidential documents were provided by the Home Office on discovery, which were subsequently read out by counsel in open court. The solicitor acting for the party to whom discovery had been given, subsequently allowed a journalist to have access to the documents which he used for the purpose of writing a newspaper article highly critical of Home Office ministers and civil servants. The House of Lords held by a majority of three to two that the solicitor had acted in breach of the implied undertaking given on discovery and was in contempt of court. The undertaking did not come to an end when the documents were read out in court. Subsequently there was a 'friendly settlement' between the solicitor (Miss Harman) and the United Kingdom of an application made by Miss Harman against the United Kingdom before the European Commission of Human Rights[13] which resulted in a change of the law. This change took the form of a new rule of court, RSC Order 24, r 14A which reads:

14A. Any undertaking, whether express or implied, not to use a document for any purposes other than those of the proceedings in which it is disclosed shall cease to apply to such document after it has been read to or by the court, or referred to, in open court, unless the court for special reasons has otherwise ordered on the application of a party or of a person to whom the document belongs.

(2) The documents and information which is subject to the implied undertaking

In *Derby & Co Ltd* v *Weldon (No 2)* (1988) *The Independent*, 2 November, the defendants had provided affidavits and exhibits as to their assets pursuant to an order of the court. Sir Nicholas Browne-Wilkinson V-C held that the affidavits and exhibits were obtained subject to the implied undertaking.[14] In principle this is true of any document prepared and served under a court order requiring disclosure of information (eg a letter or a telex). In consequence the implied undertaking, whilst it continued to apply, prohibited the plaintiffs from producing these affidavits in response to a subpoena served on them by a third party in New York. It is considered that the implied undertaking would also apply to information required to be given orally under a court order, regardless of whether the information was subsequently to be confirmed in writing. In each case the information has had to be divulged under a court order, and therefore the information is

---

12 *VDU Installations Ltd* v *Integrated Computer Systems and Cybernetics Ltd*, above.
13 The text of the settlement is set out in *Bibby Bulk Carriers* v *Cansulex Ltd* [1988] QB 155 at p 159.
14 Contrast *Ashtiani* v *Kashi* [1987] QB 888 at p 902, per Dillon LJ (obiter).

not to be used by the party who obtains discovery for purposes other than that for which production was ordered.[15]

In contrast there is no implied undertaking which is applicable to information made available voluntarily and not under compulsion of a court order by a party. Thus in *Derby & Co Ltd v Weldon (No 2)*, the defendants had sworn affidavits with exhibits and served these in order to challenge Mareva relief which had been granted against them. The defendants by their own voluntary act had destroyed the privacy in the documents. Also there were documents referred to in these affidavits, which were not exhibited, but which had to be produced pursuant to an order of the court. The Vice-Chancellor held that by swearing the relevant affidavit which referred to the documents, the documents were voluntarily relied upon and therefore were not subject to any implied undertaking. In effect the court order was merely perfecting the previous voluntary disclosure. The defendants must have known that they could not rely on the documents without being liable to produce them if required.

In the context of Mareva relief, the defendant may wish to seek a variation to the injunction in order to make a payment in the ordinary course of business or for some other justifiable purpose (eg payment of legal costs) (see pp 191–195, above). On such an application, the defendant may seek to rely on evidence which includes details of his assets and his affairs. However, such evidence is adduced by the defendant voluntarily in the sense that he is not compelled by an order of the court to disclose that information to the plaintiff. Hence the information comprised in that evidence is not protected by an implied undertaking.

In the context of Anton Piller relief, the question may arise as to the extent to which the plaintiff's representatives are bound to keep confidential information acquired by them in the course of a search. In the case of documents seen in the course of a search which fall within the scope of the order it is clear that the implied undertaking applies to them (see p 239, above). In relation to documents read for the purpose of seeing whether or not they fall within the order, but which do not, it is considered that there must be an implied undertaking not to make use of the information obtained. The defendant has been compelled by virtue of the court order to permit access to these documents, and has been required to allow the plaintiff's representatives to scrutinise them to see whether they fell within the ambit of the order. The fact that documents fell outside the ambit could provide no justification for them being accorded any less protection than documents which did fall within it. On the other hand, there is no implied undertaking given to the effect that *whatever* the representatives happen to see on the premises in the course of a search permitted pursuant to an Anton Piller order, they will keep confidential. Thus, in *LT Piver Sarl*

---

15 *Rank Film Ltd* v *Video Information Centre* [1982] AC 380 at p 447, per Lord Fraser; *VDU Installations Ltd* v *Integrated Computer Systems and Cybernetics Ltd* [1989] FSR 378 at pp 395–396.

v *S&J Perfume Co Ltd* [1987] FSR 159, a representative saw an article on the premises which he thought infringed the rights of a third party and it was held that he was at liberty to report this to the third party concerned. If a representative as a result of being admitted to the premises comes across a trade secret, then plainly he is bound not to disclose that secret. But that is because of the ordinary legal rules concerning the preservation of confidential information.

(3) The effect of RSC Order 24, r 14A

This rule came into force on 1 October 1987 and was not retrospective.[16] It has the effect of limiting the duration for which an express or implied undertaking has effect, subject to the power of the court 'for special reasons' to order to the contrary. For example, if documents are disclosed which contain confidential information as to a secret invention or process,[17] then plainly this would be capable of giving rise to 'special reasons' for keeping the documents confidential. The rule applies to 'a document' which is subject to an express or implied undertaking. Thus, for example, if an order is made requiring a party to make and serve an affidavit containing certain information then the affidavit disclosed under that order is subject to the implied undertakings, as are the exhibits. The rule also applies to the affidavit and the exhibits.

When does the rule have effect so as to cause the undertaking to cease? In *Derby & Co Ltd* v *Weldon (No 2)*, the affidavits and exhibits relating to assets situated within the jurisdiction had been included in the bundle of documents before the Court of Appeal in *Derby & Co Ltd* v *Weldon (No 1)* [1989] 2 WLR 276. The affidavits had been referred to in the skeleton argument lodged by the plaintiffs with the Court of Appeal, and the judgment of Parker LJ in the Court of Appeal had referred to those assets as being 'wholly insufficient to afford protection'. In these circumstances, the Vice-Chancellor held that the implied undertaking had ceased to apply by reason of RSC Order 24, r 14A. The affidavits had been 'read to or by the court, or referred to, in open court'. The rule is not confined to releasing the implied undertaking once a document has been read out in open court, but it applies even to documents which are read silently by the judge, or documents which are 'referred to' in open court, although not read out to the court. The reference can be by means of a skeleton argument lodged with the court which subsequently forms part of counsel's submissions in open court.

Prior to the making of the new rule of court it had been decided in *Sybron Corporation* v *Barclays Bank plc* (above), that documents obtained by

---

16 *Bibby Bulk Carriers* v *Cansulex Ltd* [1989] QB 155.
17 See *Attorney-General* v *Newspaper Publishing Plc* [1988] Ch 333 at p 389; *Werner-Lambert Co* v *Glaxo Laboratories Ltd* [1975] RPC 354; *Arab Monetary Fund* v *Hashim* [1989] 1 WLR 565 at p 577 (the need to keep confidential industrial secrets of this nature can justify the making of an order for discovery limited to a party's lawyers and experts only).

subpoena and which were referred to in a judgment given in open court were still subject to an implied undertaking. In cases governed by RSC Order 24, r 14A, in such circumstances the implied undertaking would not apply.

(4) Express undertaking on the use of information relating to assets abroad

The defendant may be ordered to disclose information about assets abroad so as to enable Mareva relief granted in respect of such assets to be made effective. This might involve the plaintiff in commencing foreign proceedings so as to preserve the assets in question. It is the practice of the court to require the plaintiff to undertake not to use such information in proceedings abroad, without the leave of the court.[18] In the absence of such an undertaking the plaintiff would not have been precluded from using the information for launching asset-preserving proceedings abroad, because such proceedings would have been directed to advancing the purpose for which the discovery had been ordered, namely preserving the assets.

The question might arise as to whether the provisions of RSC Order 24, r 14A apply to this form of express undertaking. Both the events which led to the making of the rule and its wording show that it is directed to the implied undertaking which ordinarily arises in relation to documents disclosed under an order of the court, or an express undertaking which has the same content (ie an undertaking not to use documents for some 'collateral' purpose). The express undertaking required to be furnished by the plaintiff in respect of information about assets abroad, operates as a means of enabling the court to exercise supervision and control over the plaintiff in the use of the information for preserving the foreign assets. This express undertaking is different in content from the ordinary implied undertaking described in the rule, ie 'not to use a document for any purposes other than those of the proceedings in which it is disclosed', and has a different function. The preserving of foreign assets is not a 'collateral' purpose, but is *the purpose* for which the discovery was ordered. Accordingly, it is thought that RSC Order 24, r 14A does not itself have the effect of releasing the plaintiff from this form of express undertaking, which is different both in wording and objective from the undertaking which is subject to the rule.

(5) Release of the implied undertaking

The court has jurisdiction to release a party who has received discovery under a court order, from the implied undertaking. The decision whether or not to release the recipient is one of discretion, which takes into account

---

18 *Derby & Co Ltd* v *Weldon (No 1)*, above.

the purpose for which the document is now sought to be used, and the likely consequences of releasing or not releasing the recipient from the undertaking, including any possible prejudice which might be suffered by the party who provided the discovery as a result of the release of the undertaking. If the applicant is to be released, it is necessary for him to demonstrate 'cogent and persuasive reasons'.[19] Anton Piller relief usually includes an express undertaking by the plaintiff's solicitors to retain all documents and articles obtained in their safe custody or to their order, until further order of the court, except in so far as documents or articles are to be returned to the defendant or his solicitors pursuant to the order. Precisely the same principle applies in an application to be released from this express undertaking.

In the context of Anton Piller orders the courts have not regarded the fact that the documents may evidence criminal offences as in itself providing good reason for releasing the undertaking.[20]

However, the courts have been willing to allow documents obtained on discovery to be used for the purposes of contempt proceedings. If the documents have been obtained in the same action in which contempt proceedings are to be brought then there is no restriction on their use for this purpose.[21] When the documents had been obtained in a separate, but closely connected, action between the same parties, leave was granted to use those documents for contempt proceedings in the other action.[22] The decided cases on whether or not leave should be granted in any particular circumstances are simply illustrations of the application of the same general principle that 'the court will not release or modify the implied undertaking given on discovery save in special circumstances and where the release or modification will not occasion injustice to the person giving discovery'.[23] In cases where, as a result of RSC Order 24, r 14A, the documents in question are likely to be released into the public domain in the near future, this will be a factor to be taken into account in the application of the general principle.

---

19   *Crest Homes plc* v *Marks* [1987] AC 829 at p 859, per Lord Oliver; *Bibby Bulk Carriers* v *Cansulex Ltd* [1989] QB 155 at p 161.

20   *EMI Records Ltd* v *Spillane* [1986] 1 WLR 967 at p 977, where Sir Nicholas Browne-Wilkinson V-C disagreed with the views of Falconer J in *Customs and Excise Commissioners* v *AE Hamlin & Co* [1984] 1 WLR 509. See also *General Nutrition Ltd* v *Pattni* [1984] FSR 403.

21   *Garvin* v *Domus Publishing Ltd* [1989] Ch 335 at p 342; *Crest Homes plc* v *Marks* [1987] AC 829 at p 860.

22   *Crest Homes plc* v *Marks*, above.

23   *Crest Homes plc* v *Marks*, above, at p 860.

Chapter 20

Criminal Marevas, restraint orders and receivers

(1) Introduction

At common law a constable has the right to seize goods which he reasonably believes to have been stolen.[1] This right is sufficient to enable Mareva relief to be granted to the police in respect of property which they believe on reasonable grounds to have been obtained dishonestly. Now alongside the common law jurisdiction, there is statutory jurisdiction for the civil courts to grant restraint orders or appoint receivers over property for the purpose of preserving or realising that property so that it will be available to satisfy confiscation orders made by a criminal court.

This statutory jurisdiction is analogous to the Mareva jurisdiction,[2] and involves similar procedures and concepts. Under the Drug Trafficking Offences Act 1986 there are elaborate provisions for the confiscation of the proceeds of drug trafficking and for the granting of relief by the High Court both before and after the criminal trial so as to preserve or realise property. Under the Civil Justice Act 1988 there are similar provisions modelled on the Drug Trafficking Offences Act 1986, which have wide application. This chapter reviews both the role of the ordinary Mareva jurisdiction and the statutory jurisdiction.

(2) The ordinary Mareva jurisdiction

It might have been that the civil courts would develop a general common law jurisdiction based on s 37(1) of the Supreme Court Act 1981 to act in aid of proceedings or possible proceedings before the criminal courts. However, the general rule is that Mareva relief will not be granted unless the applicant has some existing cause of action (see pp 57–59 and 110–112, above). In *Chief Constable of Kent* v *V* (below), the defendant was alleged to have stolen some blank cheques and to have forged the victim's signature. He had apparently cashed the forged cheques and the proceeds were mixed with other money of his own. Neither the victim nor her bank brought proceed-

---

1 *Chief Constable of Kent* v *V* [1983] QB 34 at p 46, per Donaldson LJ; *Chic Fashions (West Wales) Ltd* v *Jones* [1968] 2 QB 299.
2 *Re Peters* [1988] QB 871.

ings to restrain the defendant from dealing with money in his bank accounts, but the Chief Constable sought and was granted relief by the majority of the Court of Appeal. In his judgment Lord Denning MR said that s 37(1) was not subject to a limitation that the applicant must have some legal or equitable right to be protected, and he distinguished the wording of the section from its predecessors. He considered that the correct test was whether the applicant had 'a sufficient interest' (at p 42). However, this approach was rejected by both of the other members of the court, and has not subsequently been followed.[3] Accordingly, it is clearly established that the police can only obtain Mareva relief when the applicant claims a right to seize or preserve the property which is the subject of the application. Thus in *Chief Constable of Kent* v *V*, Donaldson LJ (who together with Lord Denning MR formed the majority) held that at common law the police had the right to 'detain' money which they reasonably believed had been taken from a victim in breach of the criminal law. This right enabled Mareva relief to be granted in respect of money in the form of bank notes, or money which existed in the form of a credit balance at a bank (ie in the form of a choice of action). Therefore, Donaldson LJ held that in the circumstances an injunction could be granted under s 37(1) of the Supreme Court Act 1981, but only 'if and to the extent that [the moneys in the bank accounts] can be shown to have been obtained from another in breach of the criminal law'. Donaldson LJ left open the point whether the common law right of seizure or detention would apply to money which was the proceeds of realisation of stolen goods and which had been paid into a bank account.[4]

In *West Mercia Constabulary* v *Wagener* [1982] 1 WLR 127, the defendant had been charged with fraudulently obtaining cheques from members of the public which he had paid into his bank. Forbes J granted relief limited to the proceeds of the improperly obtained cheques, and found justification for granting the relief in RSC Order 29, r 2. However, that rule only enables property to be detained or preserved when that property is the subject matter of an action. It is an ancillary power to be exercised when there are substantive proceedings on the merits before the High Court. The reasoning of Forbes J was rejected by Donaldson LJ in *Chief Constable of Kent* v *V*, because it failed to address the question whether the applicants had a substantive cause of action against the defendant. Nevertheless, with the extention of the common law right to include money taken from a victim and paid into a bank account, the actual decision of Forbes J can be justified, because the applicants did have a substantive cause of action against the defendant.

However, if a defendant is alleged to have benefited from crime, this

---

3 *Chief Constable of Hampshire* v *A Ltd* [1985] QB 132; *Chief Constable of Leicestershire* v *M* [1989] 1 WLR 20 at pp 22–23, per Hoffmann J.

4 It seems that the right would so extend: *Chief Constable of Hampshire* v *A Ltd*, above, at p 136, per Waller LJ and p 137, per Slade LJ.

does not itself confer a cause of action on the police so as to enable them to obtain Mareva relief either over the proceeds of crime or the defendant's assets. Thus in *Chief Constable of Hampshire* v *A Ltd* [1985] QB 132, the defendants were alleged to have carried on a fraudulent business involving selling motor cars with false mileometer readings. The profits of the business had been used to repay bank loans which had been used to purchase properties. The police wished to obtain Mareva relief over the proceeds of sale of the properties, but their application was dismissed. The police had not succeeded in identifying any asset which was itself property which had been stolen or obtained by fraud, or the proceeds of such property. Similarly, if a defendant is alleged to have made substantial profits as a result of obtaining mortgage advances by fraud and investing the money in properties which had substantially increased in value, the police have no common law right to detain the profits.[4A] The police have no general, common law right of detention over property held by an accused, which is not property which is the subject matter of a charge.[5] With the advent of statutory intervention in this field, it has been held by Hoffmann J that 'the courts should not indulge in parallel creativity by the extention of common law principles'.[6]

(3) The Drug Trafficking Offences Act 1986[6A]

If a convicted offender has benefited from drug trafficking he is liable to have a confiscation order made against him under s 1 of the Act. The making of the confiscation order is mandatory and, subject to s 4(3), must be for the full amount the Crown Court assesses to be the value of the proceeds of the drug trafficking.[7]

Under ss 8 to 12 of the Act, powers are conferred on the High Court to grant relief in the form of a restraint order, a charging order, and the appointment of a receiver. These powers are exercisable in civil proceedings brought before the High Court in accordance with the provisions of RSC Order 115, and constitute a jurisdiction exercised by a judge in chambers of the Chancery Division or the Queen's Bench Division for granting interim relief in aid of a confiscation order which may be made or which has been made in criminal proceedings.

The High Court proceedings are commenced by originating motion (RSC Order 115, r 3(1)) which is entitled in the matter of the defendant (naming him) and in the matter of the Act (RSC Order 115, r 3(3)). The initial application for relief is ordinarily made *ex parte* by the prosecutor (RSC Order 115, r 3(1)) to the judge, on the basis of an affidavit (RSC Order 115, r 3(2)). Under s 8(1) of the Act, the court may make a restraint order which binds 'any person' and restrains that person from

---

4A *Chief Constable of Leicestershire* v *M*, above.

5 *Malone* v *Metropolitan Police Commissioner* [1980] QB 49.

6 *Chief Constable of Leicestershire* v *M* [1989] 1 WLR 20 at p 23 and see also *Chief Constable of Surrey* v *A, The Daily Telegraph,* 11 November 1988.

6A See also Appendix 1.

7 For the definition of the value, see s 2(1).

dealing with 'realisable property' as defined in s 5(1). This definition expressly includes property held by someone other than the defendant, who has received it as a result of a 'a gift' (s 5(9) and (10)) caught by the Act. Accordingly, under s 8(1) the court has jurisdiction to freeze property held by third parties, for example by a wife or child of the alleged drug trafficker. Under s 8(6) of the Act the court also has power, when a restraint order has been made, to appoint a receiver to take possession of the property and to 'manage or otherwise deal with ' it. If a third party holds the relevant property, he can be required by an order of the court to give possession of it to the receiver. In the event of the drug trafficker being convicted and a confiscation order being made, which is not subject to appeal, the court may appoint a receiver over the property for the purpose of realising it (s 11(2) and (5)). Again provision is made for any third party who holds 'realisable' property to give possession of it to the receiver.

Thus under the Act, it is intended that the High Court should exercise jurisdiction to preserve or realise 'realisable property' not only as against an alleged or a convicted drug trafficker, but also directly against third parties who hold 'realisable property', including third parties who have received a 'gift' caught by the Act. This includes a gratuitous transfer, or a transfer at an undervalue, made out of the proceeds of drug trafficking. Through the High Court proceedings, property which would otherwise belong to a third party, may be subject to a restraint or charging order and may be used to satisfy a confiscation order made by the crown court against a convicted drug trafficker. Thus, for example, the credit balance in a wife's or child's bank account may be subject to a restraint order and can be taken in due course by a receiver under s 11(5) and dealt with by him pursuant to s 12(1).

Similarly, if a matrimonial home has been bought with money derived by a husband from drug trafficking, and his wife has been given an interest in the home, this may be made the subject of a charging order imposed under s 9(1) of the Act. Under s 8(2) of the Act a restraint order can be made in respect of property held at the date of the order or property which is subsequently received by the person specified in the order. Thus if, for example, an arrangement had been made for a drug trafficker to receive a future payment, a restraint order can be made which catches that payment when made and subjects it to the terms of the order. This mirrors the position in relation to a Mareva injunction which, whilst in force, restrains a defendant from dealing with assets, regardless of whether a particular asset has only come into being or has only been acquired since the date of the order.[8]

There is jurisdiction to grant leave for service out of the jurisdiction of the originating notice of motion, pursuant to RSC Order 11, r 1(1)(*q*).

---

8 *TDK Tape Distributor* v *Videochoice Ltd* [1986] 1 WLR 141 at p 145; *Cretanor Maritime Co Ltd* v *Irish Marine* Ltd [1978] 1 WLR 966 at p 973.

This enables the High Court proceedings to be served on a party outside of the jurisdiction.[9]

Under s 38(3) of the Act, it applies to 'property whether it is situated in England and Wales or elsewhere', and under s 5(1) the definition of 'realisable property' is formulated as extending to 'any property' within its ambit. Thus the powers of the court are exercisable in relation to property wherever situated.[10] This is also the case with Mareva relief, or relief granted under s 37(2) of the Matrimonial Causes Act 1973.[11]

It may be that an alleged drug trafficker only has a limited interest in certain property. For example, he may have a joint bank account with his wife. There is express provision in s 38(7) of the Act to the effect that 'property is held by any person if he holds any interest in it'. This has the consequence that restraint and charging orders may be imposed over any property in which a drug trafficker has an interest, even though it be only a limited interest. Thus a restraint order could be made preventing any dealings with the joint account.[12] This contrasts with the ordinary position in relation to the granting of Mareva relief.[13] However, under s 13(4) of the Act it is provided that the powers conferred on the High Court by ss 8 to 12 of the Act are to be exercised 'with a view to allowing any person other than the defendant or the recipient of any . . . gift [caught by the Act] to retain or recover the value of any property held by him'. Thus, if another person has an interest in the property, and that person has not received a gift caught by the Act, then that person should be allowed to retain his interest or recover its value. If on the other hand the other person has received a gift caught by the Act then regardless of whether his interest in the property was derived from the gift, the property is liable to be dealt with under the Act pursuant to s 13(3). Accordingly, if for example a wife has an interest in a matrimonial home which she owns together with her husband who is an alleged drug trafficker, the court has jurisdiction to make a charging order over the matrimonial home, regardless of whether the wife's interest was acquired with money which belonged to the wife and which was not in any way derived from drug trafficking.

If the husband is subsequently convicted and a confiscation order is made the question may arise as to the extent of the court's powers over the matrimonial home and how they should be exercised. Once the confiscation order is no longer subject to appeal, the court has jurisdiction to appoint a receiver under s 11(2) over the home for the purpose of selling it. If the wife has not received a gift caught by the Act then

---

9 There is an equivalent power for claims made under Part VI of the Criminal Justice Act 1988 under RSC Order 11, r 1(1)(*s*).

10 See also s 20 which provides for recognition and enforcement of orders in Scotland, and is consistent with there being power to make order in respect of property situated in Scotland.

11 See *Hamlin* v *Hamlin* [1986] Fam 11, and pp 66–67, above.

12 *Re a Defendant* (1987) *The Times*, 7 April.

13 *Z Ltd* v *A-Z and AA-LL* [1982] QB 558 at p 591, per Kerr LJ, and pp 27–28, above.

if the home is sold she should be paid out the full value of her interest. If, on the other hand, she has received a gift caught by the Act from her husband and that gift is represented by assets which have a value, then this is to be taken into account under s 13(3) of the Act in assessing how much she should be paid (if anything) in respect of her interest in the home.

(4) The *ex parte* application

Ordinarily an application is made *ex parte* to the judge in chambers by the prosecutor. Since the application is *ex parte*, the prosecutor is under a duty to make full and frank disclosure to the court of all matters which are material to the application.[14] The affidavit in support of the application must set out the information required under RSC Order 115, r 3(2), which includes the grounds for believing that the defendant has benefited from drug trafficking, details about the assets which are said to be 'realisable property' and who hold the assets, and details about—either intended criminal proceedings or criminal proceedings which have already been instituted. Under RSC Order 115, r 3(4) there is a provision corresponding to RSC Order 41, r 5(2) (see pp 75–77, above), which permits 'statements of information or belief with the sources and grounds thereof' to be contained in the affidavit. In *Re a Defendant* (above), the affidavit had been made by an investigating officer who had obtained information from a named officer who had in turn received information from members of the drug squad who had kept watch on certain premises but who were not identified by name in the affidavit. Webster J held that, at least on the *ex parte* application, the reference in the affidavit to the unnamed members of the drug squad was sufficient compliance with the rule.

It is envisaged by RSC Order 115, r 3 that the defendant to the proceedings in the High Court will be the alleged drug trafficker who is intended to be prosecuted or is being prosecuted; under RSC Order 115, r 4(3) provision is made for service of a copy of the restraint order and of the affidavit relied on its support of the application on the defendant 'and on all other named persons restrained by the order and [the plaintiff] shall notify all other persons or bodies affected by the order of its terms'.[15]

Thus, in contrast to the position under the ordinary Mareva jurisdiction where the principle is that an injunction will only be made directed to a defendant (see Chapter 11 at pp 125–126), with a restraint order it is provided under s 8(1) of the Act that a restraint order can prohibit 'any person from dealing with realisable property' and under RSC Order 115 persons may be named in the restraint order other than the defendant to the proceedings. Under RSC 115, r 5(1) anyone served with a restraint or charging order, or notified of the order, can apply to discharge or vary the order. This

14 See Chapter 8 and *Re a Defendant* (1987) *The Times*, 7 April.
15 There is a similar provision in relation to charging orders in RSC Order 115, r 4(4).

corresponds to the position of third parties under Mareva relief. The position is also dealt within ss 8(5A) and 9(8) of the Act which have been added by amendment pursuant to s 103 and Part I of Sched 4 to the Criminal Justice Act 1988. These expressly enable any person affected by a restraint order or a charging order to apply for a discharge or variation of the order.

Ordinarily, a restraint order made *ex parte* will only be made up until a return date for the application *inter partes* (RSC Order 115, r 4(2)). Similarly a charging order made *ex parte* will be an order 'to show cause, imposing the charge until such day'.

A restraint order will also usually provide for an indemnity to be given by the plaintiff to third parties in respect of expenses incurred in complying with the order (RSC Order 115, r 4(1)). This is done by way of an undertaking given by the plaintiff to the court which is equivalent to that which is usually furnished in connection with the granting of Mareva relief (see p 186, above).

(5) Living expenses, legal costs and other expenses

A restraint order will almost invariably make provision for living expenses and legal expenses of the defendant. It may also make provision for other payments by the defendant, such as for example a child's school fees. However, in exercising the discretion whether to qualify the order to allow a particular payment, the court is directed to exercise the powers conferred by ss 8 to 12 in accordance with the objectives set out in s 13. Thus under subsection (2) the statutory intent is that property subject to a restraint order should, so far as is reasonably possible, be made available to satisfy a confiscation order or any future confiscation order which may be made. In *Re Peters* [1988] QB 871, the Court of Appeal set aside an order permitting a drug trafficker[16] to make a capital payment to his son for future school fees. Whilst proceedings were at the stage that an alleged drug trafficker was facing prosecution and the court did not know whether he would be convicted, it was right that he should be able to pay for his living expenses, his legal costs, and interim expenses reasonably incurred for the period up until it was known whether he had been convicted or not, including for example school fees and medical expenses. In relation to his son's education, the defendant, whilst he was an unconvicted person, was entitled not to have his son's education interrupted. But that did not justify the making of a lump sum payment to cover future school fees which were only expected to arise after the alleged drug trafficker had either been convicted or acquitted. The jurisdiction to make or vary restraint orders was described as being 'closely analogous'[17] to the jurisdiction to grant Mareva relief, in the sense that it involved the court striking a balance between on the one hand preserving assets to satisfy a

---

16 The defendant was convicted between the hearing at first instance and the appeal.
17 At p 879, per Lord Donaldson, MR and p 880, per Nourse LJ.

confiscation order if one was made, and on the other hand meeting 'the reasonable requirements of their owner in the meantime' (at p 280, per Nourse LJ).

Section 13(6) of the Act, in contrast to s 13(2), is applicable once a confiscation order has been made. If a convicted drug trafficker is subject to a confiscation order which has not been satisfied, then he will not be allowed to use his property to satisfy other obligations. To do so would thereby reduce the amount available to be paid towards satisfaction of the confiscation order, leaving it unsatisfied. To pay the other obligations would, in the words of s 13(6), 'conflict with the obligation to satisfy the confiscation order'. Thus, provision would preclude payment of school fees when payment would conflict with a convicted drug trafficker's obligation to pay a confiscation order. It did not apply in *Re Peters*, because although there had been a conviction, the crown court had not yet dealt with the question of whether a confiscation order was to be made. Section 13(6) also applies to the property of a person who had received a 'gift' caught by the Act from the convicted drug trafficker, and whose property was liable to be taken towards satisfaction of the confiscation order. That property is liable to be taken 'with a view to realising no more than the value for the time being of the gift' (s 13(3)). So, for example, if the recipient had property worth more than 'the value for the time being of the gift', the recipient of the gift should be permitted freely to use the excess.

An analogy can be drawn between s 13(6) and the exercise of the jurisdiction to vary an injunction once the plaintiff has obtained judgment (see p 199, above). At that stage the injunction is in aid of execution of the judgment, and not merely a Mareva injunction granted for the purpose of preserving assets in contemplation of a possible future judgment. Similarly, once a confiscation order has been made it would be wrong in principle to allow the drug trafficker to use property otherwise than in connection with satisfying the confiscation order.

If the convicted drug trafficker is adjudged bankrupt, property subject to an existing restraint order, or charging order, or proceeds of property realised by a receiver, are excluded from the bankrupt's estate and are not available for distribution among the general body of creditors (s 15). This contrasts with the position where there is a bankruptcy after an injunction has been granted in aid of execution of a judgment. Such an injunction does not in any way affect property being dealt with as part of the bankrupt's estate.

(6) An undertaking in damages

No undertaking in damages is given on an application under the Act, but there is a right for compensation to be awarded in certain limited circumstances under s 19. These include a requirement that the High Court is satisfied that 'there has been some serious default on the part of a member of the police force or the Crown Prosecution Service concerned in the investigation or prosecution of an alleged drug trafficker, who was not subsequently convicted, or whose conviction was quashed on appeal, or who has been pardoned, and that 'but for that default' the criminal proceedings would not have been instituted or continued. The circumstances in which compensation may be ordered under s 19 are much narrower than would be the case if the person suffering loss had the benefit of an undertaking in damages.

It might be suggested that, independently of s 19, a claim could be brought in tort for loss caused by relief granted by the court under the Act, if the claimant could either show a case of malicious prosecution[18] of the proceedings brought under RSC Order 115, or a case that there had been some tortious abuse of the process of the court.[19] However, a claim for malicious prosecution would involve the claimant in showing, *inter alia*, that the applicant was actuated by malice and that there had been no reasonable and probable cause for bringing the proceedings. A claim for tortious abuse of the process would involve the claimant in showing that at least the predominant purpose of the applicant had been deliberately to use the proceedings to achieve some objective not within the jurisdiction's intended purposes.

Leaving aside the remote possibility of a claim being made in tort, the general rule is that if loss is caused by an order of the court, the party damaged has no claim against the person who obtained the order. That is why in the context of interlocutory injunction the plaintiff is required to furnish an undertaking in damages.[20]

Provision is made in the Act for there to be enforcement or registration of confiscation orders made abroad by a court of country or territory designated by Order in Council (ss 26 and 26A). In relation to the United States, the Order in Council[21] provides for s 19 to be omitted, so that no claim can be made under the section for cases brought by virtue of the Order in Council.

If a third party suffers loss as a result of a restraint order, which is not loss in the form of costs or expenses covered by an express undertaking given by the plaintiff to the court, then the third party has no implied right to an indemnity in respect of that loss.[22] If he can bring his case within s 19, then he could seek compensation under the provisions of that section.

---

18 Halsbury's *Laws of England* (4th ed) Vol 45, para 1368. *Metall & Rohstaff* v *Donaldson Inc* [1989] 3 WLR 563 at pp 613–614.
19 *Speed Seal Products Ltd* v *Paddington* [1985] 1 WLR 1327; *Metall & Rohstaff* v *Donaldson Inc* above, at pp 611–613; *Grainger* v *Hill* (1838) 4 Bing NC 212.
20 *Chisholm* v *Rieff* (1953) 2 FLR 211 (Supreme Court of the Northern Territory of Australia); *Digital Equipment Corporation* v *Darkcrest Ltd* [1984] Ch 512.
21 The Drug Trafficking Offences Act 1986 (United States of America) Order 1989 (SI 1989 No 485).
22 *Re R* (1989) *The Times*, 15 July.

(7) Discovery from the defendant

In proceedings under RSC Order 115, the court can order discovery to be made by the defendant for the purposes of the civil proceedings, for example the discovery may be needed so as to identify the defendant's assets and make the order effective by enabling the prosecutor to give notice of it to relevant third parties, or to take other steps to preserve the assets, for example by applying for the appointment of a receiver. The jurisdiction to order such discovery would appear to be justified by RSC Order 24, r 3(1) or by s 37(1) of the Supreme Court Act 1981. In contrast to the position on Anton Piller relief, the prosecutor can give an undertaking not to use the information obtained in the criminal proceedings and this serves to negative the invoking by the defendant of privilege against self-incrimination.[23] The undertaking prevents there being any risk of self-incrimination as a result of compliance with the order.

(8) Effect of a restraint order

A restraint order prevents any dealing (s 8(1)) with the property subject to the order by the defendant or by any person specified in the order either by themselves, their servants or agents or otherwise. This includes payment by a third party debtor to the person restrained (s 8(7)(a)).[24] It also prohibits in the case of property situated within the jurisdiction, its removal from the jurisdiction (s 8(7)(b)). A restraint order does not prevent a third party forfeiting a lease held by the alleged drug trafficker,[25] nor does it prevent a bank from exercising existing rights of set off or combination of accounts in respect of an overdraft which had been granted and drawn down prior to any restraint order being made.[26] If contempt proceedings are to be brought for breach of a restraint order, they are properly brought before a single judge of the High Court pursuant to RSC Order 52, r 1.[27]

If the powers under the Act are sought to be exercised in relation to the property of a third party who is said to have received a 'gift' caught by the Act, it will be open to the third party to put in issue whether or not there has been such a 'gift' and if so its amount. Such an issue would fall to be resolved in the High Court proceedings.

(9) Payment of the receiver

If a receiver obtains property, or proceeds of property, which are available to be paid towards satisfaction of a confiscation order, then a question

---

23 *Re a Defendant* (1987) *The Times*, 7 April.
24 Contrast, in relation to Mareva relief, *Bank Mellat* v *Kazmi* [1989] QB 541, and pp 11–14, above.
25 *Re R* (1989) *The Times*, 15 July.
26 *Re K* (1989) *The Times*, 15 July.
27 *Re H* (1988) *The Times* 1 April.

may arise as to whether the receiver is to be paid his remuneration and expenses out of the funds in his hands. It appears that under s 18(2) of the Act the prosecutor or the applicant who obtained the order appointing the receiver are responsible for paying his remuneration and expenses except when money is to be paid for these under s 12(3)(*a*) of the Act. The general principle is that if the receiver has obtained money available to be paid towards satisfaction of a confiscation order, then he is to be paid his remuneration and expenses out of these funds. This might be achieved by the court making a direction under s 12(1) of the Act for payment of these to be made to the receiver, in which case the sums so paid would not *pro tanto* reduce the amount payable by the convicted drug trafficker under a confiscation order. However, it would appear from ss 12(3)(*a*) and 18(2), that the statutory intent is that the receiver is to be paid his remuneration and expenses out of funds received by the jusitices' clerk from the receiver towards satisfaction of the confiscation order, and the convicted drug trafficker nevertheless has credit for the full amount paid to the clerk, even though part is used for this purpose. If the prosecutor has already paid the receiver pursuant to s 18(2), then the clerk must reimburse him for the sum paid.

(10) Information from third parties

There are wide powers under the Act for obtaining information from third parties for the purposes of an investigation. These powers are sufficiently wide to enable information to be obtained about 'realisable property' so that it can be preserved. Thus, for example, under s 27(2) a circuit judge has power to make an order against a bank to disclose information about a suspected drug trafficker's affairs. It is considered that a bank is not ordinarily under any duty to its customer to seek to oppose the making of an order or to apply for its discharge.[28] Furthermore, a bank would usually be well advised not to inform its customer about the making of an order in view of s 31 of the Act, which makes it a criminal offence to make 'any disclosure which is likely to prejudice the investigation'.

(11) The Criminal Justice Act 1988[29]

Part VI of the Act contains a similar scheme for the making of restraint orders, charging orders and orders appointing a receiver to that contained in the Drug Trafficking Offences Act 1986. Under s 71 the Crown Court has power to make confiscation orders in connection with any indictable offence of which the defendant is convicted, and the magistrates' court has power in relation to offences listed in Sched 4 to the Act. The defendant

---

28 See *Barclays Bank* v *Taylor* [1989] 1 WLR 1066, in relation to the position on an order made under s 9 and Sched 1 to the Police and Criminal Evidence Act 1984.
29 See also Appendix 1.

must have benefited from the offence, and the minimum amount for which
a confiscation order can be made is £10,000 (s 71(7)). A person who has
received a 'gift' caught by the Act (defined in s 74(1)) is liable to have his
property made subject to orders made under Part VI, the intention being
that his property can be applied towards satisfying a confiscation order to
the extent of 'the value for the time being of the gift' (s 82(3)). RSC Order
115, r 23 applies with certain modification the rules applicable to proceedings under the Drug Trafficking Offences Act 1986 to regulate proceedings brought under Part VI of the Criminal Justice Act 1988.

Appendix 1

Statutes

Bankers' Books Evidence Act 1879

7 Court or judge may order inspection, etc

On the application of any party to a legal proceeding a court or judge may order that such party be at liberty to inspect and take copies of any entries in a banker's bank for any of the purposes of such proceedings. An order under this section may be made either with or without summoning the bank or any other party, and shall be served on the bank three clear days before the same is to be obeyed, unless the court or judge otherwise directs.

Arbitration Act 1950

12 Conduct of proceedings, witnesses, &c

(1) Unless a contrary intention is expressed therein, every arbitration agreement shall, where such a provision is applicable to the reference, be deemed to contain a provision that the parties to the reference, and all persons claiming through them respectively, shall, subject to any legal objection, submit to be examined by the arbitrator or umpire, on oath or affirmation, in relation to the matters in dispute, and shall, subject as aforesaid, produce before the arbitrator or umpire all documents within their possession or power respectively which may be required or called for, and do all other things which during the proceedings on the reference the arbitrator or umpire may require.

(2) Unless a contrary intention is expressed therein, every arbitration agreement shall, where such a provision is applicable to the reference, be deemed to contain a provision that the witnesses on the reference shall, if the arbitrator or umpire thinks fit, be examined on oath or affirmation.

(3) An arbitrator or umpire shall, unless a contrary intention is expressed in the arbitration agreement, have power to administer oaths to, or take the affirmations of, the parties to and witnesses on a reference under the agreement.

(4) Any party to a reference under an arbitration agreement may sue out a writ of subpoena ad testificandum or a writ of subpoena duces

tecum, but no person shall be compelled under any such writ to produce any document which he could not be compelled to produce on the trial of an action, and the High Court or a judge thereof may order that a writ of subpoena ad testificandum or a subpoena duces tecum shall issue to compel the attendance before an arbitrator or umpire of a witness wherever he may be within the United Kingdom.

(5) The High Court or a judge thereof may also order that a writ of habeas corpus ad testificandum shall issue to bring up a prisoner for examination before an arbitrator or umpire.

(6) The High Court shall have, for the purpose of and in relation to a reference, the same power, of making orders in respect of—

- (*a*) security for costs;
- (*b*) discovery of documents and interrogatories;
- (*c*) the giving of evidence by affidavit;
- (*d*) examination on oath of any witness before an officer of the High Court or any other person, and the issue of a commission or request for the examination of a witness out of the jurisdiction.
- (*e*) the preservation, interim custody or sale of any goods which are the subject matter of the reference;
- (*f*) securing the amount in dispute in the reference;
- (*g*) the detention, preservation or inspection of any property or thing which is the subject of the reference or as to which any question may arise therein, and authorising for any of the purposes aforesaid any persons to enter upon or into any land or building in the possession of any party to the reference, or authorising any samples to be taken or any observation to be made or experiment to be tried which may be necessary or expedient for the purpose of obtaining full information or evidence; and
- (*h*) interim injunctions or the appointment of a receiver;

as it has for the purpose of and in relation to an action or matter in the High Court:

Provided that nothing in this subsection shall be taken to prejudice any power which may be vested in an arbitrator or umpire of making orders with respect to any of the matters aforesaid.

Theft Act 1968

31 Effect on civil proceedings and rights

(1) A person shall not be excused, by reason that to do so may incriminate that person or the wife or husband of that person of an offence under this Act—

- (*a*) from answering any question put to that person in proceedings for the recovery or administration of any property, for the execution of any trust or for an account of any property or dealings with property; or

(*b*) from complying with any order in any such proceedings;
but no statement or admission made by a person in answering a question put or complying with an order made as aforesaid shall, in proceedings for an offence under this Act, be admissible in evidence against that person or (unless they married after the making of the statement or admission) against the wife or husband of that person.

(2) Notwithstanding any enactment to the contrary, where property has been stolen or obtained by fraud or other wrongful means, the title to that or any other property shall not be affected by reason only of the conviction of the offender.

Supreme Court Act 1981

37 Powers of High Court with respect to injunctions and receivers

(1) The High Court may by order (whether interlocutory or final) grant an injunction or appoint a receiver in all cases in which it appears to the court to be just and convenient to do so.

(2) Any such order may be made either unconditionally or on such terms and conditions as the court thinks just.

(3) The power of the High Court under subsection (1) to grant an interlocutory injunction restraining a party to any proceedings from removing from the jurisdiction of the High Court, or otherwise dealing with, assets located within that jurisdiction shall be exercisable in cases where that party is, as well as in cases where he is not, domiciled, resident or present within that jurisdiction.

(4) The power of the High Court to appoint a receiver by way of equitable execution shall operate in relation to all legal estates and interests in land; and that power—

(*a*) may be exercised in relation to an estate or interest in land whether or not a charge has been imposed on that land under section 1 of the Charging Orders Act 1979 for the purpose of enforcing the judgment, order or award in question; and

(*b*) shall be in addition to, and not in derogation of, any power of any court to appoint a receiver in proceedings for enforcing such a charge.

(5) Where an order under the said section 1 imposing a charge for the purpose of enforcing a judgment, order or award has been, or has effect as if, registered under section 6 of the Land Charges Act 1972, subsection (4) of the said section 6 (effect of non-registration of writs and orders registrable under that section) shall not apply to an order appointing a receiver made either—

(*a*) in proceedings for enforcing the charge; or

(*b*) by way of equitable execution of the judgment, order or award or, as the case may be, of so much of it as requires payment of moneys secured by the charge.

72 Withdrawal of privilege against incrimination of self or spouse in certain proceedings

(1) In any proceeding to which this subsection applies a person shall not be excused, by reason that to do so would tend to expose that person, or his or her spouse, to proceedings for a related offence or for the recovery of a related penalty—

(*a*) from answering any question put to that person in the first-mentioned proceedings; or

(*b*) from complying with any order made in those proceedings.

(2) Subsection (1) applies to the following civil proceedings in the High Court, namely—

(*a*) proceedings for infringement of rights pertaining to any intellectual property or for passing off;

(*b*) proceedings brought to obtain disclosure of information relating to any infringement of such rights or to any passing off; and

(*c*) proceedings brought to prevent any apprehended infringement of such rights or any apprehended passing off.

(3) Subject to subsection (4), no statement or admission made by a person—

(*a*) in answering a question put to him in any proceedings to which subsection (1) applies; or

(*b*) in complying with any order made in any such proceedings,

shall, in proceedings for any related offence or for the recovery of any related penalty, be admissible in evidence against that person or (unless they married after the making of the statement or admission) against the spouse of that person.

(4) Nothing in subsection (3) shall render any statement or admission made by a person as there mentioned inadmissible in evidence against that person in proceedings for perjury or contempt of court.

(5) In this section—

'intellectual property' means any patent, trade mark, copyright, registered design, technical or commercial information or other intellectual property;

'related offence', in relation to any proceedings to which subsection (1) applies, means—

(*a*) in the case of proceedings within subsection (2)(*a*) or (*b*)—

(i) any offence committed by or in the course of the infringement or passing off to which those proceedings relate; or

(ii) any offence not within sub-paragraph (i) committed in connection with that infringement or passing off, being an offence involving fraud or dishonesty;

(*b*) in the case of proceedings within subsection (2)(*c*), any offence revealed by the facts on which the plaintiff relies in those proceedings;

'related penalty', in relation to any proceedings to which subsection (1) applies means—

(*a*) in the case of proceedings within subsection (2)(*a*) or (*b*), any penalty incurred in respect of anything done or omitted in connection with the infringement or passing off to which those proceedings relate;

(*b*) in the case of proceedings within subsection (2)(*c*), any penalty incurred in respect of any act or omission revealed by the facts on which the plaintiff relies in those proceedings.

(6) Any reference in this section to civil proceedings in the High Court of any description includes a reference to proceedings on appeal arising out of civil proceedings in the High Court of that description.

Civil Jurisdiction and Judgments Act 1982

24 Interim relief and protective measures in cases of doubtful jurisdiction

(1) Any power of a court in England and Wales or Northern Ireland to grant interim relief pending trial or pending the determination of an appeal shall extend to a case where—

(*a*) the issue to be tried, or which is the subject of the appeal, relates to the jurisdiction of the court to entertain the proceedings; or

(*b*) the proceedings involve the reference of any matter to the European Court under the 1971 Protocol.

(2) (*Applies to Scotland only.*)

(3) Subsections (1) and (2) shall not be construed as restricting any power to grant interim relief or protective measures which a court may have apart from this section.

25 Interim relief in England and Wales and Northern Ireland in the absence of substantive proceedings

(1) The High Court in England and Wales or Northern Ireland shall have power to grant interim relief where—

(*a*) proceedings have been or are to be commenced in a Contracting State other than the United Kingdom or in a part of the United Kingdom other than that in which the High Court in question exercises jurisdiction; and

(*b*) they are or will be proceedings whose subject-matter is within the scope of the 1968 Convention as determined by Article 1 (whether or not the Convention has effect in relation to the proceedings).

(2) On an application for any interim relief under subsection (1) the court may refuse to grant that relief if, in the opinion of the court, the fact that the court has no jurisdiction apart from this section in relation to the subject-matter of the proceedings in question makes it inexpedient for the court to grant it.

(3) Her Majesty may by Order in Council extend the power to grant

interim relief conferred by subsection (1) so as to make it exercisable in relation to proceedings of any of the following descriptions, namely—

(*a*) proceedings commenced or to be commenced otherwise than in a Contracting State;

(*b*) proceedings whose subject-matter is not within the scope of the 1968 Convention as determined by Article 1;

(*c*) arbitration proceedings.

(4) An Order in Council under subsection (3)—

(*a*) may confer power to grant only specified descriptions of interim relief;

(*b*) may make different provision for different classes of proceedings, for proceedings pending in different countries or courts outside the United Kingdom or in different parts of the United Kingdom, and for other different circumstances; and

(*c*) may impose conditions or restrictions on the exercise of any power conferred by the Order.

(5) An Order in Council under subsection (3) which confers power to grant interim relief in relation to arbitration proceedings may provide for the repeal of any provision of section 12(6) of the Arbitration Act 1950 or section 21(1) of the Arbitration Act (Northern Ireland) 1937 to the extent that it is superseded by the provisions of the Order.

(6) Any Order in Council under subsection (3) shall be subject to annulment in pursuance of a resolution of either House of Parliament.

(7) In this section 'interim relief', in relation to the High Court in England and Wales or Northern Ireland, means interim relief of any kind which that court has power to grant in proceedings relating to matters within its jurisdiction, other than—

(*a*) a warrant for the arrest of property; or

(*b*) provision for obtaining evidence.

26 Security in Admiralty proceedings in England and Wales or Northern Ireland in case of stay, etc

(1) Where in England and Wales or Northern Ireland a court stays or dismisses Admiralty proceedings on the ground that the dispute in question should be submitted to arbitration or to the determination of the courts of another part of the United Kingdom or of an overseas country, the court may, if in those proceedings property has been arrested or bail or other security has been given to prevent or obtain release from arrest—

(*a*) order that the property arrested be retained as security for the satisfaction of any award or judgment which—

(i) is given in respect of the dispute in the arbitration or legal proceedings in favour of which those proceedings are stayed or dismissed; and

(ii) is enforceable in England and Wales or, as the case may be, in Northern Ireland; or

(*b*) order that the stay or dismissal of those proceedings be conditional on the provision of equivalent security for the satisfaction of any such award or judgment.

(2) Where a court makes an order under subsection (1), it may attach such conditions to the order as it thinks fit, in particular conditions with respect to the institution or prosecution of the relevant arbitration or legal proceedings.

(3) Subject to any provision made by rules of court and to any necessary modifications, the same law and practice shall apply in relation to property retained in pursuance of an order made by a court under subsection (1) as would apply if it were held for the purposes of proceedings in that court.

SCHEDULE 1

ARTICLE 1

This Convention shall apply in civil and commercial matters whatever the nature of the court or tribunal. It shall not extend, in particular, to revenue, customs or administrative matters.

The Convention shall not apply to:

(1) the status or legal capacity of natural persons, rights in property arising out of a matrimonial relationship, wills and succession;

(2) bankruptcy, proceedings relating to the winding-up of insolvent companies or other legal persons, judicial arrangements, compositions and analogous proceedings;

(3) social security;

(4) arbitration.

ARTICLE 24

Application may be made to the courts of a Contracting State for such provisional, including protective, measures as may be available under the law of that State, even if, under this Convention, the courts of another Contracting State have jurisdiction as to the substance of the matter.

Insolvency Act 1986

423 Transactions defrauding creditors

(1) This section relates to transactions entered into at an undervalue; and a person enters into such a transaction with another person if—

(a) he makes a gift to the other person or he otherwise enters into a transaction with the other on terms that provide for him to receive no consideration;

(b) he enters into a transaction with the other in consideration of marriage; or

(c) he enters into a transaction with the other for a consideration the value of which, in money or money's worth, is significantly less than the value, in money or money's worth, of the consideration provided by himself.

(2) Where a person has entered into such a transaction, the court may, if satisfied under the next subsection, make such order as it thinks fit for—

(a) restoring the position to what it would have been if the transaction had not been entered into, and

(b) protecting the interests of persons who are victims of the transaction.

(3) In the case of a person entering into such a transaction, an order shall only be made if the court is satisfied that it was entered into by him for the purpose—

(a) of putting assets beyond the reach of a person who is making, or may at some time make, a claim against him, or

(b) of otherwise prejudicing the interests of such a person in relation to the claim which he is making or may make.

(4) In this section 'the court' means the High Court or—

(a) if the person entering into the transaction is an individual, or any other court which would have jurisdiction in relation to a bankruptcy petition relating to him;

(b) if that person is a body capable of being wound up under Part IV or V of this Act, any other court having jurisdiction to wind it up.

(5) In relation to a transaction at an undervalue, references here and below to a victim of the transaction are to a person who is, or is capable of being, prejudiced by it; and in the following two sections the person entering into the transaction is referred to as 'the debtor'.

424 Those who may apply for an order under s 423

(1) An application for an order under section 423 shall not be made in relation to a transaction except—

(a) in a case where the debtor has been adjudged bankrupt or is a body corporate which is being wound up or in relation to which an administration order is in force, by the official receiver, by the trustee of the bankrupt's estate or the liquidator or administrator of the body corporate or (with the leave of the court) by a victim of the transaction;

(b) in a case where a victim of the transaction is bound by a voluntary arrangement approved under Part I or Part VIII of this Act, by the supervisor of the voluntary arrangement or by any person who (whether or not so bound) is such a victim; or

(c) in any other case, by a victim of the transaction.

(2) An application made under any of the paragraphs of subsection (1) is to be treated as made on behalf of every victim of the transaction.

425 Provision which may be made by order under s 423

(1) Without prejudice to the generality of section 423, an order made under that section with respect to a transaction may (subject as follows)—

(*a*) require any property transferred as part of the transaction to be vested in any person, either absolutely or for the benefit of all the persons on whose behalf the application for the order is treated as made;

(*b*) require any property to be so vested if it represents, in any person's hands, the application either of the proceeds of sale of property so transferred or of money so transferred;

(*c*) release or discharge (in whole or in part) any security given by the debtor;

(*d*) require any person to pay to any other person in respect of benefits received from the debtor such sums as the court may direct;

(*e*) provide for any surety or guarantor whose obligations to any person were released or discharged (in whole or in part) under the transaction to be under such new or revived obligations as the court thinks appropriate;

(*f*) provide for security to be provided for the discharge of any obligation imposed by or arising under the order, for such an obligation to be charged on any property and for such security or charge to have the same priority as a security or charge released or discharged (in whole or in part) under the transaction.

(2) An order under section 423 may affect the property of, or impose any obligation on, any person whether or not he is the person with whom the debtor entered into the transaction; but such an order—

(*a*) shall not prejudice any interest in property which was acquired from a person other than the debtor and was acquired in good faith, for value and without notice of the relevant circumstances, or prejudice any interest deriving from such an interest, and

(*b*) shall not require a person who received a benefit from the transaction in good faith, for value and without notice of the relevant circumstances to pay any sum unless he was a party to the transaction.

(3) For the purposes of this section the relevant circumstances in relation to a transaction are the circumstances by virtue of which an order under section 423 may be made in respect on the transaction.

(4) In this section 'security' means any mortgage, charge, lien or other security.

436 Expressions used generally

In this Act, except in so far as the context otherwise requires (and subject to Parts VII and XI)—

'the appointed day' means the day on which this Act comes into force under section 433;

'associate' has the meaning given by section 435;

'business' includes a trade or profession;

'the Companies Act' means the Companies Act 1985;

'conditional sale agreement' and 'hire-purchase agreement' have the same meanings as in the Consumer Credit Act 1974;

'modifications' includes additions, alterations and omissions and cognate expressions shall be construed accordingly;

'property' includes money, goods, things in action, land and every description of property wherever situated and also obligations and every description of interest, whether present or future or vested or contingent, arising out of, or incidental to, property;

'records' includes computer records and other non-documentary records;

'subordinate legislation' has the same meaning as in the Interpretation Act 1978; and

'transaction' includes a gift, agreement or arrangement, and references to entering into a transaction shall be construed accordingly.

Drug Trafficking Offences Act 1986

(As amended by the Criminal Justice Act 1988, Sched 5.)

5 Definition of principal terms used

(1) In this Act, 'realisable property' means, subject to subsection (2) below—

    (*a*) any property held by the defendant, and

    (*b*) any property held by a person to whom the defendant has directly or indirectly made a gift caught by this Act.

(2) Property is not realisable property if—

    (*a*) an order under section 43 of the Powers of Criminal Courts Act 1973 (deprivation orders),

    (*b*) an order under section 27 of the Misuse of Drugs Act 1971 (forfeiture orders), or

    (*c*) an order under section 223 or 436 of the Criminal Procedure (Scotland) Act 1975 (forfeiture of property),

is in force in respect of the property.

(3) For the purposes of sections 3 and 4 of this Act the amount that might be realised at the time a confiscation order is made against the defendant is—

    (*a*) the total of the values at that time of all the realisable property held by the defendant, less

    (*b*) where there are obligations having priority at that time, the total amounts payable in pursuance of such obligations,

together with the total of the values at that time of all gifts caught by this Act.

(4) Subject to the following provisions of this section, for the purposes of this Act the value of property (other than cash) in relation to any person holding the property—

    (*a*) where any other person holds an interest in the property, is—

(i) the market value of the first mentioned person's beneficial interest in the property, less

(ii) the amount required to discharge any incumbrance (other than a charging order) on that interest, and

(*b*) in any other case, is its market value.

(5) Subject to subsection (10) below, references in this Act to the value at any time (referred to in subsection (6) below as 'the material time') of a gift caught by this Act or of any payment or reward are references to—

(*a*) the value of the gift, payment or reward to the recipient when he received it adjusted to take account of subsequent changes in the value of money, or

(*b*) where subsection (6) below applies, the value there mentioned, whichever is the greater.

(6) Subject to subsection (10) below, if at the material time the recipient holds—

(*a*) the property which he received (not being cash), or

(*b*) property which, in whole or in part, directly or indirectly represents in his hands the property which he received,

the value referred to in subsection (5)(*b*) above is the value to him at the material time of the property mentioned in paragraph (*a*) above or, as the case may be, of the property mentioned in paragraph (*b*) above so far as it so represents the property which he received, but disregarding in either case any charging order.

(7) For the purposes of subsection (3) above, an obligation has priority at any time if it is an obligation of the defendant to—

(*a*) pay an amount due in respect of a fine, or other order of a court, imposed or made on conviction of an offence, where the fine was imposed or order made before the confiscation order, or

(*b*) pay any sum which would be included among the preferential debts (within the meaning given by section 386 of the Insolvency Act 1986) in the defendant's bankruptcy commencing on the date of the confiscation order or winding up under an order of the court made on that date.

(8) In the case of a confiscation order made before the coming into force of the Insolvency Act 1986, subsection (7) above shall have effect as if for paragraph (*b*) there were substituted—

'(*b*) pay any sum which, if the defendant has been adjudged bankrupt or was being wound up, would be among the preferential debts.';

and in that paragraph 'the preferential debts'—

(*a*) in relation to bankruptcy, means the debts to be paid in priority under section 33 of the Bankruptcy Act 1914 (assuming the date of the confiscation order to be the date of the receiving order) and

(*b*) in relation to winding up, means the preferential debts listed in Schedule 19 to the Companies Act 1985 (assuming the date of the confiscation order to be the relevant date for the purpose of that Schedule).

(9) A gift (including a gift made before the commencement of section 1 of this Act) is caught by this Act if—

(*a*) it was made by the defendant at any time since the beginning of the period of six years ending when the proceedings were instituted against him, or

(*b*) it was made by the defendant at any time and was a gift of property—

(i) received by the defendant in connection with drug trafficking carried on by him or another, or

(ii) which in whole or in part directly or indirectly represented in the defendant's hands property received by him in that connection.

(10) For the purposes of this Act—

(*a*) the circumstances in which the defendant is to be treated as making a gift include those where he transfers property to another person directly or indirectly for a consideration the value of which is significantly less than the value of the consideration provided by the defendant, and

(*b*) in those circumstances, the preceding provisions of this section shall apply as if the defendant had made a gift of such share in the property as bears to the whole property the same proportion as the difference between the values referred to in paragraph (*a*) above bears to the value of the consideration provided by the defendant.

7 Cases in which restraint orders and charging orders may be made

(1) The powers conferred on the High Court by sections 8(1) and 9(1) of this Act are exercisable where—

(*a*) proceedings have been instituted in England and Wales against the defendant for a drug trafficking offence,

(*b*) the proceedings have not been concluded, and

(*c*) the court is satisfied that there is reasonable cause to believe that the defendant has benefited from drug trafficking.

(2) Those powers are also exercisable where the court is satisfied—

(*a*) that [whether by the laying of an information or otherwise, a person is to be charged with] a drug trafficking offence, and

(*b*) that there is reasonable cause to believe that he has benefited from drug trafficking.

(3) For the purposes of sections 8, 9 and 22 of this Act, at any time when those powers are exercisable before proceedings have been instituted—

(*a*) references in this Act to the defendant shall be construed as references to the person referred to in subsection (2)(*a*) above,

(*b*) references in this Act to the prosecutor shall be construed as references to the person who the High Court is satisfied is to have the conduct of the proposed proceedings, and

(*c*) references in this Act to realisable property shall be construed as if, immediately before that time, proceedings had been instituted against the person referred to in subsection (2)(*a*) above for a drug trafficking offence.

(4) Where the court has made an order under section 8(1) or 9(1) of this Act by virtue of subsection (2) above, the court shall discharge the order if [proceedings in respect of the offence are not instituted (whether by the laying of an information or otherwise] within such time as the court considers reasonable.

8 Restraint orders

(1) The High Court may by order (in this Act referred to as a 'restraint order') prohibit any person from dealing with any realisable property, subject to such conditions and exceptions as may be specified in the order.

(2) A restraint order may apply—

(*a*) to all realisable property held by a specified person, whether the property is described in the order or not, and

(*b*) to realisable property held by a specified person, being property transferred to him after the making of the order.

(3) This section shall not have effect in relation to any property for the time being subject to a charge under section 9 of this Act.

(4) A restraint order—

(*a*) may be made only on an application by the prosecutor,

(*b*) may be made on an *ex parte* application to a judge in chambers, and

(*c*) shall provide for notice to be given to persons affected by the order.

(5) A restraint order—

(*a*) may be discharged or varied in relation to any property, and

(*b*) shall be discharged when proceedings for the offences are concluded.

[(5A) An application for the discharge or variation of a restraint order may be made by any person affected by it.]

(6) Where the High Court has made a restraint order, the court may at any time appoint a receiver—

(*a*) to take possession of any realisable property, and

(*b*) in accordance with the court's directions, to manage or otherwise deal with any property in respect of which he is appointed,

subject to such exceptions and conditions as may be specified by the court; and may require any person having possession of property in respect of which a receiver is appointed under this section to give possession of it to the receiver.

(7) For the purposes of this section, dealing with property held by any person includes (without prejudice to the generality of the expression)—

(*a*) where a debt is owed to that person, making a payment to any person in reduction of the amount of the debt, and

(*b*) removing the property from Great Britain.

(8) Where the High Court has made a restraint order, a constable may for the purpose of preventing any realisable property being removed from Great Britain, seize the property.

(9) Property seized under subsection (8) above shall be dealt with in accordance with the court's directions.

[(10) The Land Charges Act 1972 and the Land Registration Act 1925 shall apply—

    (*a*) in relation to restraint orders, as they apply in relation to orders affecting land made by the court for the purpose of enforcing judgments or recognisances; and

    (*b*) in relation to applications for restraint orders, as they apply in relation to other pending land actions.

(11) The prosecutor shall be treated for the purposes of section 57 of the Land Registration Act 1925 (inhibitions) as a person interested in relation to any registered land to which a restraint order or an application for such an order relates.]

9 Charging orders in respect of land, securities etc

(1) The High Court may make a charging order on realisable property for securing the payment to the Crown—

    (*a*) where a confiscation order has not been made, of an amount equal to the value from time to time of the property charged, and

    (*b*) in any other case, of an amount not exceeding the amount payable under the confiscation order.

(2) For the purpose of this Act, a charging order is an order made under this section imposing on any such realisable property as may be specified in the order a charge for securing the payment of money to the Crown.

(3) A charging order—

    (*a*) may be made only on an application by the prosecutor;

    (*b*) may be made on an ex parte application to a judge in chambers;

    (*c*) shall provide for notice to be given to persons affected by the order; and

    (*d*) may be made subject to such conditions as the court thinks fit and, without prejudice to the generality of this paragraph, such conditions as it thinks fit as to the time when the charge is to become effective.

(4) Subject to subsection (6) below, a charge may be imposed by a charging order only on—

    (*a*) any interest in realisable property, being an interest held beneficially by the defendant or by a person to whom the defendant has directly or indirectly made a gift caught by this Act—

    (i) in any asset of a kind mentioned in subsection (5) below, or

    (ii) under any trust, or

    (*b*) any interest in realisable property held by a person as trustee of a trust if the interest is in such an asset or is an interest under another trust and a charge may by virtue of paragraph (*a*) above be imposed by a charging order on the whole beneficial interest under the first-mentioned trust.

(5) The assets referred to in subsection (4) above are—

(*a*) land in England and Wales, or

(*b*) securities of any of the following kinds—

(i) government stock,

(ii) stock of any body (other than a building society) incorporated within England and Wales,

(iii) stock of any body incorporated outside England and Wales or of any country or territory outside the United Kingdom, being stock registered in a register kept at any place within England and Wales,

(iv) units of any trust in respect of which a register of the unit holders is kept at any place within England and Wales.

(6) In any case where a charge is imposed by a charging order on any interest in an asset of a kind mentioned in subsection (5)(*b*) above, the court may provide for the charge to extend to any interest or dividend payable in respect of the asset.

(7) The court may make an order discharging or varying the charging order and shall make an order discharging the charging order if the proceedings for the offence are concluded or the amount payment of which is secured by the charge is paid into court.

[(8) An application for the discharge or variation of a charging order may be made by any person affected by it.].

(10) Charging orders: supplementary provisions

(1) . . .

(2) The Land Charges Act 1972 and the Land Registration Act 1925 shall apply in relation to charging orders as they apply in relation to orders or writs issued or made for the purpose of enforcing judgments.

(3) Where a charging order has been registered under section 6 of the Land Charges Act 1972, subsection (4) of that section (effect of non- registration of writs and orders registrable under that section) shall not apply to an order appointing a receiver made in pursuance of the charging order.

(4) Subject to any provision made under section 11 of this Act or by rules of court, a charge imposed by a charging order shall have the like effect and shall be enforceable in the same courts and in the same manner as an equitable charge created by the person holding the beneficial interest or, as the case may be, the trustees by writing under their hand.

(5) Where a charging order has been protected by an entry registered under the Land Charges Act 1972 or the Land Registration Act 1925, an order under section 9(7) of this Act discharging order may direct that the entry be cancelled.

(6) The Secretary of State may by order made by statutory instrument amend section 9 of this Act by adding to or removing from the kinds of asset for the time being referred to there any asset of a kind which in his opinion ought to be so added or removed.

An order under this subsection shall be subject to annulment in pursuance of a resolution of either House of Parliament.

(7) In this section and section 9 of this Act, 'building society', 'dividend', 'government stock', 'stock' and 'unit trust' have the same meanings as in the Charging Orders Act 1979.

11 Realisation of property

(1) Where—
  (a) in proceedings instituted for a drug trafficking offence, a confiscation order is made,
  (b) the order is not subject to appeal, and
  (c) the proceedings have not been concluded,
the High Court may, on an application by the prosecutor, exercise the powers conferred by subsections (2) to (6) below.

(2) The court may appoint a receiver in respect of realisable property.

(3) The court may empower a receiver appointed under subsection (2) above, under section 8 of this Act or in pursuance of a charging order—
  (a) to enforce any charge imposed under section 9 of this Act on realisable property or on interest or dividends payable in respect of such property, and
  (b) in relation to any realisable property other than property for the time being subject to a charge under section 9 of this Act, to take possession of the property subject to such conditions or exceptions as may be specified by the court.

(4) The court may order any person having possession of realisable property to give possession of it to any such receiver.

(5) The court may empower any such receiver to realise any realisable property in such manner as the court may direct.

(6) The court may order any person holding an interest in realisable property to make such payment to the receiver in respect of any beneficial interest held by the defendant or, as the case may be, the recipient of a gift caught by this Act as the court may direct and the court may, on the payment being made, by order transfer, grant or extinguish any interest in the property.

(7) Subsections (4) to (6) above do not apply to property for the time being subject to a charge under section 9 of this Act.

(8) The court shall not in respect of any property exercise the powers conferred by subsection (3)(a), (5) or (6) above unless a reasonable opportunity has been given for persons holding any interest in the property to make representations to the court.

12 Application of proceeds of realisation and other sums

(1) Subject to subsection (2) below, the following sums in the hands of a receiver appointed under section 8 or 11 of this Act or in pursuance of a charging order, that is—

(*a*) the proceeds of the enforcement of any charge imposed under section 9 of this Act,

(*b*) the proceeds of the realisation, other than by the enforcement of such a charge, of any property under section 8 or 11 of this Act, and

(*c*) any other sums, being property held by the defendant,

shall [first be applied in payment of such expenses incurred by a person acting as an insolvency practitioner as are payable under section 17A(2) of this Act and then shall,] after such payments (if any) as the High Court may direct have been made out of those sums, be applied on the defendant's behalf towards the satisfaction of the confiscation order.

(2) If, after the amount payable under the confiscation order has been fully paid, any such sums remain in the hands of such a receiver, the receiver shall distribute those sums—

(*a*) among such of those who held property which has been realised under this Act, and

(*b*) in such proportions,

as the High Court may direct after giving a reasonable opportunity for such persons to make representations to the court.

(3) The receipt of any sum by a justices' clerk on account of an amount payable under a confiscation order shall reduce the amount so payable, but the [justices' clerk shall apply the money received for the purposes specified in this section and in the order so specified.

(4) The justices' clerk shall first pay any expenses incurred by a person acting as an insolvency practitioner and payable under section 17A(2) of this Act but not already paid under subsection (1) above.

(5) If the money was paid to the justices' clerk by a receiver appointed under section 8 or 11 of this Act or in pursuance of a charging order the justices' clerk shall next pay the receiver's remuneration and expenses.

(6) After making—

(*a*) any payment required by subsection (4) above; and

(*b*) in a case to which subsection (5) above applies, any payment required by that subsection,

the justices' clerk shall reimburse any amount paid under section 18(2) of this Act.

(7) Any balance in the hands of the justices' clerk after he has made all payments required by the foregoing provisions of this section] shall be treated for the purposes of section 61 of the Justices of the Peace Act 1979 (application of fines, etc) as if it were a fine imposed by a magistrates' court.

In this subsection, 'justices' clerk' has the same meaning as in the Justices of the Peace Act 1979.

13 Exercise of powers by High Court or receiver

(1) The following provisions apply to the powers conferred on the High Court by sections 8 to 12 of this Act, or on the Court of Session by sections

20 to 22 of this Act, or on a receiver appointed under section 8 or 11 of this Act or in pursuance of a charging order.

(2) Subject to the following provisions of this section, the powers shall be exercised with a view to making available for satisfying the confiscation order or, as the case may be, any confiscation order that may be held in the defendant's case the value for the time being of realisable property held by any person by the realisation of such property.

(3) In the case of realisable property held by a person to whom the defendant has directly or indirectly made a gift caught by this Act, the powers shall be exercised with a view to realising no more than the value for the time being of the gift.

(4) The powers shall be exercised with a view to allowing any person other than the defendant or the recipient of any such gift to retain or recover the value of any property held by him.

(5) An order may be made or other action taken in respect of a debt owed by the Crown.

(6) In exercising those powers, no account shall be taken of any obligations of the defendant or of the recipient of any such gift which conflict with the obligation to satisfy the confiscation order.

19 Compensation

(1) If proceedings are instituted against a person for a drug trafficking offence or offences and either—

(*a*) the proceedings do not result in his conviction for any drug trafficking offence, or

(*b*) where he is convicted of one or more drug trafficking offences—

(i) the conviction or convictions concerned are quashed (and no conviction for any drug trafficking offence is substituted), or

(ii) he is pardoned by Her Majesty in respect of the conviction or convictions concerned,

the High Court may, on an application by a person who held property which was realisable property, order compensation to be paid to the applicant.

(2) The High Court shall not order compensation to be paid in any case unless the court is satisfied—

(*a*) that there has been some serious default on the part of a person concerned in the investigation or prosecution of the offence of offences concerned, being a person mentioned in subsection (4) below, and that, but for that default, the proceedings would not have been instituted or continued, and

(*b*) that the applicant has suffered substantial loss in consequence of anything done in relation to the property by or in pursuance of—

(i) an order of the High Court under sections 8 to 11 of this Act, or

(ii) an order of the Court of Sessions under section 20, 21 or 22 of this Act.

(3) The amount of compensation to be paid under this section shall be such as the High Court thinks just in all the circumstances of the case.

(4) Compensation payable under this section shall be paid—

(a) where the person in default was or was acting as a member of a police force, out of the police fund out of which the expenses of that police force are met,

(b) where the person in default was a member of the Crown Prosecution Service or acting on behalf of the service, by the Director of Public Prosecutions, and

(c) where the person in default was an officer within the meaning of the Customs and Excise Management Act 1979, by the Commissioners of Customs and Excise.

Criminal Justice Act 1988

PART VI

Confiscation of the proceeds of an offence

71 Confiscation orders

(1) The Crown Court and a magistrates' court shall each have power, in addition to dealing with an offender in any other way, to make an order under this section requiring him to pay such sum as the court thinks fit.

(2) The Crown Court may make such an order against an offender where—

(a) he is found guilty of any offence to which this Part of this Act applies; and

(b) it is satisfied—

(i) that he has benefited from that offence or from that offence taken together with some other offence of which he is convicted in the same proceedings, or which the court takes into consideration in determining his sentence, and which is not a drug trafficking offence; and

(ii) that his benefit is at least the minimum amount.

(3) A magistrates' court may make such an order against an offender where—

(a) he is convicted of an offence listed in Schedule 4 to this Act; and

(b) it is satisfied—

(i) that he has benefited from that offence or from that offence taken together with some other offence listed in that Schedule of which he is convicted in the same proceedings, or which the court takes into consideration in determining his sentence; and

(ii) that his benefit is at least the minimum amount.

(4) For the purposes of this Part of this Act a person benefits from an offence if he obtains property as a result of or in connection with its commission and his benefit is the value of the property so obtained.

(5) Where a person derives a pecuniary advantage as a result of or in

connection with the commission of an offence, he is to be treated for the purposes of this Part of this Act as if he had obtained as a result of or in connection with the commission of the offence a sum of money equal to the value of the pecuniary advantage.

(6) The sum which an order made by a court under this section requires an offender to pay must be at least the minimum amount, but must not exceed—

(a) the benefit in respect of which it is made; or

(b) the amount appearing to the court to be the amount that might be realised at the time the order is made,

whichever is the less.

(7) For the purposes of this Part of this Act the minimum amount is £10,000 or such other amount as the Secretary of State may specify by order made by statutory instrument.

(8) A statutory instrument containing an order made by the Secretary of State under this section shall be subject to annulment in pursuance of a resolution of either House of Parliament.

(9) In this Part of this Act—

(*a*) an order made by a court under this section is referred to as a 'confiscation order';

(*b*) 'drug trafficking offence' has the same meaning as in the Drug Trafficking Offences Act 1986;

(*c*) references to an offence to which this Part of this Act applies are references to any offence which—

(i) is listed in Schedule 4 to this Act; or

(ii) if not so listed, is an indictable offence, other than a drug trafficking offence; and

(*d*) a person against whom proceedings have been instituted for an offence to which this Part of this Act applies is referred to (whether or not he has been convicted), as 'the defendant'.

74 Definition of principal terms used

(1) In this Part of this Act, 'realisable property' means, subject to subsection (2) below—

(*a*) any property held by the defendant; and

(*b*) any property held by a person to whom the defendant has directly or indirectly made a gift caught by this Part of this Act.

(2) Property is not realisable property if—

(*a*) an order under section 43 of the Powers of Criminal Courts Act 1973 (deprivation orders);

(*b*) an order under section 27 of the Misuse of Drugs Act 1971 (forfeiture orders); or

(*c*) (*applies to Scotland only*),

is in force in respect of the property.

(3) For the purposes of this Part of this Act the amount that might be realised at the time a confiscation order is made is—

(a) the total of the values at that time of all the realisable property held
     by the defendant, less,

(b) where there are obligations having priority at that time, the total
     amounts payable in pursuance of such obligations,

together with the total of the values at that time of all gifts caught by this
Part of this Act.

(4) Subject to the following provisions of this section, for the purposes of
this Part of this Act the value of property (other than cash) in relation to
any person holding the property—

(a) where any other person holds an interest in the property, is—

(i) the market value of the first-mentioned person's beneficial interest
     in the property, less

(ii) the amount required to discharge any incumbrance (other than a
     charging order) on that interest; and

(b) in any other case, is its market value.

(5) References in this Part of this Act to the value at any time (referred
to in subsection (6) below as 'the material time') of any property obtained
by a person as a result of or in connection with the commission of an
offence are references to—

(a) the value of the property to him when he obtained it adjusted to
     take account of subsequent changes in the value of money; or

(b) where subsection (6) below applies, the value there mentioned,

whichever is the greater.

(6) If at the material time he holds—

(a) the property which he obtained (not being cash); or

(b) property which, in whole or in part, directly or indirectly rep-
     resents in his hands the property which he obtained,

the value referred to in subsection (5)(b) above is the value to him at the
material time of the property mentioned in paragraph (a) above or, as the
case may be, of the property mentioned in paragraph (b) above, so far as it
so represents the property which he obtained, but disregarding any charging order.

(7) Subject to subsection (12) below, references in this Part of this Act
to the value at any time (referred to in subsection (8) below as 'the
material time') of a gift caught by this Part of this Act are references to—

(a) the value of the gift to the recipient when he received it adjusted to
     take account of subsequent changes in the value of money; or

(b) where subsection (8) below applies, the value there mentioned,

whichever is the greater.

(8) Subject to subsection (12) below, if at the material time he holds—

(a) the property which he received (not being cash); or

(b) property which, in whole or in part, directly or indirectly rep-
     resents in his hands the property which he received;

the value referred to in subsection (7) above is the value to him at the
material time of the property mentioned in paragraph (a) above or, as the

case may be, of the property mentioned in paragraph (*b*) above so far as it so represents the property which he received, but disregarding any charging order.

(9) For the purposes of subsection (3) above, an obligation has priority at any time if it is an obligation of the defendant to—

    (*a*) pay an amount due in respect of a fine, or other order of a court, imposed or made on conviction of an offence, where the fine was imposed or order made before the conviction order; or

    (*b*) pay any sum which would be included among the preferential debts (within the meaning given by section 386 of the Insolvency Act 1986) in the defendant's bankruptcy commencing on the date of the confiscation order or winding up under an order of the court made on that date.

(10) A gift (including a gift made before the commencement of this Part of this Act) is caught by this Part of this Act if—

    (*a*) it was made by the defendant at any time after the commission of the offence or, if more than one, the earliest of the offences to which the proceedings for the time being relate; and

    (*b*) the court considers it appropriate in all the circumstances to take the gift into account.

(11) The reference in subsection (10) above to an offence to which the proceedings for the time being relate includes, where the proceedings have resulted in the conviction of the defendant, a reference to any offence which the court takes into consideration when determining his sentence.

(12) For the purposes of this Part of this Act—

    (*a*) the circumstances in which the defendant is to be treated as making a gift include those where he transfers property to another person directly or indirectly for a consideration the value of which is significantly less than the value of the consideration provided by the defendant; and

    (*b*) in those circumstances, the preceding provisions of this section shall apply as if the defendant had made a gift of such share in the property as bears to the whole property the same proportion as the difference between the values referred to in paragraph (*a*) above bears to the value of the consideration provided by the defendant.

76 Cases in which restraint orders and charging orders may be made

(1) The powers conferred on the High Court by sections 77(1) and 78(1) below are exercisable where—

    (*a*) proceedings have been instituted in England and Wales against the defendant for an offence to which this Part of this Act applies;

    (*b*) the proceedings have not been concluded; and

    (*c*) either a confiscation order has been made or it appears to the court that there are reasonable grounds for thinking that a confiscation order may be made in them.

(2) Those powers are also exercisable where—

(*a*) the court is satisfied that, whether by the laying of an information or otherwise, a person is to be charged with an offence to which this Part of this Act applies; and

(*b*) it appears to the court that a confiscation order may be made in proceedings for the offence.

(3) For the purposes of sections 77, 78 and 92 below at any time when those powers are exercisable before proceedings have been instituted—

(*a*) references in this Part of this Act to the defendant shall be construed as references to the person referred to in subsection (2)(*a*) above;

(*b*) references in this Part of this Act to the prosecutor shall be construed as references to the person who the High Court is satisfied is to have the conduct of the proposed proceedings; and

(*c*) references in this Part of this Act to realisable property shall be construed as if, immediately before that time, proceedings had been instituted against the person referred to in subsection (2)(*a*) above for an offence to which this Part of this Act applies.

(4) Where the court has made an order under section 77(1) or 78(1) below by virtue of subsection (2) above, the court shall discharge the order if proceedings in respect of the offence are not instituted (whether by the laying of an information or otherwise) within such time as the court considers reasonable.

77 *Restraint orders*

(1) The High Court may by order (referred to in this Part of this Act as a 'restraint order') prohibit any person from dealing with any realisable property, subject to such conditions and exceptions as may be specified in the order.

(2) Without prejudice to the generality of subsection (1) above, a restraint order may make such provision as the court thinks fit for living expenses and legal expenses.

(3) A restraint order may apply—

(*a*) to all realisable property held by a specified person, whether the property is described in the order or not; and

(*b*) to realisable property held by a specified person, being property transferred to him after the making of the order.

(4) This section shall not have effect in relation to any property for the time being subject to a charge under section 78 below.

(5) A restraint order—

(*a*) may be made only on an application by the prosecutor;

(*b*) may be made on an *ex parte* application to a judge in chambers; and

(*c*) shall provide for notice to be given to persons affected by the order.

(6) A restraint order—

(*a*) may be discharged or varied in relation to any property; and

(*b*) shall be discharged when proceedings for the offence are concluded.

(7) An application for the discharge or variation of a restraint order may be made by any person affected by it.

(8) Where the High Court has made a restraint order, the court may at any time appoint a receiver—

    (*a*) to take possession of any realisable property, and

    (*b*) in accordance with the court's directions, to manage or otherwise deal with any property in respect of which he is appointed,

subject to such exceptions and conditions as may be specified by the court; and may require any person having possession of property in respect of which a receiver is appointed under this section to give possession of it to the receiver.

(9) For the purposes of this section, dealing with property held by any person includes (without prejudice to the generality of the expression)—

    (*a*) where a debt is owed to that person, making a payment to any person in reduction of the amount of the debt; and

    (*b*) removing the property from Great Britain.

(10) Where the High Court has made a restraint order, a constable may for the purpose of preventing any realisable property being removed from Great Britain, seize the property.

(11) Property seized under subsection (10) above shall be dealt with in accordance with the court's directions.

(12) The Land Charges Act 1972 and the Land Registration Act 1925 shall apply—

    (*a*) in relation to restraint orders, as they apply in relation to orders affecting land made by the court for the purpose of enforcing judgements or recognisances; and

    (*b*) in relation to applications for restraint orders, as they apply in relation to other pending land actions.

(13) The prosecutor shall be treated for the purposes of section 57 of the Land Registration Act 1925 (inhibitions) as a person interested in relation to any registered land to which a restraint order or an application for such an order relates.

78 Charging orders in respect of land, securities, etc

(1) The High Court may make a charging order on realisable property for securing the payment to the Crown—

    (*a*) where a confiscation order has not been made, of an amount equal to the value from time to time of the property charged; and

    (*b*) in any other case, of an amount not exceeding the amount payable under the confiscation order.

(2) For the purposes of this Part of this Act, a charging order is an order made under this section imposing on any such realisable property as may be specified in the order a charge for securing the payment of money to the Crown.

(3) A charging order—

    (*a*) may be made only on an application by the prosecutor;

    (*b*) may be made on an *ex parte* application to a judge in chambers;

    (*c*) shall provide for notice to be given to persons affected by the order; and

    (*d*) may be made subject to such conditions as the court thinks fit and, without prejudice to the generality of this paragraph, such conditions as it thinks fit as to the time when the charge is to become effective.

(4) Subject to subsection (6) below, a charge may be imposed by a charging order only on—

    (*a*) any interest on realisable property, being an interest held beneficially by the defendant or by a person to whom the defendant has directly or indirectly made a gift caught by this Part of this Act—

    (i) in any asset of a kind mentioned in subsection (5) below; or

    (ii) under any trust; or

    (*b*) any interest in realisable property held by a person as trustee of a trust if the interest is in such an asset or is an interest under another trust and a charge may by virtue of paragraph (*a*) above be imposed by a charging order on the whole beneficial interest under the first-mentioned trust.

(5) The assets referred to in subsection (4) above are—

    (*a*) land in England and Wales; or

    (*b*) securities of any of the following kinds—

    (i) government stock;

    (ii) stock of any body (other than a building society) incorporated within England and Wales;

    (iii) stock of any body incorporated outside England and Wales or of any country of territory outside the United Kingdom, being stock registered in a register kept at any place within England and Wales;

    (iv) units of any unit trust in respect of which a register of the unit holders is kept at any place within England and Wales.

(6) In any case where a charge is imposed by a charging order on any interest in an asset of a kind mentioned in subsection (5)(*b*) above, the court may provide for the charge to extend to any interest or dividend payable in respect of the asset.

(7) The court may make an order discharging or varying the charging order and shall make an order discharging the charging order if the proceedings for the offence are concluded or the amount payment of which is secured by the charge is paid into court.

(8) An application for the discharge or variation of a charging order may be made by any person affected by it.

79 Charging orders: supplementary provisions

(1) The Land Charges Act 1972 and the Land Registration Act 1925 shall apply in relation to charging orders as they apply in relation to orders or writs issued or made for the purpose of enforcing judgments.

(2) Where a charging order has been registered under section 6 of the Land Charges Act 1972, subsection (4) of that section (effect of non- registration of writs and orders registrable under that section) shall not apply to an order appointing a receiver made in pursuance of the charging order.

(3) Subject to any provision made under section 80 below or by rules of court, a charge imposed by a charging order shall have the like effect and shall be enforceable in the same courts and in the same manner as an equitable charge created by the person holding the beneficial interest or, as the case may be, the trustees by writing under their hand.

(4) Where a charging order has been protected by an entry registered under the Land Charges Act 1972 or the Land Registration Act 1925, an order under section 78(7) above discharging the charging order may direct that the entry be cancelled.

(5) The Secretary of State may by order made by statutory instrument subject to annulment in pursuance of a resolution of either House of Parliament amend section 78 above by adding to or removing from the kinds of asset for the time being referred to there any asset of a kind which in his opinion ought to be so added or removed.

(6) In this section and section 78 above, 'building society', 'dividend', 'government stock', 'stock' and 'unit trust' have the same meanings as in the Charging Orders Act 1979.

80 Realisation of property

(1) Where—

   (*a*) a confiscation order is made;

   (*b*) the order is not subject to appeal; and

   (*c*) the proceedings in which it was made have not been concluded,

the High Court may, on an application by the prosecutor, exercise the powers conferred by subsections (2) to (6) below.

(2) The court may appoint a receiver in respect of realisable property.

(3) The court may empower a receiver appointed under subsection (2) above, under section 77 above or in pursuance of a charging order—

   (*a*) to enforce any charge imposed under section 78 above on realisable property or on interest or dividends payable in respect of such property; and

   (*b*) in relation to any realisable property other than property for the time being subject to a charge under section 78 above, to take possession of the property subject to such conditions or exceptions as may be specified by the court.

(4) The court may order any person having possession of realisable property to give possession of it to any such receiver.

(5) The court may empower any such receiver to realise any realisable property in such manner as the court may direct.

(6) The court may order any person holding an interest in realisable property to make such payment to the receiver in respect of any beneficial

interest held by the defendant or, as the case may be, the recipient of a gift caught by this Part of this Act as the court may direct and the court may, on the payment being made, by order transfer, grant or extinguish any interest in the property.

(7) Subsections (4) to (6) above do not apply to property for the time being subject to a charge under section 78 above.

(8) The court shall not in respect of any property exercise the powers conferred by subsection (3)(*a*), (5) or (6) above unless a reasonable opportunity has been given for persons holding any interest in the property to make representations to the court.

81 Application of proceeds of realisation and other sums

(1) Subject to subsection (2) below, the following sums in the hands of a receiver appointed under this Part of this Act or in pursuance of a charging order, that is—

> (*a*) the proceeds of the enforcement of any charge imposed under section 78 above;
>
> (*b*) the proceeds of the realisation, other than by the enforcement of such a charge, of any property under section 77 or 80 above; and
>
> (*c*) any other sums, being property held by the defendant;

shall first be applied in payment of such expenses incurred by a person acting as an insolvency practitioner as are payable under section 87(2) below and then shall, after such payments (if any) as the High Court may direct have been made out of those sums, be applied on the defendant's behalf towards the satisfaction of the confiscation order.

(2) If, after the amount payable under the confiscation order has been fully paid, any such sums remain in the hands of such a receiver, the receiver shall distribute them—

> (*a*) among such of those who held property which has been realised under this Part of this Act, and
>
> (*b*) in such proportions,

as the High Court may direct after giving a reasonable opportunity for such persons to make representations to the court.

(3) The receipt of any sum by a justices' clerk on account of an amount payable under a confiscation order shall reduce the amount so payable, but the justices' clerk shall apply the money received for the purposes specified in this section and in the order so specified.

(4) The justices' clerk shall first pay any expenses incurred by a person acting as an insolvency practitioner and payable under section 87(2) below but not already paid under subsection (1) above.

(5) If the money was paid to the justices' clerk by a receiver appointed under this Part of this Act or in pursuance of a charging order, the justices' clerk shall next pay the receiver's remuneration and expenses.

(6) After making—

> (*a*) any payment required by subsection (4) above; and

(*b*) in a case to which subsection (5) above applies, any payment required by that subsection,

the justices' clerk shall reimburse any amount paid under section 88(2) below.

(7) The justices' clerk shall finally pay any compensation directed to be paid out of any sums recovered under the confiscation order under section 72(7) above.

(8) Any balance in the hands of the justices' clerk after he has made all payments required by the foregoing provisions of this section shall be treated for the purposes of section 61 of the Justices of the Peace Act 1979 (application of fines, etc) as if it were a fine imposed by a magistrates' court.

(9) Where under subsection (3) above a sum falls to be applied in payment both of compensation and of other outgoings—

(*a*) the person entitled to the compensation shall be liable to pay to the Secretary of State such an amount as bears to the remuneration or expenses the same proportion as the amount payable in accordance with the direction under section 72(7) above bears to the total amount payable under the confiscation order;

(*b*) the justices' clerk shall deduct from the amount falling to be applied in payment of the compensation an amount equal to the amount of any liability arising by virtue of paragraph (*a*) above;

(*c*) notwithstanding the deduction under paragraph (*b*) above, the person entitled to the compensation shall be treated as having received the whole amount which falls to be applied in payment of it; and

(*d*) the amount deducted shall be treated for the purposes of section 61 of the Justices of the Peace Act 1979 as if it were a fine imposed by a magistrates' court.

(10) In this section, 'justices' clerk' has the same meaning as in the Justices of the Peace Act 1979.

82 Exercise of powers by High Court or receiver

(1) This section applies to the powers conferred on the High Court by sections 77 to 81 above or on the Court of Session by sections 90 to 92 below; or on a receiver appointed under this Part of this Act in pursuance of a charging order.

(2) Subject to the following provisions of this section, the powers shall be exercised with a view to making available for satisfying the confiscation order or, as the case may be, any confiscation order that may be made in the defendant's case the value for the time being of realisable property held by any person by the realisation of such property.

(3) In the case of realisable property held by a person to whom the defendant has directly or indirectly made a gift caught by this Part of this Act the powers shall be exercised with a view to realising no more than the value for the time being of the gift.

(4) The powers shall be exercised with a view to allowing any person other than the defendant or the recipient of any such gift to retain or recover the value of any property held by him.

(5) An order may be made or other action taken in respect of a debt owed by the Crown.

(6) In exercising those powers, no account shall be taken of any obligations of the defendant or of the recipient of any such gift which conflict with the obligation to satisfy the confiscation order.

89 Compensation

(1) If proceedings are instituted against a person for an offence or offences to which this Part of this Act applies and either—

   (a) the proceedings do not result in his conviction for any such offence, or

   (b) where he is convicted of one or more such offences—

   (i) the conviction or convictions concerned are quashed, or

   (ii) he is pardoned by Her Majesty in respect of the conviction or convictions concerned,

the High Court may, on an application by a person who held property which was realisable property, order compensation to be paid to the applicant if, having regard to all the circumstances, it considers it appropriate to make such an order.

(2) The High Court shall not order compensation to be paid in any case unless the court is satisfied—

   (a) that there has been some serious default on the part of a person concerned in the investigation or prosecution or the offence concerned, being a person mentioned in subsection (5) below; and

   (b) that the application has suffered loss in consequence of anything done in relation to the property by or in pursuance of an order under this Part of this Act.

(3) The Court shall not order compensation to be paid in any case where it appears to the Court that the proceedings would have been instituted or continued even if the serious default had not occurred.

(4) The amount of compensation to be paid under this section shall be such as the High Court thinks just in all the circumstances of the case.

(5) Compensation payable under this section shall be paid—

   (a) where the person in default was or was acting as a member of a police force, out of the police fund out of which the expenses of that police force are met;

   (b) where the person in default was a member of the Crown Prosecution Service or acting on behalf of the service, by the Director of Public Prosecutions;

   (c) where the person in default was a member of the Serious Fraud Office, by the Director of that Office;

(*d*) where the person in default was an officer within the meaning of the Customs and Excise Management Act 1979, by the Commissioners of Customs and Excise; and

(*e*) where the person in default was an officer of the Commissioners of Inland Revenue, by those Commissioners.

Appendix 2

Practice Directions and Official Precedents

(As issued by the Lord Chancellor's Department for the Commercial Court, and by the Chancery Division)

Practice Note (Court of Appeal: Anton Piller Orders)
Practice Direction (Chancery Division: Motions Procedure)
Practice Direction (Chancery Division: Motions Procedure (No 2))
Practice Direction (Evidence: Document)
Practice Direction (Judge in Chambers: Procedure)
Guide to Commercial Court Practice, including official Precedent for Mareva relief.
Chancery Division Official Precedent for Mareva Injunctions.
Chancery Division Official Precedent for Anton Piller relief.

[COURT OF APPEAL]
PRACTICE NOTE
(COURT OF APPEAL: ANTON PILLER ORDERS)[1]

1982 Nov 5

Sir John Donaldson MR,
Watkins and May LJJ

Open Court—Anton Piller order—Application for hearing in camera—Appeal from refusal to make order—Procedure on application for hearing in camera

November 5. Sir John Donaldson MR made the following statement. We have been discussing how this court should deal with *Anton Piller* orders. The applications are made *ex parte* in the court below. They are by their nature applications whose purpose could in some circumstances be frustrated if an appeal was heard in open court, although experience has shown that it is often possible to consider the matter in open court, relying upon the great responsibility and discretion which is always shown by those who report the cases on a regular basis (the members of the High Court Journalists' Association). Accordingly something out of the ordinary has to be shown before it would be right for the court to go into camera.

We would like it to be known that where counsel forms the view that is necessary in the interests of justice that a preliminary application for an appeal against an *ex parte* refusal of an *Anton Piller* or similar order should

---

1 [1982] 1 WLR 1420

be heard in camera, he should approach the registrar, indicating his view. The reasons should be put into writing, signed by counsel and handed to the registrar. In so doing it should be understood that counsel is expressing his personal professional view and is not making a submission on behalf of his client. This will enable the court to make a preliminary decision on whether the application should initially be made in camera or in open court. This procedure will avoid the problem which arises when the very reasons which justify a hearing in camera must themselves be put forward in camera if they are to be put forward at all.

[CHANCERY DIVISION]
PRACTICE DIRECTION (CHANCERY DIVISION: MOTIONS PROCEDURE)[2]
[No 2 of 1980]
Practice—Chancery Division—Motion—Revised procedure for listing and hearing motions

The judges of the Chancery Division have decided that as from October 1, 1980, the procedure for bringing motions in the Chancery Division should be revised. The new procedure is set out below. It is substantially on the lines of the proposals which were circulated in the profession for comment last year. The new procedure will apply until further notice, though it will be kept under review, and will, if necessary, be revised in the light of experience.

1. *Motion days*
Instead of the normal motion days being Tuesdays and Fridays, every week-day (except the last day of each sittings) will be a motion day.

2. *Motion judges*
(*a*) For each sittings, two judges will, as at present, be assigned to hear motions. One of these judges ('the motions judge') will sit to hear all motions, whether in Group A or Group B, on each court day for a period of two weeks. If the volume of motions requires it, the other judge ('the stand-by judge') or any other judge then available to assist with motions will hear such motions as the motions judge directs.

(*b*) Subject to this, the stand-by judge will hear such of the ordinary work of the Division (usually the short non-witness work hitherto heard by the motions judges on Mondays, Wednesdays and Thursdays) as may be required.

(*c*) At the end of the first two weeks, the motions judge and the stand-by judge will exchange functions for the ensuing two weeks, and so on

---

2 [1980] 1 WLR 751

until the end of the sittings. As at present, the Easter and Trinity Sittings will for this purpose be treated as a single sittings.

(*d*) Minor variations in these periods may be made from time to time, eg, to equalise the burdens on the judges. Notices in the Term List or Daily Cause List will show the periods for which each judge will be motions judge and stand-by judge.

3. *Notices of motion*

Notices of motion will continue to be given for the same period as at present, though they may be given for any court day, whether or not a Tuesday or Friday, except the last day of each sittings.

4. *Listing motions*

(*a*) *Motions book*. As far as possible, all motions will be listed. For this purpose, the clerk to the motions judge for the time being will maintain a motions book.

(*b*) *Entry in motions book*. A motion will be entered in the motions book only if (i) two copies of the writ, (ii) two copies of the notice of motion, and (iii) the best estimate of duration that counsel can give, signed by counsel for the applicant, are lodged with the clerk to the motions judge not later than 12 noon on the day before the date for which notice of motion has been given, or on the preceding Friday if the notice has been given for a Monday. If there is any difficulty in reaching the clerk to the motions judge, the documents may instead be lodged with the Clerk of the Lists (Room 165), who will record the time of lodging and transmit the documents to the clerk to the motions judge.

(*c*) *Revised estimate of duration*. Counsel for the applicant must ensure that the clerk to the motions judge is at once informed of any material revision to an estimate of duration entered in the motions book. This applies equally to shortening, as where the parties come to terms or agree an adjournment, and lengthening, as where substantial last-minute affidavits are to be adduced. If a revised estimate is given orally, it should be confirmed in writing as soon as possible.

(*d*) *'Short' motions*. As soon as it becomes apparent that a motion will take less than 5 minutes to dispose of, as where terms have been agreed or the motion is to be stood over, the clerk to the motions judge should be informed and requested to mark the motion 'short' in the motions book. This will not alter the sequence of motions in the book, but it will usually ensure that the motion will be taken before the more lengthy motions: see paragraph 6 below.

(*e*) *Daily Cause List*. Each motion duly entered in the motions book will be listed in the Daily Cause List for the day on which it is to be heard. Where possible, the motions judge will direct the later motions in the list to be marked 'Not before' a stated time, though in view of the unpredictability of motions, this will be done only where counsel for all parties have given the clerk to the motions judge telephone numbers which will make it possible for counsel to be in court on ten minutes notice. There will be no warned list of motions, but information about motions listed for future days can be obtained from the clerk to the motions judge.

5. *Standing over and saving motions*

(*a*) *In court*. When a motion is stood over in court, or it is saved in court, the clerk to the motions judge will forthwith enter it in the motions book for the day for which it has been stood over or saved; and in due course the motion will be listed for that day.

(*b*) *Out of court*. If a motion is saved by agreement, or if by consent it is stood over before a registrar (see *Practice Direction (Chancery Division: Motions)* [1976] 1 WLR 441 and *Practice Direction (Chancery Division: Motions) (No 2)* [1977] 1 WLR 228), it will be entered in the motions book for the day for which it has been stood over or saved only when the clerk to the motions judge has been notified of this by the parties, and the documents mentioned in paragraph 4(*b*) above have been lodged with him, if that has not already been done. Before arranging the future date, it will normally be advisable for the parties to consult the clerk to the motions judge in order to ascertain what other motions there will be on that date.

6. *Order of hearing*

The judge hearing motions will continue to exercise his discretion as to the order in which he hears them, so that he may, for instance, give priority to any application that he considers to be sufficiently urgent, as may be the case with some *ex parte* applications. Subject to this—(*a*) motions affecting the liberty of the subject will continue to take priority over all other motions. (*b*) Motions marked 'Short' in the motions book will usually be taken next. If it becomes apparent that a motion is not in fact 'short', the judge will normally cease to hear it and let it resume its normal priority. (*c*) All other listed motions will be heard in the order of listing, irrespective of the seniority (or juniority) of counsel. (*d*) All unlisted motions will then be heard, according to the seniority (or juniority) of counsel as at present. But if the clerk to the motions judge or the registrar in court is informed that an unlisted motion is or has become 'short' (see paragraph 4(*d*) above), he will mention this to the judge, and the judge may take it after motions listed as 'short' and before other listed motions. (*e*) Motions likely to last more than three hours will still normally be made motions by order unless the state of work permits the judge to deal with them as they arise. (*f*) When another judge is available to assist with motions, the motions judge may transfer to him such motions as he considers appropriate, irrespective of priority. (*g*) Any motion which at the end of a day, is part-heard will normally head the listed motions for the next court day, followed by any listed motions that have not been reached. (*h*) The judge will usually give effect to any variation in this order of priority which is agreed by all who are affected.

7. *Ex parte motions*

The procedure under this practice direction will apply to *ex parte* motions. If it is desired to have an *ex parte* motion listed, two copies of the order sought should be lodged under paragraph 4(*b*)(ii) above in place of a notice of motion. If the application is to be made otherwise than in open court, it can be listed under the applicant's name alone, without that of the defendant. Where it may be unjust to the defendant or some other party if the application is heard in public, the judge may exercise his discretion to sit otherwise than in open court. Where an application is very urgent and the motions judge is unable to hear it promptly, it may be heard, as at present, by any judge who is available, though the request for this must be made to the clerk to the motions judge, or, in default, to the Clerk of the Lists.

8. *Excepted motions*

This new procedure is intended to apply only to what may be called ordinary interlocutory motions made during the usual sittings. It does not apply to motions made during the vacations, nor to motions for judgment, or motions in the Patents Court, in the Companies Court, in bankruptcy, or in the revenue paper. In all these matters, the present procedure will remain unchanged. The same applies to originating motions, save that applications for directions as to the hearing of such motions which at present come before the judge hearing motions may be made under the procedure of this direction, with the originating notice of motion taking the place of the writ and notice of motion under paragraph 4(*b*) above; and agreed directions may be given out of court under paragraph 9 below.

9. *Trade marks: agreed directions on originating motions*

(*a*) Certain proceedings by originating motion at present come before the judge hearing motions for directions as to the conduct of the proceedings. Where the parties are agreed as to the directions that should be given, then instead of being obliged to obtain those directions from a judge in court, they may obtain them from a registrar of the Division out of Court, subject to the registrar's discretion to require the application to be made in court. This is an extension of the procedure for agreed adjournments of motions by a registrar: see the practice directions cited in paragraph 5 above.

(*b*) Any application under this head must be made to the registrar in chambers either by counsel or solicitors for all parties, or else by counsel or solicitors, representing all parties. The applicant must produce a document setting out the agreed directions; and these, where appropriate, may include liberty to apply to the master if any further directions are required. On this being done, the registrar will give the necessary direction to the Clerk of the Lists for setting the matter down in the appropriate list for hearing. In simple cases it will not be necessary for any order to be drawn up.

(*c*) This procedure applies to the following proceedings—(i) any appeal from the Registrar of Trade Marks under Order 100 from the refusal of an application to register a trade mark, or from his decision in opposition or rectification proceedings; (ii) any application for rectification of the register of trade marks under the Trade Marks Act 1938, sections 26, 27 or 32; and (iii) any case referred to the court by the Registrar of Trade Marks or the Board of Trade under sections 12(2), 53 or 54 of that Act.

By the direction of the Vice-Chancellor.

[CHANCERY DIVISION]
PRACTICE DIRECTION (CHANCERY DIVISION: MOTIONS PROCEDURE) (No 2)[3]
[No 1 of 1985]

Practice—Chancery Division—Motion—Lodging notice of motion and documents—
Amendment of procedure

Under the present practice direction governing motions (*Practice Direction (Chancery Division: Motions Procedure)* [1980] 1 WLR 751), the necessary papers have to be lodged with the clerk to the motions judge not later than 12 noon on the day before the date for which notice of motion has been given, or on the preceding Friday if the notice has been given for a Monday.

From 11 February 1985 the notice of motion and other documents must instead be lodged at the office of the Clerk of the Lists, Room 163, Chancery Chambers, Royal Courts of Justice, and paragraph 4(*b*) of the practice direction is amended accordingly.

By direction of the Vice-Chancellor.

[SUPREME COURT OF JUDICATURE]
PRACTICE DIRECTION (EVIDENCE: DOCUMENTS)[4]

Practice—Documents—Form—Marking, numbering and binding of documents—
Marking of exhibits—RSC, Ord 41

This practice direction applies to the Court of Appeal and to all divisions of the High Court. Any affidavit, exhibit or bundle of documents which does not comply with RSC, Ord 41 and this direction may be rejected by the court or made the subject for an order for costs.

Affidavits

1. *Marking*

At the top right hand corner of the first page of every affidavit, and also on the backsheet, there must be written in clear permanent dark blue or

---

3 [1985] 1 WLR 244
4 [1983] 1 WLR 922

black marking: (i) the party on whose behalf it is filed; (ii) the initials and surname of the deponent; (iii) the number of the affidavit in relation to the deponent; and (iv) the date when sworn.

For example: 2nd Dft: EW Jones: 3rd: 24.7.82.'

2. *Binding*

Affidavits must not be bound with thick plastic strips or anything else which would hamper filing.

Exhibits

3. *Markings generally*

Where space allows, the directions under paragraph 1 above apply to the first page of every exhibit.

4. *Documents other than letters*

(i) Clearly legible photographic copies of original documents may be exhibited instead of the originals provided the originals are made available for inspection by other parties before the hearing and by the judge at the hearing.

(ii) Any document which the court is being asked to construe or enforce, or the trusts of which it is being asked to vary, should be separately exhibited, and should not be included in a bundle with other documents. Any such document should bear the exhibit mark directly, and not on a flysheet attached to it.

(iii) Court documents, such as probates, letters of administration, orders, affidavits or pleadings, should never be exhibited. Office copies of such documents prove themselves.

(iv) Where a number of documents are contained in one exhibit, a front page must be attached, setting out a list of the documents, with dates, which the exhibit contains, and the bundle must be securely fastened. The traditional method of securing is by tape, with the knot sealed (under the modern practice) by means of wafers; but any means of securing the bundle (except by staples) is acceptable, provided that it does not interfere with the perusal of the documents and it cannot readily be undone.

(v) This direction does not affect the current practice in relation to scripts in probate matters, or to an affidavit of due execution of a will.

5. *Letters*

(i) Copies of individual letters should not be made separate exhibits, but they should be collected and exhibited in a bundle or bundles. The letters must be arranged in correct sequence with the earliest at the top, and properly paged in accordance with paragraph 6 below. They must be firmly secured together in the manner indicated in paragraph 4 above.

(ii) When original letters, or original letters and copies of replies, are exhibited as one bundle, the exhibit must have a front page attached, stating that the bundle consists of so many original letters and so many copies. As before, the letters and copies must be arranged in correct sequence and properly paged.

6. *Paging of documentary exhibits*

Any exhibit containing several pages must be paged consecutively at centre bottom.

7. *Copies of documents generally*

It is the responsibility of the solicitor by whom any affidavit is filed to ensure that every page of every exhibit is fully and easily legible. In many cases photocopies of documents, particularly of telex messages, are not. In all cases of difficulty, typed copies of the illegible document (paged with 'a' numbers) should be included.

8. *Exhibits bound up with affidavit*

Exhibits must not be bound up with, or otherwise attached to, the affidavit itself.

9. *Exhibits other than documents*

The principles are as follows. (i) The exhibit must be clearly marked with the exhibit mark in such a manner that there is no likelihood of the contents being separated; and (ii) where the exhibit itself consists of more than one item (eg, a cassette in a plastic box), each and every separate part of the exhibit must similarly be separately marked with at least enough of the usual exhibit mark to ensure precise identification.

This is particularly important in cases where there are a number of similar exhibits which fall to be compared. Accordingly:

(*a*) The formal exhibit marking should, so far as practicable, be written on the article itself in an appropriate manner (eg, many fabrics can be directly marked with an indelible pen), or, if this is not possible, on a separate slip which is securely attached to the article in such a manner that it is not easily removable. (NB Items attached by Sellotape or similar means are readily removable.) If the article is then enclosed in a container, the number of the exhibit should appear on the outside of the container unless it is transparent and the number is readily visible. Alternatively, the formal exhibit marking may be written on the container, or, if this is not possible, on a separate slip which is securely attached to the article in such a manner that it is not easily removable). If the article is then enclosed in a container, the number of the exhibit should appear on the outside of the container unless it is transparent and the number is readily visible. Alternatively, the formal exhibit marking may be written on the container, or, if this is not possible, on a separate slip securely attached to the container. If this is done, then either—(i) the number of the exhibit and, if there is room, the short name and number of the case, the name of the deponent and the date of the affidavit must be written on the exhibit itself and on each separate part thereof; or (ii) all these particulars must appear on a slip securely attached to the article itself and to each separate part thereof.

(*b*) If the article, or part of the article, is too small to be marked in accordance with the foregoing provisions, it must be enclosed in a sealed transparent container of such a nature that it could not be reconstituted once opened, and the relevant slip containing the exhibit mark must be inserted in such container so as to be plainly visible. An enlarged photograph or photographs showing the relevant characteristics of each such exhibit will usually be required to be separately exhibited.

10. *Numbering*

Where a deponent deposes to more than one affidavit to which there are exhibits in any one matter, the numbering of such exhibits should run consecutively throughout, and not begin again with each affidavit.

11. *Reference to documents already forming part of an exhibit*

Where a deponent wishes to refer to a document already exhibited to some other deponent's affidavit, he should not also exhibit it to his own affidavit.

12. *Multiplicity of documents*

Where, by the time of the hearing, exhibits or affidavits have become numerous, they should be put in a consolidated bundle, or file or files, and be paged consecutively throughout in the top right hand corner, affidavits and exhibits being in separate bundles or files.

Bundles of documents generally

13. The directions under 5, 6 and 7 above apply to all bundles of documents. Accordingly they must be (i) firmly secured together, (ii) arranged in chronological order, beginning with the earliest, (iii) paged consecutively at centre bottom, and (iv) fully and easily legible.

14. Transcripts of judgments and evidence must not be bound up with any other documents, but must be kept separate.

15. In cases for trial where the parties will seek to place before the trial judge bundles of documents (apart from pleadings) comprising more than 100 pages, it is the responsibility of the solicitors for all parties to prepare and agree one single additional bundle containing the principal documents to which the parties will refer (including in particular the documents referred to in the pleadings) and to lodge such bundle with the court at least two working days before the date fixed for the hearing.

Lord Lane CJ

July 21, 1983.

[QUEEN'S BENCH DIVISION]
PRACTICE DIRECTION (JUDGE IN CHAMBERS:
PROCEDURE)[5]

1983 March 30

Lord Lane CJ, Taylor
and McCowan JJ.

Practice—Chambers applications—Queen's Bench Division—Inter partes applications and appeals estimated to last more than 30 minutes—Special appointments—Ex parte applications—New procedure

LORD LANE CJ, at the sitting of the court, gave the following practice direction.

A Queen's Bench judge in chambers: special appointments

1. A sharp increase in the volume of work listed to be heard by the Queen's Bench judge in chambers has led to unacceptable delays in the hearing of inter partes applications and appeals estimated to last more than 30 minutes. The following steps will be taken to reduce these delays.

2. All inter partes applications and appeals to the Queen's Bench judge in chambers will initially be entered in a general list. Whenever it appears or is agreed that any application or appeal is likely to last more than 30 minutes, it will in future be immediately and automatically transferred to a list of matters requiring special appointments. This will be a floating list and fixed dates will not be granted save on application to the judge when special circumstances have to be shown. The unavailability of counsel will not, save exceptionally, amount to a special circumstance. Every effort will be made to give at least seven days' notice before cases in this list are listed for hearing.

3. Cases for which fixed dates have already been given will retain those dates unless earlier dates acceptable to both parties can be granted. Any outstanding applications and appeals (estimated to last more than 30 minutes) and not already entered in the special appointment list should be entered in it at once. *Counsel's clerks must take particular care to ensure that such outstanding applications and appeals do not remain in suspense.*

4. In order to ensure that a complete set of papers is available for perusal by the judge before hearing such applications and appeals, it shall hereafter be required that not less than five clear days before the date fixed for a special appointment (where a date has been fixed) and not later than 24 hours after a case in the floating special appointment list has been warned for hearing, (*a*) each party shall bespeak the affidavits already filed which it proposes to use: (*b*) each party shall lodge in room 128, Royal Courts of Justice, the exhibits to the affidavits referred to in (*a*); (*c*) the appellant or applicant shall lodge in room 128 a bundle of the pleadings and previous court orders. Except with the leave of the judge, no

---

5 [1983] 1 WLR 433

document may be adduced in evidence or relied on unless it has been bespoken or lodged as required.

B Queen's Bench judge in chambers: ex parte applications

A large increase in the number of applications made *ex parte* to the Queen's Bench judge in chambers makes it necessary to introduce a new and clearly understood procedure, which will be strictly followed.

1. The standard procedure, suitable for all ordinary *ex parte* applications, will be: (1) that the applicant shall lodge with the clerk to the judge in chambers by 3.00 pm on the day before the application is to be made, papers which should include (*a*) the writ (*b*) the affidavit in support and (*c*) a draft minute of the order sought; (2) that the judge in chambers will hear the application at 10.00 am on the following morning before embarking on his published list.

2. There will be some cases where the 3.00 pm deadline specified in paragraph 1(1) *cannot* be met and where the urgency is too great to permit up to 24 hour's delay. Such applications should be dealt with in one or another of the three following ways. (1) The applicant's advisers shall attend on the clerk to the judge in chambers at 9.50 am and lodge with him the papers listed in paragraph 1(1) and also a certificate signed by counsel (or solicitor if counsel is not instructed) that the application is of extreme urgency. The application will be heard by the judge in chambers at 10.00 am. (2) The applicant's advisers shall lodge the papers with the clerk to the judge in chambers by 12.30 pm (such papers to include all those specified in paragraph 1(1) and attend on the clerk at 1.50 pm. The application will be heard at 2.00 pm. (3) In the very rare case where the application is of such urgency as to preclude either of the foregoing procedures the applicant's advisers may give notice to the clerk to the judge in chambers and the judge in chambers will hear the application at once, interrupting his list if necessary. In such a case the applicant's counsel or solicitor must be prepared to justify taking this exceptional course.

3. (1) Attention is drawn to the provisions of RSC, Ord 29, r 1 which ordinarily requires the issue of a writ or originating summons and the swearing of an affidavit in support of an *ex parte* application for an injunction before it is made. (2) The affidavit in support should contain a clear and concise statement: (*a*) of the facts giving rise to the claim against the defendant in the proceedings; (*b*) of the facts giving rise to the claim for interlocutory relief; (*c*) of the facts relied on as justifying the application *ex parte*, including details of any notice given to the defendant or, if none has been given, the reasons for giving none; (*d*) of any answer asserted by the defendant (or which he is thought likely to assert) either to the claim in the action or to the claim for interlocutory relief; (*e*) of any facts known to the applicant which might lead the court not to grant relief *ex parte*; (*f*) of the precise relief sought. (3) Applicants for *ex parte* relief should prepare and lodge with the papers relating to the application a draft minute of the order sought. Such minute should specify the precise relief which the court

is asked to grant. While the undertakings required of an applicant will vary widely from case to case, he will usually be required: (*a*) to give an undertaking in damages; (*b*) to notify the defendant of the terms of the order forthwith, by cable or telex if he is abroad; (*c*) in an application of *Mareva* type, to pay the reasonable costs and expenses incurred in complying with the order by an third party to whom notice of the order is given; (*d*) in the exceptional case where proceedings have not been issued, to issue the same forthwith; (*e*) in the exceptional case where a draft affidavit has not been sworn, or where the facts have been placed before the court orally, to procure the swearing of the affidavit or the verification on affidavit of the facts outlined orally to the court.

The order should as a general rule contain provision for the defendant to apply on notice for discharge or variation of the order and for costs to be reserved.

GUIDE TO COMMERCIAL COURT PRACTICE

Appendix to Order 72
Sections

This Guide has two objects.

The first is to summarise certain practical recommendations of a Working Party of the practitioner members of the Commercial Court Committee under the chairmanship of Mr Nicholas Phillips QC. The report was adopted by the Commercial Court Committee and then approved by the Lord Chief Justice. It was considered at an open meeting of Commercial Court users held on 25 February 1986 and, despite some reservations, received the overwhelming endorsement of those present. Following this meeting the Commercial Court Committee considered the representations made orally and in writing, and substantially reaffirmed its adoption of the Working Party's recommendations.

The second object of the Guide is to draw attention to certain Rules of the Supreme Court and Practice Directions which tend to be overlooked, and to give notice of certain proposed practices.

I *Commercial actions* (O.72)

1. 'Commercial action' is defined in O.72, r 1(2) to include 'any cause arising out of the ordinary transactions of merchants and traders and, without prejudice to the generality of the foregoing words, any cause relating to the construction of a mercantile document, the export or import of merchandise, affreightment, insurance, banking, mercantile agency and mercantile usage.'

2. The resources available to the Commercial Court do not permit the transfer into the commercial list or the retention in the commercial list of every action falling within the wide language quoted above.

3. In deciding whether to exercise his discretion under O.72, r 5 or r 6, the commercial judge is likely to consider

(1) Whether the subject matter of the action falls within one of the fields with which the Court habitually deals, which may (very broadly) be summarised as being
  (i) the carriage of goods by land, sea and air;
  (ii) contracts relating to ships and shipping;
  (iii) insurance and re-insurance;
  (iv) banking, negotiable instruments and international credit;
  (v) the purchase and sale of commodities;
  (vi) the operation of international markets and exchange;
  (vii) the construction and performance of mercantile contracts; and
(2) whether the case raises a question of fact or law with which the Court is particularly well fitted to deal.

4. Applications relating to arbitration under O.73, r 2 and r 3 are required by O.73, r 6 to be heard by a commercial judge unless any such judge otherwise directs. Such directions are ordinarily made, if no significant point of arbitration law or practice is raised, in rent review arbitrations for transfer to a Judge of the Chancery Division and in building and civil engineering arbitrations to an Official Referee.

IV *Ex parte applications for injunctions*

On 30 March 1983 the Lord Chief Justice made a Practice Direction governing *ex parte* applications to the Queen's Bench Judge in Chambers. Paragraph 3 of that practice is equally appropriate where application is made to a Commercial Judge:

3. (1) Attention is drawn to the provisions of RSC Ord 29, r 1, which ordinarily requires the issue of a writ or originating summons and the swearing of an affidavit in support of an *ex parte* application for an injunction before it is made.

(2) The affidavit in support should contain a clear and concise statement (*a*) of the facts giving rise to the claim against the defendant in the

proceedings, (*b*) of the facts giving rise to the claim for the interlocutory relief, (*c*) of the facts relied on as justifying application *ex parte*, including details of any notice given to the defendant or, if none have been given, the reasons for giving none, (*d*) of any answer asserted by the defendant (or which he is thought likely to assert) either to the claim in the action or to the claim for interlocutory relief, (*e*) of any facts known to the applicant which might lead to the court not to grant relief *ex parte*, (*f*) of the precise relief sought.

(3) Applicants for *ex parte* relief should prepare and lodge with the papers relating to the application a draft minute of the order sought. Such minute should specify the precise relief which the court is asked to grant. While the undertakings required of an applicant will vary widely from case to case, he will usually be required (*a*) to give an undertaking in damages, (*b*) to notify the defendant of the terms of the order forthwith, by cable or telex if he is abroad, (*c*) in an application of Mareva type, to pay the reasonable costs and expenses incurred in complying with the order by any third party to whom notice of the order is given, (*d*) in the exceptional case where proceedings have not been issued, to issue the same forthwith, (*e*) in the exceptional case where a draft affidavit has not been sworn, or where the facts have been placed before the court orally, to procure the swearing of the affidavit or the verification on affidavit of the facts outlined orally to the court.

The order should as a general rule contain provision for the defendant to apply on notice for discharge or variation of the order and for costs to be reserved.'

See [1983] 1 WLR 433; [1983] 1 All ER 1119, 1120.

No single form of order will be appropriate in all cases. Annex A is a standard draft which will, amended as appropriate, be suitable in many cases of extreme urgency.

ANNEX A

IN THE HIGH COURT OF JUSTICE
QUEEN'S BENCH DIVISION
COMMERCIAL COURT
THE HON MR JUSTICE
IN CHAMBERS
BETWEEN:

........................Plaintiffs
   and
........................Defendants

UPON hearing Counsel for the Plaintiffs and upon reading the (draft) affidavit(s) of..............

AND upon the Plaintiff by their Counsel undertaking:
  (1) to issue and serve the writ herein forthwith

(2) to swear and file (an affidavit) in the form of the draft(s) initialled by the Judge

(3) to abide by any Order of the Court as to damages should the Defendants suffer any by reason of this Order which the Plaintiffs ought to pay

(4) to pay to any Third Parties served with notice of this Order their reasonable costs and expenses incurred in complying with the same, and to indemnify any such Third Parties against liability arising from such compliance

(5) to give notice to the Defendants by telex forthwith of the contents of this Order (and of the said draft affidavit(s)) (and of the telephone number of a representative of the plaintiff's solicitors to whom any notice of an application to set aside or vary this Order may be given out of office hours).

IT IS ORDERED THAT

1 The Defendants be restrained until trial or further order by themselves their servants or agents or otherwise howsoever from:

(*a*) removing their assets from the jurisdiction or disposing of or dealing with the same within the jurisdiction save in so far as such assets exceed the sum of £........

(*b*) drawing on their (current) account at the.........

.... Branch of the

.... Bank

so as to reduce the balance in such account below £.......

Provided however that nothing in this Order shall prevent..........

Bank from exercising any right of set off it may have in respect of the facilities afforded by it to the Defendants before the date of this Order.

2 (Notwithstanding paragraph 1 hereof, the Defendants shall be entitled to draw on their (current) account

(*a*) a sum not exceeding...............pounds per week for ordinary living expenses;

(*b*) a sum not exceeding...............pounds per week for ordinary trade outgoings;

(*c*) such further sum or sums, if any, as the plaintiffs' solicitors may from time to time agree in writing.

Provided however that nothing in subparagraph (*a*) or (*b*) of this paragraph shall impose any obligation on the Bank to enquire into the purpose or purposes for which any sum or sums drawn by the Defendants thereunder are in fact required or used.)

3 (The plaintiffs have leave to issue and serve the writ on the Defendants at......................

or elsewhere in

The time for the Acknowledgment of Service shall be days.)

4 Liberty to the Defendants or to any other person affected by this

Order to apply (on notice to the Plaintiff's solicitors) to set aside or vary this Order or to seek further directions hereunder.

5 Costs reserved.

Official Mareva Injunction Precedent: Chancery Division

IN THE HIGH COURT OF JUSTICE
CHANCERY DIVISION
MR JUSTICE
   the   day of   19
In The Matter of an Intended Action
Between

Intended Plaintiff

and

Intended Defendant

ORDER

UPON MOTION made by Counsel for the Intended Plaintiff(s) (hereinafter called the Plaintiff(s))

AND UPON READING the Court File

AND the Plaintiff(s) by his her its Counsel undertaking

(1) forthwith on or before . . . to issue a Writ of Summons claiming relief similar to or connected with that hereafter granted

(2) to make and file an Affidavit verifying what was alleged by Counsel in the terms of the draft Affidavit of

(3) to serve upon the Intended Defendant(s) (hereinafter called the Defendant(s) a copy of the said Affidavit and Notice of Motion for

(4) to pay the reasonable costs incurred by any person other than the Defendant(s) to whom notice of this Order may be given in ascertaining whether any assets of this Order applies are within the power possession custody or control and in complying with this Order and to indemnify any such person against all liabilities which may flow from such compliance

(5) to obey any Order this Court may make as to damages if it shall consider that the Defendant(s) shall have sustained any damages by reason of this Order which the Plaintiff(s) ought to pay

IT IS ORDERED

(1) that the Defendant(s) [and each of them] be restrained until after or until further Order in the meantime from doing (as regards the whether by . . . directors or by . . . servants or agents or any of them or otherwise howsoever and as regards the Defendant(s) whether by . . . or by . . . servants or agents or any of them or otherwise howsoever) the following acts or any of them that is to say removing from the jurisdiction of this Court or otherwise disposing of or dealing with his her its their [respective or

joint] assets within the jurisdiction of this Court including and in particular

 (i) the freehold property known as . . . or (if the same has been sold) the net proceeds of sale thereof after discharge of any Subsisting mortgage of charge

 (ii) the property and assets of the business known as . . . carried on by the Defendant(s) from premises at . . . or (if and in so far as the same have been sold) the proceeds of sale thereof

 (iii) any monies in [any] account(s) [numbered . . .] at . . . at . . . and without prejudice to the foregoing pledging charging or otherwise parting with title to or possession of SUCH ASSETS

(A) SAVE and in so far as the said assets of [each of] the Defendant(s) exceeds £ . . .

(B) SAVE that the Defendant(s) [and each of them] is/are to be at liberty to expend a sum not exceeding £ . . . [each] per week/month for ordinary and proper business expenses

AND not otherwise in each case upon informing the Plaintiffs Solicitors of the source or accounts from which such sums are to be drawn and

(D) THAT the Defendant(s) [and each of them] may expend [a sum not exceeding £ . . . [each] [such reasonable sum] on Legal Advice and representation as may requisite

(E) PROVIDED nothing in this injunction shall prevent any bank from exercising any rights to set off it may have in respect of facilities afforded by any such bank to the Defendant(s) or any of them prior to the date of this Order

(2) that the Defendant(s) [and each of them] do forthwith disclose the full value of his her its their [respective and joint] assets within [and without] the jurisdiction of this Court identifying with full particularity the nature of all such assets and their whereabouts and whether the same be held in his her its their own names or by nominees or otherwise on his her its their behalf and the sums standing in such accounts such disclosures to be verified by affidavit(s) to be made by the Defendant(s) [and in the case of Defendants by its their proper officer] and served on the Plaintiff's Solicitors within . . . days of service of this Order or notice thereof being given [PROVIDED that no person other than the Defendant(s) shall in any wise be affected by the terms of this Order or concerned to inquire whether any instruction given by or on behalf of the Defendant(s) or by anyone else or any other act or omission of the Defendant(s) or anyone else whether acting on behalf of the Defendant(s) or otherwise is or may be a breach of this Order by the Defendant(s)]

(3) that the Defendant(s) [and each of them] do forthwith upon the service of this Order deliver up or cause to be delivered up into the custody of the Plaintiffs' Solicitors the . . . specified in the Schedule hereto

AND the Plaintiff . . . is are at . . . liberty to serve Short Notice of Motion for

AND the Plaintiff . . . is are at . . . liberty to move to discharge or vary

this Order upon giving to the Plaintiff . . . days Notice of . . . intention so
to do

Official Anton Piller Precedent: Chancery Division

IN THE HIGH COURT OF JUSTICE
CHANCERY DIVISION
MR JUSTICE
    the   day of 19
    In The Matter of an Intended Action
    Between

Intended Plaintiff

and

Intended Defendant

ORDER

UPON MOTION made by Counsel for the Intended Plaintiff(s) (hereinafter called the Plaintiff(s)).
    AND UPON READING
    AND the Plaintiff(s) by [his her its their] Counsel undertaking
    (1) forthwith on or before . . . to issue a Writ of Summons claiming
relief similar to or connected with that hereafter granted
    (2) to make and file an Affidavit [verifying what was alleged by Coun-
sel] [in the terms of the draft Affidavit of . . .]
    (3) to serve upon the Intended Defendant(s) (hereinafter called the
Defendant(s)) by a Solicitor of the Supreme Court of Judicature a copy of
the said Affidavit and the copiable Exhibits thereto and Notice of Motion
for
    (4) to obey any Order this Court may make as to damages if it shall
consider that the Defendant(s) shall have sustained any damages by
reason of this Order which the Plaintiff(s) ought to pay
    (5) to obey any Order this Court may make as to damages if it shall
consider that any innocent parties other than the Defendant(s) shall have
sustained any damages by reason of this Order which the Plaintiff(s)
ought to pay]
Note: the U/T in respect of innocent 3rd parties is only to be inserted if it is
expressly given.
    AND the Solicitors for the Plaintiff(s) by Counsel for the Plaintiff(s)
being their Counsel for this purpose undertaking
    (1) to offer to explain to the person or persons served with this Order its
meaning and effect fairly in everyday language and to advise the person
on whom the same is served of his right to obtain legal advice before complying with this Order provided that such advice is obtained forthwith

(2) to retain in their safe custody until further order all articles and documents taken or delivered to them pursuant to this Order

(3) to answer forthwith any query made by the Defendant(s) as to whether any particular [document/article] is within the scope of this Order

(4) to make a list of all articles and documents obtained as a result of this Order prior to removal of any such articles or documents into their safe custody and to provide to the Defendant or the person served with this Order a copy thereof prior to such removal

(5) to return the originals of all documents obtained as a result of this Order within 2 working days of removal of the same

(6) where ownership of any article obtained as a result of this Order is disputed to deliver up any such article to the custody of solicitors acting on behalf of the Defendant within 2 working days of receipt of an undertaking in writing from the Defendant's solicitors to retain the same in safe custody and production if required to the Court

IT IS ORDERED

(1) that the Defendant(s) [and each of them] be restrained until after . . . or until further Order in the meantime from doing (as regards the . . . Defendant(s) whether by . . . directors or . . . servants or agents or any of them or otherwise howsoever and as regards the Defendant(s) whether by . . . or by . . . servants or agents or any of them or otherwise howsoever) the following acts or any of them that is to say

(*a*) directly or indirectly informing or notifying any person company or firm of the existence of these proceedings or of the provisions of this Order of the Plaintiffs interest in these proceedings or otherwise warning any person company or firm that proceedings may be brought against [him her it them] by the Plaintiff(s) otherwise than for the purpose of seeking legal advice from [its his her their] lawyers

(2) that the Defendant(s) do disclose forthwith to the person serving this Order upon [him her its them]

(*a*) the whereabouts of all . . . which are in [his her its their] possession custody power or control

(*b*) to the best of the Defendants' knowledge and belief

(A) the names and addresses of all persons who have supplied or offered to supply [him her it them] with . . .

(B) the names and addresses of all persons to whom [he she it them] had/have supplied or offered to supply any . . .

(C) full details of the dates and quantities of each offer to supply and supply referred to in (A) and (B) hereof

(3) that the Defendant(s) do deliver forthwith to the Plaintiffs' Solicitors all . . . which are in [his her its their] possession custody or power and if any such item exists in computer readable form only the Defendant(s) shall cause it forthwith to be printed out and deliver the print out to

the Plaintiffs Solicitors (or failing a printer) to be displayed in a readable form

(4) that the Defendant(s) and each of them whether by [himself herself itself themselves] or by any person appearing to be in control of the premises hereafter mentioned do permit the person serving this Order upon them and such other persons duly authorised by the Plaintiffs (such persons not to exceed [four] in number altogether) to enter forthwith at any time between . . . o'clock in the morning and . . . o'clock in the evening the premises known as . . . [and any other premises or vehicles to the extent that any of the said vehicles or premises are in the power possession occupation or control of the Defendant(s)] for the purpose of looking for inspecting photographing and taking into the custody of the Plaintiffs' Solicitors all items and materials referred to in paragraph . . . above or which appear to the Plaintiffs' Solicitors to be such items or materials

(5) that within 7 days after service of this Order the Defendant(s) do make and serve on the Plaintiffs' Solicitors an Affidavit or affidavits setting out all of the information to be disclosed pursuant to this Order and exhibiting thereto all relevant documents

AND the Defendant(s) is/are to be at liberty to move to vary to discharge this Order upon giving to the Solicitors for the Plaintiff 24 hours notice of intention so to do

The material in Apendix 2 is reproduced with the kind permission of Sir Nicholas Browne-Wilkinson V-C.

Appendix 3

Precedents

1 High Court order granting a Mareva Injunction and requiring the intended defendant to disclose information about his assets
2 Affidavit in support of an application for a Mareva injunction
3 Anton Piller Order
4 Draft Affidavit in support of an application for an Anton Piller Order
5 Letter of Explanation of Anton Piller Order
6 Mareva injunction—arbitration proceedings
7 Angel Bell order
8 Originating Summons seeking interim relief under section 25(1) of the Civil Jurisdiction and Judgments Act 1982
9 Order made *inter partes* in proceedings brought under section 25(1) of the Civil Jurisdiction and Judgments Act 1982 continuing world-wide Mareva relief which had been granted *ex parte* with modifications
10 Order made *ex parte* in the Chancery Division which includes world-wide Mareva relief, the appointment of a Receiver, and an order for disclosure of information about assets world-wide
11 Ancillary Order preventing a Defendant from leaving the jurisdiction and requiring delivery up of the Defendant's passport

1. High Court order granting a Mareva Injunction and requiring the intended defendant to disclose information about his assets

IN THE HIGH COURT OF JUSTICE
QUEEN'S BENCH DIVISION
Mr Waterloo QC
(sitting as a Deputy Judge of the High Court)

19—No—

In The Matter of the Supreme Court Act 1981
And
In The Matter of an Intended Action
Between:—

Duke Wellington

Intended Plaintiff

—and—

Napoleon Bonaparte

Intended Defendant

ORDER

Upon Hearing Counsel for the above named Intended Plaintiff
And upon reading an affidavit in draft to be sworn by Prince Blucher
And upon the Intended Plaintiff by Counsel undertaking as follows:—

(1) to issue forthwith a writ of summons in the form of the draft produced to the Court and initialled by the Judge for service upon the Intended Defendant out of the jurisdiction, pursuant to RSC Order 11 Rule 1(2) and to serve a copy thereof upon the Intended Defendant as soon as practicable thereafter;

(2) to procure that an affidavit is sworn forthwith in the terms of the draft affidavit, such affidavit also to include the further matters relied upon in the course of the application before the Judge or alternatively such further matters to be verified in a separate affidavit to be sworn forthwith;

(3) to give notice forthwith to the Intended Defendant of the terms of this order by facsimile to the Palace of Versailles, France and by delivering a copy of this order together with a copy of the affidavit evidence, including exhibits, sworn pursuant to undertaking (2) above to the Intended Defendant at Red Square, Moscow or elsewhere in Russia;

(4) to inform the Intended Defendant forthwith of his right to apply to discharge or vary this order on notice to the Intended Plaintiff;

(5) to abide by any order that the Court may make as to damages should the Intended Defendant suffer any by reason of this order, which in the opinion of the Court, the Intended Plaintiff ought to pay;

(6) to pay to any Third Parties served with or given notice of this order their reasonable costs and expenses incurred in complying with this order and to indemnify them against any liability reasonably incurred in order to comply with this order;

(7) to inform any Third Party of his right to apply to discharge or set aside this order on notice to the Intended Plaintiff;

NOW IT IS HEREBY ORDERED AND DIRECTED THAT:—

1 The Intended Defendant whether by himself his servants or agents or otherwise howsoever be restrained and an Injunction is hereby granted restraining him until trial of the Intended action or further order from dealing with or disposing of or removing from the jurisdiction any of his assets within the jurisdiction including without prejudice to the generality of the foregoing:—

(1) Account No 1815 at the Paris Bank Ltd, Cannon Street, Sandhurst

and any other accounts at the said Bank in the name of the Intended Defendant or in his name together with one or more third parties;

(2) his interest in property situated at 4, Victory Street, London SW1.

Save in so far as the unencumbered value of his assets within the jurisdiction exceeds the sum of F francs 100 million or the sterling equivalent.

Provided however that nothing in this order shall prevent a Bank exercising any right of set off which it may have in respect of loan facilities made available to the Intended Defendant before the making of this order.

2 Notwithstanding paragraph 1 hereof the Intended Defendant:—

(1) shall be entitled to use his assets to pay ordinary living expenses not exceeding £250 per week;

(2) shall be at liberty to continue to make payments in the ordinary course of his business as a designer carried on under the name 'Emperor of the French' and to obtain receipts in the course of that business.

3 The Intended Defendant shall within 7 days from service of this order upon him make and file with the Court, and serve a copy upon the Intended Plaintiff's solicitors, Guards & Co of 1, Whitehall, London SW1 an affidavit stating precisely what assets he has within the jurisdiction and their whereabouts, and whether the same are in his name alone and if not, how and in whose name and names the same are held. In the case of any bank, building society or similar account the Intended Defendant is to include in the affidavit in respect of each account:—

(1) the name or names in which it is held;

(2) the name of the bank, building society or other entity;

(3) the address of the branch at which the account is held;

(4) the number of the account;

(5) the balance in the account at the date of swearing the affidavit. If there is any change in the balance prior to service of the affidavit, this is to be notified to the Intended Plaintiff on service of the affidavit.

4 Liberty to the Intended Defendant or any third party affected by this order to apply on notice to the Intended Plaintiff to discharge or vary this order, or to seek further directions hereunder.

5 Costs Reserved.

Dated——.

2 Affidavit in support of an application for a Mareva injunction

For: Intended Plaintiffs
W A Dodson
Affidavit No 1
Sworn: 24.12.89[1]

IN THE HIGH COURT OF JUSTICE
QUEEN'S BENCH DIVISION
COMMERCIAL COURT
In the matter of an intended action
Between:

David Copperfield and Company Ltd

Intended Plaintiffs

—and—
Little Emily Inc of Utopia
'The Little Emily'

Intended Defendants

AFFIDAVIT

I, WILLIAM ANDREW DODSON of Freeman's Court, Cornhill, London EC3 MAKE OATH AND SAY as follows:

1 I am a partner in the firm of Dodson & Fogg of Freeman's Court, Cornhill, London EC3, solicitors for the Intended Plaintiffs. I have the care and conduct of this matter and I am duly authorised to make this Affidavit on behalf of the Intended Plaintiffs.

2 The contents of this Affidavit are derived from documents and information supplied to me by or on behalf of my clients, in particular by Mr David Copperfield, a director of my clients, and are true to the best of my information and belief.

3 There is now produced and shown to me marked 'WAD 1' a paginated bundle containing true copies of relevant documents, to which I shall refer by page number in the course of my Affidavit.[2] Numbers in brackets appearing in the course of this Affidavit are references to pages in this bundle.

---

1 The endorsement on the top right-hand corner of the affidavit follows the procedure required under para 1 of the Practice Direction set out at [1983] 1 WLR 922. The text is set out in Appendix 1.

2 Where a number of documents are contained in one exhibit a front page must be attached, setting out a list of documents, with dates, which the exhibit contains, and the bundle must be securely fastened (para 4 (*iv*) of the Practice Direction (above)). If the originals of copy documents exhibited are available, then they should be held ready to be shown to the Judge on the *ex parte* application if so required (para 4(*i*) of the Practice Direction (above)).

Application

4 I make this Affidavit in support of an application by the Intended Plaintiffs for:

(1) Leave to be granted to issue a Writ of Summons for service on the Intended Defendants out of the jurisdiction, in the form of the draft produced to this Honourable Court;

(2) Leave to be granted to serve the said Writ on the Intended Defendants at their registered office at Pantechnicon House, Utopia City or elsewhere in the Republic of Utopia;

(3) A Mareva injunction to be granted against the Intended Defendants in the terms of the draft order, or in such other terms as may be just and convenient.

Facts concerning the claim

5 The Intended Plaintiffs have their head office at 18 Windsor Terrace, London EC3 and are well-established commodity traders and part of a group of companies having an annual turnover of US$ in the year November 1988-November 1989. The consolidated audited accounts of the Group (pages   ) disclose group assets of   . The Intended Plaintiffs made a profit of [US$500,000] in the last accounting year (page   ) and I am advised by Mr Copperfield and verily believe that they have continued to trade at a profit in the present financial year.[3]

6 By a Charterparty dated 3 February 1989 the Intended Plaintiffs chartered vessel 'Little Emily' from the Intended Defendants for a time charter trip via safe ports from Mombasa, Kenya to Folkstone. There is now produced and shown to me marked 'WAD 2' a copy of the Charterparty.[4] In particular, I refer the attention of this Honourable Court to clauses   (For ease of reference these clauses have been typed at pages of 'WAD 2').[5]

7 The vessel was loaded at Mombasa with a cargo of coffee in bulk and a Bill of Lading dated 19 April 1989, was issued by the Master acknowledging shipment of the cargo in apparent good order and condition (page   ). The Bill of Lading was retained by the Intended Plaintiffs, who were also the owners of the cargo, having purchased it from their associated company Barkis and Peggotty Mocca Traders of Kenya Ltd under a contract on fob terms dated 15 March 1989, under which title to the goods passed to the Intended Plaintiffs on shipment (page   ).

---

3 Information about the plaintiff's financial standing is relevant to the question whether the cross-undertaking in damages is of any value.

4 The Charterparty (and any addenda) should be exhibited separately from the other documents in the case pursuant to para 4(*ii*) of the Practice Direction (above).

5 The relevant clauses in the Charterparty should be referred to in the affidavit (*Bakarim* v *Victoria P Shipping Co* [1980] 2 Lloyd's Rep 193 at p 199). Similarly any relevant statutory provisions should be referred to in the affidavit, and, in appropriate cases, set out in the affidavit or the exhibit for ease of reference.

8 On 23 April 1989 the Intended Plaintiffs received a telex from the managers of the Intended Defendants, Odios Heepos SA of Piraeus, notifying them that the vessel had sunk on the previous day in calm seas only three days after leaving port (page   ). No explanation has been given by the managers or the Intended Defendants for the loss, despite the Intended Plaintiffs' numerous requests by telex and a letter dated asking for an explanation, addressed to the London agents of the Greek managers of the vessel, Wickfield & Heep (pages   to   ).

9 Inquiries have been commenced by Perker & Co on behalf of the Intended Plaintiffs, as to the cause of the loss. I am advised by Mr George Bucket of Perker & Co and verily believe that he was informed by the Master of the vessel, Captain Steerforth, that water had entered the vessel through a hole in the shell plating in the engine-room and that the crew had been unable to control the ingress of water because the pumps were unserviceable. Captain Steerforth also informed Mr Bucket that the fact that the pumps were unserviceable had been reported by him to Odios Heepos SA of Piraeus, some three weeks before the casualty. However, nothing had been done to rectify the problem on the grounds of expense.

10 Accordingly, I verily believe that the Intended Plaintiffs have a good arguable case against the Intended Defendants in support of a claim for damages for breach of the Charterparties, for breach of their duties as bailees of the cargo and for negligence. In particular, at all material times the vessel was unseaworthy. (Expand here on the nature of the alleged breaches/negligence.)

Quantum of the Intended Plaintiffs' claim

11 The value of the cargo at the date of the casualty, 21 April 1989, would have amounted to US$. I say this because (fill in details). The Intended Plaintiffs also wish to claim interest pursuant to section 35A of the Supreme Court Act 1981 at a commercial rate of   % per annum (which to date amounts to US$ and continues at the daily rate of $), and costs. (Expand here on why the claimed rate of interest is said to be justified.)

Defences to the claim[6]

12 Since the loss, the Intended Defendants have sought to reject the claim, relying (page   ) upon clause 13 of the Charterparty which provides as follows:

The Owners only to be responsible for loss or damage to goods on board the vessel if such loss or damage has been caused by personal want of due diligence on the

---

6 Possible defences should be set out in the affidavit if they may be material to the consideration of the application by the court. A possible defence of limitation of liability is an obvious one, and in a case of this nature should be specifically addressed.

part of the Owners or their Managers in making the vessel seaworthy and fitted for the voyage or any other personal act or omission or default of the Owners or their Managers. The Owners not to be responsible in any other case for damage or delay whatsoever and howsoever caused even if caused by the neglect or fault of the Master or crew or their servants or agents.

13 However, in view of Captain Steerforth's account of the loss the Intended Plaintiffs believe that the loss was caused by the personal want of due diligence of the Intended Defendants or their Managers. I would also draw the attention of this Honourable Court to section 503 of the Merchant Shipping Act 1894 (page   ). The tonnage of the 'Little Emily' was   tons, as appears from the entry in Lloyd's Register of Shipping (page   ). The limitation fund would be approximately £   . However, in view of the Master's statement and the fact that no explanation has been offered by the Intended Defendants to date as to why the loss occurred, there is a real prospect that the Intended Defendants will be unable to avail themselves of limitation of liability under this section. I do not know of any other defences which are being relied upon or are likely to be relied upon by the Intended Defendants.

Assets

14 I am informed by Mr Copperfield and verily believe that he was informed by Mr Robert Cratchit of Wickfield & Heep, the London agents of the vessel's managers, that the vessel was insured for US$ through their insurance brokers Martin Chuzzlewit & Co of Lombard Street, and that the whole or a substantial part of the hull and machinery insurance was placed at Lloyds. The lead underwriter was a Mr Wilkins Micawber.

Risk of disposal of assets

15 The Intended Defendants are incorporated and have their registered office at Pantechnicon House, Utopia City, Utopia. A search of the Utopian companies register has shown that the directors of the company are Uriah Heep and John Wickfield (page   ). Other than the wreck, the only asset of the Intended Defendants known to the Intended Plaintiffs consist of the claim on hull underwriters. The vessel was registered in Utopia and there are no mortgages entered on the register (page   ). I verily believe that if hull underwriters pay the claim to Wickfield & Heep it will be remitted by them to the vessel's managers, Odios Heepos SA of Piraeus.

16 The 'Little Emily' was traded as part of a fleet of vessels known as Uriah Heep Tramping, all of which were managed by Odios Heepos SA with Wickfield & Heep as their London agents. Each vessel in the fleet is owned by a different Utopian company. There is a history of default on arbitration awards and judgments by companies within the group. For example, a London arbitration award for US$250,000 made in July last year in respect of a claim for damaged cargo carried on board the vessel

'Big Emily' has remained unsatisfied. The vessel is still trading as a member of the fleet but has since changed her name to 'Agnes Wickfield' (page   ). (Expand here on other defaults by companies within the group.)

17 In all circumstances, I verily believe that unless a Mareva injunction is granted in appropriate terms against the Intended Defendants there is a real risk that any judgment obtained by the Intended Plaintiffs against the Intended Defendants would remain unsatisfied.

Leave to serve the writ out of the jurisdiction

18 I would draw attention to clause   of the Charterparty (page   ) which provides that the Charterparty is to be governed by English Law and that all disputes arising in connection with the Charterparty shall be referred to the jurisdiction of the Commercial Court in London. There is jurisdiction to grant leave to issue the intended writ for service out of the jurisdiction and for service of that writ out of the jurisdiction pursuant to RSC Order 11, r 1(1)(*d*)(iii) and 1(1)(*d*)(iv) on the grounds that the intended action falls within the jurisdiction clause in the Charterparty, and the Charterparty was expressly governed by English Law. I believe that the Intended Plaintiffs have a good cause of action. I therefore request leave to issue a writ in the form of the draft produced to the Court for service on the Intended Defendants out of the jurisdiction and leave to serve the said writ on them at Pantechnicon House, Utopia City or elsewhere in the Republic of Utopia. The prescribed time for acknowledgment of service is   days.

Sworn, etc

3 Anton Piller Order

IN THE HIGH COURT OF JUSTICE
CHANCERY DIVISION
  Mr Justice Clarence
  ——the——day of——
In The Matter of an Intended Action
Between:

Henry Seventh plc

Intended Plaintiff

—and—
Richard Third

Intended Defendant

ORDER

UPON MOTION made by Counsel for the Intended Plaintiff (hereinafter called 'the Plaintiff')

AND UPON READING the draft affidavit to be sworn herein by Warwick Kingmaker;

AND UPON the Plaintiff by Counsel as aforesaid undertaking:—

(1) forthwith on or before . . . to issue a writ of summons in the form of the draft produced to the Court and initialled by the Judge;

(2) forthwith to procure that an affidavit is sworn in the terms of the said draft [which also incorporates the further evidence relied upon in the course of the application];

(3) to abide by any order the court may hereafter make as to damages should the Intended Defendant (hereinafter called 'the Defendant') suffer any by reason of this Order which in the opinion of the Court the Plaintiff ought to pay;

(4) to serve this Order by a Solicitor of the Supreme Court, and at the time of service of the Order to serve upon the Defendant or the person served with the Order a copy of the said affidavit and the copiable exhibits thereto, and either a copy of the writ or (if not yet issued) a copy of the intended writ.

AND UPON the Solicitors to the Plaintiff by Counsel for the Plaintiff being their Counsel for this purpose, undertaking:—

(1) to offer to explain to the person or persons served with this Order in everyday language, fairly and accurately its meaning and effect, and to advise any person served with the Order of his right to obtain legal advice before complying with paragraphs 3 and 4, provided that such advice is obtained forthwith;

(2) to answer forthwith any questions asked by the Defendant as to whether any document (including any computer record) falls within the scope of this Order;

(3) to make a list of all articles and documents (including computer records) obtained as a result of implementation of this Order prior to their removal from the premises referred to in the Schedule to provide a copy of the list to the Defendant or person served with the Order prior to removal and to retain in their safe custody all articles and documents obtained, prior to their return to the Defendant or his solicitors;

(4) to offer to return the documents obtained by reason of this Order following photocopying and in any event within 3 working days of removal, to the Defendant's Solicitors against their undertaking to retain the documents in their safe custody and to produce them to the Court if so required;

(5) to offer to return all articles obtained by reason of this Order within 3 working days of removal to the Defendant's Solicitors against their undertaking to retain the articles in their safe custody and to produce them to the Court if so required, and their signed receipt for the articles received by them.

IT IS ORDERED THAT:—

1   The Defendant whether by himself his servants or agents or otherwise howsoever be restrained until after . . . or further order, and an injunction is hereby granted restraining him from destroying, mutilating, damaging, altering, hiding or removing from the premises referred to in the Schedule or removing from the jurisdiction articles, or documents (including computer records) falling within the categories or classes set out in the Schedule hereto.

2   The Defendant whether by himself his servants or agents or otherwise be restrained until after . . . or further order, and an injunction be granted restraining him from directly or indirectly informing, notifying or warning any person (including any company or firm) of the intention to bring or the bringing of these proceedings, or of the making of this Order or of its provisions, or of the Plaintiff's interest in these proceedings, or warning in any manner whatsoever any person (including any company or firm) that proceedings may be brought against them by the Plaintiff, except for the purpose of seeking legal advice from his lawyers.

3   The Defendant do disclose forthwith to the person serving this Order upon him:—

(1) the whereabouts of all articles or documents (including computer records) in his possession custody or power falling within the categories or classes set out in the Schedule hereto.

(2) to the best of the Defendant's knowledge information and belief the names and addresses of all persons (including companies or firms) who have supplied or offered to supply him with articles falling within the categories specified in the Schedule, or to whom he has supplied or offered to supply such articles, with full details as to each and every supply or offer to supply including in relation to each supply, the date of delivery of the articles, where delivery was made, and the quantity of articles supplied.

4   The Defendant by himself his servants or agents or by any person appearing to be in control of the premises referred to in Part 2 of the Schedule do permit forthwith the person serving this Order and such other persons duly authorised by the Plaintiff (such other persons not to exceed 2 in number) to enter, or re-enter the said premises and remain there at any time between . . . o'clock in the morning and . . . o'clock in the evening, Monday to Friday inclusive, and to have access forthwith to the Defendant's motor vehicle registration number RIC 3, for the purpose of looking for, and removing from the premises or vehicle all articles and documents falling within the categories or classes set out in the Schedule hereto. In the case of computer records, the Defendant is to provide forthwith a print out of all records falling within the Schedule or (failing a printer) to display forthwith the records in a readable form.

5   Within 7 days after service of this Order upon him the Defendant is to make and serve on the Plaintiff's Solicitors an affidavit setting out all of the information to be disclosed pursuant to paragraph 3(2) above and exhibiting thereto all relevant documents, concerning any supply or offer to supply.

6   The Defendant is to be at liberty to move to vary or to discharge this Order or any part thereof on 24 hours notice to the Plaintiff's Solicitors.

Schedule

Part 1: Articles and Documents

(A) Articles

Video tapes of 'The King and I'.

(B) Documents

(1) Originals or copies of order forms, invoices or delivery documents relating to the purchase or resale of video tapes of 'The King and I'.

(2) All records (including computer records) relating to the purchase or resale of such video tapes, including records concerning stock, delivery, orders, invoices, payments, and names and addresses of suppliers or customers.

Part 2: Premises

(1) Bosworth Field House,
    Lancaster Road,
    York
    YK1 485

(2) Room 41, Kingdom House,
    4A Horse Street,
    London, W1

4 Draft Affidavit in support of an application for an Anton Piller Order

(i)	Filed for: Plaintiff
(ii)	W Kingmaker
(iii)	No 1
(iv)	Date sworn:

IN THE HIGH COURT OF JUSTICE
CHANCERY DIVISION
    In The Matter of an Intended Action

Between:—

Henry Seventh plc

Intended Plaintiff

—and—
Richard Third

Intended Defendant

AFFIDAVIT

I Warwick Kingmaker of 2A Crown Street, London SW1 make oath and say as follows:—

1 I am a Solicitor of the Supreme Court and a partner of Henry King & Co, of 4A Tudor Street, London EC2. I have the conduct of this intended action on behalf of the Intended Plaintiff. I make this affidavit to the best of my knowledge information and belief being derived from documents and information provided to me by Mr E Richmond who is the managing director of Henry Seventh plc. There is now produced and shown to me and marked 'WK 1' a numbered bundle of copy documents to which I wish to refer in the course of this affidavit. Numbers in brackets in the course of this affidavit are references to pages in this bundle.

2 Henry Seventh plc carries on business making and marketing films and has its head office at Pink Rose House, Lancaster Street, Richmond. In the last accounting year up until 30th April, the business made profits of £1,483,000. The business has substantial assets (. . .) and I am informed by Mr Richmond and believe it to be the case that Henry Seventh plc has adequate assets from which it could honour any order that might be made against the company under a cross undertaking as to damages.

3 Henry Seventh plc owns the copyright in a film called 'The King and I', which it markets under the label 'Tudor Records'. This is a highly successful film (. . .). Unfortunately the marketing of video tapes of the film has been adversely affected by the availability of unauthorised copies of the film which are sold at much lower prices to members of the public than the retail price set by the company. These illicit copies do not have the markings or wrappings of video films produced by 'Tudor Records' and tend to be of low quality. An example of such a tape is now produced and shown to me and marked 'WK 2'. Such has been the adverse effect of the availability of these copy tapes that the company has employed the professional investigators, Gaunt & Co, to try to obtain information about who is responsible for producing and selling such tapes. I understand from Mr John who is a partner in Gaunt & Co, that it has been very difficult to obtain this information, because the copies are not made available openly on the shelves of retail shops and outlets. A report has been prepared by Mr John of the nature and results of the inquiries which have been carried out so far (. . .).

4 I am informed by Mr John and believe it to be the case that as a result of his inquiries it is clear that copy tapes of 'The King and I' are being sold by a certain Richard Third, from Room 41, Kingdom House, 4A Horse Street, London W1, which appears to be a rented room, and also from a flat at Bosworth Field House, Lancaster Road, York YK1 485, at which there is a large stock of unmarked video tapes kept in a back room. Richard Third does not appear to have any substantial assets. When an investigator from Gaunt & Co visited Room 41, there was a

large stock of unlabelled video tapes, and a counter with a portable personal computer. There were also some leaver-arch files. Richard Third uses a motor vehicle, registration No RIC 3 for travelling between his premises in London and York and has been seen carrying the tapes to and from this vehicle.

5 Gaunt & Co have found out, as a result of their inquiries, that Richard Third is also selling other copy tapes which include poor copies of films made by Edward Fifth Ltd, which recently went into liquidation. Examples of these tapes have been shown by me to the liquidator Mr R Brackenbury, who has informed me that they appear to be illicit copies of tapes which were marketed under the 'White Rose' label. I am also informed by the liquidator that proceedings were brought against Richard Third by Edward Fifth Ltd before it went into liquidation concerning illicit copying and marketing of tapes on the 'White Rose' label but that Richard Third denied the allegations advanced in those proceedings (. . .) and did not produce any relevant discovery (. . .).

6 I believe that unless 'Anton Piller' relief is granted against 'Richard Third' in respect of video tapes of the 'King and I' and his acquisition and marketing of such tapes, there is a substantial danger that if proceedings are brought against him illicit copy tapes will be hidden and that documents including computer records will be destroyed or otherwise made not available. Gaunt & Co have advised Henry Seventh plc that in their opinion the tapes sold by Richard Third are similar to other tapes of 'The King and I' which they have come across in the course of their inquiries and that it is likely that there is a central source for these tapes. It would be extremely valuable to them for the purposes of their inquiries to have access to order forms, invoices and delivery documents and all records, in the possession, custody or power of Richard Third relating to the purchase or resale of video tapes of 'The King and I', and to have full information from him concerning the names and addresses of the suppliers of the tapes and those who have purchased the tapes from him.

7 Accordingly I respectfully ask for orders to be made *ex parte* against the Intended Defendant in the terms of the draft minute of order which has been prepared.
Sworn etc.

5 Letter of Explanation of Anton Piller Order

Richard Third or the person appearing to be in charge of the premises,
Kingdom House,
4A, Horse Street,
London W1

Henry Seventh plc v *Richard Third*

Dear Sir or Madam,
    On . . . the Hon Mr Justice Clarence made an order ('the Order') in

proceedings to be commenced in the High Court of Justice, Chancery Division by Henry Seventh plc against Richard Third. We are the Solicitors acting for Henry Seventh plc in this matter and we have undertaken to the Court to offer to explain to any person served with the Order in ordinary everyday language its meaning and effect. An explanation will be given orally, and the purpose of this letter is to set out an additional explanation in writing.

1 The order was made by the judge sitting in camera on the application of Henry Seventh plc. The evidence on which he relied is incorporated in an affidavit which has been sworn by Warwick Kingmaker of this firm. Certain undertakings have been given to the Court by Henry Seventh plc and these are set out after the words 'AND the Intended Plaintiff by his Counsel undertaking as follows: . . . '

Certain undertakings have been given to the Court by ourselves personally and these are recorded after the words in the order which read 'AND UPON the Solicitors to the Plaintiff by Counsel for the Plaintiff, being their Counsel for this purpose undertaking . . . '.

2 A person who has been served with a copy of the Order is entitled to seek immediate legal advice from his or her legal advisers concerning it, before carrying out its requirements. However, subject to this, paragraphs 3 and 4 of the Order state that they must be complied with 'forthwith', ie immediately and without delay.[1]

3 Paragraphs 1 and 2 of the Order contain injunctions, which prohibit certain acts. These injunctions apply now. Their purpose is:

(1) to prevent documents or articles being destroyed or damaged, or removed from the premises referred to in the Schedule, or removed from the jurisdiction;

(2) to prevent third parties (except legal advisers) being told of the bringing of these proceedings or of the Order.

4 Paragraph 3 of the Order requires the Defendant to tell us where certain documents and articles are to be found and to provide us with information about his suppliers and his customers and the transactions entered into with each of them. The documents and articles referred to are specified in Part 1 of the Schedule to the Order.

5 Paragraph 4 of the Order is commonly called an 'Anton Piller' order. It requires permission to be given to us for the solicitor who served the Order and up to 2 additional persons to enter the premises listed in Part 2 of the Schedule between certain hours for the purposes of searching them for the documents and articles referred to, and for removing such documents and articles into our custody. If permission is not given we will not

---

1 'Forthwith' is preremptory and permits of no interval of time save such as may be imposed by circumstances which cannot be avoided: *Re Muscovitch* [1939] Ch 694. See also *Sameen* v *Abeyewickrema* [1963] AC 597, *Re Southam, ex parte Lamb* (1881) 19 ChD 169 and *Hillingdon London Borough* v *Cutler* [1968] 1 QB 124.

enter the premises, but the withholding of permission in breach of the Order is a contempt of Court.

6 Paragraph 4 of the Order contains in its second sentence an order that computer records falling within Part 1(B) of the Schedule to the Order are made available immediately in the form of a computer print out, or failing that are displayed in a readable form (ie so that notes can be made of their contents).

7 One of our representatives will compile a complete list of all documents and articles which we intend to remove from the premises. This list will be available for you to look at and to make sure that it is accurate.

8 Under the Order we will be returning all documents removed to the Defendant's solicitors after the documents have been photocopied, provided that the solicitors provide an undertaking to keep them safe and produce them to the Court if required to do so. We will also be offering to return to the Defendant's solicitors all video tapes of 'The King and I' removed from the premises provided that the solicitors provide a similar undertaking in respect of the video tapes and a receipt for the tapes returned to them.

9 We would be pleased to answer any questions you may have. It is necessary to read the Order to find out precisely what its requirements are.

10 We hope that the Order can be implemented without any problems. However, we would point out that if its terms are broken then this could lead to proceedings being brought against the person or persons involved for contempt of Court.

Yours sincerely,
Henry King & Co.

6 Mareva injunction—arbitration proceedings

IN THE HIGH COURT OF JUSTICE
QUEEN'S BENCH DIVISION
COMMERCIAL COURT
   The Honourable Mr Justice Stareleigh
   In The Matter of The Arbitration Acts 1950–1979
   And
   In The Matter of an Arbitration
   Between:

                                                                19— D No 1234
                        Dombey and Son Limited
                                                        Intended Plaintiffs
                                              (Claimants in the Arbitration)
                        —and—
                  Doyce and Clennam SA of Utopia
                                                        Intended Defendants
                                           (Respondents in the Arbitration)

ORDER

Upon hearing Counsel for the Intended Plaintiffs (hereinafter called 'the Plaintiffs')

And upon reading the Affidavit sworn herein on the . . . by Paul Dombey,

And upon the Plaintiffs by their Counsel undertaking:

(1) Forthwith to issue an Originating Summons[1] claiming the injunctive relief granted herein against the Intended Defendants (hereinafter called 'the Defendants'), and to serve the said Summons as soon as is reasonably practicable, thereafter upon the Defendants out of the jurisdiction at their registered office at 2, Marshalsea Road, Erewhon or elsewhere in the Republic of Utopia;[2]

(2) Forthwith to give notice of the terms of this order to the Defendants by sending a copy of this order by first class post to their registered office at the aforesaid address and by telexing a copy of this order to the Defendants' managers Tite, Barnacle & Co (UK) Limited at their business address namely Circumlocution House, 24 Mews Street, London SW1 and by telexing to or serving a copy of this order on the Defendants' solicitors Tulkinghorn & Co of 4 Equity Square, Lincoln's Inn, London WC2;

(3) To notify the Defendants of their right to apply to the Court on notice to the Plaintiffs' solicitors to vary or set aside this order;

(4) To abide by any order which this Court may make as to damages in case this Court may hereafter be of the opinion that the Defendants have suffered any by reason of this order which the Plaintiffs ought to pay;

(5) To pay the reasonable costs and expenses incurred by any Third Party to whom notice of this order has been given, by reason of this order or his compliance therewith and to indemnify any such Third Party against any liability reasonably incurred for the purpose of complying with this order;

(6) To notify any Third Party to whom the Plaintiffs or their solicitors

---

1 If the plaintiff has not commenced arbitration proceedings prior to the *ex parte* application, he should give a further undertaking to 'commence arbitration proceedings against the intended defendant forthwith'. It is usually unnecessary to specify the exact steps which he should take, eg appointing an arbitrator, although the plaintiff may, if he so chooses, include in the undertaking an express reference to the relevant arbitration clause.

2 If the plaintiff obtains *ex parte* Mareva relief in respect of arbitration proceedings he must issue an originating summons. If he wishes to apply for an extension of the injunction at a later stage (eg in aid of execution of the arbitration award) he should issue a summons in the action commenced by his originating summons. Unless the court grants the Mareva injunction for a short period pending an *inter partes* hearing, the return date on the plaintiff's originating summons is usually left blank. If the defendant wishes to apply for the injunction to be discharged or varied he may (*a*) require a date to be fixed for the hearing of the originating summons, or (*b*) issue his own summons in the action, or (*c*) apply to the court in accordance with the liberty to apply granted in the Mareva order. In practice the defendant will usually choose the last of these options.

may give notice of this order, of his right to apply to the Court upon notice to the Plaintiffs to set aside or vary this order in so far as it affects him;

(7) To provide security in the sum of £   in the form of a first class London Bank Guarantee in the form set out in the Schedule hereto for their cross-undertaking in damages under (4) above herein within 48 hours from the date of this order;[3]

NOW IT IS HEREBY ORDERED AND DIRECTED THAT

1 The Defendants be restrained and an injunction be granted restraining them until 21 days after the publication of the Final Award in the arbitration proceedings commenced between the Plaintiffs and the Defendants on . . . , or until order, whether by themselves, their directors, servants, agents or otherwise howsoever from (1) removing from its present location namely [   ], and (2) selling, disposing of, mortgaging, charging, encumbering or otherwise dealing with howsoever the vessel named "Son and Heir" or their beneficial interest therein.[4] For the avoidance of doubt an Interim Award shall not be regarded as the Final Award in the arbitration proceedings.

2 The Plaintiffs have leave to issue an Originating Summons [in the form of the draft produced to the Court] and to serve the said Originating Summons on the Defendants out of the jurisdiction at their registered office at 2, Marshalsea Road, Erewhon, Utopia or elsewhere in the Republic of Utopia and that the time for acknowledgement or service thereof be [days] after service of the said Originating Summons on the Defendants.

3 Liberty to the Defendants and any Third Party served with notice of this order to apply to the Court upon notice to the Plaintiffs' solicitors to vary or set aside this order:

4 Costs reserved.

Dated, etc

---

3 This precedent gives an example of an undertaking to provide security for the cross-undertaking in damages. The amount of the security will be determined by the court on the assessment of the potential loss which the defendant may suffer by reason of the injunction. The court is usually in a better position to assess the likely loss and damage to the defendant at the *inter partes* stage than at the *ex parte* application and therefore that is the time at which security for the cross-undertaking is usually considered. If security is required at the *ex parte* stage, the court may require it to be put up within a short period (eg 48 hours) as a condition of granting the injunction. If it is likely that the plaintiff will be required to furnish security, then an appropriate form of security (eg a bank guarantee) should be drafted by the plaintiff and attached to the draft order and the plaintiff should satisfy himself that there will be no practical difficulties in complying with the undertaking within the specified time. If the court does not stipulate a particular form of security, the words 'in a form acceptable to the defendants' should be omitted from the order, otherwise the plaintiff may be unable to comply with his undertaking because the defendant refuses to approve the form of the security.

4 The injunction is normally granted until a specified time after publication of the final award. This period varies, but 21 days is common, this being the period during which the respondent has the opportunity to commence proceedings seeking leave to appeal or to commence proceedings for the remission or setting aside of the award.

7 Angel Bell order

19— M No 1234
IN THE HIGH COURT OF JUSTICE
QUEEN'S BENCH DIVISION
The Honourable Mr Justice Tulkinghorn
Between:

(1) Wilkins Micawber
(2) Elizabeth Ann Trotwood

Plaintiffs

(3) David Copperfield
—and—
Wickfield & Heep (a firm)

Defendants

ORDER

Upon Hearing Counsel for the Plaintiffs and Counsel for the Defendants

And upon reading the Affidavits sworn herein by Thomas Edwin Traddles on behalf of the Plaintiffs and by Uriah Heep on behalf of the Defendants

And upon the Defendants by their said Counsel undertaking:

(1) To provide to the Plaintiffs' solicitors within the first 7 days of each calendar month (including within those 7 days Saturdays and Sundays) a list of all the office expenses and trade debts falling due in the ordinary course of business which were paid by the Defendants during the previous calendar month pursuant to proviso (3) to paragraph 1 of this order, together with the sum or sums paid in respect of each item of expenditure or trade debt;

(2) To provide to the Plaintiffs' solicitors within the first 7 days of each calendar month copies of all invoices or bills relating to the said office expenses or trade debts together with any receipts issued to the Defendants in respect of the said payments;[1]

---

1 This precedent includes a provision for notification by the defendant of payments made in accordance with the variation, by way of safeguard for the plaintiff. Whether the court will impose a requirement of prior or subsequent notification as a condition of granting the variation sought by the defendant, will depend on the facts of the particular case. It is usual for a provision for notification to be embodied in an undertaking given by the defendant, although it may be included as a proviso to the variation in the terms of the order.

NOW IT IS HEREBY ORDERED AND DIRECTED THAT:

1 Paragraph 1 of the order herein of Mr Serjeant Buzfuz QC (sitting as a Deputy Judge of the High Court) dated the   day of   be varied into the following form:[2]

The Defendants be restrained and an injunction be granted restraining them until trial or further order, whether by themselves their servants or agents or otherwise howsoever from removing from the jurisdiction, disposing of, mortgaging, assigning, charging or otherwise dealing with howsoever any of their assets within the jurisdiction including but not limited to, the following:

(*a*) Such sums as may or may hereafter be held to the account of the Defendants (whether in the name of the Defendants or in the names of one or both of the partners in the Defendants, namely John Wickfield and Uriah Heep, whether separately or jointly with each other or with some other person) at Murdstone & Grinby's Bank, High Street Branch, 104 High Street, Dover, Kent or at some other branch of the said Bank in Dover, including but not limited to the personal accounts and trading accounts specified under provisos (2) and (3) below.

(*b*) The interest of the Intended Defendants or one or both of the aforementioned partners in the property known as [address of office premises] save in so far as the unencumbered value of those assets exceeds [£50,000].

PROVIDED THAT

(1) Nothing in this order shall prevent the exercise by Murdstone & Grinby's Bank of any right of set-off which such Bank may have in respect of facilities afforded by it to the Defendants or the aforesaid partners prior to the date of this order or the date on which such Bank was notified of this order (whichever is the later):

(2) Each of the aforesaid partners shall be at liberty to withdraw and expend the sum of up to [£1,000] per week in respect of his ordinary living expenses from his personal account, namely current account no ABC 1234567 at Murdstone & Grinby's Bank, High Street Branch, Dover, in the name of John Wickfield, and current account no DEF 8912345 at Murdstone & Grinby's Bank, St John's Street Branch, Dover, in the name of Uriah Heep.

(3) The said partners shall be at liberty to draw on the trading account of the Defendants, namely account no XYZ 7654321 at Murdstone &

---

2 When the order is drawn up the terms of the injunction as varied should be set out in full so that it is clear on the face of one document what the defendant is enjoined from doing and what he is permitted to do. It is unsatisfactory for a defendant or third party to be obliged to cross-refer to another document before he can ascertain the full extent of his obligations: see *In re a Bankrupt, Rudkin-Jones* v *Trustee of the Property of the Bankrupt* (1965) 109 SJ 334. If the full terms of the varied injunction are not set out in the order then this omission may be significant should the plaintiff subsequently bring proceedings for contempt against the defendant or a third party, and it is said that there was some confusion as to what were the precise terms of the injunction.

Grinby's Bank, High Street Branch, Dover, Kent sums not exceeding in total [£2,000] per week for the purpose of paying the said firm's office expenses and trade debts falling due in the ordinary course of business including, but not limited to:

(a) mortgage repayments on the aforementioned office premises due to Murdstone & Grinby's Bank;

(b) accrued rentals of office equipment due to Mr Ebenezer Scrooge;

(c) the weekly salary of Mr Robert Cratchit, the office manager;

(d) sums due in respect of the rates, water rates and gas and electricity services in respect of the said premises; and such further sums (if any), as the Plaintiffs' solicitors may from time to time consent in writing to the Defendants drawing from the said account and expending in excess of the weekly limit of [£2,000].

2 Liberty to the Defendants to apply to the court upon notice to the Plaintiff's solicitors to [discharge or] vary the order of Mr Serjeant Buzfuz QC herein dated . . . as varied by this order.

3 In the event that the Defendants pay the sum of [£50,000] into court, or provide security in that sum in a form acceptable to the Plaintiffs' solicitors, paragraph 1 of the Order of Mr Serjeant Buzfuz QC as varied herein shall be discharged forthwith from the time that the Plaintiffs' solicitors have been notified in writing by the Defendants' solicitors that the said sum has been paid into court or that the said security has been provided.

4 [Provision for costs].

Dated, etc

8 Originating Summons seeking interim relief under section 25(1) of the Civil Jurisdiction and Judgments Act 1982

IN THE HIGH COURT OF JUSTICE
QUEEN'S BENCH DIVISION
COMMERCIAL COURT

In the Matter of the Civil Jurisdiction and Judgments Act 1982

And

In the Matter of proceedings pending before the Tribunal de Grande Instances at Grasse

Between:

Henry Fifth & Company Limited

Plaintiff

—and—

(1) Charles Sixth
(2) Louis Dauphin

Defendants

ORIGINATING SUMMONS

To: (1) Charles Sixth of 14, Rue de Palace, Agincourt, France

(2) Louis Dauphin of 15, Rue de Bourbon, Orleans, France

Let the First and Second Defendants, within   days after service of this summons upon him, counting the day of service return the accompanying Acknowledgment of Service to the appropriate Court Office.

By this Summons which is issued on the application of the Plaintiff, Henry Fifth & Company Limited, of Exeter House, Westmoreland Street, Bedford, BED 42, the Plaintiff seeks the following relief:—

1 An Injunction against the First and Second Defendants in such terms and subject to such qualifications as may be just and convenient, restraining each of them whether by himself his servants or agents or otherwise howsoever from dealing with his assets wherever situated, save in so far as the same may exceed such sum as may be fixed by the court, until further order of the court.

2 An Order against each of the First and Second Defendants requiring him to disclose to the Plaintiff forthwith or within such time as may be specified full information about the nature and location of his assets wherever situated, and all documents within his possession custody or power relating to the nature and location of such assets.

3 Further or other relief may be granted by way of interim relief pursuant to section 25(1) of the Civil Jurisdiction and Judgments Act 1982 against the First and Second Defendants or either of them in relation to the relief sought in paragraphs 1 and 2 above, or otherwise by way of interim relief in connection with proceedings pending before the Tribunal de Grande Instances at Grasse brought by the Plaintiff against the Defendants.

4 The Defendants be ordered to pay the costs of these proceedings.

If the First or Second Defendant does not acknowledge service, etc.

9 Order made *inter partes* in proceedings brought under section 25(1) of the Civil Jurisdiction and Judgments Act 1982 continuing world-wide Mareva relief which had been granted *ex parte*, with modifications

IN THE HIGH COURT OF JUSTICE
QUEEN'S BENCH DIVISION
COMMERCIAL COURT
   The Honourable Mr Justice Canterbury
   Between:—

Henry Fifth & Company Limited

Plaintiff

—and—
(1) Charles Sixth
(2) Louis Dauphin

Defendants

ORDER

Upon Hearing Counsel for the Plaintiff and Counsel for the Defendants

AND UPON Reading the Affidavits sworn in these proceedings by Thomas Erpingham (Nos 1 and 2) on . . . and . . . , and by Charles Sixth (No 1) on . . . , Louis Dauphin (Nos 1, 2 and 3) on . . . , . . . and . . .

And Upon Reading the summonses issued herein by the Plaintiff on . . . and by the First and Second Defendants on . . .

IT IS HEREBY ORDERED AND DIRECTED THAT:—

1 The Injunction granted by the Hon Mr Justice Ely on . . . against the First and Second Defendants, is to continue until 21 days after the final conclusion of the proceedings brought against them by the Plaintiff before the Tribunal de Grande Instances at Grasse, or further order, in the following terms:—

The First and Second Defendants be restrained and an injunction is hereby granted restraining them whether by themselves or by their respective servants or agents or any of them or otherwise howsoever, until 21 days after the final conclusion of the said proceedings before the Tribunal de Grande Instances at Grasse or further order, from disposing of, transferring, charging, diminishing in any way howsoever or dealing with any of their assets wheresoever the same may be situate save in so far as the unencumbered value of such assets exceeds the sum of US $

PROVIDED ALWAYS THAT:

(i) In so far as this order purports to have any effect outside England and Wales, no person shall be affected by it or concerned with the terms of it until it shall have been declared enforceable or shall have been recognised or registered or enforced by a foreign court (and then it shall only affect such person to the extent of such declaration or recognition or registration or enforcement) unless that person is:

(1) a person to whom this Order is addressed or an officer or an agent appointed by power of attorney of such a person; or

(2) a person who is subject to the jurisdiction of this Court and who:

(A) has been given written notice of this order at his or its residence or place of business within the jurisdiction; and

(B) is able to prevent acts or omissions outside the jurisdiction of this Court which assist in the breach of the terms of this order.

(ii) The First and Second Defendants may make such payment as may be necessary in respect of their reasonable legal costs in defending the said proceedings at Grasse and any other payment with the consent of the Plaintiff's solicitors, in any case from a current account or other source the identity of which has first been notified by it in writing to the Plaintiff's solicitors.

(iii) Nothing in this Order shall prevent any Bank from exercising any right of set-off it may have in respect of facilities given to the Third

Defendant before . . . including any interest which has accrued or may hereafter accrue in respect of such facilities.

(iv) The First and Second Defendants may each pay ordinary living expenses of up to £750 each per week.

2 The summons issued by the First and Second Defendants on . . . be dismissed.

3 The First and Second Defendants do pay the costs of each of the said summonses issued herein by the Plaintiffs and the First and Second Defendants in any event.

4 There is liberty to apply.

Dated, etc.

10 Order made *ex parte* in the Chancery Division which includes world-wide Mareva relief, the appointment of a Receiver, and an order for disclosure of information about assets world-wide

IN THE HIGH COURT OF JUSTICE
CHANCERY DIVISION
Mr Justice Cicero
  . . . the . . . day of . . .
  In The Matter of an Intended Action
    Between:—

(1) Octavius Caesar Bank Inc
(2) Augustus Trading Company Inc

Intended Plaintiffs

—and—

(1) Marcus Brutus
(2) Metellus Cimber
(3) Cassius and Company SA

Intended Defendants

ORDER

UPON MOTION made by Counsel for the Intended Plaintiffs (hereinafter called 'the Plaintiffs')

AND UPON READING an affidavit in draft to be sworn by Mark Anthony

AND the Plaintiffs by their Counsel undertaking:—

(1) forthwith on or before . . . to issue a writ of summons herein in the form produced to the Court by their Counsel for service upon each of the Intended Defendants (hereinafter called 'the Defendants') pursuant to RSC Order 11, Rule 1(2) in Rome or elsewhere in Italy, and thereafter to serve the same forthwith upon each of the Defendants;

(2) forthwith to procure that the said affidavit is sworn and filed;

(3) to abide by any order as to damages should the Defendants or any of

them suffer any by reason of this Order which in the opinion of the Court, the Plaintiffs ought to pay;

(4) to pay any Third Party served with or given notice of this order their reasonable costs and expenses, and to indemnify them against any liability, reasonably incurred for the purpose of complying with this order;

(5) to be answerable for all assets and sums received by the Receiver hereby appointed, and for all sums that the Receiver may become liable to pay;

(6) to give notice of the terms of this order forthwith on or before . . . to the Defendants by facsimile transmission to Fax No   and to deliver copies of this order, and the affidavit to be sworn by Mark Anthony and its exhibits to the Defendants by courier, by leaving the same in an envelope addressed to the Defendants at . . . ;

(7) not to use any information obtained by reason of paragraph 6 of this Order except for the purposes of these proceedings, save with the leave of the Court.

NOW IT IS HEREBY ORDERED AND DIRECTED THAT:—

1 The First, Second and Third Defendants be restrained and an injunction is hereby granted restraining them until after judgment in this action or further Order in the meantime whether by themselves or by their respective servants or agents or any of them or otherwise howsoever from disposing of or transferring, charging, diminishing or in any way howsoever dealing with any of their assets wheresoever the same may be situate save in so far as the value of such assets exceeds the sum of £25,000,000 (twenty-five million pounds) respectively PROVIDED ALWAYS THAT:

(*a*) In so far as this order purports to have any effect outside England and Wales, no person shall be affected by it or concerned with the terms of it until it shall have been declared enforceable or shall have been recognised or registered or enforced by a foreign court (and then it shall only affect such persons to the extent of such declaration or recognition or registration or enforcement) UNLESS that person is:

(i) a person to whom this order is addressed or an officer or an agent appointed by power of attorney of such a person, or

(ii) a person who is subject to the jurisdiction of this court and who:

(A) has been given written notice of this order at his or its residence or place of business within the jurisdiction; and

(B) is able to prevent acts or omissions outside the jurisdiction of this court which assist in the breach of the terms of this order

(*b*) The Defendants may make such payments as may be necessary in respect of their reasonable legal costs in defending this action and any other payment with the consent of the Plaintiffs' solicitors, in any case from a current account or other source the identity of which has first been notified by them in writing to the Plaintiffs' solicitors;

(*c*) That nothing in this Order shall prevent any bank from exercising any right of set-off it may have in respect of facilities given to the Defendants before including any interest which has accrued or may hereafter accrue in respect of such facilities.

(*d*) The First and Second Defendants may each pay ordinary living expenses of up to Italian Lira 1,500,000 per week each.

2 Mr Flavins Marullus of Artemidorus and Partners, Chartered Accountants, be appointed until further order Receiver without security of all assets of the Defendants including without limitation the following assets:—

(Set out the relevant assets)

PROVIDED ALWAYS THAT:

(i) In so far as this order purports to have any effect outside England and Wales, no person shall be affected by it or concerned with the terms of it until it shall have been declared enforceable or shall have been recognised or registered or enforced by a foreign court (and then it shall only affect such persons to the extent of such declaration or recognition or registration or enforcement) unless that person is:

(A) a person to whom this Order is addressed or an officer or agent appointed by power of attorney of such a person; or

(B) a person who is subject to the jurisdiction of this Court and who:

(1) has been given written notice of this order at his or her or its residence or place of business within the jurisdiction; and

(2) is able to prevent acts or omissions outside the jurisdiction of this Court which assist in the breach of the terms of this order.

(ii) The Receiver shall not without the leave of the Court take any steps relating to the conduct of these proceedings on behalf of or in the name of the Defendants.

(iii) Subject to the terms of paragraph 1(*b*) above, the Receiver shall not raise any objection to the Defendants at their own expense instructing solicitors and counsel to conduct these proceedings.

(iv) This Order shall not extend to any papers in the possession of the solicitors of the Defendants, which come into their possession for the purposes of these proceedings.

(v) The Receiver shall not without the leave of the Court or the consent of the Defendants disclose:

(A) to the Plaintiffs any information which has come or comes into his possession as such Receiver;

(B) to any other person (other than his legal and other professional advisers and counsel) any information which has come or comes into his possession as such Receiver save for the purposes of carrying out his investigatory functions.

(vi) The Receiver shall not raise any objection to the First and Second Defendants paying ordinary living expenses of up to Italian Lira 1,500,000 each per week.

3 The Defendants do procure so far as it lies jointly or severally within their power:—

(*a*) that their assets forthwith delivered up or transferred to the Receiver, except that the First and Second Defendants are to be at liberty to retain Italian Lira 6 million each for the purpose of paying ordinary living expenses; and

(*b*) that none of the said assets is disposed of by any person until after judgment in this action or further order in the meantime save with the consent of the Receiver or the leave of the Court.

4 The Receiver be authorised:

(*a*) to take such steps as may seem to him to be appropriate for the purpose of getting in recovering and preserving the assets to which his appointment extends and (with the leave of the Court) any assets formerly held directly or indirectly by or to the order of or for the benefit of the Defendants or any present or former direct or indirect subsidiary or associated company of the Third Defendants;

(*b*) to take proceedings in any jurisdiction in the name of the Defendants or in his own name (as may be appropriate) for the aforesaid purpose;

(*c*) to retain independent legal advice both inside and outside England and Wales to assist him in the aforesaid purpose;

(*d*) to retain the services of Messrs Artemidorus & Partners, Chartered Accountants, including overseas offices, for the like purpose.

5 The Receiver and any party be at liberty to apply to a Judge of the High Court for directions concerning the conduct of the receivership.

6 The Defendants do forthwith upon service of this order on each of them disclose to the Plaintiffs and to the Receiver full information concerning the nature and location of their assets wherever situate, and do disclose all relevant documents in their possession custody or power concerning such assets.

7 There be liberty to apply to vary or discharge this Order.

11 Ancillary Order preventing a Defendant from leaving the jurisdiction and requiring delivery up of the Defendant's passport

This type of ancillary order was first approved by the Court of Appeal in *Bayer AG* v *Winter* [1986] 1 WLR 497. The relief will be granted as part of an order which will be served personally upon the Defendant by a Solicitor of the Supreme Court and it is intended that the Solicitor will himself receive the passport from the Defendant and keep it in safe custody pursuant to an undertaking given by his firm to the Court so to do. The undertaking could be formulated as follows:—

'And upon the Solicitors to the Plaintiff, by the Plaintiff's Counsel who for this purpose acts as Counsel for the said Solicitors, undertaking to serve this order upon the Defendant by a Solicitor of the Supreme Court and to retain in safe custody any passport delivered up to them by the

Defendant, and to produce the same to the Court or to return the same to the Defendant or his agent, if directed so to do by the Court, and in any event, subject to further order to the contrary, to return the passport to the Defendant or his agent on . . . ;'

The relevant part of the Order could be formulated as follows:—

'1 The Defendant be restrained and an injunction be granted restraining him from leaving the jurisdiction until . . . or further order.

2 The Defendant do forthwith deliver up his passport to the person who serves this order upon him.'

The order will include an undertaking in damages.

Index